MW00466439

BECOMING BIG LEAGUE

Becoming
BIG LEAGUE

SEATTLE, THE PILOTS, *and* STADIUM POLITICS

William H. Mullins

UNIVERSITY OF WASHINGTON PRESS

Seattle and London

© 2013 by the University of Washington Press
Printed and bound in the United States of America
Design by Thomas Eykemans
Composed in Chaparral, typeface designed by Carol Twombly
18 17 16 15 14 13   5 4 3 2 1

All rights reserved. No part of this publication may be reproduced or transmitted in any form or by any means, electronic or mechanical, including photocopy, recording, or any information storage or retrieval system, without permission in writing from the publisher.

UNIVERSITY OF WASHINGTON PRESS
PO Box 50096, Seattle, WA 98145, USA
www.washington.edu/uwpress

LIBRARY OF CONGRESS CATALOGING-IN-PUBLICATION DATA
Mullins, William H., 1946–
Becoming big league : Seattle, the Pilots, and stadium politics / William H. Mullins.
    p. cm.
Includes bibliographical references and index.
ISBN 978-0-295-99252-5 (hardcover : alk. paper)
1. Seattle Pilots (Baseball team)—History.
2. Baseball—Washington (State)—Seattle—History.
3. Seattle (Wash.)—Social life and customs.
4. Seattle (Wash.)—Politics and government.
I. Title.
GV875.S433M85 2013   796.357'6409797772—dc23   2012046032

Frontispiece: University of Washington Libraries, Special Collections, UW 25985z

The paper used in this publication is acid-free and meets the minimum requirements of American National Standard for Information Sciences—Permanence of Paper for Printed Library Materials, ANSI Z39.48–1984.∞

FOR EDITH

CONTENTS

ACKNOWLEDGMENTS

A FIRST-YEAR history grad student sat on the wooden planks in the left field bleachers in the bright May sun. The Mountain, Mount Rainier, was out. The Pilots were playing the Detroit Tigers in what would be one of the most exciting games of the year. The previous winter had seen heavy snow and then record cold in January and February that caused the student, who had moved from Southern California, to wonder about life in the Northwest. But the spring was a Puget Sound spectacular of blooms, long twilights, and gentle warmth. The newcomer was falling in love with Seattle. It was not Dodger Stadium, but the greens and blues of this pastoral scene made an idyllic setting for playing baseball. Seattle was a big city that did not seem to realize it—and that was appealing. Traffic seemed light. The acknowledged ills of the city looked quaint: the police vice squad practiced vice. There was a plethora of neighborhoods all worth exploring. Most of the real problems were in abeyance. The economy flew pretty much on a single engine, but Boeing appeared to be going strong. There was racial inequality and consequent tensions, most evident on the University of Washington campus, but viewed through the lens of the Watts riots, race relations were less strained than in other large cities.

After forty years and a career as a historian spent away from Seattle, and then retirement to the Northwest, writing about that time, that city, and that team seemed like a worthy project. The warm glow of personal experience in the late 1960s and early 1970s is still evident at many points in this book. But the process of reading through the newspapers again, looking at the evidence, thinking about the leadership that put the Pilots in place and lost the team to Milwaukee, and then built the Kingdome, yields a story of greater complexity. Civic virtue is mixed with apathy and some selfishness. The inadequacy of those planks in the bleachers are as much a part of the story as the ballplayers on the greensward in the sunshine. Circumstances surrounding the loss of a team after one year might explain why the fifteenth largest market did not feel like a big city.

So this is a story of remembrance, but it is also a historical record woven out of research, thought, and analysis. Inevitably, such a work is not the product of a single writer. Plenty of colleagues, friends, editors, librarians, and archivists have lent a hand. Dona Bubelis of the Seattle Central Library spent considerable time working up a packet of research suggestions. At Seattle Municipal Archives, Anne Frantilla supplied valuable sources on the Pilots and Sicks' Stadium, while Julie Kerssen provided guidance in locating sources in the reorganized files. Janette Gomes led the way expertly through finding aids and retrieved scrapbooks and boxfuls of materials at the King County Archives, and Rebecca Pixler brought out an array of King County photos. James Copher at the Northwest Regional Branch of the Washington State Archives retrieved the records, more than once, of the lengthy trial that brought the Mariners to Seattle, and Philippa Stairs expanded my scope of research and retrieval at the Puget Sound Regional Branch. Carolyn Marr at the Museum of History and Industry and Nicolette Bromberg at the University of Washington Libraries Special Collections dug into their troves of images to help find illustrations for the book. Patrice Hamiter of the Cleveland Library made it much easier to find photos of William Daley. Tim Jenkins was enthusiastic and generous in sharing his knowledge and extensive collection of Pilots memorabilia.

I express thanks to those who were willing to talk with me, sometimes for hours. Bill Sears, Rod Belcher, Jim Kittlesby, Lew Matlin, and Eddie O'Brien of the Pilots provided context and much to consider in telling the team's story. James Ellis represented the perspective of civic leaders with grace. John Owen added his memories to his insightful *Seattle Post-Intelligencer* columns. John O'Brien, Slade Gorton, and John Spellman were willing to share information and perceptions that went well beyond the written records. I express my appreciation, as well, to Mike Fuller, the proprietor of the extensive website honoring the Seattle Pilots, where he shares interviews of those who have passed away.

Because a number of people have read through parts or all of the manuscript at various stages, the book is more streamlined, a better read, and burdened by fewer errors, and as any author should, I bear the responsibility for any errors that still exist. Kent Anderson read the first draft, caught some crucial mistakes, and suggested ways of condensing the narrative. John Findlay, who has been an encouragement from the outset, read several of the first chapters early on and proffered helpful advice on characterizing midcentury Seattle. Karen Anderson read the entire book and made helpful suggestions on enlivening the narrative. David Eskenazi, who probably knows more Seattle baseball history than anyone, has read much of the text, made corrections, supplied a raft of Pilots documents, shared his collection of photos, and given his moral support throughout the project. His assistance has been essential. Marianne Keddington-Lang has gone beyond the duties of an acquisitions editor, offering her vision and her counsel on how to bring this book to fruition. Laura Iwasaki, as copy editor, worked with remarkable diligence, precision, and empathy for the project. My daughter Julie Mullins was a willing in-house (literally) professional editor who did as much as anyone to make this a more tightly written, more readable work. My deepest thanks are to her for supplying her talents and her time.

Finally, it is not just those who have an impact on a book directly by assisting with research or lending their expertise and a keen eye that make such a project possible. Friends and, especially, family provide an atmosphere of encouragement that keeps an author going or furnish support that gives an author time to gather materials, write, and rewrite. And so it is with this work. Thanks to those who asked after the project over its years of gestation. Thanks to Julie and son, Michael, who knew the importance of completing the job. And I thank my wife, Edith, who has been with me from shortly after that first spring in Seattle, who loves the Northwest just as much or more than I do, whose patience is enduring and encouragement sustaining, and to whom I dedicate this book.

ABBREVIATIONS

CASH   Citizens Against Stadium Hoax
CHECC   Choose an Effective City Council
ERA   earned run average
MLBPA   Major League Baseball Players Association
NBA   National Basketball Association
NCAA   National Collegiate Athletic Association
NFL   National Football League
PCL   Pacific Coast League
PNSI   Pacific Northwest Sports, Inc.
RBIs   runs batted in
SRI   Stanford Research Institute

BECOMING BIG LEAGUE

INTRODUCTION

GOING OVER THE GROUND RULES

> It breaks your heart. It is designed to break your heart. The game begins
> in the spring, when everything else begins again, and it blossoms in the
> summer, filling the afternoons and evenings, and then as soon as the
> chill rains come, it stops and leaves you to face the fall alone.
>
> —A. Bartlett Giamatti

EVERY season, every spring, everything is new. The sense of starting fresh was stronger than most years in Tempe, Arizona, in February 1969. The batteries, the pitchers and catchers, were reporting for the first time for the Seattle Pilots. As they arrived at the newly built training complex in Arizona, they donned their plain spring training uniforms, white with a blue "Pilots" stitched across the front. A number of players, coaches, and front office officials were meeting for the first time. General manager Marvin Milkes called out to Darrell Brandon, a pitcher whom he had selected that winter in the expansion draft, to come over and tell his boss who he was. The camp filled in successive waves starting February 20, the first reporting day, through March 1, the first official day of spring training. Because the Major League Baseball Players Association had asked major leaguers not to sign their contracts until several issues between players and owners could be resolved, minor league pitchers and catchers and a few position players were mainly the ones who showed up as camp opened. Marvin Miller, Players Association executive director, finally gave the go-ahead to sign on February 25. Most did and soon reported to camp. Several latecomers trickled in during the last days of February as they negotiated and then inked their contracts. Only holdout Rich Rollins, a few players who had permission to arrive late, and a smattering of others who had played winter ball were absent from Tempe by the March 1 deadline.

In the first week, manager Joe Schultz and his coaches led the players in calisthenics, then schooled them in fundamentals until a few intrasquad games interrupted the monotony. The Ron Plazas beat the Frankie Crosettis 4–1 in the Pilots' first organized ball game. The players who had been in camp the longest made up the two squads, while the bigger names continued to work, not play, their way into shape. Mike Hegan, Greg Goosen, Ray Oyler, Wayne Comer, and Steve Hovley, soon to be familiar names to Pilots fans, populated the inaugural intrasquad rosters. A few, more marginal players participated in the second practice tilt. Infielders Mike Ferraro and Gus Gil got off to good starts in the pre-exhibition contests.

It was a cool, windy March 7 when the Pilots opened up their first Cactus League season in Tempe against the Cleveland Indians. All manner of dignitaries turned out to celebrate the newly minted franchise. Commissioner Bowie Kuhn, American League president Joe Cronin, Arizona governor John Williams, and Tempe mayor Elmer Bradley joined Milkes and owners William Daley and Dewey Soriano for the game. Cleveland manager Alvin Dark bused up from Tucson, bringing mainly his aspiring minor leaguers. Seattle sportswriters recognized several familiar faces from the 1968 Portland Beavers on the field. Seattle took advantage of Dark's decision. The Pilots scored early and often for a 19–3 victory. Ferraro got hotter, going four for six with three runs batted in (RBIs). Five other Pilots got two hits each. Pitcher Mike Marshall started the game and gave up two runs over three innings. This was the first of several exhibition games in which the Pilots experimented with the designated hitter, Soriano's brainchild.[1]

In the first weeks of March, the weather in Arizona is still iffy; in Seattle, the gloom of winter lingers on. Still, a fan can sense spring and the baseball season just around the corner, and spirits begin to lift. Spring training is the harbinger of hope. It was never truer than in March 1969 as the Pilots' exhibition season got under way in Tempe. The visiting dignitaries, the spiffy training complex, the pristine home whites, and, above all, the team on the field marked the culmination of years of hard work and the beginning of a new era in the city's history. The voters of King County had finally approved a new stadium, Seattle had a big-league ball club, and the city had established itself as truly major league. Sports fans and Seattleites in general could sense a future about to blossom, redolent of hope. Yet by fall, baseball and the Pilots would break the hearts of Northwesterners. At the end of a discouraging season, the franchise itself would be in jeopardy. By the next spring, the Pilots would be gone, the stadium project at risk, and the reputation of the city in tatters.

This is a baseball story. It is about the dreams of the Soriano brothers to bring a baseball team to their hometown and their ill-fated efforts to shape the Pilots into a solid organization. The American League team owners bumble their way through the narrative. But it is also the story of a city. Scholars who have written about the business of sports focus on the doubtful economic benefits of acquiring a new franchise or building a stadium. They mention the intrinsic rewards only in passing, yet these are at the heart of this story. Seattleites who pushed for a team and a new stadium were less concerned about the financial impact and more attracted to the prestige of becoming a big-league city, and they were crushed by the ignominy of losing the Pilots after one year. The story is also an investigation of municipal leadership. Foot-dragging politicians, cautious to the point of obstruction, were replaced by more aggressive elected administrators. Boosters such as the indefatigable Ford dealer Joe Gandy and more circumspect movers and shakers such as Ed Carlson and James Ellis urged their city on. Local sportswriters, such as Hy Zimmerman and John Owen, and columnist Emmett Watson acted as both Greek chorus and fervent cheerleaders. Finally, this story revolves around the challenges of using public money to construct stadiums for private owners. The voters—some of whom were fans, many who were not—Mayor Dorm Braman, gadfly and initiative writer Frank Ruano, and King County Executive John Spellman collided, occasionally cooperated, and cajoled one another for a decade and a half until the King County Stadium, the Kingdome, was finally completed.

By the mid-twentieth century, there were established ground rules for bringing a team to town. Three essential conditions had been set out for Seattleites as early as the summer of 1960. The Seattle City Council and King County had put up twenty thousand dollars and hired Stanford Research Institute (SRI) to investigate the feasibility of a first-rate stadium and determine whether the Puget Sound region was ready for a major league baseball or football team. The SRI staff spread out across the United States, visiting twelve major league baseball cities, viewing seven municipal stadiums, speaking with nearly fifty baseball and football officials, and interviewing the presidents of both major baseball leagues, the commissioner of baseball, and the presidents of the National and American Football Leagues. They looked deeply into the city's recent sporting history and examined the demographics of the region.

In September, SRI shared its findings. The researchers found Seattle to be a decent sports town. The Triple-A Rainiers had led the Pacific Coast League (PCL) in attendance for several years since the Second World War, and Husky fans turned out at the same rate as other West Coast university football crowds. SRI concluded that with a population base of 1.1 million in the Seattle-Everett area, the region could potentially support a major league franchise and that it would likely take two professional teams, baseball and football, to meet the projected operating expenses of a major league stadium. At the least, a baseball franchise was a must for maintaining a facility. SRI set three nonnegotiables for obtaining major league baseball: a palpable interest on the part of the city, owners with sufficient finances, and a stadium with at least twenty-five thousand seats.[2]

Seattle whiffed on all three. Over the course of a decade, hopes grew, reached a high point in the spring of 1969, then turned to despair in 1970. The citizens of Seattle and their leaders ranged from avid to ambivalent about the prospect of a major league franchise. The owners who tried to bring baseball to the Northwest were well meaning but underfunded. And, above all, several cycles of stadium politics delayed Seattle's permanent admission into the major leagues for years—a holdup that caused some in the city to bemoan their municipality's second-rate status until the arrival of the Seahawks and the Mariners. This story describes the springtime of rising aspirations in a growing city, the bleak autumn of despair that followed the one-year stand of the Seattle Pilots, the reemergence of hopes, and the new teams that finally grew out of a fruitful round of stadium politics in the Northwest.

Chapter 1

SEATTLE: CITY OF RESTRAINT

THE terms "big league" and "major league" have become metaphors for excellence. Cities of middling size—growing urban centers a little unsure of themselves—are most anxious to be esteemed as big league. Woe to the aspiring municipality that is described as "minor league" or, worse, "bush league." Sports fans, especially, are convinced that a city, regardless of size or attainment, requires at least one major league team if it is to be big league. In the 1960s, when Seattle first began to dream of a franchise, that meant a major league baseball or a National Football League (NFL) club.

Most cities in the American West were out of luck until the late 1950s. The prospect of days-long train trips meant that the world of major league baseball ended at the Mississippi River. The Los Angeles Rams and the San Francisco 49ers were the only NFL teams in the Far West. But the relocation of the Dodgers and the Giants from New York City to the West Coast for the 1958 baseball season signaled that transportation restraints had come to an end. Passenger airplanes and emerging jet service made jaunts across the continent feasible. Now western cities could become big league by snagging an established team or, within a couple of years, by riding the wave of expansion. For Seattle, it would be an unusually rough journey, filled with as much angst as opportunity. Ultimately, Houston, Oakland, San Diego, Seattle, Dallas, then Seattle again, and finally Denver and Phoenix would attract National League or American League teams and prove, to themselves at least, that they had arrived.

Actually, luring major league baseball or football does not make a city big league. Franchises come to cities that have already attained a certain size and standing. Seattleites filled with the booster spirit, for example, aspired to major league status even before 1960. But the Stanford Research Institute team tugged at the reins of reality by posing key questions: Was the city of Seattle capable of supporting major league baseball? Was the city big league? The answers to these questions are central to the Seattle Pilots' story and its aftermath.

Seattle is one of the most beautiful cities in the United States. Its climate is temperate. Rain is frequent but usually merely annoying. The Cascade Range and Olympic Mountains backdrop views east and west. Mount Rainier looms to the south. Puget Sound, lakes, and rivers sparkle on sunny days. The mountains and water provide abundant recreation. To those who embrace the city, the greens and blues of forest, sky, and water offer ample distractions from the gray of the clouds.

By the end of the 1960s, when the Pilots began their one-year sojourn in the city, Seattle was gaining a reputation as one of the most livable cities in the nation. It was not only the natural setting. The burdens of an urban environment rested easily on the city. Seattle seemed unpretentious, a little isolated, perhaps, yet only mildly afflicted by the crowding and violent crime larger cities endured. A north-to-south freeway was equipped with a set of extra "express lanes" that were hardly needed to speed the flow of traffic. The city was characterized by neighborhoods, not sprawl. It was a big city that did not quite realize it was a big city. In 1975, *Harper's*, in the incongruously themed story "The Worst American City," rated Seattle the most livable American metropolis, basing its conclusions not only on residents' access to natural surroundings but on crime statistics, affluence, education, and the health of the population.

What did not come with this inviting image was preeminent stature. For its boosters, Seattle's lack of status was galling. After all, it was growing, it was a capital of the air transportation industry, and it was a portal to Asia. Seattle's champions believed that their city should be acknowledged as a rising city of the West. And as part of its burgeoning maturity, it deserved—some said required—a major league sports team.

From the start, settlers of what would become Seattle entertained visions of glory. White pioneers optimistically named their first settlement on the shores of Elliott Bay "New York Alki," or "New York By and By." Seattleites worked hard to seize the terminus of the Great Northern railroad from Tacoma. During the Klondike Gold Rush, an assay office and a boatload of advertising made Seattle what the ads claimed it to be: the jumping-off point to the Alaska gold fields. The city transformed itself from a mill town into a bustling port, a permanent gateway to Alaska, and a commercially thriving city. It celebrated itself and its attainments in 1909 with the Alaska-Yukon-Pacific Exposition. The string of geographic adjectives in the fair's title hints at Seattleites' sense that their city was the center of an important part of the world, not merely perched on the rim of the United States. The Boeing aircraft company, established in 1916, expanded through the early twentieth century and took Seattle with it. During the Second World War, the Puget Sound region burgeoned as airplane fabrication and shipbuilding brought workers to the Northwest. "In the 1950s," one newspaperman observed, "Seattle was poised on the threshold of the big time."[1]

As the airplane and shipbuilding industries continued to thrive, the city experienced growth that continued into the early 1970s. Except for a slump in 1962–63, jobs, wages, and population multiplied in the region from 1950 through 1968. In the second half of the 1960s, unemployment was consistently under 5 percent and usually closer to 3 percent. The growth of Washington wages in 1966 was the highest in the nation. Boeing, by far the dominant local business, gave Seattle its place in the postwar global economy.[2]

Seattle was maturing, but it was doing so in its own restrained way. By the 1960s, the city was still only a regional economic center, remote from northeastern and midwestern markets and pressing forward economically less vigorously than other West Coast cities. As late as 1975, the *Atlantic Monthly* located Seattle in the "Far Corner," not just geographically, but in the consciousness of Americans as well. To be sure, a number of residents embraced Seattle's reputation as something of a backwater. A sizable portion of Seattleites balked at their neighbors' ambitions for major league status. Some hoped the city's population would not exceed 600,000 and thought Seattle's King County should not surpass 1,000,000. (Only a mass exodus from the county could have achieved the latter at the time these opinions were published in 1969.) This "Lesser Seattle" contingent, as Emmett Watson, a mildly sympathetic *Seattle Post-Intelligencer* columnist, dubbed them, had a significant impact on the city's character and development throughout the 1960s.[3]

Observers through the 1960s considered the residents and their city quiet, prosperous, orderly, respectable, sedate, provincial (as characterization tipped over into castigation), sleepy, and lethargic. The city's homogeneity likely contributed to this. Seattle of the 1960s was well over 80 percent white and deemed "quintessentially middle class" by U.S. senator Slade Gorton. Outside consultants found the Northwest full of outdoor-loving provincialists who did not mind being governed by conservative nonpartisans. University of Washington English professor Roger Sale summed it up best: "Many [newcomers] who didn't want to come to a city-like city were content in Seattle." He added that even readers of the progressive *Seattle Magazine* were somewhat complacent parochials who liked the 1962 world's fair, knew nothing about blacks, loved Husky football and hydroplane racing, and were proud of their new freeways.[4]

Aspects of Seattle's midcentury development contributed to citizen ambivalence about the city's development. Pacific Highway, Aurora Avenue, Bothell Way, and Marginal Way—Seattle's highways and major arterials—were becoming annoyingly crowded. More and more sewage poured into Lake Washington, threatening to turn it into a municipal cesspool. Schools were becoming crowded, housing was in short supply, and rising crime afflicted the city. California-style sprawl and, for that matter, Californians themselves were the bane of the "Lesser Seattle" element. For some—lumbermen, for example—losing clout to newcomers added to their fear of spreading pavement, endless suburbs, and pollution of their green valleys. In short, Seattle was an emerging metropolis, but its citizens did not exactly throb with a passion for growth.[5]

If Seattle had any claim on world-class status by the mid-twentieth century, it was a result of the success of the Boeing Company. Boeing was the economic engine of the region. The corporation had located in Seattle because William Boeing lived in western Washington and saw several advantages of setting up shop there. He could manufacture his planes out of the cheaper spruce abundant in the region. Seattle was large enough to furnish electric power to his plant, and the University of Washington could supply engineers. The labor pool was sufficient and transportation adequate. By the Cold War era, Boeing had made itself into a successful defense and commercial aviation enterprise.[6]

William Allen became president of the company in 1945. He was aware of his public relations role, writing in his diary, "Try to improve feeling around Seattle toward Boeing" and "above all else be human— keep your sense of humor—learn to relax." It was good advice that went largely unheeded. Allen was personally conservative, and described by some as humorless, but he was pragmatic and willing to take big gambles from time to time. In 1952, Allen bet the very future of the company on building a jet plane that could compete in the commercial aviation market. The wager on the Boeing 707 was a roaring success, propelling the company to leadership of the commercial aviation industry in the United States. For Seattle, it was an important step that helped ameliorate its "Far Corner" isolation in two ways: commercial jets linked the city to the rest of the country, and the Boeing Company put it on the map as the center of U.S. aviation.[7]

Boeing's hiring habits were almost manic, however, and created a roller-coaster effect in the company and throughout the Puget Sound. In 1964, a down year for the company, 90,000 worked at Boeing. In the later 1960s, when times were flush, Boeing hired at a feverish rate, projecting expansion plans that Governor Dan Evans proclaimed "would stagger you." The company hit a high of more than 148,000 employees in 1968. Then the airplane industry sank into a steep decline. By the end of 1970, there were only 62,000 employees at Boeing. These cycles affected Seattle dramatically. By the late 1960s, Boeing accounted for as much as 60 percent of the area's growth, and the aerospace industry as a whole furnished more than 90 percent of King County's manufacturing jobs. When Boeing production flagged, the entire Seattle economy entered the doldrums. Seattleites sardonically told one another, "I hear they are hiring at Boeing so they'll have enough to lay off at Christmas." While Boeing was a boon, Seattle's lack of economic diversity was not a hallmark of a mature city.[8]

Though the city was grateful for Boeing, the company held the city at arm's length. Allen told a Chamber of Commerce audience in 1965, "We at Boeing are in a rather specialized sphere of activity and . . . most of you . . . are more closely identified with community affairs than we are. Our best contribution to community affairs is in endeavoring to make a success of our own affairs." The company gave to local cultural and charitable causes, but not bountifully. One young city activist expressed both hope and dismay, stating, "Boeing, I think, is a sleeping giant. Many of us involved in community affairs ask each other what we must do to awaken it. Boeing has considerably more potential for constructive contribution to community affairs [than] it chooses to exercise." Boeing contributed by wooing well-educated engineers and highly skilled workers to Seattle, but it was not a source of corporate dollars or open-handed magnates who would fund an opera company, a new hospital—or a baseball team.[9]

The Boeing story, along with the histories of many of the prominent firms in the Puget Sound region, should have given pause to those who touted Seattle's growth. Many companies established headquarters around Seattle only because their founders were locals. Outsiders, even if enamored with the region's natural beauty, measured that against Seattle's sparsely populated hinterland and its remoteness from most other markets. Several potential investors remarked on the reluctance of local banks to take on much risk or, even more of an indictment, the bankers' disinclination to see beyond the Cascades and the Columbia River. Moreover, by 1969, high interest rates, a slowing economy, and the beginning of the flight of commerce from downtown to the edges of the city and beyond shook the confidence of even the most avid boosters. Though Seattle's economic foundation was expanding, it was still not entirely firm.[10]

In Kansas City, it started with a sportswriter. In Minneapolis, a group of businessmen got the ball rolling. For Anaheim, the mayor was the catalyst. But in each case, several elements from the community joined together to secure a team for their city. In Seattle, teamwork was tentative at best. The city's leadership was uneven leading up to the arrival and departure of the Pilots. When it came to sports, Seattle's movers and shakers were divided into three factions. The elected politicians—languorous, even quiescent, about most municipal matters—had little time for negotiations with major league teams. In contrast, a group of private civic leaders grew increasingly active and assertive through the 1960s, energizing the community with the "Seattle Spirit." The third faction was the boosters, whose zeal to lure big time sports to the region outstripped the ardor of the other two leadership groups and, frequently, exceeded the passion of most Seattleites. Seattle's booster in chief was Joe Gandy. The local Ford dealer assumed leadership of several stadium campaigns, working himself to a frazzle promoting bond issues for a new arena. Dave Cohn, a Seattle restaurateur, persistently beat the drum for a team, assembling delegations that traveled nationwide to major league baseball and NFL meetings where they touted their city to team owners. Bill Sears, the University of Seattle sports information director who had also served as the minor league Seattle Rainiers team publicist, supplied the copy for these presentations. Economist Dewayne Kreager detailed the city's financial prospects, while former Seattle University basketball and baseball star and county commissioner John O'Brien added his knowledge and influence. Others, such as brothers Dewey and Max Soriano, professional baseball men, worked behind the scenes and became instrumental in obtaining a franchise. Local sportswriters, as fans themselves, yearned to watch big-league sports but also stood to gain prestige if Seattle acquired a professional team. John Owen, the venerable Royal Brougham, and Lenny Anderson of the *Seattle Post-Intelligencer* speculated occasionally about what it would be like to have a major league franchise in Seattle. Rarely did a month or two go by without Hy Zimmerman of the *Seattle Times* floating some kind of rumor about baseball or football coming to town. When SRI gave its presentation, the *Times'* front-page headline read "Seattle Qualifies for Major League Baseball, Research Group Reports: $15,000,000 Sports Stadium Held Justified." *Times* sports editor Georg Meyers revealed his hopes several days later, as he looked forward to a vote: "Seattle has been trying to persuade herself and her neighbors that she is 'big time.' Now comes the time to find out if it was all talk." Meyers caught the fundamental belief of the boosters, that Seattle could not be a great city without a major league sports franchise.[11]

The second group of Seattle notables, the private civic leaders, had a wider perspective. They made up the city's most vital leadership group in the 1960s. They generated the idea for the 1962 Seattle World's Fair and then substantially carried it out. They were at the core of the visionary Forward Thrust bond campaign in 1968, which funded capital improvements throughout King County, including construction of a domed stadium. They took pride in the new baseball franchise, yet they were not heavily involved in acquiring or promoting the team. But in the fall of 1969, because they understood that losing the Pilots would adversely affect their city's reputation, they stepped forward to launch a stirring, yet unsuccessful, last-minute campaign to save the team for Seattle.

These civic leaders could be counted on for time and energy, but they did not represent vast wealth. Seattle was populated with middle-class millionaires—wealthy people who were not flashy spenders. There were pockets of affluence but no neighborhood or club restricted to the elite. When in need, the city could not call on any exceedingly rich group or wealthy individual. The most likely financial source, the Boeing family, like the company, held itself substantially aloof from city affairs.[12]

Seattle's civic leaders were upper-middle-class businessmen, professionals mainly associated with downtown Seattle, aided by a few community volunteers who worked for good government or promoted cultural activities. Though mostly corporate, they did not unduly favor downtown business interests. They usually worked for the interests of the region, extending to the boundaries of King County. They had a good deal of power but do not appear to have used it to further themselves financially.

The relationships among these city fathers were neither formal nor strict. One could be easily initiated into the group by working on chamber of commerce projects, pitching in to help the United Good Neighbors (United Way) campaign, or volunteering for whatever ad hoc committee was working at the time. Although Seattle had a reputation for aloofness, its openness to newcomers willing to work was typical of a much smaller community. If there was an inner circle, it was the Monday luncheon group whose leaders discussed ideas and plans to benefit the city. Out of this emerged a purported Big Ten. Ten is probably an apocryphal number—the *Atlantic Monthly* thought it was about a dozen middle-aged managerial types—but it is clear that Ed Carlson of Western International Hotels was the key figure. Bond attorney James Ellis was a member. Joe Gandy operated in both the booster and civic leader circles. Ross Cunningham, editor of the *Seattle Times*, observed, "If you want to get anything done in Seattle, you get about six members of the 'Big Ten' together and tell them it's a good project. If you convince them you're in. That's the way the town is run." Cunningham seemed to identify himself as among the Big Ten by adding that the *Times* was instrumental in cultivating such support. Crusty Seattle author Bill Speidel was less formal in his description of the city leaders: "There are a certain number of people in this town who get things done, who know what's important and what's going on. The rest we just keep around for bulk."[13]

These men, and it was certainly all men, were remarkably self-effacing. They enjoyed working behind the scenes and manning committees, and, above all, they relished the opportunity to further their city. Ellis affirmed that they were not the wealthiest Seattleites, and he considered them the people willing to work the hardest for the public good. In a more telling comment, he maintained that nonpolitical leaders were needed to inject creativity into city decision making and to rise above the restraints of politics. In something of a counterpoint, a University of Washington political science professor observed, "They don't know what conflict of interest is here because they don't know they have it." The civic leaders were a unique leadership cadre that did much to advance the reputation of Seattle yet represented qualities that marked Seattle as less than top rank in the eyes of many. Seattle historian Murray Morgan described their efforts as "flashes of creative imagination from prosaic professionals." Another writer was even less complimentary: "Doing-it-by-citizen-committee is highly congenial to the Protestant middle class. Whether it accomplishes anything or not, they like it that way."[14]

Vigorous elected officials are essential to achieving and maintaining municipal preeminence. In any bid for a professional sports franchise, City Hall generally takes the lead and certainly provides crucial support. Throughout most of the 1960s, political leadership was largely apathetic about transforming Seattle into a major league metropolis or luring a big-league franchise to the region.

In an effort to stem corruption in the 1930s, reformers created a weak-mayor–strong-council city government. With power diffused and initiative dampened, the council concentrated on seeing that the city was running smoothly. Council members were older, constrained, and careful with the budget. The result was a municipal government starved of vision and ambition—even inattentive to problems that might ordinarily elicit action.[15]

In the mid- to late 1960s, there were signs that the government was stirring, even as early as Mayor Dorm Braman's term (1964–69). By the end of the decade (though too late to save major league baseball in Seattle), change was afoot. Although he was open to some innovation, Braman's governmental needle was essentially set on "status quo." Consequently, he is not only a key player in the story of the Pilots but also a good representative of the political establishment during the first slow-moving part of the transformation of Seattle into a big-league city. James d'Orma Braman had been a hardware dealer in Seattle and was elected to the city council in 1954. He served on the council, notably on the budget committee, until 1964, when he was elected mayor. In 1966, a new state law allowed him to take over budget creation, and he won the authority to create new city departments. With the prodding of his talented assistant, Ed Devine, Braman, though always cautious, brought some initiative to the executive's office. Devine convinced Braman to apply for a federal Model Cities grant for urban development, which the city secured. At Devine's insistence, Braman became, a bit belatedly, an active supporter of the Forward Thrust capital improvement election campaign in 1968. Though the mayor dragged his feet in responding to growing racial tensions in the Central Area and was reluctant to initiate police reform, he was able to stir the city government to some action. When Braman left for Washington, D.C., to become assistant secretary of the Department of Transportation in February 1969, Councilman Floyd Miller replaced him. Miller took up the role of caretaker for the rest of the year (some claimed he wintered in Southern California), and city government briefly turned from moderate activity to lethargy until Seattle could elect a new mayor.[16]

As the 1960s came to a close, significant reform was brewing. A bipartisan group of mostly younger attorneys formed Choose an Effective City Council (CHECC) in 1966. Phyllis Lamphere and Tim Hill were the first CHECC-supported candidates to win seats on the council in 1967. Lamphere promised to get beyond the city council's caretaker mentality and seek a stronger executive. Hill supported the Model Cities initiative and campaigned for higher pay as a way of attracting better officers to the corruption-ridden police department. Neither was interested in spending taxpayer money for sports arenas. Between 1967 and 1973, voters replaced the entire city council. Although not all the new members were supported by CHECC, the council was younger, less doctrinaire, and more questioning of city operations—all of which comported with the CHECC vision. They did not care much about putting their community on the sports map but supported expansion of social programs. A CHECC board member claimed credit for a battery of initiatives including expansion of community services, housing rehabilitation, arts funding, historic preservation, and parks renovation.[17]

The other infusion of vibrancy into the municipal government came with the mayoral election of December 1969. Again, youth was served. Wes Uhlman, a thirty-four-year-old, modish state senator, appealed to those who felt left out of government. His platform ran to environmental issues—such as protecting Lake Union—education, efficiency in government, and a simple promise to form a vision for the city. Uhlman won handily over the older Mort Frayn, a printer whose policies were not that much different from Uhlman's but whose style and conservative personal appearance represented a Seattle that was passing. The *Argus* hailed Uhlman's win as a victory over the establishment, and his administration turned out to be much more dynamic than his predecessors'. Uhlman's vision paralleled that of the new city council members. Though he dutifully worked to retain the Pilots for Seattle, baseball was not a priority. Uhlman's idea of advancing the city was to improve life for its residents. He established a department of community development that would work to lure industries to Seattle and help already established businesses expand, created a department of human resources, and enforced affirmative action, furthering civil rights at a crucial juncture in the city's history. Though he endured setbacks—including the loss of the Pilots and more police corruption—and though he labored through one of Seattle's toughest economic times, he pushed Seattle a good way toward becoming more nationally renowned. Historian Norbert MacDonald asserts that by the end of his tenure as mayor, Uhlman "had become a symbol of a more self-confident, urbane, and tolerant Seattle. It was a long way from the tensions and anxiety of 1968–69." The arrival and departure of the Pilots spanned the terms of Braman, Miller, and Uhlman, and the transition to a CHECC-dominated council. All the occupants of the seats of Seattle power would have a major impact on the place of baseball in the city.[18]

One of SRI's three criteria for acquiring a major league franchise was an adequate stadium. By the 1960s, this almost surely meant a publicly constructed arena. Building a stadium, in turn, necessitated a number of new public works—traffic revisions, parking lots, and utilities, for example. Maintenance and improvement of a city's infrastructure are signs of its readiness for a major league franchise. Once again, Seattle's record was mixed. The Evergreen Point Floating Bridge (Highway 520), a second link connecting Seattle to the eastern suburbs across Lake Washington, opened in 1963. Construction of the Interstate 5 freeway moved through the eastern part of downtown and to full completion by 1967.

In addition, there was a master plan to build ring roads around downtown. The R. H. Thomson Expressway would extend from the northern border of the city south along the western edge of Lake Washington to Renton. The Bay Freeway was projected to run from the interstate along the northern edge of downtown near the Seattle Center to connect with Highway 99 at the viaduct, near the waterfront. Only a bit of this vision came to pass. The private civic leaders were not enthusiastic about the ring road scheme, distracted by their own initiatives to build rapid transit, add to the park system, and finish cleaning up Lake Washington.[19]

Some Seattleites sought a thorough renovation of the historic Pioneer Square downtown district and Pike Place Market, to make way for the gentrification of the two downtown areas. Others, more preservation minded, pushed for needed structural repair yet hoped to retain the ambience of the two landmarks. The two sides fought each other to a standstill for several years. All of this, combined with the city's typical reluctance to act, slowed redevelopment to a crawl. Both the highway projects and the arguments over renovation versus renewal would affect stadium planning. [20]

Jim Bouton, Pilots relief pitcher, thought Seattle's cultural priorities were in the right order, observing in his best-selling *Ball Four*, "A city that seems to care more for its art museums than its ballpark can't be all bad." Bouton may have been onto something. A city's capacity to sustain high culture might be an indication of its ability to maintain a team. Some of the same dynamics that are necessary to maintain a thriving arts scene are crucial for backing a baseball team: sufficient individual wealth, ongoing support from an array of businesses, and steady attendance (whether it's opera lovers or baseball fans). Seattle's support for culture balanced out its sometimes tepid political leadership and rows over public works, bolstering its argument that the region was ready for the major leagues. The city's cultural arts scene burgeoned from the time of the world's fair in 1962 into the late 1960s. The fair had provided new or much improved facilities, which various performing arts groups happily occupied. Allied Arts, created in 1954 as a clearinghouse for donations to the arts, pushed successfully for the refurbishment of the buildings on the fairgrounds when the exposition concluded. In a move that presaged the effort to save baseball in Seattle, Allied Arts, attuned to the middle-class culture of the city, effectively solicited a large number of less-than-well-heeled donors as well as business interests. Glynn Ross, Seattle Opera general director beginning in 1963, marveled at the condition of the arts in the city. "I came to Seattle and found that the parade had already begun; my job was to get out in front and to stay out in front."[21]

There were caution signs as well. By the late 1960s, enthusiasm and support for the arts had plateaued. John Hauberg, Weyerhaeuser board member, suggested that the problem was that the most prosperous families living in Seattle represented first-generation wealth. Sustaining the arts took second-generation wealth—sons and daughters who had been raised with an appreciation for the fine arts and, consequently, were more eager to support cultural activities. A similar analysis could apply to the failure to establish local ownership for the Pilots.[22]

Another boon for Seattle in the late 1960s was its media base. In addition to the three requisite TV network channels and a public broadcasting outlet, there were independent stations that served Seattle and Tacoma. The AM radio dial was full of stations. One, KVI, proved to be a crucial source of revenue for the Pilots when it agreed to a generous broadcasting deal. Seattle had two citywide daily newspapers, the *Seattle Post- Intelligencer* and the *Seattle Times*. The *Post-Intelligencer* was the morning paper, with a circulation of 200,000 in 1969. The afternoon *Times* went out to 251,000. Neither paper was prone to publicize problems in Seattle, but both had energetic sports departments that reported on games, held contests, staged Man of the Year banquets, and generally supported the local sporting community. The two papers would treat the Pilots and its ownership with proprietary affection until rumors about the team's move began to surface. The *Argus*, a weekly, aspired to be a high-brow publication with a social conscience and frequently offered prickly observations that were often discomfiting to the city's formal and informal leadership.[23]

Seattle Magazine sought to go where its media counterparts trod with restraint. The weekly, published from 1964 through 1970, covered black militancy, homosexuality, police harassment, and county prosecutor Charles O. Carroll winking at corruption. It also presented several articles on Seattle's relationship with major league baseball. *Seattle Magazine* seemed committed to bringing Seattle into the ranks of great cities singlehandedly. Stimson Bullitt, whose family owned KING broadcasting, envisioned a Seattle version of *Saturday Review*. Editor Peter Bunzel, brought in from Time-Life, was more than game to achieve his employer's goal quickly, noting, "We were charged with writing down our noses from an eastern point of view." Maybe it was because a large number of the staff was from the East—not a sound strategy in a city that did not warm quickly to critical outsiders—but Bunzel, writing down his nose, observed that it was easier to teach the transplanted staff about Seattle than to teach Seattleites how to write.[24]

Finally, what about the fans? Were Northwesterners ready to support major league baseball? Seattleites enjoyed their sports, but that was the point. It was *their* sports. Each year, 200,000 went skiing, often taking off in midweek to populate the slopes. One in seven owned a boat. Whether there were really more boat owners per capita in Seattle than anywhere else, this was an article of faith among a populace grateful to be surrounded by water. The same pride of ownership was true for spectator sports. The University of Washington's football team, the Huskies, was Seattle's team. To numerous Husky fans and university administrators, the NFL was merely a potential interloper. A Husky game was the place to go and be seen. Attendance ranged between 35,000 and 40,000—a large crowd for a middling team in the mid- to late 1960s. The annual summer spectacle of hydroplane races was major league for Northwesterners. Perhaps 150,000 or more turned out on a usually sunny Sunday in August to watch the boats race. By the late 1960s, detractors like *Post-Intelligencer* columnist Emmett Watson deemed Seafair a stodgy imitation of midwestern winter carnivals, but local folks were enthralled by parades, hoopla, and, mainly, the prospect of watching, for free, the thunderboats roar around Lake Washington. Royal Brougham cut the difference between a desire for major league sports and Seattle's first loves in response to his skeptical colleague. Brougham believed that even in the face of future competition from major league baseball and football teams, the hydroplanes would continue to enjoy undying support and the Huskies would be fine if they could produce a winner. ABC's famed broadcaster Keith Jackson, who worked for Seattle's KOMO early in his career, thought it would be Huskies and hydros forever in Seattle and staked his career on it, moving up by moving out. He said that if he thought Seattle would ever become a big-league sports town, he would stick around, but with the water sports and hiking, there was no chance.[25]

The Pacific Coast League Seattle Angels, originally the Rainiers, had played in Sicks' Stadium since 1938. Local fans seemed happy with their minor league team, so much so that some wondered (presciently) if the city could ever develop a taste for major league baseball once it arrived. The fans came out to see good baseball and their local heroes, such as Fred Hutchinson and Edo Vanni. The Rainiers topped the PCL attendance charts in 1945, 1949–51, and 1955. Attendance reached its peak in Seattle in 1947, with a season turnout of 548,368. Seattle, once a star baseball town, by the mid-1960s seemed just mediocre. Despite a PCL pennant in 1966, attendance slumped. There were plenty of people, though, who remembered the postwar heydays and were sure the city was ripe for major league baseball.[26]

Pro football came in the shape of the Ramblers of the Pacific Football League, then the Rangers of the Continental Football League, two wobbly minor leagues. Occasionally, much to Seattleites' chagrin, major league baseball and football owners on the make threatened to relocate to Seattle as a way of leveraging a better deal at home. The one great surprise was the Sonics basketball team, which arrived with almost no advance ballyhoo (and a Los Angeles owner) in 1967. Despite the local sports establishment's startled joy, the National Basketball Association (NBA) did not yet count as major league. In short, Seattle's quest, what there was of it, to acquire a major league franchise summed up the citizens' aspirations to become a big-league city. They would gladly welcome it, maybe thinking in passing that it was about time, but were hardly consumed with the idea.

So the question remains, by 1969, was Seattle ready for big-league status? Boeing was a world-class company and, when healthy, a powerful economic engine. Seattle was already a major entrepôt on the Pacific Ocean. The region was growing. Seattle was the fifteenth-largest media market in the country, and metropolitan Seattle was the eighteenth-largest urban area, surpassing the likes of Atlanta, Cincinnati, Milwaukee, and San Diego. It seemed to be a city at least on the threshold of the kind of recognition that includes a sports franchise.

But perceptions are trickier than realities, and perceptions play a big part in determining status. Commentators' opinions varied—and it often was a commentator's geographic perspective that made the difference. The tendency of *Seattle Magazine*'s Peter Bunzel to inform Seattle of its shortcomings as a real city derived from his comparing it to New York. Walt Crowley, who came to love Seattle and documented it in his online HistoryLink project, arrived in 1961, after living in Michigan, Connecticut, and Washington, D.C. He initially found Seattle "puny, provincial, and puritanical." Likewise, Malcolm Cowley, an East Coast man of letters, thought Seattle fell short in politics, ethnic diversity, and journalism. He found it bourgeois—not meant as a compliment. Cowley softened his criticism a bit, observing, "Everyone seemed to be middle class and literate no matter what his trade." For *New York Times* sportswriter Neil Amdur, Seattle was the last sports frontier, still operating very much in the shadow of Los Angeles and San Francisco. Quoting a New York cabby on the arrival of the Pilots in 1969, Amdur noted that ten years earlier, people thought Seattle was in the rain forest. By the end of the 1960s, it was still a place that did not let women sit at a bar and had twice defeated proposals for a sports stadium. Amdur concluded that Seattle did not know what it had in the Pilots, implying that it was not yet figuratively major league enough to operate in the big leagues.[27]

In contrast, Earl Pomeroy, whose vantage point was Eugene, Oregon, portrayed the city as a metropolis. Pomeroy, a historian of the Pacific Northwest from the University of Oregon, considered Seattle afflicted with big-city ills, such as automobiles and ad agencies. Portland State University historian Carl Abbott similarly envisioned Seattle of the 1960s and 1970s as a good deal more advanced than his own city. Abbott found Portland regional, while Seattle was transforming itself into one of the country's major links with Asia. Further, Seattle leadership was much more dynamic and full of civic optimism than Portland's.[28]

Not surprisingly, the commentators who most incisively assessed Seattle's big-league status were established residents. Roger Sale, literature professor at the University of Washington, published his history *Seattle: Past to Present* in 1976. The *Post-Intelligencer*'s Emmett Watson was the insider's insider. As they looked back at 1969, the year the Pilots brought major league baseball to Seattle, they substantially agreed. Seattle was making its way toward national prominence but had not yet attained it. Watson saw Seattle as young and beautiful but in need of a healthy sense of skepticism; its citizens needed to be less self-satisfied about their community. Watson did believe Seattle had begun to move in some progressive directions in the 1960s. It was becoming a city that welcomed diversity, where business interests were not the only ones with influence, and whose citizens were willing to pay for their betterment. For Sale and many others, the 1962 Seattle World's Fair, more formally the Century 21 Exposition, marked the beginning of a forward-looking spirit. He observed that the Puget Sound region had been growing quantitatively (economically and in population) and was now catching up to itself qualitatively in fits and starts. The capital improvements campaign Forward Thrust, the private refurbishing of Pioneer Square, approval of a sports stadium, and the modernization of the Port of Seattle impressed him. But the city's limited response to the black community's outcries, its deteriorating schools, a do-little city government, and the economic dominance of Boeing remained disturbing problems. Uhlman's new administration and the significant turnover in the city council were strides toward maturity.[29]

Did Seattle merit a big-league franchise? It was populous enough, it was usually economically and culturally vibrant, but it was still a bit provincial and somewhat lethargic. And there were real doubts about support for a team. Where were the monied interests outside of the reluctant Boeing Company? Was there sufficient fan interest? The city was on the verge, but there remained serious questions about whether Seattle had everything a city needs to be a big-league metropolis.

Chapter 2

THE SEATTLE SPIRIT AND A WORLD'S FAIR

A T first, the sketches made it look like a tethered balloon. Then it evolved into a shaft and a saucer. When someone called it a "space needle," it took on a life of its own. Seattle hotelier Ed Carlson had visited Stuttgart, Germany, in 1959 and eaten in a restaurant atop a television broadcast tower. He was impressed that people would pay just to go up into the tower and order dinner. Carlson sketched out his vision for the structure and shared it with his friend James Douglas, a shopping center manager. Soon, architects Jack Graham and Victor Steinbrueck were in on the design. The Space Needle became an image rich in meaning. It was an icon of the 1962 Seattle World's Fair and has represented the city in the national mind ever since. Its inception was emblematic of the workings of the city in the 1960s. When the county turned down a funding proposal, a private consortium of civic leaders built the Space Needle. The Pentagram Corporation, which financed the $4.5 million project, included arts patron Bagley Wright; Ned Skinner, head of Alaska Steamship Corporation; Norton Clapp, of Weyerhaeuser; contractor Howard Wright; and Graham. Carlson's Western International Hotels got a twenty-year contract to operate the restaurant. The Bank of California supplied the lead loan.[1]

Because it was a private enterprise, the Space Needle could not be built on public property. The city agreed to sell an old fire alarm station next to the fair site. Skinner and Wright took a helicopter to see how high the Needle should be. One thousand feet provided a good view but was too expensive to build. At 607 feet, "the economic and aesthetic lines converged." As the Needle began to rise out of the ground in 1961, many Seattleites really believed for the first time that their city was going to hold a world's fair. The Space Needle embodied what Seattleites were beginning to call the "Seattle Spirit." Dean Leffler, dean emeritus of St. Mark's Cathedral, summed it up: "The Space Needle symbolizes the fair and the fair marks when the city began to grow up and develop culturally."[2]

Through the 1960s, Seattle made strides toward maturity, but these steps were halting and awkward. In 1962, the Seattle World's Fair and its Space Needle drew the admiration of the nation. Then the Forward Thrust bond election of 1968 enlivened the city and promised capital improvements. Yet, in the midst of the visionary plans and emergent Seattle Spirit, the city failed to find consensus on transportation, renewal projects, and Central Area problems, and voters thwarted repeated efforts to build a sports stadium that would attract a major league sports franchise.

Before the fair, the Seattle Spirit did not seem to be in abundant supply. It was mainly avid sports fans who pushed for a stadium. Their enthusiasm was kindled as the Dodgers and Giants proposed their moves west. In 1957, Dewey Soriano—who later became the president of the Pacific Coast League and then owner of the Seattle Pilots—not only urged construction of a multipurpose stadium but suggested it have a plastic dome. Again, in 1959, Soriano, by then general manager of the minor league Seattle Rainiers, cast an eye toward attracting major league baseball, proposing a city-county-state coalition to build a sixty thousand–seat stadium. Football fans envisioned the University of Washington Huskies playing in a dome; conventions and trade shows would be willing to make the costly trip out to the Northwest to spread their wares or their delegates across the floor of a large arena; and concerts, revivals, circuses, and rodeos would fill the dates between sports seasons. (It was not yet clear how the grass surface would be cared for.) Washington governor Albert Rosellini caught Soriano's vision and formed the Governor's Sports Advisory Council.

Entrepreneurship and the dream of major league sports in Seattle touched off a brief boomlet for stadium building in 1960. The city council's parks and public grounds committee instructed the city planning commission to study the desirability of erecting a stadium near the civic center north of the central business district. This led to the Stanford Research Institute study that brought the good news that Seattle could build a stadium for about $15 million that would operate in the black.

Boosters felt that the SRI requirements were in place and believed that Seattle, with a stadium, would be irresistible to major league baseball by the time the second wave of baseball expansion hit, probably in 1962 or 1963.[3]

The Pre-Stadium Citizens Committee, charged with making a recommendation on the basis of the SRI report, urged county commissioners to hold a bond election, knowing that the county had bonding capacity to spare. Attentive to SRI's admonition about securing a team for the arena, the committee and commissioners briefly engaged in a chicken-and-egg argument. Should Seattle wait to be granted a franchise before it committed to build? Could the city get a franchise without a stadium? Eric Duckstad of the SRI team assured the committee and the county commissioners that if they built a stadium, major league baseball would respond very positively—not a guarantee, but good enough. The King County commissioners unanimously adopted a resolution that authorized a vote on November 8, 1960, for $15 million worth of bonds. The resolution explained that the purpose of building a stadium was to bring major league football and baseball to western Washington, "thereby adding to the social and economic interests of Seattle." It would be one of the few times the economic argument was used in Seattle to promote stadium construction. The commissioners prudently took SRI's advice and added that they would sell the bonds only if there was a real prospect of luring major league teams.[4]

There was no groundswell of support for the measure. A modest committee composed of three restaurant owners (including Dave Cohn), publicist Bill Sears, and philanthropist Paul Friedlander exhausted its $4,000 budget on some flyers and a few bumper stickers. One labor leader liked the fact that it promised more jobs, and the president of Seattle University thought it would lift the city's morale. Seattle sportswriters, the most visible among the sports booster crowd, championed the measure in telling terms. The stature of the city rode on the vote. The *Seattle Times'* Hy Zimmerman enthused that a stadium would nicely complement Seattle's natural amenities. But bigger things than being crowned as a leisure capital might be in the offing. "Perhaps," Zimmerman wrote, "Seattle can be Boston's equal instead of its underling." Georg Meyers of the *Times* calmed letter writers' fears that the stadium would stand empty. The bonds were contingent on obtaining a team. The real risk, Meyers warned, was that "if the bond issue fails, this neck of the woods can kiss good-bye all hopes of attracting major league baseball or football here in this generation." Royal Brougham agreed with Meyers, writing that with the rejection of the bond, "we'll settle back into being a nice sleepy minor league town for the next decade or so."[5]

For Dan Walton, sportswriter for the *Tacoma News Tribune*, the perspective from the south was a little different. He thought that major league baseball was more interested in saving the Pacific Coast League and would shy away from ruining both Seattle and Tacoma as baseball towns by prematurely bringing a major league franchise to Seattle. A new stadium might just kill a good minor league town.[6]

Though it did not take a firm stand, the *Times* editorial page was not on the same wavelength as its sports department. There were several other bond issues on the ballot in 1960. The *Times* rhetorically asked if schools, parks, and the port of Seattle were critical to the city. It advised readers to weigh the tax propositions and vote for the ones they thought they could afford—stopping one step short of rejecting the stadium. The *Seattle Post-Intelligencer* editors were likewise noncommittal but more evenhanded, merely describing the cost and likely outcomes of a positive vote.[7]

Seattleites counted the cost and found an extra amenity too expensive. The final vote in King County was 176,362 against to 159,432 for. The bond needed 60 percent approval but won less than 48 percent. The lack of vigorous leadership and the competing bond issues, especially the ones for schools, sapped support for the issue. While sports columnists saw baseball's movement west as a great opportunity that would enable Seattle to enter the top echelons of sports, most Seattleites did not yet consider financing a stadium particularly worthwhile.[8]

That attitude, whether born of a sense of priorities, caution, or apathy, began to shift in 1962. Seattle surprised itself with a roaring success—the Seattle World's Fair. Historian John Findlay describes the magnitude of this transformation in civic self-perception: "In the months preceding the exposition, some residents thought of Seattle as a small, remote, relatively unsophisticated community, struggling against long odds to become 'a major world's fair host city.' After basking in the success of the fair and the praise of the nation in 1962, the metropolis perceived itself to be maturing, not simply in terms of economic and physical growth, but also by developing the amenities that characterize cosmopolitan living and major league status." With the fair, Seattle had a new vision. Ensuing events in the 1960s demonstrated a determination to fulfill it.[9]

The Seattle Spirit had emerged as early as the Alaska-Yukon-Pacific Exposition of 1909. Simply put, the Seattle Spirit was civic boosterism coupled with a willingness to work to accomplish goals. The planners of the exposition were prominent Seattle businessmen who almost off-handedly decided to celebrate Seattle and the Gold Rush and bring some business to town, but before long, they had recruited King County, the state legislature, and exhibitors from around the United States and from Asia. The spirit had been roused from time to time since then. Initial responses to the Great Depression, for instance, included a brief flurry of civic activism from both businessmen and the down-and-out them-selves. It showed up again in the mid-1950s. In a virtual reenactment of the first Alaska-Yukon-Pacific Exposition meeting, city councilman Al Rochester bumped into *Times* political reporter Ross Cunningham and Chamber of Commerce manager Don Follett at the Washington Athletic Club. Rochester casually mentioned that a celebration of the fiftieth anniversary of the Alaska-Yukon-Pacific Exposition might stimulate a little business for the city. Follett promised that the chamber would get behind the idea, and Cunningham pledged the *Times'* support. By early 1955, the state senate was busy on the project, and Governor Arthur Langlie had persuaded Ed Carlson to head the Fair Feasibility Commit-tee. The original plan was to host a regional fair in 1959, the Festival of the West. Seattle could have some fun, reap a little profit from tourists, and enhance its economic reputation. But the Seattle Spirit seized the leadership group, and it expanded the vision. One of the planners, man-agement consultant and economist Dewayne Kraeger, marveled at the spontaneity of the change: "We really had no business trying to put on a World's Fair. Seattle wasn't supposed to be big league enough for that kind of operation. But we were just cocky and ignorant enough to give it a try." Historian of Seattle Murray Morgan was less reticent and more col-orful, lauding the group of "practical dreamers who undertook to paddle their canoe across a vast sea of apathy, Seattle in tow."[10]

At the time, Eddie Carlson was emerging as a key leader of the civic-minded set. His role in organizing the fair fully established his reputa-tion. Carlson started in the hotel business as a messenger boy, a position beneath even that of bellhop, while attending the University of Washing-ton. A lack of funds cut short his college career. He signed on as an able-bodied seaman and then returned to the hotel business, rising swiftly to manager of the President Hotel in Mount Vernon, Washington, in 1935, and manager of the Rainier Club in Seattle in 1937. After a stint in the navy during the Second World War, Carlson returned to Western Hotels (later Western International and, later still, Westin Hotels & Resorts), where he became assistant to the president by 1946 and president in 1960. Everyone in a leadership position in Seattle seemed to know the diminutive, curly-haired man with horn-rimmed glasses. Friends and colleagues admired his competence, energy, and drive. A good listener, Carlson had a special talent for getting people to work in harmony. Throughout the 1960s, those qualities served both him and Seattle well. Ultimately, after Western International Hotels merged with United Airlines, Carlson became the chairman of UAL, the holding company for the hotels and the airline.[11]

Carlson mobilized Seattle's civic leadership to work on the feasibility study for the fair and then to organize the exposition itself, recruiting a group whose names would pepper reports of civic enterprise for the next decade and more: Norton Clapp, the chairman of Weyerhaeuser; developer Henry Broderick; James Douglas, president of Northgate shopping center; Vic Rosellini, owner of one of the leading restaurants in the city; Joe Gandy; William Blethen of the *Times* family; Lawrence Arnold, Seattle First National Bank chairman; Harry Carr, vice president of the King County Labor Council; Paul Friedlander; Seattle banker and business icon Joshua Green; and political leaders including city council members Dorm Braman, Myrtle Edwards (notably, the only woman and always referred to in the newspapers as Mrs. Harlan Edwards), and Senator Warren Magnuson. Unpublicized financial contributions from Rainier Brewing owner Emil Sick, developer Ben Ehrlichman, and Western Hotels founder Frank Dupar kept the study committee going until fair planners were able to secure commitments from local firms and tap into significant public funding. Ned Skinner, declaring that he liked to work on projects with long odds, was in charge of soliciting private funds from community leaders. To support the early effort, he cajoled an advance of $1,000 out of those whom he expected to pledge a good deal more. Architect and city planning commission member Paul Thiry signed on as the chief architect of the fair. Thiry had already designed the Museum of History and Industry and the Frye Art Museum. The Seattle Spirit was coming alive.[12]

Besides establishing financial support, the committee's top priority was finding a suitable site for the exposition. The obvious choice combined the need for a fair site, the clear interest of the Fair Feasibility Committee in keeping the fair near downtown (a *vested* interest according to the *Argus*), and the city council's visions of an expanded civic center, or, in Skinner's words, the choice was a combination of "political sagacity, business acumen, and desperation." The civic center was several acres smaller than the other possibilities. When fair organizers discovered that a 1951 festival site in Britain was even smaller, they happily declared that the exposition would be a jewel-box fair. In retrospect, the size of the fair was probably instrumental in limiting costs and producing a profit.[13]

It was hardly a privately run enterprise. The city underwrote the world's fair after the electorate approved a $7.5 million bond issue. The state followed with $7.5 million more. Local businesses underwrote $5 million in bank loans. The banks and, even more, the businesses making the pledges were sticking their necks out four years before the fair opened its gates. It turned out to be a good bet. Because the exposition made a profit, no one had to pay on the pledged guarantees.[14]

Senator Magnuson took responsibility for federal dollars, coming up with a $9 million appropriation. The fair committee made his task easier by shrewdly emphasizing science as a central theme of the fair, drawing strong support from the U.S. science community in the aftermath of Sputnik. The fair would be a tribute to American technology, a glorification of progress through science, and a testament to the ability of humans to manage their environment on earth and in outer space. The Seattle World's Fair was transforming from a commercial display into the Century 21 Exposition.[15]

As Carlson, Skinner, and the others rallied increasing community support, there was one important holdout. Boeing CEO William Allen, forgetting his promise to relax and lighten up, played the curmudgeon. He did not like fairs and thought that the Seattle effort would be a financial disaster. He refused to be a part of it. William Street, of Frederick & Nelson department stores, assured Allen that the fair would be held with or without Boeing and pointed out that since the major theme was science, Boeing would be conspicuous by its absence. Allen gave in. Boeing made no cash contribution or pledge, but it built a major exhibit, the Spacearium, in the Science Pavilion. In an almost too predictable move, the company placed an ad in the fair's program inviting visiting engineers to stop by the Boeing employment center, conveniently located on the grounds.[16]

The Century 21 Exposition had been scheduled for 1959 to commemorate the Alaska-Yukon-Pacific Exposition's fiftieth anniversary. There was too much to do. The organizers postponed the fair twice, finally aiming for a 1962 opening. The Seattle Spirit was going dormant. Civic disbelief seemed total. In the midst of all the pressures, Carlson, newly president of Western International Hotels, found that he could not both do his job and lead the effort for the fair. In mid-1960, he turned the reins over to Joe Gandy, who later remembered, "The fair was a dying dog. And a lot of people thought I'd be the one to bury it." Though Carlson hardly absented himself from the project, Gandy's efforts proved that the "dog" had plenty of bark left. He flew to Paris and, through extensive diplomacy, convinced the Bureau of International Expositions that Seattle, Washington (not Washington, D.C., as the bureau members had believed), deserved recognition as a certified world's fair. He traveled hundreds of thousands of miles recruiting exhibits from fifty-five nations. Domestically, he and his team convinced U.S. companies, including Ford Motor Company, to participate. Gandy pointed out that if the local Ford dealer was the head of the project, the company could not very well ignore the event. He persuaded fellow committee member Harry Carr of the King County Labor Council to make a no-strike pledge and committed the fair organization to practicing racial equality and upholding fair hiring practices. The public relations machinery cranked into operation, and the exposition made it into *Look*, *Sunset*, the *Saturday Evening Post*, and the *New York Times*. The other iconic image of the fair, the monorail line that whisked people from Fifth Street downtown to the fairgrounds, joined the Space Needle on the cover of *Life*. Like the fair, the monorail was a financial success.[17]

On April 21, 1962, even as laborers worked feverishly to put the last elements in place, President John Kennedy tapped a telegraph key in the White House, triggering a radio telescope that picked up an impulse from a star and sent it to the fairgrounds to signal the opening of the Century 21 Exposition. This was the same telegraph key decorated with gold nuggets that President Taft had used to open the Alaska-Yukon-Pacific Exposition 103 years earlier. Cannons fired, whistles blew, and jets flew overhead (one crashed). From their perch in the Space Needle, city councilman Al Rochester and Ned Skinner looked down on nearly empty parking lots. What seemed to presage disaster at first was actually no worse than an isolated error—there was too much parking. Though attendance started off spotty, ultimately 9.6 million people walked through the gates, and another 400,000 bought tickets but failed to attend. Seven million of the fairgoers came from out of state, adding 8.3 percent more revenue to the state's economy, compared to 1961. Summing all this up, Findlay concluded—not critically—"It was a thinking man's fair. The Seattle World's Fair presented middlebrow culture to middle-class fairgoers." Another observer remarked, "It was large enough to impress, but not so large as to intimidate—much like the city itself." The fair operated within closely controlled margins. Had the Clearing House Association, which furnished the bank loan, actually run the exposition, it would have been hamstrung, but it did watch over the books. Even as the Seattle Spirit soared, the restraint that marked the city's endeavors was also in force.[18]

But it was a success. To the relief and surprise of many Seattle businessmen who had put much of their money and all of their reputation on the line, the fair made $1 million. Further, the city was left with a legacy of buildings, which meant it had a decision to make. For this purpose, the city created the Century 21 Center Corporation and asked Carlson, who had earned the deep trust and admiration of the people of Seattle, to head the group. Would the grounds become an entertainment venue? A cultural center? A tourist destination? A memorial to the fair? "All of the above" seemed to be the corporation's response. The grounds closed for a year and a half and then reopened as the Seattle Center. The federal government leased the science pavilion to the corporation for one dollar, so that it could become an educational facility, the Pacific Science Center. The Coliseum would provide a sports venue and a home for the Seattle Supersonics basketball team for forty years. The Seattle Symphony, the Seattle Opera, and the newly formed Repertory Theater occupied several buildings. The grounds became a large park and a site for festivals and functions throughout the year. The Seattle Center became, if not a Central Park, an anchor for city life and a place that spoke of a sophisticated urban center.[19]

Euphoria spawned by the financial and artistic success of the fair swept Seattle—the city of restraint, the community that seemed to believe "pretty good" would be the pinnacle of *its* success, a people who suspected something would go wrong if one dared to build too high. Seattle had done it. Historians of the fair paint it as a catharsis. Inferiority complex? "Seattleites, typifying the traditional cultural insecurity of the West, tended to think that theirs was a minor league city, but afterwards they felt that they had arrived in the big leagues." Too self-effacing? "The city proved to itself and to the world that it could do a professional piece of work of international moment and, moreover, do it with style." Afflicted with a certain Scandinavian pessimism? "The paralysis of shared doubts was supplanted by a 'we can do it' courage that even today [in 1971, in the midst of the Boeing recession] gives us strength to overcome sobering economic reverses." Too boring, too middle class? "The fair was a catalytic event in the history of Seattle, sparking new self-awareness in the city, awakening new tastes, higher ambitions, and even a keener sense of this area's destiny." More than anything, it was the reemergence of the Seattle Spirit—a phenomenon that became truly vital only after the success of the fair—that stirred leading Seattleites to believe that their city was on the rise. Seattle was now much more well known than before the world's fair. Though most leaders understood that Seattle was not yet a world-class city, many became confident that they could be a catalyst for making it so. Gandy, who would play a major role in that quest, expressed his ambitions in terms of an entrepreneurial past. The fair, he declared, "has re-kindled civic spirit . . . the spirit that built a community out of the ashes, that moved hills and spanned lakes and waterways and sent its commerce around the world." Ned Skinner looked toward the future: "People applauded the world's fair and wanted more. 'What will we do for an encore?' became the oft-repeated popular cliche."[20]

For some, especially Gandy, a major league baseball team for a major league city would have been an ideal encore. It would not be. The next move toward obtaining a team for Seattle illustrates aspects of the Seattle Spirit. This spirit had more of an effect on business leaders—the "civic leadership"—than on most local politicians. And even among the civic-minded, there was no consensus about what would boost the city's reputation. Further, the spirit might be moving, but caution and restraint had not been thrown to the winds.

Impressed by the success of the fair, the Seattle Chamber of Commerce launched the Citizens Committee for Major League Baseball in 1962. William Woods, past chamber president, headed the committee initially. Its purpose was to rally a newly confident populace to build a stadium. This time, there would be a well-orchestrated campaign aimed especially at persuading women and people on fixed incomes to support stadium bonds.[21]

In March 1963, probably at the behest of the Citizens Committee, the Seattle Junior Chamber of Commerce mailed a questionnaire to city organizations drawn from its list and to individuals selected at random from the phone book. The poll asked Seattleites and residents of King County about their interest in pursuing a sports team. The return rate, 18 percent for individuals and 15 percent for organizations, was typical of a mailing, but the results may have made sports boosters think twice. Only about 50 percent of the respondents were extremely interested in a major league franchise coming to Seattle. A slightly larger majority strongly favored a bond issue to build a stadium, although around 70 percent would at least be supportive of such an undertaking. (It took 60 percent for a measure to pass.) County residents were both more likely to attend sporting events than city respondents and much more willing to vote for a stadium (88 percent, compared to 66 percent of Seattleites). Other cities often registered 70 percent majorities when asked to approve stadium issues. One wonders if, at the end of the decade, Citizens Committee member and, later, Pilots' president Dewey Soriano, recalled this early warning sign of a city that was clearly interested in but not passionate about baseball.[22]

The target date for the second stadium vote of the decade was set for 1964, then 1965, and finally 1966. But the unexpected possibility of drawing an established team excited Puget Sound sports fans and, for a few months, redirected the committee's efforts. The Cleveland Indians appeared to be on the move. A new ownership group, chaired by William Daley, had lost about one-third of a million dollars in 1963 in Cleveland and was looking for a more lucrative market. With the Braves moving to Milwaukee, the Dodgers and Giants to the West Coast, and the Twins to Minnesota, the era of owners demanding concessions and threatening to take their franchises elsewhere was in full swing. Daley had visited Seattle on a business trip and was impressed. Gabe Paul, president of the Indians, was familiar with the city from his time with the Cincinnati Reds, who had been affiliated with the minor league Seattle club. Paul was also well acquainted with Dewey Soriano, who was the Rainiers general manager at that time. Daley sought a $4 million renovation to

Cleveland's Municipal Stadium and warned the mayor, "I have a chance to move to Seattle. I'll move if I don't get what I want." Though Daley and Paul also entertained offers from Oakland and Dallas–Fort Worth, Seattle appeared to be at the top of their list.[23]

At the urging of the Citizens Committee, the two baseball executives flew to the Northwest in early October 1964 to look around and allow themselves to be solicited by representatives of the fifteenth-largest market in the United States, who were currently operating in a can-do mode. The first matter of business was determining a place to play. The Cleveland group toured Sicks' Stadium, owned by Alan Ferguson's Sicks' Rainier Brewing Company. The stadium, located in the Rainier Valley neighborhood southeast of downtown Seattle, was the home of the Pacific Coast League Seattle Rainiers. It seated eleven thousand fans, not a sufficient capacity for a major league club. Moreover, parking was minimal. The question of who would pay for remodeling the park to seat at least twenty-five thousand was thorny. Ferguson was unwilling. Instead, he offered to let the Indians use the park rent-free if they would undertake the estimated $900,000 upgrade. The Citizens Committee lined up area residents to pay for the upgrade, but the commitments were not very solid. Committee members and Paul sat down with Mayor Dorm Braman to see what the city could do. Braman was clear. It was a privately owned ballpark, and the city would neither contribute anything nor seek a formal legal opinion about whether municipal funds could be used.[24]

Braman had no enthusiasm for bringing a baseball franchise to the city and did not intend to expend any political capital on (or accrue any from) attracting the Indians to Seattle. Paul reported that when Indians executives met with Braman and other political leaders, the city officials "just sat there," and when he asked the mayor when Seattle would be ready for major league baseball, Braman replied laconically, "Oh, in about five years." Mayoral assistant Ed Devine chimed in with "Seattle is not panting with excitement, mind you, but is in favor of [a franchise]." (Not much Seattle Spirit there, but, to be fair, Braman's assessment turned out to be optimistic by about seven years.) Braman and the other political leaders were not the only ambivalent Seattleites. *Seattle Magazine* believed that "a small but fervent group hoped Seattle would not get baseball because the city was attractive *because* it was not big league." Some half-hearted comments about holding a $25 million bond vote for a stadium as early as November 1964 and a trip to Federal Way to inspect a potential stadium site at 320th Street did little to draw the Indians ownership or bring about a substantive solution to the stadium problem.[25]

If Braman and like-minded others were not much interested, the Citizens Committee was still hopeful and worked to entice the Indians to Seattle. Bert West of Golden West Broadcasting thought that he had heard Paul call for an advance sale of eight thousand season tickets and started a drive to reach that goal. Ticket coupons appeared daily in the *Seattle Post-Intelligencer* and, at times, in the *Daily Journal of Commerce* and the *Washington Teamster*; the committee distributed ten thousand "GO MAJORS—SEATTLE" bumper stickers and presented Mayor Braman with a baseball cap. William Woods, in a statement that rang with newfound Seattle confidence, declared, "A successful campaign can have a lasting impact greater than the Seattle World's Fair. No other civic project in sight has the potential for bringing Seattle full national recognition." The confidence was misplaced. Individuals responded more readily than businesses but bought only single-seat or partial-season-ticket packages. The drive ended with $731,000 pledged, which represented the equivalent of only 2,400 season seats, less than a third of the goal. (The committee thought the Indians owners' lack of activity squelched enthusiasm.) The boosters rolled out one other inducement. Otto Brandt, general manager of KOMO broadcasting, traveled to Cleveland to pledge $1 million in broadcast rights if the Indians moved west. That exceeded the Cleveland media deal by $200,000. All of this worried Cleveland writers. Hal Lebovitz of the *Cleveland Plain-Dealer* predicted that there was a fifty-fifty chance that the team would move and that "if the Indians leave, Cleveland becomes a bush league town."[26]

On October 16, Gabe Paul sat down with his board of directors to give his report. He praised Seattle as "one of the best baseball markets in the country" and said that he saw "tremendous potential." But Seattle needed a stadium. On the way back to Cleveland, he had also visited Oakland, California, a city that would have a stadium ready by 1966. He also stopped by Dallas, where Lamar Hunt promised to underwrite a guaranteed revenue minimum. The board discussed a new offer from Cleveland that included a longer lease on Municipal Stadium along with stadium and parking upgrades. Heeding a recommendation from Paul and Daley, the board voted to stay in Ohio.[27]

Had Seattle just been used as a bargaining chip? Paul told Soriano, "Look, Dewey, I am ready to go." Soriano's gut feeling was that the prospect of the Indians coming to Seattle came to a halt after Paul had seen Sicks' Stadium. Zimmerman added that neither the brewing company nor the city would come up with the money needed to improve the stadium. A sweetheart lease deal was not attractive enough. The weak ticket sales must have given Daley and Paul some pause as well.[28]

Whatever Paul's and Daley's motivation, the episode revealed something to Seattle about itself and about attracting major league baseball. Three realizations emerged. Two signaled that, even with the world's fair euphoria still in the air, the city was not yet ready to host a team. First, Seattleites were not red-hot for baseball. During the dalliance with the Indians, the eagerness of people like Dewey Soriano, Dave Cohn, and William Woods caused them to believe that the community was as eager for a team as they were. But the ticket drive went poorly, and a number of key civic activists were nowhere to be seen during the scramble to lure the Indians west. Men such as Ed Carlson, Ned Skinner, and Norton Clapp did not exert their leadership, and the politicians continued to be models of Seattle restraint rather than Seattle Spirit. Seattle had fallen short on citizen support, the first of the three Stanford Research Institute's criteria. Gabe Paul bluntly enunciated the second lesson. "Seattle has muffed its chance," he said. "Here's the best advice I can give Seattle. If it wants a major league club, it has to build a ball park." That spoke to the second SRI criterion. (Paul and Daley would have filled SRI's third stipulation, a call for well-heeled ownership, though not local, of course.) Finally, the third instructive insight brought some hope: the Seattle market was attractive to baseball ownership. Though he chose to stay put in 1964, Daley was affected by this brief October episode. He would be back, next time without the Indians, but he would be bringing baseball with him.[29]

Chapter 3

FOR WANT OF A STADIUM

OVER the next three years, Seattleites eager for major league sports grew keenly aware of the three lessons that had emerged from the 1964 effort to snare the Cleveland Indians. The National and American Leagues had their eyes on Seattle—that was an article of faith for sportswriters Hy Zimmerman and Georg Meyers and sports boosters such as Joe Gandy, Dave Cohn, and Dewey Soriano. It was also achingly obvious to these men that the lack of a suitable playing field was the only impediment to major league baseball or professional football coming to the Northwest. And, yes, Seattle fans needed to get more excited about attracting a team and paying for a stadium.

The expectation that the public, not the team owner, would furnish a place to play grew in strength after the Second World War. Baseball commissioner Ford Frick predicted in 1951 that cities would be required to provide stadiums for their teams, arguing that the economic advantages of a park in or near a city merited public assistance. By 1970, 70 percent of major league sports stadiums were publicly financed. As more cities joined the trend and pressure mounted to keep up, the *Seattle Times* and *Seattle Post-Intelligencer* sports departments grew antsy. In November 1965, the headline across the front page of the *Times* sports section read "Another City Chooses Progress." San Diego had voted 3–1 for a new stadium in order to keep the NFL's Chargers and entice major league baseball to the city. The *Post-Intelligencer* groused that although the San Diego market—hemmed in by Los Angeles, Mexico, the desert, and the ocean—was inferior to Seattle's, the stadium meant that the California city was first in line for the next expansion franchise on the West Coast. As plans materialized for the Superdome in New Orleans, the *Post-Intelligencer* warned, again in headline form, "We Have a Strong Rival." Seattle sports lovers worried even more as Louisianans voted 3–1 for their stadium. Zimmerman reminded Seattleites that the Twin Cities, Houston, Atlanta, Anaheim, and Oakland had all built stadiums and now had major league baseball. To underline the point, the *Times* sports department surveyed baseball officials about Seattle's prospects in fall 1966. Bill DeWitt, owner of the Cincinnati Reds, and Charlie Metro, manager of the Tulsa Oilers, a minor league team, separately agreed that Seattle would be a "shoo-in" with a stadium. California Angels executive Bob Reynolds thought that the American League would be foolish to let the National League get to Seattle first, if the city had a stadium. Marvin Milkes, Angels vice president, assured Zimmerman that he would not turn down a job with a Seattle major league team. Not everyone surveyed was as positive as the *Times* writers would have liked. George Weiss of the New York Yankees would not promise a franchise but made it clear that Seattle did not stand a chance without a stadium. Walter O'Malley counseled risk taking—if people want a stadium, go ahead and build it and see what happens.[1]

Zimmerman urged the city council to take the lead. He railed at their do-nothing attitude, especially while the economy was moving ahead. As a goodwill gesture, city councilman Charles M. Carroll suggested spending $2 million and expanding Sicks' Stadium to thirty thousand or even forty-five thousand seats. Zimmerman, who wanted a new arena, labeled Carroll's suggestion as more council penny-pinching, writing derisively, "Charlie, wasn't it a namesake of yours who wrote 'Alice in Wonderland'?" Others poked fun at Seattle's halting ways. Melvin Durslag of the *Los Angeles Times* declared Seattle ready for expansion. The city was just rustic enough to support a losing team while building a stadium. Harry Glickman, Portland, Oregon, sports promoter, doubted Seattle's ability to build a stadium or capture a team. The city was big and beautiful, Glickman conceded, but it was a town of amateurs. This is what Seattleites hated—and dreaded: outsiders scorning them for their lack of sophistication. Into all this ballyhoo and angst came a pair of opportunities. The NFL began to consider Seattle for expansion, and King County finally set a date for a vote on a stadium.[2]

Word began to circulate in late 1965 that the NFL would expand the next year. The NFL's franchise derby pitted Seattle against New Orleans, Houston, Portland (Oregon), Cincinnati, Phoenix, and Boston for one expansion team. Gandy headed up a governor's committee to bring the NFL to the Northwest. Zimmerman praised Governor Dan Evans for tapping the dynamo of the world's fair to get the job done. Local officials, who understood what it would take for a successful bid, again set up a committee to make a multipurpose stadium a reality. Leading it were Dave Cohn, chairman of the sports and recreation division of the Chamber of Commerce; Wilbert Lewis, chairman of the Washington State Athletic Commission; and Junior Chamber of Commerce president Eric Van. Gandy, Cohn, several politicians, and the sportswriters assured fellow citizens that they thought Seattle's chances would be good if it had a stadium. The NFL sent a Stanford Research Institute representative to the contending cities to gather data. Some Seattle leaders took heart—SRI was a familiar face. Others remembered that the earlier study had concluded that a stadium needed baseball, not football alone, to break even. Industrialist John Fluke got on the bandwagon immediately, proclaiming to the Rotary Club that a city with vision cannot always stick with pay-as-you-go. It has to assume debt sometimes if it wants to realize stadium-sized dreams.[3]

May 1966 brought the applicants to the NFL hearings. The Seattle delegation included Gandy ("Go, Joe, Go," a *Post-Intelligencer* editorial cheered), economist H. Dewayne Kraeger, Cohn, Governor Evans, Senators Warren Magnuson and Henry Jackson, and Mayor Braman. (Zimmerman, commented the mayor, who had dropped the ball with the Indians in 1964, was now exercising some leadership.) The presentation kicked off with a color film shot from a helicopter highlighting the beauties of the Puget Sound area. Then Kraeger extolled the economic advantages of Seattle, and the politicians weighed in with supporting statements. Gandy waxed optimistic about the stadium bond vote slated for September. The day concluded with a reception hosted by the governor and the two U.S. senators. At the end of the series of hearings, Scripps-Howard sports columnist Murray Olderman rated Seattle the top contender, with New Orleans and Houston next. Things looked particularly bright when NFL commissioner Pete Rozelle later told the city that his league would delay its decision until after the stadium vote. A visit to Seattle by Max Winter, president of the Minnesota Vikings, and Elroy Hirsch, assistant general manager of the Los Angeles Rams, was one final positive sign before the bond election. The *Post-Intelligencer* featured the visit on the front page, where voters would be sure to notice.[4]

One question still needed to be addressed. Where would the new football team play until a stadium was built? The obvious answer was Husky Stadium. University of Washington administrators were resistant, arguing that the campus should not be used for private gain and that public education and private sports did not mix. Obvious, but left unsaid, was that Husky football was the number one game in town and facilitating a competing pro team would be financially disadvantageous, if not ruinous. Tangled up in this concern was a fear that Seattle was too small to be anything more than a top college sports town.[5]

Meyers indulged his sportswriter's bent for sarcasm as he wrote, "The university's Board of Regents . . . has envisioned an educational program inundated by a wave of delinquency, should hired football players set foot on Lower Campus. Overzealous legislators have hinted darkly of cutting the university off at the pockets, unless the regents recognize the simple rectitude of leasing for profit a quasi-public structure on days when it otherwise lies idle." Under pressure, the regents finally hedged their bets. They declared that the stadium could not be a permanent site for the NFL, but they might consider temporary occupancy—if a battery of questions could be answered: When will they leave? Will they leave for a defined venue? Will the team be financially responsible for the lease? How much will rent be? What will be done about the parking? The regents were being prudent, but their reluctance to share, on a temporary basis, a taxpayer-financed stadium smacked of Seattle's aversion to change.[6]

Momentum for another stadium vote had been building before the NFL's overtures commenced. In 1964, the sports and recreation division of the Chamber of Commerce pressed for an update of the 1960 SRI stadium study. When nothing came of that, Eric Van, president of the Junior Chamber of Commerce, and Bob Robertson, president of the Puget Sound Sportswriters and Sportscasters Association, asserted that it was "not only admirable, but imperative" that a bond election for a multipurpose stadium be held by fall 1965. The Chamber of Commerce added its voice, urging the county commissioners to do a feasibility study. Not everyone was on board. Mayor Braman prudently promised to follow the will of the people but made it clear that a number of more important issues demanded his attention. In November 1965, expanding on his earlier comment to Gabe Paul, Braman wrote, "Seattle will not be a contender for either a new or existing franchise for from three to five years in the future . . . if ever." Almost a year later, as pressure for a stadium grew, Braman remained skeptical about baseball's staying power and said that support for a stadium had been "inflated" by local sportscasters and journalists. He also argued, not unreasonably, that the stadium was the county's issue, not the city's.[7]

But when the NFL announced its expansion plans, the desire to build a stadium caught fire in January 1966. The time had come, many thought, for Gandy and his Stadium Now Committee to show the Durslags and Glickmans who the rustics and amateurs were. The city and county had recently put up ten thousand dollars each for another feasibility study. Sportswriters recited the familiar litany that Seattle would not only be minor league without a stadium, but this time, if the vote failed, it would be minor league forever. Discussion, debate, and jockeying began over where the stadium would be built. Would the city supply the site and the county build the structure? Perhaps the cities in the south end of King County could come up with enough money to build it, with the county's aid. Tacoma and Pierce County considered offering assistance if the stadium were built in south King County. Eager imaginations projected everything from a stadium located in Federal Way to one floating on Elliot Bay.

Frank Ruano made his first appearance on the stadium-building scene in early 1966. Ruano was a middle-aged real estate developer who operated a strip mall at Twenty-Third and Madison in Seattle. Born in Florida, he had spent some time in New York and worked for RKO Radio Pictures and American Express before settling in the Puget Sound area around 1950. He was to become an uninvited fixture in stadium deliberations for the next decade. Ruano proposed forming a private holding company in which citizens could purchase subscriptions to build a downtown stadium in the open space above the sunken railroad tracks near King Street. Though railroad executives were intrigued, most stadium supporters dismissed Ruano's scheme as financially unlikely. Ruano— wedded more to the private ownership aspect than the location—felt he never got a fair hearing and vowed to make those in power regret the snub. The gadfly would buzz around and occasionally sting the body politic for the next decade.

Opposite Ruano was the familiar figure of Joe Gandy, who headed the 1966 campaign. Gandy consistently brushed off Ruano and his suggestions. Ruano countered, not without justification, that Gandy was hogging the limelight. Gandy was in his sixties, rugged-looking, and had been prominent in Seattle civic affairs since the Second World War. He was best known as a proprietor of Smith-Gandy Ford, but he had a law degree from the University of Washington and was a community leader by inclination. An outgoing man, he had been president of the Chamber of Commerce during the second half of the 1950s, a leader of Greater Seattle, the organization that put on Seafair, and was involved with the symphony, Urban League, Municipal League, and the Seattle Central Association. In 1964, attempting to trade on his success in leading the Seattle World's Fair, he initiated a short-lived run for governor. He saw himself as a key city actor—even though he had not quite cracked the innermost ring of civic leaders. Talking about the challenge of winning the bond vote for a stadium, Gandy said, "The World's Fair was a sicker cat than this is now when I took it over." He was a perennial optimist who was determined to lead Seattle to world-class status, vowing, "I'm going to get this accomplished. Don't ask me how but it'll get done. If we don't now, our children in grade school will be doing this at much greater expense than today. And they will be wondering what kind of leadership their fathers had." If this was a little overblown, Georg Meyers was forgiving. While he wondered if Gandy was preparing a political bid, Meyers thought it was an asset to have men with large egos attempt what more timid folk would not.[8]

Praeger, Kavanagh, and Waterbury and Western Management Consultants researched and produced feasibility, design, and cost studies during the first three months of 1966. Western Management rated the Puget Sound region as a prime market for major league sports. The consultants estimated that by the time a stadium could be completed, the greater Seattle area would rival Houston and the Twin Cities in population and income. Season attendance of 1 million for baseball (an attractive prospect in 1966) could be expected immediately. Less optimistic than SRI in 1960, Western Management reported that it would take both baseball and football franchises and other revenue-generating events to cover the operating expenses of a multipurpose stadium. The consultants' predictions of the economic impact of new teams were conservative. Calculating only media rights and expenditures flowing into the city, they estimated anything from an income of $20 million a year to a negative return, depending on the nature and number of stadium tenants.[9]

The Praeger group furnished construction calculations. The cost of the completed structure ranged from $23 million (an open stadium in the suburbs) to $32 million (a dome downtown). Seating capacity would be forty-five thousand for baseball and forty-nine thousand for football. Play could begin with baseball on opening day 1969. Neither consultant offered much in the way of site recommendations, although Western advised that, for baseball, the arena should be highly accessible to middle-class folks or they would opt not to come.[10]

Gandy took a hard-sell approach in his stadium campaign. His notes read, "Right now Seattle is the biggest city in the bush leagues." He exhorted voters to move their city into the big leagues. He called for public financing—increasing interest rates eliminated the possibility of a privately constructed stadium. And he argued strongly for a domed multipurpose stadium as the best investment because it would provide a roof for both fans and conventioneers. There was some foot-dragging. The *Times* supported a bond election for a stadium without endorsing the proposal. Meyers predicted that vigorous arm-twisting lay ahead if voters were to endorse a building estimate that had doubled since 1960. As head of the committee to recruit the NFL as well as the stadium drive, Gandy was stretched thin and a little testy even before the campaign started. He demanded that the Seattle Chamber of Commerce endorse the stadium bonds or he would step down from both positions. The chamber came through, and Gandy stayed on.[11]

Once the stadium committee had examined the studies, it decided on a fifty thousand–seat domed stadium. That upped the cost to $38 million. In August 1966, the county commissioners resolved: "Because of rapid growth of King County there is immediate need for an all-purpose or multi-purpose stadium." The vote was set for September, and bonds would be sold contingent on acquiring a professional sports franchise. More than a year earlier, county commissioner John O'Brien saw the risks. Prophetically, he warned, "When we put a stadium bond issue on the ballot, it must include a stipulation that we won't spend a penny until the club has signed a contract to remain in Seattle for, say, twenty-five years. If we put up a stadium and soon lost our team, we might just as well paint the stadium white then stick a trunk and tail on it."[12]

The campaign swung into action. Advocates stressed that the NFL's delay in granting a franchise until after the election was a good sign for Seattle. Gandy hammered at the idea of a multipurpose stadium, undoubtedly to draw in as many supporters as possible, especially women who might not see much return out of a property tax increase for sports alone. He proclaimed that the stadium would be worth more to the economy than the world's fair. It was not entirely clear who his audience was when he averred, "From a cold-blooded viewpoint, I'd rather have two weeks of Billy Graham than the entire NFL season." Gandy also pointed out that building sooner rather than later would save in steadily rising construction costs. Wisely, he dodged speculation about an arena site. He reiterated that the use of private funds, even from a franchise owner, was not feasible, and he assured that no bonds would be sold unless Seattle obtained a franchise. Gandy also realized that Portland would vote on a stadium in November and needed only a 50 percent "yes" vote, while King County required 60 percent. If Seattle turned down the proposal and Portland voters endorsed their bonds, Gandy warned, the center of sports in the Northwest would shift south.[13]

The campaign set up forty-three distribution points for bumper stickers, yard signs, buttons, and pamphlets. The *Post-Intelligencer* carried a photo of a leggy young woman in shorts bending over to pound a campaign sign into her lawn. More than one hundred speakers signed on to work for approval, including Paul Friedlander, Dave Cohn, county commissioners Scott Wallace, John O'Brien, and Ed Munro, and *Post-Intelligencer* sports editor John Owen.[14]

Endorsements for the bonds came from all over. Sportswriters, even from Tacoma, called for Seattleites to seize the opportunity to become major league. Rolf Stramberg, cultural critic of the *Post-Intelligencer*, and Owen agreed that a stadium would complete Seattle's cultural landscape. Emmett Watson acknowledged that there were higher priorities but then demanded rhetorically when anyone ordered life strictly on priorities. Ed Donohoe, leader of the Teamsters Union, endorsed the bonds, though Gandy jokingly rejected his support, noting that Donohoe consistently picked the wrong side of a vote. The Central Labor Council got behind the bond, as did the Aero Mechanics. The Central Association and the Business Owners and Managers Association were among the commercial organizations lending support. Even revered attorney Alfred Schweppe—cantankerous when it came to taxes—thought a stadium would make Seattle well-rounded. University of Washington president Charles Odegaard was for it. Organizations as diverse as the Municipal League, which had withheld support in 1960, the Knights of Columbus, and former Husky football stars called for passage of the bonds. The city council voted to endorse it, Senators Magnuson and Jackson wired their support, and Governor Evans called it a "must." Even Mayor Braman allowed, "If we're going to have a stadium we better be at it." The *Post-Intelligencer* backed it, and the *Times* OK'd it but asked its readers to vote for the $43 million in school bonds, which were also on the ballot, if they had to make a choice.[15]

If so many were for it, who could be against it? KOMO set up three televised debates on the "$38 million Question." Gandy and Dewayne Kraeger faced off against attorneys Steven Chadwick and Donald Schmechel. The first debate did not go well for the stadium proponents. Clearly, Chadwick and Schmechel were better prepared. Gandy's energy was flagging from countless days of speaking to any group that would listen. It was a turning point in the campaign. The two attorneys brought up a number of questions. If the stadium is such a good deal, why don't private investors come forward? Can the arena be self-supporting? Why not wait to see if the first domed stadium, the Astrodome, is workable? Does Seattle really need a dome on its stadium? What if the team leaves? Where will it be built? (Several of these questions turned out to be quite germane a couple of years later.) Gandy had been handling these questions for weeks but could not articulate convincing answers. He stumbled so badly that John Owen felt compelled to review the questions and offered up his own considered responses in his column after the debate. Owen argued that public funding was appropriate for a stadium, just as it was appropriate for cultural venues. Moreover, the stadium was probably only a break-even proposition, which would not attract private capital. Owen pointed out that the threat of a rainout was significant enough to justify a dome so that those who were traveling long distances could be confident that the game would be played. A long-term contract would solve the problem of a team leaving abruptly. County commissioner John O'Brien assured voters that management consultants and plenty of citizen comment would be a part of the siting process. Hy Zimmerman simply pleaded with his readers to pay attention to the stadium, not Gandy's performance. Despite the fact that stadium supporters believed that Gandy and Kraeger excelled in the succeeding two debates, the opponents had made an impact. At the end of the campaign, Gandy was on the verge of nervous collapse. Significantly, it took two people, Schweppe and publicist Bill Sears, to carry on in his stead.[16]

In 1932, property owners in the depths of the depression, concerned that they could lose their homes to onerous tax levies, endorsed an initiative that prescribed that no government entity could impose a tax of more than 40 mills without 60 percent approval from 40 percent of those who had voted in the last general election. This super-majority provision defeated the stadium. The final tally was 118,099 in favor and 111,380 against. A 51.5 percent approval of the stadium bonds was not enough. (The school bonds won with 60 percent.)[17]

There was some finger-pointing, but the main reaction was gloom. The voters had diverged from their leaders. Maybe it was the debate. Chadwick and Schmechel helpfully offered advice for a second go-around: find a broader financing base, determine a site, plan for parking and transit, and get yourself a guaranteed franchise. Not everyone was sure there would be a next time. Royal Brougham grumbled sarcastically that Seattleites had a "nice quiet little village," and it would be spoiled by swarms of people coming in for a game. Earl Luebker, sportswriter for the *Tacoma News Tribune*, observed, "The vote was interpreted by some as sounding the death knell for this area's big time dreams" and suggested that Tacoma and Pierce County might have a try at going big-league. An exhausted Gandy agreed. "This is the end of it," he sighed. "It's a good thing the World's Fair didn't have to go on the ballot. It never would have made it." He went on, "We've been running scared from the start. Just getting a majority vote on a money measure is difficult. Getting 60 percent approval is a hideous thing." He had a point. Those who counted sports as a necessary part of a progressive city concluded that Seattle was suffering from an excess of democracy. Dorm Braman probably depressed Gandy all the more in a letter of consolation, writing, "We had to sell something to the mass of voters on the basis of a somewhat intangible value to them. Whereas the opponents had all kinds of close to home arguments." John Owen thanked Gandy for sticking his neck out and pointed out that he had done well to get the NFL to delay its decision until Seattle could vote. Others, such as Hy Zimmerman, thought that Gandy was the problem. He charged the campaign leader with acting too much on his own and losing what had become a personality contest.[18]

After the election, there was little hope of obtaining a pro football team. The plucky Gandy, nonetheless, continued to work with the NFL and the University of Washington to keep the league interested. Pete Rozelle tantalized local franchise hopefuls, telling them that Seattle's presentation in May had been so impressive that he wanted to see the place for himself. In October, accompanied by Buffalo Bills owner Ralph

Wilson and Dan Reeves, owner of the Los Angeles Rams, the commissioner came to the Northwest, looked around, and then read from the familiar script: if Seattle built a suitable stadium for professional football, it would certainly be in the running for a new team.[19]

Only two years after major league baseball arrived on the West Coast, the 1960 vote for a stadium was visionary, even surprising, but for Seattleites, it was clearly premature. The flirtation with the Cleveland Indians in 1964 came after the fair had boosted Seattle's confidence and instilled an urge for even greater recognition, but it had not gone well. Political leaders made it clear that the city would not bend over backward to entice the club to Seattle. When a few chamber of commerce types sought to rally the populace with a ticket drive, it elicited a lukewarm response. The episode was instructive in a number of ways, but the primary lesson for Seattle sports advocates was the crying need for an adequate place to play. As the NFL took serious interest in the city, the desire to build a multipurpose stadium for baseball and, now, for football and as an activity center became overwhelming. The Seattle Spirit was invoked, and Joe Gandy, the epitome of that spirit and self-styled savior of the fair, stepped in to lead in 1966. Despite a good economic climate, and even with respected leaders urging them on, the people of Seattle were not ready to add the $6.50 per year to their property tax bill required to bring pro sports to their city. Consciousness had been raised, but Seattle seemed a long way from bringing home a major league franchise.

In the gloom of defeat, Royal Brougham grumped that it might be ten, twenty, or even thirty years before the city got a team. It did take ten years to get a team that would stay, but the Puget Sound region was too big and too tempting a market to be ignored by professional sports. In 1967, less than a year after the failed stadium vote, Charlie Finley came knocking. An insurance executive from Chicago, Finley had bought a controlling interest in the Kansas City Athletics in 1960. By the mid-1960s, the mercurial owner and Kansas City leaders had fallen out. Finley had spent perhaps half a million dollars on stadium renovations, for which the city declined to reimburse him. When he thought he had negotiated a one-dollar-a-year lease with the city, a newly elected city council voted it down. He tried to move to Louisville, Kentucky. The American League said "no," so he signed a four-year lease to stay in Kansas City. As the lease came to an end, Finley condemned the stadium as a "pig pen" and declared he would go bankrupt if he stayed. He was on the move again.[20]

Mayor Braman's executive assistant, Ed Devine, and then Dewey Soriano urged Finley to take a look at Seattle. Soon, Soriano brought Finley, Braman, and Governor Evans together in a conference call. Finley accepted their invitation to visit in August. He was impressed. "It's the best place I've seen," he enthused after spending Sunday watching the Seafair hydroplane races in front of some 200,000 at Lake Washington. (Did Finley know that admission was free?) On Monday, he met with municipal and county officials and the governor. He exclaimed, "My eyes are twice as big as they've ever been after seeing this city and this area." (Did his hosts know that Finley "hollers loudest when he is not sure of something"?) Once again, the Seattle sports world was in a tizzy. Dave Cohn was already setting up a retinue to attend the American League meetings. Sportswriters knew Finley's reputation for flightiness but were flattered that their city was the object of his admiration and, perhaps, his desire. They were also encouraged by the efforts of the city administration. The city had purchased Sicks' Stadium, Seattle's minor league ballpark, at the end of 1965 (see chapter 7), and Mayor Braman in particular seemed more motivated to deal with a prospective owner and tenant than he had with the Indians.[21]

The team's owner may well have been wide-eyed during his visit, but he was no rube. He had paid $25,000 to consulting firm Booz, Allen & Hamilton for a report on Seattle, which portrayed it as a prime location for professional baseball, especially if there was a suitable place to play. (Some believed that Finley actually asked the consulting firm to skew its analysis toward Oakland.) There was another stadium bond election scheduled for February 1968, and Finley stated that he'd "take that gamble [on voter approval] every day." There was also a "big wad" of media money available to entice the A's. Negotiations lasted well into September. The team would play in Sicks' Stadium until the new stadium was completed. Sicks' had to be both refurbished and expanded by more than ten thousand seats to a capacity of twenty-five thousand. Ed Devine, negotiating for the city, offered a $20,000-per-year lease if the A's would do the renovations. Finley declined. Devine then gave the owner a choice of a $10 lease if the club did the construction or a five-year lease at $165,000 a year with the city spending $1.6 million on expansion and remodeling, excluding a scoreboard and new seats. Finley had estimated that it would take almost $2 million to get the park into shape. The team's owner was tempted, but he wanted an out. If the stadium bonds did not pass or if construction on the new stadium did not begin within a year of bond approval, he wanted the freedom to walk out on the contract and, presumably, Seattle. On September 22, Braman announced, "I'm personally inclined to doubt that it will work out even though Finley wants to come here." Negotiations had come to an end.[22]

Finley seemed genuinely put out. He claimed that he had been tempted to play even in that "pigsty" of a stadium but city officials, whom he now thought were worse than the two-bit politicians in Kansas City, had given him the run-around. Finley believed he had a deal on renovating Sicks', but then the mayor and governor reneged on it. Partly, Braman was reluctant, with good reason, to permit the A's to be mere sojourners. But it was largely the mayor's penny-pinching ways that won out over securing a major league team. Braman estimated that upgrading the stadium would cost the city only $30,000 by the time the team moved into the new stadium, since rent plus the salvage of stadium equipment would cover most of the renovation costs. For this to work out, of course, the A's would have to stay out the lease. So Finley left for Oakland and its already completed stadium, and several baseball writers across the United States congratulated Seattle on its good fortune. But the city remained without a major league team. Upon leaving, Finley tendered the same advice that Gabe Paul had given three years earlier: if it wanted to be major league, Seattle must have a major league stadium.[23]

Can a professional basketball team bring a city into top-tier status? Opinions in Seattle were mixed when the Sonics suddenly appeared. Even sportswriters, who maintained more than anyone that it took a pro sports franchise to make a city first-class, were ambivalent. Georg Meyers proclaimed Seattle as big-league—"The National Basketball Association confirmed that," he wrote as the season opened—but his next sentence indicated that the NBA flew just a bit below the radar. "Uninvited, [the NBA] thrust a team into Seattle—so eagerly, so simply it caught most of the populace by surprise." The perennials who trolled for baseball or football franchises were nowhere to be seen when the Sonics came to town. There was no negotiating with the mayor, no delegations sent off to NBA headquarters to extol the Seattle market, and virtually no speculation about pro basketball in the Northwest on the sports pages.[24]

Quietly, TV writer Don Richman and stockbroker Dick Vertleib, both from California, plotted it out and worked with the NBA. Then they sold Gene Klein, owner of the San Diego Chargers, and Los Angeles businessman Sam Schulman on the idea of bankrolling a new franchise in Seattle. In 1965, the NBA was in the process of expanding from ten teams to twenty-five by 1968. There was a ripple of rumor in March 1966, when Golden State owner Franklin Mieuli mentioned Seattle as an expansion candidate at a sports luncheon. After that, there was no news until the mid-December announcement that Seattle had a team. Significantly, there was a place for the team to play. The Washington State Pavilion of the world's fair was now the Seattle Coliseum, with fourteen thousand seats (more than Sicks' Stadium at the time). If the Sonics did not endow Seattle with enough respect to be ranked as a major sports city, they were a step in that direction. Hy Zimmerman revealed his personal tastes, writing that only major league baseball could get Seattle to the true big leagues, but the Sonics would allow Seattle to show that it was deserving of other professional teams. As a stalking horse, the team did reasonably well. In the 1967–68 season, two crowds exceeded 10,000. By December 1967, in fifteen dates, the Sonics were drawing just under the NBA average of 6,953. Zimmerman was partially correct. The early Sonics story did give some insight into how Seattle was measuring up to the SRI criteria by the late 1960s. But the indicators were not as compelling as the *Times* sportswriter might have wished. The Sonics had an NBA-quality arena, but that pointed up the lack of an outdoor stadium. Although fans enjoyed the new team, they did not come out in large numbers. And local leadership had played little part in bringing the team to town. Nonetheless, by 1968, if not quite major league, Seattle was maturing, and, ready or not, a big-league franchise was finally in the offing.[25]

Chapter 4

COME, AND THEY WILL BUILD IT

ISSOURI senator Stuart Symington was a force in U.S. government in the late 1960s. He was a veteran senator and a longtime member of both the Senate Armed Services Committee and the Foreign Relations Committee. Symington was a consistent advocate for the U.S. military, especially the air force, and, as a Cold Warrior and a hawk, he was increasingly critical of the restraints President Lyndon Johnson placed on bombing operations in Vietnam. He had much more important issues to deal with than baseball. But if there was any individual who brought the Pilots to Seattle, it surely was not Dorm Braman, nor was it Joe Gandy or Ed Carlson or even Dewey Soriano. Improbably, the catalyst that brought major league baseball to the Northwest in 1969 was Stuart Symington.

By 1967, baseball had spanned the continent for almost a decade, but there were still only three teams west of Houston, and the American League needed a companion on the West Coast for the Angels. Baseball was both relocating franchises and expanding. After the Dodgers and Giants moved west in 1957, the Braves moved south to Atlanta, the Senators went north to Minneapolis–Saint Paul, and Charlie Finley was ready to move anywhere out of Kansas City. Like Johnny Appleseed, owners spread major league baseball across the landscape by sowing the seeds of expansion. In 1961–62, they planted the Mets in New York, the Angels in Los Angeles, and the Colt .45s in Houston and restored the Senators to Washington, D.C. It was time to expand again. The process was lucrative for established owners, created new markets, and, as necessary, could placate riled senators who threatened hearings on baseball's antitrust exemption as retribution for a lost franchise.

There were drawbacks. Because baseball kept a tight grip on its anti-trust exemption, it was a given that, except for cities such as New York and Los Angeles, owners would not permit new teams to invade the territories of established franchises. Consequently, the newly hatched franchises would be placed in smaller markets. That meant lower attendance, which, in turn, meant less revenue for the visiting team and inferior nines on the field, at least for several years. But most baseball officials saw expansion as a winning proposition. The prospect of several competing cities ready to offer lucrative concessions—especially publicly financed stadiums—for the honor of obtaining a major league team attracted new potential owners. Franchise fees for new clubs beckoned established owners. Smart local politicians who could bring home the bond issues to build stadiums reaped accolades. Quality owners who were able to market even a losing team became wealthy. Finally, by 1967, American League owners felt that they had fallen behind. Attendance at their games was lower than it was for teams of the rival National League; the junior circuit had fewer new parks and had missed out on the best untapped markets. American League owners were looking to grab the best territories so that they could close the gap. Seattle had no major league competitors nearer than San Francisco to the south and Minneapolis–Saint Paul to the east and would soon vote for a domed stadium. The Northwest was an alluring market.[1]

At the time of the October 1967 American League meeting in Chicago, many owners saw expansion happening slowly, maybe a couple of years or more down the road. As often happened, they failed to anticipate Finley, who had been wanting to get out of Kansas City for years. The league had refused him permission to move to Louisville, but by the end of the 1967 season, he had had it with Kansas City. Though city officials promised to extend the option for a stadium lease renewal and pointed out that a new stadium was in the planning stages, Finley was adamant. After his late summer dalliance with Seattle, he flirted with Oakland and struck a deal. He came to his fellow American League owners in October 1967 demanding permission to move. After some discussion, the league voted 7–3 to let Finley shift the A's to the East Bay.[2]

This was where Stuart Symington's influence came to bear. With the departure of the A's, Symington threatened to initiate a suit or antitrust legislation. Rather than take a risk, the league voted for expansion and awarded Kansas City a new team. In the interests of maintaining a balanced schedule, the league needed a second expansion city. Dallas–Fort Worth made a presentation at the Chicago meeting, and Milwaukee sent an observer. Seattle brought its full crew just in case opportunity knocked. Dewey Soriano, Dave Cohn, and Bert West of the governor's stadium commission, city councilman Floyd Miller, county commissioner John O'Brien, Dewayne Kraeger, and Chamber of Commerce member Jack Keene were ready to put on their full show.[3]

Things got off to a rocky start when the film projector failed to operate. Keene fixed it, and the American League owners watched a film highlighting the beauty and vibrancy of Seattle. Kraeger praised the Seattle economy as healthy and growing. The group reminded the owners that the stadium vote was only a few months away, and even if it were defeated, there were other ways of financing the stadium—a bit of news that would have surprised a number of people back home. The Seattleites also assured the American League that Sicks' Stadium could easily be expanded from eleven thousand seats to twenty-eight thousand, in order to accommodate the team while the domed stadium was being built (no one seems to know exactly how many seats Sicks' actually had, but eleven thousand is a number that was often mentioned). Miller, representing Mayor Braman, who was at the Western Regional Highway Conference, proclaimed Seattle's joy at being considered. He noted that the city had worked with Finley on crafting a deal to convert Sicks' into a usable stadium. There is no record that Finley shared any of his thoughts with his owner colleagues about the "pigsty" of a stadium or his disdain for Seattle city officials. On behalf of the city, Miller offered to lease Sicks' Stadium for one dollar a year if the new team would refurbish it, or the city could bring it "up to major league standards and enter into a mutually agreeable lease arrangement." He pointed out Seattle's reputation for getting things done (the fair, for example) and promised that the city would fully cooperate with major league baseball.[4]

Hy Zimmerman, sounding like an expectant father in the waiting room, described the league's decision. "It was a long vigil, 13 hours long," he reported. "From 7 pm on, officials promised sportswriters that American League President Joe Cronin would make an announcement soon. Finally it came at 11:30."

The American League has approved the transfer of the Kansas City Athletics to Oakland, California, effective for the 1968 season. The league also voted to adopt an expansion plan under which the league will expand to 12 clubs as soon as practical, but not later than the 1971 season, and awarded the expansion franchises to Kansas City and Seattle. The award will be subject to applicable baseball rules and procedures, and to other terms acceptable to the league and, in the case of Seattle, to the city's being able to provide suitable stadium facilities.

Proud papa Zimmerman noted that the press release was typed on his typewriter.[5]

Others were not quite so giddy. Years later, in a rambling deposition, apparently given in Stengalese, Dorm Braman remembered his reaction.

> As far as I was concerned from my own personal enjoyment, it wasn't material that we have [the expansion team] here, but as administrator of the city in listening to the voices of the city, listening to the responsibility of the leaders of the city who are telling us in no uncertain terms that the city would be downgraded not only in prestige but in economic progress if we didn't take steps to acquire a major league franchise, this caused us to give an attention priority that far exceeded what we normally would give to a city problem because overriding the physical arrangements that were necessary was the fact that we were told and we believed from our own knowledge that the economic benefits to the city . . . would be so great that we should give every effort to not find reasons why we couldn't do this and to give in to what appeared to be almost insurmountable problems, but rather to find ways in which we could do it.

The *Seattle Post-Intelligencer*'s Lenny Anderson caught the tone of Braman's statement as he ventured that the Seattle delegation deserved some credit for bringing major league baseball to Seattle, but it was mainly Finley forcing the league to let him move to Oakland (and Senator Symington's looming presence) that accomplished the task. The pattern had been set in 1964 when the Indians came looking and was reinforced in September 1967 when Finley sought a deal with Seattle. A coterie of citizens (made up of substantially the same people each time) was ready to push the city into the big leagues. But the political leadership, especially Mayor Braman, exhibited only mild interest, especially if it meant an outlay of municipal funds.[6]

Symington not only forced the league's hand on expansion; he also sped up the process. The senator from Missouri was incensed that the league had let Finley move and would not stand for Kansas City to be without baseball for more than a year. Symington, who attended the Chicago meeting, invited Cronin and his advisers up to his room. After a tongue-lashing, the chastened officials announced that expansion, which had been scheduled for 1971, would be moved up to 1969.[7]

Though Finley's move to Oakland and Symington's pressure were the dominant forces behind league expansion, they were not the only impetus. American League owners saw Seattle's market as highly desirable, and they wanted to stake a claim before the National League. Bob Reynolds of the Angels promised that he would not let the Chicago meeting end until Seattle obtained the expansion team. The Yankees' Mike Burke said, "Seattle is vital to the future of the American League, and we just very well can't lose it." More colorfully, Finley later looked back on what turned out to be an ill-fated decision and asserted, "We wanted Seattle, and we wanted Seattle badly. We made every effort to get Seattle before the National League, we approved a move to Seattle to a group that we thought would paddle their own canoe for more than one year."[8]

Major league baseball's guidelines for expansion were not well established. Theoretically, expansion happened through negotiation. One league was supposed to notify the other of its intentions several months before expansion took place; then the two leagues would parley over territories. This had not happened in the early 1960s. Though the American League expanded first, the National League had already laid claim to New York and Houston. The American League, feeling betrayed, had no compunctions about disregarding the guidelines in 1967. Mayor Braman played coy with the American League, announcing, "We are not the property of the American League. . . . We can be almost like prima donnas. We know we will have a baseball team whichever the league." Indeed, on the one hand, National League president Warren Giles sent up a trial balloon. A rumor circulated that Emil J. "Buzzie" Bavasi, general manager of the Dodgers, was interested in operating a team in Seattle. (Bavasi had looked around but astutely noted that Sicks' Stadium had no office space and little parking available.) On the other hand, Dave Cohn said that Commissioner of Baseball William Eckert had told him that Seattle would have an American League team, but that was not much of a guarantee, since Eckert was the weakest commissioner in the history of baseball. Most significantly, Warren Magnuson warned the National League not to throw a monkey wrench into the process. After a month of speculation, the National League announced that, although the other league had breached the rules, it would not contest the American League's decision. Bavasi had moved on to part-ownership of the National League's San Diego expansion team. Looking back, many agreed that, in its eagerness, the American League had stumbled over itself to nab Seattle. And the city had probably obtained the franchise too easily for its own good.[9]

How had Seattle, almost absentmindedly, turned the tables on the American League? Commentators on the business aspects of sports write of commercial leaders who press for major league teams as a way of boosting their city's reputation. The new home team is supposed to be at the nexus of creating civic pride. As well as establishing a city as major league, the team is a symbol of a progressive community. As long as franchises are limited, so the notion goes, the acquisition of a team sets the community apart as a winner. For politicians, bringing in a franchise demonstrates leadership. The economic stimulus a team will bring is always a major point. The media, with the prospect of more readers and viewers, broadcast rights, and ad sales, are among the strongest boosters. The public is entertained, and special-interest groups who long for a team are satisfied. With all this incentive, it is normally the city that bends over backward to acquire the franchise, not the league that pursues the city.[10]

On the surface, as a city enthralled by the attention it had received from the world's fair and consciously striving to be regarded as a major commercial player on the West Coast, Seattle seemed to fit the standard profile well. There was plenty of evidence of a yen for a team. But support for obtaining a big-league franchise, especially among the city's political leaders, and even among a number of civic notables, did not reach the intensity portrayed by scholars. For example, many Seattleites thought that Washington Husky football was sufficient validation of place and prominence. It was the league, not the city, that had become the suitor, and American League owners were making haste to be sure they had secured the prize. They would come to rue their rashness.

It appeared that the city was set up to get the best of the deal. If the Western Management Consultants 1966 study was accurate, a major league baseball team with a lease reasonably favorable to the city would likely keep a new stadium's operating budget in the black. In concert with most present-day sports business economists, Western Management Consultants did not count local fans' expenditures as income, since this discretionary income would be spent on something else if baseball were not in town. But it expected out-of-town spectators to leave about $700,000 a year in the region. In addition, the study concluded that a major league franchise would bring good publicity to the city and produce intangibles—for example, good feelings, especially if the home team won fairly often. In short, Seattle got a good deal. It had achieved a coveted position and probably would have come out ahead financially in the long run, had there been a long run.[11]

The *Seattle Times* did its own research, conducting person-in-the-street interviews. This less-than-scientific sample yielded some insight into the future. Exhibiting typical Seattle restraint, Kathy Crosby, age twenty-two, thought a big-league ball club would be "nice." A newsstand dealer, Paul Darlington, forty-two, said it was great but wished the city had gotten an established club, like the A's. Bill Carey, twenty-four, was happy to get a team but thought Seattle was more of a football town. Taxi driver Robert Madison, sixty, saw the pragmatic side—having a team would generate more fares from the airport. And Dave Cohn noted that instead of being lauded as a conquering hero, he came home to "Why couldn't you get a National League team?"[12]

While they may have been overeager in bestowing the franchise, the American League owners were not entirely imprudent. They recognized that, in their haste to satisfy Senator Symington's demands for a 1969 expansion, they had assigned a franchise to a city in need of a major league playing field. They sought to solve the problem in their agreement with the franchise holders. The voters had to approve the February 1968 stadium bond issue, and construction had to be under way by 1970. In the meantime, the team needed an adequate site for games, which everyone understood to be Sicks' Stadium. "Adequate" meant that the field must be in major league condition, and the seating capacity would be enlarged from eleven thousand to, probably, twenty-eight thousand. It was risky business. The league might end up revoking the franchise, a public relations nightmare. Most Seattle sportswriters hailed the demand for a stadium as an advantage. A major league stadium and a major league franchise had long been a chicken-and-egg riddle, wrote Georg Meyers in the *Seattle Times*. The American League had now provided the egg. This was the incentive needed to approve the stadium. Some doubt, if not outright sportswriter cynicism, crept into John Owen's column at the *Post-Intelligencer*. Seattle offered a minor league stadium that seated eleven thousand, a history of twice defeating a stadium issue, but gobs of potential, Owen wrote. What will happen if the voters defeated the stadium this time? Dave Cohn, a "most optimistic man," American League president Joe Cronin remembered, was not worried. All the hard work by Cohn, "Mr. Bond Issue himself" (another Cronin sobriquet), was going to pay off. Voters could not turn down the stadium with a major league team in the offing.[13]

The next step for the American League was to approve an ownership group. There are a couple of unusual aspects to baseball team ownership. First, despite the fact that the city or county where a team plays usually owns the playing field and although the team works hard to convince local fans that it is "their" team, neither the fans nor their governments have any say in how the team is run or who runs it. Owners, adhering to their entrepreneurial rights, brook no interference with how they stock the rosters or market the team, or even whether they remain in the city. Second, baseball owners, though their teams vie against each other on the field, depend on their compatriots to furnish worthy and entertaining competition, because home teams split the revenue for each game with the visitors. For the sake of the league's reputation in the city and for the good of their own bottom lines, established owners are particular about who their partners or rivals will be. Above all, prospective owners must be well funded. Beyond that, the group or individual must not have an interest in other teams, be free of gambling interests, preferably be local, and have some baseball sense. The ownership group of what would become the Seattle Pilots seemed to exceed those qualifications.[14]

Joe Cronin had contacted Dewey Soriano as early as September 1967, suggesting that he put together an ownership group in case Finley's peregrinations resulted in expansion. Dewey Soriano, his brother Max, and William Daley formed Pacific Northwest Sports, Inc. (PNSI), while the American League deliberated. Dewey Soriano announced that the group was capitalized for $10 million, that "only local capital will be involved," and that the Sorianos would be the majority stock holders. None of the three statements was accurate. Daley, from Cleveland, ended up as the primary stockholder, and PNSI was not as financially solid as Soriano maintained.[15]

If the story of the Pilots possesses aspects of tragedy, the tragic hero is Dewey Soriano—the Seattle boy who had dreamed for years of bringing major league baseball to his city, who as a man saw his dream come true only to have team finances spin out of control, and who bore the stigma of losing the franchise after only one season. The Sorianos had been around the Seattle baseball scene all their lives. They came from a family of six boys and four girls. Their father, who operated a halibut boat, was Spanish-born, and their mother was Danish. Dewey was a Franklin High School classmate of James Ellis's. Though he had always been heavyset, he was athletic, graduating from selling peanuts at the local ballpark to being on the playing field of Sicks' Stadium as a right-handed pitcher for the Rainiers. Baseball was his life. By 1968, he had been in the game for twenty years as owner and general manager of Yakima, general manager of the Mounties, from Vancouver, British Columbia, and the Rainiers. He was married to Royal Brougham's daughter. When PNSI formed, he was president of the Pacific Coast League and an active harbor pilot (with a couple of accidents on his record). Soriano was one of the first proponents anywhere of a domed stadium, and he deserves as much credit (or discredit) as anyone for the designated hitter idea. At one point, he was a candidate for assistant commissioner under William Eckert, which might have vaulted him into the top office when Eckert was fired. He was one of the boosters who had been working to bring major league baseball to Seattle and had already made an effort on behalf of his city as early as 1965, when he filed for a National League franchise. Though well known among the civic leaders, he was not a member of the Central Association nor was he really a part of the more elite groups, and he probably suffered for being connected more to the locker room than to the boardroom. Brother Max had also been an aspiring pitcher, but after hearing his elbow crackle one too many times, he opted for the law. He worked alongside Dewey as counsel for the Pacific Coast League and was an official with two financial institutions. Hy Zimmerman waxed enthusiastic about the potential leader of the Seattle franchise. "No man in Seattle is as eminently qualified as Dewey Soriano [to run the team]. The man knows every aspect of baseball from the field through the front office and to the presidency of the Pacific Coast League." Dewey and Max "won't let the plum turn sour."[16]

William Daley and Dewey Soriano were acquainted before Daley accompanied Gabe Paul to Seattle to have a look around on behalf of the Indians, but the relationship was solidified during the visit. Daley told Charlie Finley that he had checked out the Sorianos and "would enjoy the opportunity of getting in bed with them." (Daley was seventy-five years old at the time and was using language that probably had not sounded quite so odd in his youth.) He also assured Finley that he would bail out the Sorianos if necessary.[17]

William R. Daley was born in Ashtabula, Ohio, in 1892. He received a law degree from Case Western Reserve University (as it is known today) and fought in the First World War. He joined with Cyrus Eaton, one-time president of Republic Steel, and rose to become president of Otis and Company, a Cleveland investment firm. Daley was also a director of Detroit Steel and chairman of the board of the Reading Railroad and two mining companies. He bought an interest in the Cleveland Indians in 1949 and became owner in 1955. Though associated with the game for a long period of time, he did not win accolades for his baseball acumen. He was the antithesis of a promoter and, with the Indians, had to follow in the footsteps of the flashy Bill Veeck. Locals criticized his lack of marketing savvy. Though he was a hard worker and full of determination, the diminutive dynamo—he was five feet seven and weighed 140 pounds—was also a penny-pincher. A chronicler of the Indians writes that Gabe Paul "had only one problem: Bill Daley did not want to spend any money on the Cleveland Indians." Max Soriano put it more gently but came to the same conclusion: "Sure he had money . . . but I don't think he was a careless person with his dollars." What Daley did understand was that an owner could depreciate his players over a five-year period (a tax provision that Veeck was the first to discover). Daley also understood how to use leverage against a city administration. In the late 1950s, he began to talk about the necessity of moving the Indians, and, of course, in 1964, he and Gabe Paul were on the road again checking out greener pastures. The Indians stayed, but the owners got a good portion of what they wanted from the city of Cleveland. So it was Daley who provided the bankroll for the Pilots and, even with Dewey Soriano's reputation among baseball insiders, helped PNSI with admittance to the lodge. To Seattle observers, he was just a businessman from Cleveland.[18]

Daley asserted several times that he traveled to Seattle early on for the purpose of selling a portion of his holdings to those "who represented the business and community leaders of Seattle," but without success. Yet somehow he missed key people. Ed Carlson had not heard of Daley's efforts. Joe Cronin told Dave Cohn that he would be able to purchase a 25 percent share, but Cohn and Dewey Soriano did not get along and Cohn was left out. (Dewey later claimed that Cohn wanted to be a team official but declined to put up any money.) Being left out was devastating for Cohn, who was a little starstruck about sports—he had once gloried in Charlie Finley inviting him to stay overnight in Finley's suite. Daley ended up with a 47 percent ownership, other Cleveland interests controlled the 13 percent Daley wanted to sell to Seattle investors, and the Sorianos held 33 percent. Other minority owners included William Patterson, chairman of United Airlines; Chinn Ho, a Honolulu land developer; Dr. William Hutchinson, the late Fred Hutchinson's brother; Vern Courson, a Seattle realtor; John Talminson, a local attorney; and W. G. Campbell of the Bank of California, which had staked PNSI to a large loan.[19]

The structure of the syndicate was complex. The American League estimated that it would take $8 million to run the operation, so that was the level of capitalization the league required for PNSI. Daley would underwrite the group. The league preferred that one person be majority owner. Though he owned only 47 percent of the club, the league felt comfortable with Daley as the representative of the franchise. Daley signed a letter in early 1968 guaranteeing that he would be good for 62 percent of the $8 million. In fact, in a screening interview with Gabe Paul, Daley asserted that he was committed to the entire $8 million needed to run the club, if necessary. (That Paul would "screen" his friend and former partner suggests rather casual due diligence but demonstrates how clubby an atmosphere surrounded the league owners.) Daley's guarantee that he would totally underwrite the franchise if need be became a source of contention later on.[20]

Initially, the $8 million capitalization consisted of $1 million in stock, a loan from the Bank of California for $4 million, and $3 million in loans at 7 percent, furnished principally by Daley and the Sorianos. In May 1969, Sportservice, the team's concessionaire, provided a $2 million loan in exchange for a twenty-year concessions contract that would follow the team wherever it moved—presumably from Sicks' Stadium to the new domed stadium. The Sportservice loan essentially paid off $2 million of the $3 million in personal loans from the owners. The transfer of debt obligation to the concessionaire was a sign that ownership was getting jumpy about finances only a month into the season. The *Tri-City* (Washington) *Herald*, looking back, reported, "'At that point [opening day] they were adequately financed,' says one of the few men who had a good look at the Pilot books. 'They had equity capital then, but they took some of it out [with the Sportservice loan]. If that money had been left in, I seriously doubt the later crisis would have developed.'" It got worse. From January to July 1969, PNSI paid down the bank loan by $500,000. To make the payments, Daley loaned PNSI $300,000 and Max Soriano loaned another $200,000 in July, both at a relatively stiff 9.5 percent interest. Daley's holdings were up to $1.24 million in stock and debt. He felt the obligations of ownership becoming onerous.[21]

All this was to come. Back in the December 1967 league meeting in Mexico City, the American League, satisfied with the baseball reputation of the Sorianos and comforted by the presence of former colleague William Daley, ratified PNSI as the franchise owner in Seattle, subject to the stipulations about a playing site. Not everyone was so sure that the Sorianos were the best choice. Jerry Hoffberger of the Baltimore Orioles was slightly uneasy at the meeting before the vote, complaining, "We are actually convinced there is no other group in Seattle, they have been scared off for some reason. It is probable that the Sorianos' participation in baseball in the past might have given them a leg up on any decision this league might take in this and has scared off any other potential prospects here." Finley echoed Hoffberger, saying, "Soriano is known as 'Mr. Baseball' up there," and so no one else had shown any interest.[22]

Later, Hoffberger expressed regret that he did not heed his instincts and press for a more careful review of PNSI finances. It might have been that the Sorianos had, indeed, stolen the march, although it was telling that they had to look to Cleveland to find someone to bankroll their dream. The Boeing and Weyerhaeuser fortunes were too new and too spread out among those families for either to provide an obvious candidate for ownership, or even partnership, with the Sorianos. Later, the Nordstrom family would join a consortium that brought the Seahawks football team to Seattle, which makes another point: Seattleites enjoyed baseball but loved football. The American League owners, in their ardor for the Seattle market, were able to suppress a nagging awareness that they were getting themselves into a sticky situation. They had breached each of the Stanford Research Institute's three nonnegotiable criteria. They had voted a franchise to a city without a major league stadium, in an area that had not pursued a team avidly, and with an ownership group that was, at best, financed by a penny-pincher and, at worst, insufficiently capitalized.[23]

Because no other groups seemed to be bidding for the Seattle franchise, PNSI could act as though it was the designated owner even before formal American League approval. Its first action was to purchase the Seattle Angels from the California Angels. That would secure territorial rights. Bob Reynolds, co-owner of the California Angels, was happy to sell his minor league team. The major league Angels, of course, were delighted to have a third American League team to join them and the Oakland A's on the West Coast, but there was a particularly strong relationship between the two clubs. The Angels took an almost paternal interest in the Seattle franchise throughout its existence. PNSI also purchased Northwest Guarantee Savings and Loan, one of the financial institutions connected to Max Soriano. The idea was to make PNSI appear more financially robust.[24]

The price of admission was $5.35 million. The PNSI partners had to pay a $100,000 membership fee and purchase thirty players from their newly affiliated American League brethren at $175,000 each. Making the player draft such a hefty part of the entrance payment yielded tax advantages. Since an owner could depreciate a team's roster over a five-year period, the draft allowed the new owners to take a tax write-off for the expenditure and permitted the established owners to treat the purchase price of the players they lost as capital gains. There were other provisions. The newly formed team had to pay several other charges and forgo national television revenue for three years. The established teams considered expansion a money-making venture and sought to put off any sharing of revenue streams for as long as they could. Indemnity to the Pacific Coast League was another start-up cost. Bill McKechnie, Jr., the league president after Dewey Soriano stepped down, asked for $1.1 million from Seattle and San Diego, a National League expansion team. Soriano was probably a little miffed, since the Tacoma Cubs would continue to play, and the Mounties, from Vancouver, B.C., were actually the Seattle Triple-A farm team. The Pilots' first offer for their part of the indemnity was $30,000. Not surprisingly, the indemnity negotiations went on longer than the Pilots' tenure in Seattle and became part of the bankruptcy settlement. The Pilots' extensive radio broadcasts and regionwide promotion did not sit well with PCL owners, either. The Portland Beavers complained that the Pilots' newspaper advertising in the Oregon city was encroaching on their domain and bewailed the loss of KEX to the Pilots' radio network. The Spokane Indians echoed the Beavers' concerns about encroachment on their broadcast territory and criticized local advertising that referred to "*Your* Seattle Pilots." Dewey Soriano wrote an apology.[25]

Many of these were expected nuisances that attend the inception of any new franchise, although any major expenditure loomed as something of a crisis because PNSI was operating on a relatively thin margin. But at the time, it appeared that getting the stadium bond approved was the primary hurdle to a successful operation in Seattle.

Play-by-Play

S PRING training is always a time of trying out new players, fitting new pieces together, and replacing aging veterans with rookies. The established players go a few innings in the games early in the spring, then stretch out their stints as the season nears. Their reputations provide them with the benefit of the doubt, but they have to do well enough to show they haven't "lost it." Young hopefuls must use their early playing time well and impress management. With an expansion team, this winnowing and vying increases exponentially. Management hoped the team's big-name players would be starters in April, but as castoffs, none was a sure thing.

A mid-February confidential memo asking for glossy photos of the manager, his coaches, and a dozen players was a tip-off as to who general manager Marvin Milkes and field manager Joe Schultz thought were probably going to be on the team. The memo listed Jack Aker, Steve Barber, Gary Bell, Tommy Davis, Larry Haney, Tommy Harper, Jerry McNertney, Don Mincher, Ray Oyler, Rich Rollins, Chico Salmon, and Diego Segui. Only Salmon was absent from the opening-day roster. There were plenty of sore knees, gimpy ankles, not-so-sturdy arms, and aging muscles that could alter the starting lineup. At the opening of the Cactus League exhibition season, pitchers Steve Barber and Gary Bell seemed to be sure starters. Marty Pattin was a likely candidate for the third spot. Pitching coach Sal Maglie was impressed with Dick Baney, whom Maglie knew from his sojourn as the pitching coach for the Red Sox. Diego Segui could round out the rotation in a pinch, but he was more likely a bull-pen stalwart with Jack Aker. Bill Henry, a forty-one-year-old relief pitcher whom the Pirates had released at the end of the 1968 season, sought to hook on with the expansion team for a last fling at the game. Henry looked good and began making his case to become a spot reliever. Most baseball-savvy observers thought that pitching would be the new team's weakness.[1]

Tommy Harper was almost sure to start, but spring training would determine if he would be in the infield—most likely at second base—or the outfield. Early arrival Mike Hegan impressed both the coaches and the sportswriters during the first days of the exhibition season. Top draft pick Don Mincher was probably going to be the team's first baseman, so Hegan would be in the outfield with Tommy Davis and who knows who else.[2]

By the end of the first week of Cactus League games, trends were emerging. The Pilots had no trouble hitting, for both average and power. Wayne Comer, Hegan, Mincher, Lou Piniella, and Jose Vidal had several multi-hit games. As feared, the pitching was suspect. Jim Bouton's knuckleball was not behaving, and Mike Marshall was touched up for runs. Diego Segui and Jack Aker were the steadiest of the staff. Infield defense was iffy: Tommy Harper continued to work on his skills, and Chico Salmon was hampered by a slow-healing surgically repaired knee.

The nadir of the exhibition season was a game against the Arizona State University Sun Devils. The college squad scored four runs, three unearned, in the seventh to put away the Pilots 5–4. Had the Pilots known that the two Sun Devils pitchers were headed to decent major league careers, perhaps they would not have felt chagrined. Larry Gura and Craig Swan (a freshman) limited them to three earned runs.[3]

The good-hitting–poor-pitching trend continued into mid-spring. Not counting B games, the Pilots had four wins and six losses and were in fifth place in their division (the *Seattle Post-Intelligencer* lumped Florida and Arizona teams together based on regular season divisions). Seven Pilots were hitting .300 or better. Mike Hegan, with the most at bats, was clearly the star of the camp. The free agent pickup turned out to be a bargain. Son of longtime Cleveland Indians catcher Jim Hegan, Mike had been taught how to hit by Wally Moses. Hegan continued to be a Pilot stalwart through the season, hovering around .300 until leg injuries in July and a military reserve obligation curtailed his playing time. Rollins, Piniella, and Davis were also hitting over .400. Mike Ferraro, Vidal, and Jim Gosger were .300 or better, and John Kennedy was at .296. Even Ray Oyler had hit a home run.[4]

But the pitchers were getting bombed. Thirteen-, nine-, and eight-run games were becoming a staple. Maglie decried a crew of hurlers who walked eighty while striking out forty. Bouton and Barber were particularly hard hit. Bill Edgerton went to the minor league camp after being roughed up by the Sun Devils. Gary Bell's ailing back limited his appearances. The walks were probably due to the new, tighter strike zone. The thin air in Arizona was also having an effect. The pitchers were pressing. And it was possible that some were reaching the tired-arm stage, when velocity drops for a start or two during spring training (though it came a week or two early). But the reality was that the pitchers were just not that talented. Ineffective pitching would be a season-long plague for the Pilots. Defense had become a worry as well. In an 8–5 loss against the Cubs at the halfway point of spring training, Oyler, who was drafted purely for his glove, made an error, while Rollins, in his second start, made two at third. These errors plus spotty play from Salmon, Gus Gil, and Harper at second had manager Joe Schultz perplexed about his infield.[5]

Las Vegas was setting odds for the season. The Pilots and the Royals were installed at 200 to 1 to win the World Series. The two National League expansion franchises, the San Diego Padres and the Montreal Expos, came in at 300 to 1. In the Pilots' American League Western Division, bettors favored Oakland at 2 to 1. Chicago, Minnesota, and California were established at 3 to 1.[6]

The Pilots' hitting prowess and pitching woes kept up. On March 21, the team hit five home runs against the Indians—Harper, Oyler (again!), Piniella, Salmon, and Freddie Velazquez. But Schultz could only eye the pitching staff and say, "Just let them play and they'll eliminate themselves." Even Segui was hit hard in the 10- 9 loss to Cleveland. Schultz continued to be perturbed about the fielding as well. He was ready to give up on the Harper experiment at second and chewed out Piniella, who made an error in the game, for mental mistakes.[7]

Back in Seattle, Bob Hardwick of KVI, the Pilots' flagship radio station, created the Ray Oyler fan club. Though it was an effort by funnyman Hardwick to stir up a little ironic humor at the expense of a .135-hitting shortstop, the fan club picked up steam as Oyler batted .300 in spring training and popped a couple of home runs. In a rainout against the Cubs, Oyler cracked a grand slam, and the fan club grew to 1,800. Oyler was appreciative and flattered. Whether he hit in the actual season or not (he ended up batting a lowly .165), Ray Oyler would be the Pilots' shortstop.[8]

In a sign that the season was nearing, the general manager plotted some trades. The Kansas City Royals had drafted Seattle native Wally Bunker. The Pilots needed pitching, and a local talent would draw fans. Milkes offered right-hand hitters to Cedric Tallis, his former Angels front office colleague, but the Kansas City general manager indicated that he was as thin in pitching talent as Milkes was. Milkes also sounded out his old club about outfielder Roger Repoz, but the Pilots didn't have anyone the Angels needed or wanted.[9]

As spring training moved into the last week of March, the roster began to take shape. Wayne Comer continued to impress Milkes with his toughness and his bat, and he made the twenty-five-man roster. Marty Pattin pitched five strong innings against Cleveland. He credited Maglie with making his windup more efficient, boosting his effectiveness. He won the opening-day starting assignment since Barber was struggling and Bell was just emerging from his late start. Though Barber claimed he was having off-and-on shoulder trouble, a few days later, the press reported that he was in constant pain—a story Bouton later confirmed in *Ball Four*. In the outfield, Vidal returned from injury to hit with authority and reasserted himself as the fifth outfielder over Piniella, who was in an ill-timed slump. Infielder Kennedy's versatility gave him the edge over Mike Ferraro, who had started the exhibition schedule with a hot bat. By the end of the week, every outing was crucial for those whose futures were still undetermined. Outfielder Steve Hovley, catcher Merritt Ranew, and pitcher Gary Timberlake were sent down to Vancouver, but more cuts were necessary. Dick Baney looked like another candidate for the Vancouver Mounties after he could not get the last out in the ninth inning against the Angels. Bouton closed out the game and upped his major league stock. Marty Pattin had started the game, which Seattle won 4–3, that was now referred to as a tune-up for his opening-day start.[10]

Trade rumors turned into realities in the last days of spring training. There had been speculation about Chico Salmon for some time. His knee was still painful. He could play but lacked range and agility. The Pilots did not want to carry someone who would be a question mark until he healed. And they needed pitching. Milkes sent Salmon to Baltimore for six foot seven, 227-pound (or more) Gene Brabender and minor league shortstop Gordy Lund. The big twenty-seven-year-old right-hander had not pitched much for the Orioles in spring training because he was not in pitching shape, not really in shape generally. When ready, Brabender would be a starter, which the Pilots needed, especially if Barber could not pitch regularly. Brabender's addition ensured that Segui would bolster the bull pen.[11]

Milkes, Schultz, and the coaches met in a motel room in Tempe to finalize the roster. When they came to Lou Piniella, a long discussion ensued. Piniella was out of options. He would have to stay with the club or be traded if he were to retain any value. He had already shown signs of his later irascibility and had rubbed even the affable Schultz the wrong way. He seemed to have a weak arm but maintained that he had hurt it the previous year and was bringing it along gradually. He was a good hitter. Finally, they reached full agreement: Piniella would be a Pilot. The next morning the staff woke up to find that despite the previous evening's consensus, Milkes had dealt Piniella to the Kansas City Royals for outfielder Steve Whitaker and pitcher John Gelnar. Jim Bouton claims that Dewey Soriano almost fired Milkes when he got the news. Whitaker was a serviceable outfielder and a local boy from Tacoma. Gelnar pitched steadily for the Pilots. Piniella hit .282 and won rookie of the year for the Royals.[12]

There was one more subtraction. Bill Henry had probably won a place on the team as a spot reliever but was not entirely satisfied with himself. At the end of spring training, he surprised Joe Schultz by telling the manager he was packing it in. John Morris, also a left-handed reliever, surmised with good reason that Henry had quit to open the roster spot for him. Onetime Angels playboy Bo Belinsky gave Milkes a call when he was released by the Cardinals at the end of their spring training. Milkes turned him down, saying that Belinsky did not really fit the Pilots' pitching needs.[13]

The Pilots ended spring training with a rush, winning six of their last eight games, five of them consecutively. Pattin's last start of the spring was against the Angels, whom he would face opening day. It was a sloppy performance for him and the team. Pattin gave up seven hits and four runs in five innings. He was followed by the usually steady Jack Aker, who gave up a grand slam to Dick Stuart. But Seattle was equally as adept at the plate as the Angels, scoring five in the third inning and seven in the sixth to win 14–9. It would turn out to be good practice for the regular season. In a 6–4 loss to California, Barber was sluggish and sore but gave up only two runs. There was more good news than bad in a double-header against the Padres in San Diego that completed the spring schedule. The Pilots split the twin bill, forced by a rainout, to finish with a 12-and-16 Cactus League record. Bell was sharp in the nightcap, allowing three earned runs in six innings. Aker steadied himself with one inning of shutout relief, and Segui demonstrated that his thumb injury of a few days before had healed by throwing a few pitches in the bull pen. Barber could go only one inning and gave up six runs. His next stop was Los Angeles, to visit orthopedist Dr. Robert Kerlan.[14]

The clubhouse was coming together. Jim Bouton admired Tommy Davis, who had established his team leadership: "Tommy Davis is loose and funny and a lot of guys look to him, not only the Negroes," Bouton wrote. "Everybody sort of gravitates toward him and his tape machine and he is asked his opinion about things." The team elected Jack Aker to be player representative.[15]

Joe Schultz saw several pluses and a few minuses during the Pilots' first spring training. Hegan was a surprise. Rollins and Davis, who had begun to sting the ball at the end of the exhibition season, were also coming through. Among the second-line players, outfielders Jim Gosger and Wayne Comer and infielder Gus Gil made themselves assets. Of these six, all but Comer and Gil had hit over .300 in the preseason. Catcher Jerry McNertney and third baseman Mike Ferraro had also topped .300. Schultz was relieved that Tommy Harper had made real progress at second. That left another spot in the outfield for a good hitter. Pitching, especially his hurlers' control, was a negative for the manager. Overall, Schultz complained that evaluating so many players was just a difficult task.[16]

Spring training had accomplished its purpose. It had sifted out the players who were not ready, not adept, or simply not physically able to play. It had put some pieces together: Tommy Harper would be an infielder and pitcher Gene Brabender was needed more than shortstop Chico Salmon. And it had sketched out the contours of the season. The Pilots would usually have to outhit the opposition to win.

TIME LINE OF PILOTS AND STADIUM POLITICS

PILOTS AND MARINERS	STADIUM
OCTOBER 1967 American League grants franchise to Seattle	
DECEMBER 1967 American League selects Pacific Northwest Sports, Inc., as owners.	
	FEBRUARY 1968 First Forward Thrust vote.
	JUNE 1968 Consultants recommend South Park neighborhood in Seattle for stadium.
	AUGUST 1968 Stadium Commission selects Seattle Center for stadium.
SEPTEMBER 1968 Seattle City Council approves lease agreement.	
	JANUARY 1969 Renovation of Sicks' Stadium begins.
APRIL 1969 Home opener for Pilots.	
OCTOBER 1969 Handshake agreement with Milwaukee Brewers; Danz bid to buy Pilots announced.	
JANUARY 1970 Carlson bid to buy Pilots announced.	
FEBRUARY 1970 American League rejects Carlson bid.	
APRIL 1970 Pilots declared bankrupt and sold; Pilots move to Milwaukee.	

PILOTS AND MARINERS	STADIUM
	MAY 1970 Second Forward Thrust vote; vote on Seattle Center site.
	JANUARY 1971 New Stadium Commission chooses King Street for stadium.
	NOVEMBER 1972 Groundbreaking for Kingdome.
JANUARY 1976 Trial begins, *Washington et al. v. American League.*	
FEBRUARY 1976 Seattle granted Mariners.	
	MARCH 1976 Kingdome opens.
APRIL 1977 Home opener for Mariners.	

Chapter 5

BUILD IT, AND THEY WILL COME

THE boosters had failed twice in the 1960s to persuade Seattle and King County voters to build a stadium to lure major league sports to the area. In 1968, it was the turn of the civic leaders. In the midst of their campaign, a major league baseball franchise dropped into their laps. Because of the American League's eagerness to put a franchise in Seattle, all that remained to secure the team was a positive vote on the domed stadium in the February 1968 Forward Thrust election. (Key moments in the brief existence of the Pilots and many of the important events in Seattle stadium politics overlapped in time. For a chart that tracks them all, see the time line, pp. 72–73.) This effort would be very much unlike the previous two. Forward Thrust was a multifaceted campaign to gain funding for a whole array of capital improvements for Seattle and King County. It was a sign that Seattle was moving toward maturity even as it drew on a decades-old tradition of citizen participation.

The Northwest had been one of the bastions of the Progressive Era. At the turn of the twentieth century, democracy broadened. Middle-class professionals, especially, stood up to combat corruption and inefficiency in their governments. They sought to regulate and rationalize business and governmental processes. By the 1960s, at least two aspects of the Progressive Era were still evident in the fabric of Seattle as it came of age.

First, the people's ability to legislate was well established through the referendum and initiative processes, which had been in place since 1912. Joe Gandy's bitter observation about being glad that the world's fair had not been subject to a ballot becomes a significant commentary on how far out in front of the community the boosters stood. They were activists; the community was cautious. The city council and the mayor might have dragged their heels when it came to projects like the fair, a stadium, or renovating an existing baseball park, but they reflected the will of many of their constituents. If obtaining a major league sports franchise was the mark of a big-league city, and if it took a stadium to do it, a sizable minority of the voting public was willing to forgo the honor. Nonetheless, the civic leaders, whether or not they were privately wary of citizen participation, honored the Progressive tradition and placed the fate of the stadium and the promised team in the hands of the voting public.

Second, another remnant of Seattle's Progressive past was the band of civic activists such as Gandy, Carlson, and a bevy of other private citizens who were instrumental in putting on the world's fair. These men, and a very few women, like their forebears, believed that citizens—especially professional, well-educated members of the community—had a certain responsibility to pitch in to improve their city, at least according to their own priorities for improvement.

Attorney James Ellis was another of these civic leaders. Ellis was a graduate of Franklin High School in Seattle and then Yale University. He finished his education with a law degree at the University of Washington. As a leader, he was neither imposing, wealthy, nor charismatic, but he had a keen sense of what problems were lurking down the road, and, blessed with an organized mind that could manipulate a mass of information, he was able to fashion innovative responses. He was an optimist, a pragmatist, and an apostle of efficiency who believed there were numerous people of goodwill ready to reform and mold society into providing more livable surroundings. "Young men and women looking for a cause beyond self can find it here," Ellis proclaimed. He was convinced that "the quality of urban environment is within our power as citizens to change for good or ill," and with advances in technology, the means for doing so was within the grasp of reasonable men and women.[1]

As a man well connected with businessmen and politicians, Ellis could get things going, sometimes successfully, sometimes not. His efforts spanned county charter reform, a cleanup of Seattle's Lake Washington, a mass transit initiative, and, in 1968, Forward Thrust. There were detractors. Some said that Ellis had a personal political agenda, but he never ran for office. Others saw a conflict of interest for a bond attorney who pushed public works, but no one ever demonstrated that his firm gained any advantages from his campaigns. "In sum," wrote an interviewer from *Harper's*, "he is a walking contradiction of everything that C.

Wright Mills has told us about the Power Elite." More than anyone in the 1960s, James Ellis and Ed Carlson embodied leadership that could bring the city to new heights.[2]

In the first week of November 1965, Ellis combined his progressive sensibilities with optimism about the willingness of Seattle leaders to match his work ethic and vision. He kicked off Forward Thrust in a speech to the Rotary Club. While local governments merely reacted to problems on a short-term basis, Ellis rallied civic leaders to a long-range master plan. Sounding a little Babbitt-like, he called his listeners to exercise "world's fair zip and area-wide effort." His prescription for action, though, was far more sophisticated than anything Sinclair Lewis's realtor could come up with. True to his decadelong outlook, he was convinced that the Puget Sound region would move ahead through cooperation on a grand scale. He encouraged collaboration in planning among his fellow visionaries, saying, "If each person or group who has sought a limited objective for the city were to join together to develop a total program of capital financing and secure its approval by the taxpayers we could take a step into the future that would transform the city."[3]

Ellis ticked off a list of likely projects: rapid transit, a multipurpose stadium, street improvements, parks, a trade center, and urban redevelopment. Then he predicted the lasting impact of participation in a unified project, declaring, "The objective of the Forward Thrust committee would not simply be rapid transit or big league sports, or parks, but rather a joint effort to weld all of these elements into a total urban design which will challenge a great community effort." Finally, he exhorted his audience with an image of Seattle transforming itself into a top-flight city. "The heart of the metropolitan area should serve as the rallying point for this forward thrust," he proclaimed, "but the welfare of the entire area will be its aim. With the tools of the urban designer, a regard for human values and plenty of work we could see the beginning of a golden age for Seattle. We could build one of the great cities of man." Now he sounded like Theodore Roosevelt or even Jane Addams. Technical expertise infused with humanism and honest toil were the ingredients to bring about a great society. In the 1960s, many of these ideals were sharply questioned, but for Ellis and many Seattleites, it was still a can-do society. The Seattle Spirit was very much alive. Both daily newspapers reacted with enthusiasm. Ellis had touched a nerve, and as word of the Rotary speech spread about town, many were ready to pitch in, do some creative thinking, and get their city, and region, on the move.[4]

As Ellis's carefully selected group assembled the ambitious array of projects, cooperation continued to be the watchword. The citizens who drove the program forward were still in harness with their government leaders, though Mayor Braman dragged his heels a bit. The group was self-consciously aware of the times. "In this era of clamor and complaint, successful civic action represents thoughtful communication between official and citizens," reads a 1970 Forward Thrust booklet. "It is not officials telling citizens what's good for them, nor is it citizens demanding more than they are willing to pay for. It is a continuing dialogue. It is listening, learning, and hard work on both sides." Next, while Forward Thrust focused on the pragmatic matter of improving infrastructure needed to sustain a burgeoning population, the committee never lost sight of the fact that they were in the business of building a great city. The Forward Thrust policy analysis committee described how quality of life merged with improved infrastructure: "while some may suggest that these [cultural and social service] items be deferred for more 'essential' needs, the committee is convinced that the attractiveness of the metropolitan area and the quality of urban life depend critically upon adequate cultural, recreation, and entertainment opportunities. Many of these opportunities can only be provided by public capital investment." Finally, Ellis thought that an assortment of projects authorized simultaneously should compel governments at the federal, state, and, particularly, local level to act together and accomplish something magnificent for everyone.[5]

Ellis envisioned a community effort, but since he was recruiter in chief, the committee reflected his network. A majority were businessmen, attorneys, and elected officials. Housewives, college professors, real estate investors, and bankers each made up 5 percent of the committee. The group was almost 90 percent male and only 5 percent minority. The Forward Thrust committee was about evenly split between Republicans and Democrats. Representatives from all over King County were sprinkled throughout, but most shared Ellis's view that the continued vibrancy of the downtown core was critical for the well-being of the outlying areas. While it is clear that most members had answered the call to a civic obligation and were eager to solve municipal problems and shape a city, it was not entirely a selfless outpouring of municipal concern. For some, it was a stepping-stone to political office. Forward Thrust was a grand networking opportunity not seen since the fair, and, at the very least, it was a chance to be seen doing good.[6]

The first step was to enlist the state legislature. Olympia signed on. Beginning in January 1967, the legislature enacted all but one of the nineteen bills that would facilitate the Forward Thrust proposals. Many of the bills granted local governments greater flexibility in their powers to tax and spend. Others added state funding to a number of projects that Forward Thrust was considering. For example, for the proposed stadium project, the state in essence allocated to King County almost half of the 4.5 percent state sales tax on hotel and motel revenue generated in the county. This meant that a 2 percent tax levy from every King County lodging bill would help pay off stadium bonds, thereby reducing the impact on property taxes. Ed Carlson noted that his Washington Plaza Hotel alone would contribute $60,000 a year.[7]

With this helpful legislative framework in place and a myriad of ideas in front of the committee, the next step was to decide what would actually go to the voters. Rapid transit topped the list. Though Ellis was quite serious in his request for a broad and coordinated program of works, this was the initiative dearest to his heart. Seattle traffic had been increasing by 4 percent a year. The transit system would be expensive: $1.15 billion. But two-thirds of that could be paid by a federal grant provided by the Urban Mass Transportation Act of 1964. So what King County needed was the remaining $385 million in matching funds. That made transit the largest single item on the ballot. Aside from the stadium, the rest of the slate included money for parks, an aquarium, community centers, infrastructure repairs, and low-income housing. There were thirteen separate issues. The price tag would be $820 million if citizens approved everything.[8]

Campaign officials were aware that it would be a hard sell. The package stretched the debt capacity of the governments and the willingness of voters to pay higher property taxes. Part of the economic argument was that the local economy was strong and growing. Forward Thrust literature sought to soothe the anxious. "The homeowner will pay a substantially lower tax on his home," the argument went, "than the owner of a similar home in any western city of comparable size." If these reassurances were not enough, then that average homeowner needed to remember that it would never be cheaper to accomplish all these projects. Moreover, the Forward Thrust literature argued, now was the time to spend, because the federal government would add millions to the pot if local governments were willing to provide the ante.[9]

Forward Thrust was visionary. Ellis's horizon for the project stretched ahead about twenty years, but Forward Thrust projects continue to have an impact on the region's livability more than forty years later. Most of the committee's attention was focused on preparing the Puget Sound region for an influx of people without destroying its ambience. The Economic Analysis Committee, struggling to come up with a cost-benefit equation, described the dream: Forward Thrust "will create substantial economic and social benefits, even though it is very difficult to put a specific value on benefits such as the aesthetic quality of green space in urban areas, the value of clean air and water, or the social values available at the community centers." To a great degree, it succeeded.[10]

The stadium was one of the big drawing cards, if not the centerpiece, of the Forward Thrust campaign. The committee hoped that the stadium would lure voters to the polls and that, once there, they would endorse most or all the pieces of the program. In fact, in 1966, Ellis, thinking ahead, appealed to Joe Gandy to postpone that year's vote on an arena so that it could be part of the package of projects he would be proposing. At the time, the NFL was dangling the prospect of a franchise for Seattle, and Gandy believed he could gain approval. Two days after his campaign failed, the Ford dealer broke out of his depression and declared that he wanted to give it another go. He petitioned a very willing Ellis to include a multipurpose stadium in Forward Thrust. Then, in October 1967, as the committee was finalizing its slate of bond propositions, the American League granted Seattle a franchise contingent on a successful vote. It was all coming together. The committee asked voters for $40 million for stadium construction.[11]

Municipal stadium development has never been an easy process. Politicians and their constituencies must be persuaded that it is worth the enormous outlay, especially if they are mindful of other competing uses for the funds. There are also ancillary costs of a facility, including reconfiguring traffic patterns, sewerage, and police and safety services on game days. Siting is another challenge, especially for political leaders. Some areas take a "not in my backyard" attitude, forcing the arena into the hinterlands. Others campaign hard for a nearby facility and pursue vengeance through lawsuits if they are thwarted. Downtown elements often see the new stadium as a chance for urban renewal or a catalyst for development and apply pressure, even if parking and access are next to impossible. Finally, financing is a major challenge. Does a stadium mean a tax increase? Yes, almost surely. Whose taxes will go up? Revenue bonds (taxes on the use of the stadium) most likely will not cover both construction and operation costs. Usually, it is general obligation bonds, which incur the lowest interest rate, that come into play—and that means higher property taxes. Spreading the tax burden as widely as possible is a desirable strategy, and that often means some kind of sales tax—a tax on visitors is especially appealing to local residents. A 4 percent hotel/motel tax helped build the New Orleans Superdome; a 1 percent restaurant and bar tax contributed to the Hoosier Dome in Indianapolis. Half the funds for an arena in Orlando came from a resort tax. Lotteries, naming rights, seat licenses, and racetrack taxes have subsidized other playing venues. In short, a stadium is a necessity for obtaining a franchise, it is likely to be built by local governments, and someone has to pay for it. Authorizing and siting a building can be a daunting process, especially for the political establishment. Such was the case in Seattle.[12]

For a third time, Gandy was the man to lead Seattle through this maze of stadium issues. He was an inevitable choice for cochairman of Forward Thrust's Culture and Entertainment Committee, and, of course, he headed the campaign's Multipurpose Stadium Sub-committee. There was speculation, which had pretty well evaporated by the end of the summer of 1967, that the arena could be built with private funds and then leased to the county. For a short time, Gandy hoped that revenue bonds combined with operations income might be enough to pay off the stadium. But as early as August 1967, he was arguing against that notion and advocating general obligation bonds.[13]

Even with the hotel/motel tax picking up some of the obligation, the stadium was behind in the polls a month before the February 1968 vote. Potential voters were more familiar with the stadium than with any other Forward Thrust issue. It proved a boon and a curse. The stadium had the highest "yes" vote in the January 1968 polls, 50 percent, but it had the highest negative vote as well, 35 percent. Men, younger voters, and the upper middle class were most supportive. The biggest negative was the suspicion that the owners of the new baseball franchise were just out to make a buck. The American League was very concerned. Gerald Hoffberger was stewing again. A friend in Seattle warned him that the issue looked iffy. Hoffberger advised Joe Cronin to have a contingency plan ready if the stadium vote failed. No matter how clever the plan, the league knew that it would look foolish if it had to revoke the franchise. It commissioned Kraft pollsters to survey the situation. They came to the same conclusions as the Forward Thrust opinion takers: the stadium issue was running behind the needed 60 percent approval rate and generated a strong negative vote. The pollsters thought a 60 percent margin could be achieved by turning out the vote among men, younger voters, and the upper middle class.[14]

The league and Pacific Northwest Sports, Inc., decided it was time to roll out the big guns. With a month to go, PNSI donated $10,000 to the Forward Thrust publicity campaign. It paid for ballplayers Mickey Mantle, Jimmy Piersall, and Carl Yastrzemski and umpire Emmett Ashford to canvass Seattle. Many of their presentations were intentionally oblique. High pressure could backfire, so just making people feel good about baseball was the order of the day. Ashford, an African American, spoke on race relations, asserting that blacks should make their own way. Yastrzemski recalled good memories of going out to games as a boy and assured Seattleites that being big-league was important to any city. Mantle and Piersall dropped by Children's Orthopedic Hospital and Boeing to proclaim Seattle as major league, implying that since it was truly a major league city, Seattle would naturally vote for a stadium. The players also visited high schools and junior high schools. The object, of course, was to turn the kids into effective proselytizers of their parents on the stadium issue.[15]

Joe Cronin came west as well. He claimed to have just decided to come to Seattle on his own to see for himself, but the American League paid for the trip. Chauffeured by Dave Cohn, he made five or six speeches to civic groups throughout the county and met with Mayor Braman and the county commissioners. Unlike the players, Cronin campaigned hard for the stadium. When asked what might happen if the vote failed, he refused to entertain the possibility. Later, referring to his optimism, he asserted, "You don't sell bad fish." Statement after statement assured the public that Joe Cronin was all about the freshest catch. He appealed to the city's pride: "We can have any city. We want Seattle." "Seattle is a big league town. This is a major league territory and the American League is happy to be a part of it." He assured the worriers: "The American League is in Seattle to stay, given a place to stay," and "The American League is not a jumper." And he warmed Jim Ellis's heart with "I congratulate the people of this community for the foresight they are showing with the conception of the Forward Thrust program. Your community needs it, all thirteen parts. It's the proper manner of progress." Cronin's visit, along with those of the others, established positive momentum. In the days following the visits, the stadium issue rose in the polls from a 58 percent approval level to over 60 percent.[16]

Other sports figures joined the campaign. Though he did not come to town, National Football League commissioner Pete Rozelle reminded Seattleites that they would already have an NFL team had they approved the stadium in 1966. He assured fans that the league still looked upon their market with eager eyes. Along with the good possibility of an expansion team, the Houston Oilers, Boston Patriots, and Buffalo Bills were rumored as candidates for the new arena. NFL star and former Husky Rick Redman was sure that a domed stadium would bring football. Former quarterback Y. A. Tittle came to town to push for the issue, and major league baseball commissioner William Eckert let Seattleites know that he had been talking with Warren Magnuson about baseball in the Puget Sound region ever since he had become commissioner (it was probably the other way around).[17]

Officials thoroughly understood Seattleites' concerns that the new arena was a boondoggle benefiting mainly sports franchise owners. Accordingly, Forward Thrust leadership, true to its philosophy, presented the stadium as serving everyone. As consistently as possible, speakers called it the "multipurpose stadium." In conjunction with the Coliseum at Seattle Center, the domed stadium would complete the region's "full range of cultural and entertainment facilities," according to Forward Thrust literature. There would be conventions, Billy Graham crusades, auto shows, boat shows, home shows, and rodeos, along with major league sporting events. Political leaders took this tack as well. When it looked as though the stadium was failing, Mayor Braman felt that his task was to convince non–sports fans, like himself, that the arena with its dome promised much more than games and would take the pressure off the Coliseum. City Council chairman Floyd Miller echoed the mayor's arguments as he emphasized the multipurpose aspect of the stadium. An article in the *Seattle Post-Intelligencer*'s women's section ("She Changed Her Mind: But It Was Not Due to Women's Prerogative") detailed Councilwoman Phyllis Lamphere's conversion to the project. She had voted "no" in 1966 but now believed that a fair-minded citizen, recognizing the balance of Forward Thrust, would vote for the stadium. With the hotel/motel tax, it was too good a deal to turn down. Others raised the banner of major league over the stadium. Councilman Charles M. Carroll and Alfred Schweppe said they endorsed the stadium because it made Seattle major league, Councilman Sam Smith thought the stadium was necessary to keep Seattle an "All American city," columnist Emmett Watson promised that isolated Seattle would be a thing of the past, and Secretary of State A. Ludlow Kramer saw the stadium as imperative for the development of the state and the community.[18]

Royal Brougham wrote that the stadium vote paled in the face of greater issues such as the Vietnam War, but a number of soldiers stationed in Southeast Asia had written him, anxious to see the bond pass. Brougham, who had been a sportswriter for decades, demonstrated that he was more at home in the 1930s than the 1960s, writing that the multipurpose facility would have a little something for the ladies. He predicted that a visit from Lawrence Welk, a fashion show with Twiggy and the Gabor sisters, or afternoon tea with Ann Landers would be in the offing when the project was complete. (He let his imagination run for a full column. There is no record of James Ellis's reaction to the article.) Not to be outdone, Sally Raleigh, the *Seattle Post-Intelligencer*'s women's editor, called her counterpart in Houston to ask about the Astrodome. The *Houston Post*'s Virginia McCallan told her that she had a skybox and dressed formally for games, and that other women seated in the stands appreciated not getting wet or having the wind blow their hair in the dome. Such was the *Post-Intelligencer*'s contribution to securing the crucial women's vote for the stadium.[19]

The Forward Thrust campaign sought to pick up the religious vote. Archbishop Connolly averred that Seattle would not be big-time until it got major league baseball and football. Billy Graham telegrammed, "If I were a citizen of Seattle, I would vote for such a stadium at the earliest possible time. If such a facility is built, we would gladly accept an invitation to hold a major evangelistic crusade in your city."[20]

Most of the media pitched in with support. KVI, owned by Golden West Broadcasting, which also owned the California Angels—and very much in the running for baseball broadcasting rights—called for a "yes" vote as a civic duty, much like supporting the Seattle Opera House or other public venue, and pointed out once again that almost everyone would profit from its construction since it was a multipurpose stadium. The *Post-Intelligencer* argued that the stadium would yield a net profit in the long run. The *Seattle Times*, less enthusiastic, still thought the proposal did "hold promise" with its "sound approach." The *Argus* finally argued itself into support, pointing out that the stadium was not a solution to a civic crisis (i.e., it was not a testament to being major league) but a sound business deal. The African American community's newspaper, the *Facts*, was for the stadium, mainly because Sam Smith, the only African American city councilman, endorsed it. Lenny Anderson spoke for all the sportswriters, declaring, "In short, it seems inconceivable that the Seattle area could reject a stadium costing the average taxpayer less than $2 a year." The *Tacoma News Tribune* reminded its friends to the north that Kansas City had approved stadium bonds by a 70 percent majority, and Oakland OK'd its stadium by 66 percent. Finally, the counterculture paper, the *Helix*, ever disdainful of the establishment, simply saw the stadium as "a lasting memorial to man's insurmountable stupidity." [21]

Active opposition came from others besides the *Helix*. City council candidate George Cooley feared that the Forward Thrust program would exceed the bonding capacity of the city and thought that the stadium should be privately built. He apparently ignored the fact that the county was going to be issuing the stadium bonds. Steven Chadwick again had reservations about stadium expenditure. While he approved the stadium because it would be partially funded by the room tax, he wondered at the necessity and cost of a dome, ignoring the multipurpose aspect of the proposal.[22]

During the campaign, the newly appointed Washington State Stadium Commission began looking for a building site. Jim Ellis had sought to delay the final decision on the site until after the funding vote, to avoid alienating voters who might have been counting on a particular site or others who may have opposed a certain location. Ellis had a keen sense of human nature. Sure enough, the siting process later became a great wrangle and verged on complete disaster. Governor Dan Evans appointed the commission, which the legislature had authorized in 1967. By September 1967, Evans had appointed two city councilmen, Floyd Miller and Clarence Massart; two county commissioners, John O'Brien and John Spellman; and two citizens from King County, Dave Cohn and, inevitably, Joe Gandy. This group, working with a consulting firm, would choose the site and send its selection to the King County Commissioners for final approval. The bonds would then be sold and construction begun. In September 1967, still six months out from the bond vote, stadium commission chairman Gandy called for any and all nominations for a site in King County. Eighty-five firms and individuals answered the call with everything from architects' renderings to scrawled postcards.[23]

In a remarkable bid to launch a cooperative effort, Pierce County, south of King County, chimed in with a proposal. County officials authorized a vote for $10 million to contribute toward a facility in King County, if it would be built in south King County, preferably just south of Kent. The commission was cordial to the proposal but clearly discomfited. The *Times* was concerned that the stadium could be built well out of town; the *Post-Intelligencer* approved, welcoming the possible infusion of funds and finding pleasure in twitting the *Times*. Seattleites, especially the downtown leadership, breathed a sigh of relief when the $10 million measure did not get even 50 percent approval from Pierce County voters. The *Tacoma News Tribune* lamented, "This county isn't as major league conscious as some had thought."[24]

In the meantime, the Seattle Central Association (the downtown association) suggested three sites: Yesler and Jackson at Fifth (in the heart of the Pioneer Square, Skid Road district), Interbay in northwest Seattle, and next to the King Street Station, at the southern edge of downtown. Paul Thiry, Seattle World's Fair architect, advocated the Seattle Center as the site, explaining that the new stadium would complement the Coliseum. The stadium commission selected Western Management Consultants from the nine firms that bid for the job of assisting the selection process. By voting day in February 1968, Western Management and the commission had winnowed the possible sites from twelve to six but had not made a choice or ranked the options. On the eve of the election, Gandy predicted that the decision on a location would take another 30 to 45 days, or maybe 45 to 60, or maybe up to 120 days (depending on which edition of the newspaper one read). It would be a battle.[25]

Tuesday, February 13, 1968, was exceptionally balmy, and the voters came out in droves to cast their votes on Forward Thrust. It was the largest turnout for a special election in Washington State history, with around 50 percent of eligible voters in King County making their way to the polls. Every one of the measures received more than 50 percent of the vote, but only seven bond issues out of the thirteen ballot measures garnered the requisite 60 percent. Rapid transit, the keystone for Ellis, failed, leaving Seattle without an extensive commuter rail system until the twenty-first century. But the stadium passed with 62 percent. It found its greatest support among the better-off neighborhoods. African Americans were strong supporters. Neighborhoods with average incomes of $12,000 or more voted 67 percent in favor of the stadium; precincts with average incomes of $8,000 or less gave it a 65.6 percent approval; and those in the middle of this range just barely endorsed the stadium with a 60.9 percent "yes" vote. It appears that the stadium lagged among the blue-collar population, who probably saw little value in trading higher property taxes for the opportunity to pay additional hard-earned dollars to see baseball or football in a new sports facility.[26]

Among the city leaders, there was frustration, if not gloom. Ellis's pet project, rapid transit, had failed, and he had promised to disband Forward Thrust after the election. Citizen reform in the Puget Sound region seemed to have ended with a whimper. But Mayor Braman sought to persuade Ellis and his committee to stage an encore. Ellis agreed. Between 1968 and 1970, Forward Thrust did it all over again. The second Forward Thrust vote would draw the civic leaders into the effort to save the Pilots.

Meanwhile, the sports community in Seattle celebrated. John Owen declared that the city would now have one of the best sports arenas in the world. Colleague Royal Brougham, thanking *Post-Intelligencer* editors for permission to push hard for the stadium, wrote, "In one 12-hour span our town grew up." Hy Zimmerman likewise saw the vote as a sign of the city's growth and maturity. On the East Coast, Joe Cronin stayed up until 3 a.m. to get the news that the American League's premature bet on Seattle had paid off. Cronin thanked Seattleites for their vote, declaring, "I know this will be a fine association for many years to come."[27]

On a broader level, Forward Thrust was another important step toward maturity for Seattle, even if voters failed to pass some issues. On the sports front, it appeared that the city had arrived—it was now one of those young western cities on the move, establishing itself as a big-league sports town. The criteria that the 1960 Stanford Research Institute study had set out—sufficient interest from city leadership and fans, a credible ownership, and a stadium—seemed to have been fulfilled. The American League thought so and was more than happy to officially grant the franchise. But a closer look might have given Joe Cronin and the American League owners pause.

Neither the fans nor Seattle leaders were that enthused about big-league sports if they came with any kind of price tag attached. It took three tries to push through stadium bonds. By the third attempt, the civic leaders had joined the sports boosters in persuading the public to approve the stadium, but many of them supported it only because it was part of the Forward Thrust package and was described as a multiuse facility. Even then, it took a tax subsidy from the state legislature and a publicity campaign by Cronin and several baseball stars to elicit the required 60 percent approval. Few local politicians were at the forefront of the stadium campaign, and several remained skeptical about baseball in the city. Compared to the vigor of leadership in Anaheim, Oakland, or Minneapolis when the Twins came to town, the situation in Seattle was not all that propitious. It should have worried the American League that Seattle could not produce sufficient financial capital to form a totally homegrown ownership group. Finally, stadium politics would play out badly in the Northwest. Almost as important as what took place on the field, the difficulties involved in getting Sicks' Stadium ready for major league baseball and then siting and constructing the domed stadium would progressively become an unwelcome focus of the Seattle sports story.[28]

All of this was clearer in hindsight, of course, although Orioles owner Jerry Hoffberger was astute enough to see the outlines of a number of these problems on the eve of the stadium vote in 1968. The American League was blinded in its rush to beat the National League to the Northwest. It had not really examined the situation, optimistically assuming that anyone would welcome a team with joy. Unfortunately for them, Kathy Crosby, the *Times* person in the street, probably represented a substantial number of Seattleites when she judged it merely "nice" that the American League had awarded her city a major league baseball franchise. The league would pay for its careless optimism.

Play-by-Play

APRIL AND MAY

T HE Pilots' opener was an away game in Anaheim against the California Angels. Five hours before the first pitch, Hy Zimmerman suffered a mild heart attack and was taken to Cedars of Lebanon hospital. He would recover and resume his post during the season, but he must have been frustrated to miss the moment for which he had campaigned so intensely.

Seattle fielded a veteran lineup for its inaugural game. Only two players, starting pitcher Marty Pattin and right fielder Mike Hegan, had fewer than four seasons in the majors. Tommy Harper, at second, would lead off, followed by Hegan, Tommy Davis in left, and Mincher at first base hitting cleanup. Third baseman Rich Rollins came next, then Jim Gosger in center, Jerry McNertney behind the plate, Ray Oyler at short, and Pattin. If the team knew that one of its beat writers had been sidelined, it was not a distraction. After Angel starter Jim McGlothlin's first pitch sailed over Harper's head, the second baseman hit a sizzler down the left field line for a double. Hegan followed with a homer, giving the team a two-run lead. Pattin allowed two runs on eight hits, including a shot that Hegan dropped when he slammed into the outfield wall and lay crumpled on the turf for several minutes. X-rays showed that nothing was broken. Had the phrase been in vogue, he would have been listed as "day-to-day." Following the spring training pattern, Diego Segui relieved Pattin when the starter ran out of gas after five innings, and Jack Aker finished the game when Segui lost his command in the ninth. The Pilots won 4–3 and were undefeated. The next night against the Angels, the Pilots got off to a 3–0 start, including a Mincher home run, but Mike

Marshall, Gene Brabender, and Johnny Morris were ineffective, giving up seven runs, while the team committed four errors. The Seattle club sank to .500.[1]

Although workmen were still refurbishing Sicks' Stadium, the team opened at home on April 11. All the appropriate pregame hoopla attended the first-ever home game. Fans welcomed the Pilots back from California at the airport. A downtown parade and luncheon at the Olympic Hotel honored the team the day before the game. Dignitaries of every sort showed up to the luncheon: Senators Warren Magnuson and Henry Jackson; Governor Dan Evans, who had proclaimed April 6–12 "Baseball Week"; Mayor Floyd Miller; baseball commissioner Bowie Kuhn; American League president Joe Cronin; ex-pitcher Lefty Gomez, who was the banquet's keynote speaker; Dewey Soriano; William Daley; Chicago White Sox owner John Allyn; and Angels owner Gene Autry. Tables were arranged in the shape of a baseball diamond and decorated with eighty autographed baseballs from the Pilots. President Nixon sent a congratulatory telegram. Joe Schultz was all "aw, shucks" when he got a kiss from Miss Seafair, received the key to the city, and was crowned king of baseball. Bridget Hanley, star of the TV show *Here Come the Brides*, loosely based on Seattle's nineteenth-century Mercer Girls, asked starting pitcher Gary Bell to wear her garter on the mound. (There is no record that he complied.) It was a great time for Seattle to celebrate itself.[2]

Clear skies and sixty-degree weather greeted the teams the afternoon of April 11. The *Seattle Post-Intelligencer* published a forty-one-page opening-day insert with room for plenty of corny baseball-themed ads. ("Give her a ring, then take her out to the ballgame" to show it off, suggested one jewelry store.) Magnuson threw three first pitches to Evans as Jackson stood at bat. Rod Belcher sang his song "Go, Go, You Pilots." And the workmen laid down their hammers.[3]

The game itself was as rewarding as the congratulatory ceremonies. Gary Bell pitched a complete-game shutout. Don Mincher hit his second home run—caught by one of the carpenters in right field—Tommy Harper had two hits and a stolen base, and the Pilots beat the White Sox 7–0. The Pilots split their two remaining games with Chicago. Segui demonstrated that he could start as well as relieve, taking the ailing Barber's spot and going seven and two-thirds innings in a 5–1 victory. But Pattin, Brabender, and Bouton were pummeled the next day for eleven runs in a homerfest (Chicago hit five and Seattle two) that ended 12–7. In an effort to accommodate more seats, the fences at Sicks' Stadium had been brought in from where they had been during the minor league days. Early in the season, there was talk of home run records, but although there were some high-scoring games, records did not materialize.[4]

The Pilots ended the home stand one game under .500 after a complete-game loss by Mike Marshall to Kansas City and a rainy late-inning collapse against Minnesota. (Someone selling ad space in Sicks' was on the ball. The stadium tarp read "It never rains in Southcenter.") The team was beginning a season of adjustments. To take up the pitching slack left by Barber's sore shoulder and Brabender's excess girth, Milkes shipped Jim Bouton to Vancouver on twenty-four-hour recall and brought up Bill Edgerton. Edo Vanni slipped out from behind the group sales desk to give some advice about going the other way to Jim Gosger, who promptly went three for three.[5]

Reality began to set in on the ensuing six-game road trip to Chicago and Kansas City. The Pilots got good pitching from Pattin, Marshall, and Segui, who was again pressed into duty as a starter. But the hitting went dormant, and the fielding continued to be spotty. The Pilots averaged three runs a game and lost four of the six. The season record sank below .500 and would stay there the rest of the way. Barber and Brabender gave up thirteen runs in Chicago. Back at home, Bell could not get out of the fourth inning against the A's, victimized in part by his own throwing error. Oakland then lit up Bill Edgerton and put away the Pilots 14–2.

"We are very disappointed in some of the members of this club," Milkes told the press. In what would become a familiar refrain, he promised player changes. Mike Ferraro, who hit over .300 in spring training but had gotten only four at bats so far, was outrighted to Vancouver. When he refused to go down, he was traded to Baltimore for pitcher John O'Donoghue. Dick Bates took Ferraro's place on the roster; then, in a couple of days, Bates went back to Vancouver to make way for O'Donoghue. Bill Edgerton was also returned to the minors, exchanged for pitcher Darrell Brandon. The players joked grimly about the bus to Vancouver pulling out from Sicks' nightly.[6]

Next it was Marshall's turn to face the hitting prowess of the A's and the wrath of his manager. Marshall went to one and two on the season, giving up five runs in six innings. The A's ended up with thirteen runs. When Schultz went out to get his laboring starter, Marshall began to walk off the mound. Irritated, the manager summoned him back to wait for Bates. Marshall was studying for a Ph.D. in kinesiology (his research focused on the impact of physical maturation on the self-esteem of adolescents) and was rather self-consciously intellectual. He had started baseball as an infielder but wanted to pitch. The Detroit Tigers gave him a chance after the Phillies cut him. In a feature column on the *Post-Intelligencer* Style page, Marshall had told editor Bobbi McCallum that his priorities were family, education, and baseball, in that order. He found traditional baseball authority suspect, disdained Schultz, and said he felt like a "piece of meat in uniform." It is likely that Schultz was not as dense as Marshall thought and realized he had a nonconformist in his starting rotation. It would cause tension for both men.[7]

Meanwhile, Lenny Anderson, *Post-Intelligencer* beat writer, was detecting a home-run hitting pattern. At night, homer production was relatively normal, but during day games, in the drier, warmer air, the ball jumped out of Sicks'. Factoring in the uneven pitching of the Pilots, Sunday home games began to bring a sense of foreboding.[8]

The Pilots split their final two games in April but saw hopeful signs on the pitching front. Marty Pattin got his breaking stuff over and shut out the Angels 1–0, and Jim Bouton, back from Vancouver, pitched two shutout innings in relief in a losing effort against the Twins. By the end of April, only 65,335 fans had come out to see the Pilots, who had compiled a 7–11 record. Marvin Milkes blamed low attendance on cool weather and promised that upcoming promotions would stimulate crowds, but an average turnout of 7,250 had to worry the front office.[9]

May started badly. The Pilots began the month 1–6. Steve Barber's arm throbbed, and he pitched to only three batters before coming out of a game. Bouton, perhaps feeling a little insecure after taking his turn on the Vancouver shuttle, wondered why his teammate didn't just go on the disabled list or work out his problems in the minors, leaving a roster spot for someone else. Tommy Davis and Ray Oyler were also injured and sat out some games. Do-everything Diego Segui injured a finger and was used sparingly. There were some highlights. Tommy Harper was stealing bases regularly, Mike Hegan hit around .300, and Don Mincher socked five home runs. But Mincher and Davis were in deep slumps averagewise, and Rollins was batting below .250. The pitching was in its normal condition: uneven. The defense continued to be ragged. By May 7, the Pilots were at the bottom of the Western Division and had the poorest record of the four expansion clubs. Milkes was peeved. He told the press that he "would rather make a bum deal than die with some of these fellows"—a comment certain to be discussed in the clubhouse. Bouton's take was that "Marvin Milkes is not a guy who will sit around in a situation that calls for panic." In a newspaper question-and-answer column, broadcaster Jimmy Dudley assured a letter writer that "Seattle is proud to be a major league city and the negative attitude you speak of is fast disappearing." Interestingly, the letter had not made reference to any "negative attitude." The Pilots needed steady pitching, but the only trade possibility Milkes mentioned was one that would be counterproductive—Segui going to Oakland for shortstop Ted Kubiak.[10]

Then the Pilots' fortunes suddenly improved. Seattle went on a five-game winning streak, their longest of the season. A Saturday night tilt against the Washington Senators fueled the skein. It started off poorly for the home team. The Senators had an 11–3 lead going into the bottom of the sixth. Mincher got to starter Camilo Pascual for a two-run homer. Then after a hit and three walks, Rollins hammered a grand slam off reliever Dave Baldwin. The Pilots pulled ahead in the seventh, but the Senators came back to take the lead 13–12. And then the Pilots took advantage of two walks and some poor fielding in the eighth to score four runs, three unearned, winning 16–13. Things seemed to be looking up. The next day, Mincher hit a dramatic ninth-inning home run for a 6–5 victory, but the front office was surely more excited by the 14,363 fans who turned out for bat day. The *Post-Intelligencer* began to run a "Harper-O-Graph" comparing Tommy Harper's steals to Ty Cobb's American League record pace of 1915. Mincher declared that he was beginning to feel comfortable at the plate.[11]

The struggling New York Yankees came to town on the heels of the Senators, and the Pilots took two games out of three from them. In the first game, Bobby Murcer slid hard into Ray Oyler at second, inciting a brawl. As benches cleared, two Burns Detective Agency guards hustled onto the field. Edo Vanni later claimed that he had told them to wait by the gate, but they thought they had been ordered to go onto the playing field. Yankee manager Ralph Houk made it clear in his best Marine vernacular that the guards were an unwelcome breach of baseball etiquette. The next night, 19,072 came out to see local boy Mel Stottlemeyer, originally from Mabton, Washington. The Pilots beat the Yankees' ace and were in fifth place.[12]

Seattle played .500 ball the second half of May and, for most of the period, inspired optimism. Third place did not seem so farfetched. In twenty-first-century baseball parlance, Mike Marshall was an "innings eater." By the end of the month, he was 3–6, but he had the third-lowest ERA (earned run average) on the club and regularly went deep into games. The coaching staff may have had other terms for the headstrong starter. Marshall had irked Schultz by throwing a fastball to Roy White, just after the manager instructed him not to throw the heater. White stroked the ball into center field for a go-ahead run. Then, in a win against Boston, Schultz pulled Marshall in the ninth after he gave up a grand slam to Carl Yastrzemski. Marshall complained to the press, "I shouldn't have come out when I did." Schultz retorted, "What am I supposed to do—just sit there and lose the game?" Things took a bad turn off the field the last week of May when the right hander was mugged in Cleveland. Later, Marshall revealed that he had dislocated his pitching shoulder in the attack but told no one. His ERA inflated about a run and a half over the next month.[13]

With the team winning games, the clubhouse was loose. Mike Hegan described a typical day during a home stand: Get to the park about 4 p.m. From 4:15 to 5:20, get dressed, get any therapy needed, go over the opposing team. Then shag flies in the outfield until 6:00. From 6:00 to 6:40, take batting practice. Lounge around in the clubhouse from 6:40 to 7:10; then take the infield and check on conditions. Game time was 8:00. Hegan normally ate dinner after the game and got to bed by 1 a.m. With so much routine seasoned with idle time, the players endeavored to keep themselves entertained. Games in the outfield, a kangaroo court with fines for silly things like base-running gaffes or awkward fielding plays, and batting practice contests for the pitchers helped kill time at the park.[14]

Though it was a good month for the expansion club, the Pilots still had problems. Barber's sore arm was healing slowly. The team's fielding, especially in the outfield, was somewhere between poor and atrocious. Rich Rollins strained knee ligaments in Boston and returned to Seattle for treatment. There was more player movement, mainly in trades. Jose Vidal, so promising in the spring, was hitting .192. He went to the Yankees in exchange for Dick Simpson. Jack Aker's ERA was over 7.00, and he was shipped to the Yankees, for pitcher Fred Talbot. Catcher Merritt Ranew came up from Vancouver to replace Fred Velazquez, who was claimed by Oakland when he was sent down. Gary Bell replaced Aker as player representative, and Don Mincher was elected his assistant. Bouton thought that Marshall, bright and organized, should have gotten the assistant job.[15]

The good news on the field was that Mincher's bat was heating up, and Tommy Davis, club RBI leader with twenty-two, moved back over .200. The bull pen seemed to be stabilizing. Segui, used only in relief in late May, was developing into the top pitcher on the staff. John O'Donoghue settled in as the left-handed relief specialist. The team was still searching for a fourth starter after Pattin, Marshall, and Bell, who were workmanlike, and occasionally masterful, in their performances. On May 21, Gene Brabender, finally working himself into pitching shape, went into the sixth inning against the Washington Senators and won his first game 7–3.

Indians manager Alvin Dark was the first to make note of a major weakness: the Pilots were susceptible to left-handed pitching. In fact, as the team arrived in Cleveland, Seattle was 3–6 against lefties and 14–15 against right-handed pitching. Dark started three left-handers against the Pilots. Even so, Seattle, on a relative hot streak, won two of three. The big match-up was supposed to be Mincher against lefty Sam McDowell, who had beaned Mincher early in the 1968 season, endangering the first baseman's career. But any drama was defused by Schultz, who played it by the book and sat down the left-hand-hitting Mincher and put Hegan at first. The Pilots knocked out McDowell after one and one-third innings and won the game 8–2. Another bit of good news: Steve Barber started for the first time since May 2, went four innings, and said he felt good.

It might have been Harper's legs as much as anyone's bat that did the damage to McDowell. In the second inning, Harper stole home. McDowell lost his concentration, and Dark took him out. Harper was on a tear. The next day, he swiped three bases for a league-leading twenty-five on the season. He was becoming the offensive star of the team. He had come from Cleveland, where he had stolen eleven bases in 1968 in only 235 plate appearances. Harper was from Oakland, California, had debuted in the majors with Cincinnati, hitting .278 in 1966, and hoped he was returning to that form. He was a natural athlete who had quarterbacked his high school football team and was a good shooter on the basketball team. Harper cherished the opportunity to play regularly in Seattle and liked the city. "This is a pretty town, when you can see it," he observed. The fans were equally intrigued with "Tailwind Tommy."[16]

The Pilots returned from their eastern road swing May 27 and promptly defeated the Baltimore Orioles, who were already looking like the class of the American League. Brabender hurled a 153-pitch complete game, allowing only one run. If he hadn't been in game shape before, he undoubtedly was after this game. Euphoria reigned. Even the sportswriters were on the third-place bandwagon. The Pilots had won twelve of their last sixteen games, putting them a half game out of third and only four out of first place in the West.

Milkes was still on the prowl, especially for starting pitching. In the meantime, he purchased Jim Pagliaroni from the A's. The catcher had a broken finger, so he went on the disabled list, but that did not stop Merritt Ranew from questioning the need for another player at his position. Pitcher John Gelnar, who had come to the Pilots in the Piniella trade, was summoned from Vancouver on Mounties manager Bob Lemon's recommendation. Darrell Brandon was sent down.

Just as the Pilots peaked, Joe Schultz slumped. When the Orioles' Jim Palmer stiffened up before the May 28 game, Baltimore switched to Dave McNalley as its starter. Schultz rejiggered his lineup, substituting Dick Simpson for Don Mincher against the lefty. But he gave Baltimore manager Earl Weaver and the home plate umpire the original lineup card. Weaver saw the mistake and bided his time until the fifth inning. Tommy Davis doubled in two runs, hitting from the spot Mincher occupied on the official scorecards. Weaver brought it to umpire Jake O'Donnell's attention. Davis was out, and the two runs were nullified. While it was not a turning point in the game, the Pilots lost 9–5; it brought great embarrassment to Schultz. "I keep saying that it was just one of those things," despaired the manager, "but I'm just talking to myself. It's tough to shake." One wonders what Marvin Milkes was thinking. It could have been the beginning of the end for Schultz. One bright spot—it was Elks night at Sicks', and 21,679, a new attendance record, turned out to watch the game.[17]

The last game of the month was on a gloriously sunny Saturday afternoon. The Pilots were on NBC's nationally televised Game of the Week against the American League champion Detroit Tigers. Emmett Watson's Lesser Seattle movement was taking a beating as people around the nation gazed at a ballpark backed by Mount Rainier. Mickey Mantle, doing color, thought the ballpark was certainly compact—he figured that he could have broken the all-time home run record by 180 homers had he played his career in Sicks' Stadium. Even with all this, the excitement was on the field. Detroit's Joe Sparma almost no-hit the Pilots. He started off raggedly, walking Tommy Harper on four pitches. Harper was called out while trying to steal. Mike Hegan walked on four pitches; then Tommy Davis grounded a pitch out of the strike zone into a double play. Before it was over, Sparma had walked seven. The Seattle club helped Detroit with five errors. Two of the errors led to two Tiger runs in the fifth without a hit. The Pilots scored one in the bottom of the fifth on a walk, a wild pitch, and an error. By the ninth, it was Tigers 3, Seattle 1, and the home team was without a hit. Davis hit a one-and-two pitch to left for the first out. Don Mincher came to bat and took two balls, then lined the next pitch to right center. Center fielder Mickey Stanley raced to the wall, but the ball bounded off the fence for a double. Sparma had gone eight and one-third innings pitching no-hit ball. Another error and a fielder's choice scored a run, and now the 15,395 could hope that Sparma was in danger of losing his win. Larry Haney flied out, and the 3–2 victory was Detroit's.[18]

Chapter 6

SETTING THE COURSE

THE Seattle ownership was well aware of the hurdles the team faced even before it took the field. A picture of William Daley and a letter to the fans from the principal owner greeted visitors to the ballpark as they opened their copies of the *Seattle Pilots Official Scorebook* throughout the 1969 season. The letter was telling. Daley wrote:

> It is a privilege—just that—for us to be able to bring you BASEBALL at the Major League level. Both the stadium we play in (temporarily) and our win-and-loss balance sheet may, at first, require your patience, but as our talent scouts explore, and our coaches teach, and our baseball mechanics (we think we have the best) tinker and adjust . . . so, most surely will our product, the PILOTS, match the magnificent backdrop against which they perform. This is our hope and more than that, our promise.[1]

That the owner believed an apology was necessary before the season even began demonstrates that he grasped the problems facing an expansion team. The difficulties were not limited to Seattle. Baseball as a whole was feeling a financial pinch. By the end of the 1960s, the National Football League was replacing baseball in the hearts of the public. A 1971 *Forbes* article was typical. While admitting that baseball was drawing as many fans as ever, it accused the sport of being languid, devoid of new ideas, and on the verge of becoming passé. League owners were aware that the national pastime was slipping from its singular place in the sports universe. Before the 1969 season, they fired Commissioner Eckert (a personality so bland that the press unkindly nicknamed the former general "the unknown soldier"); they lowered the pitching mound and narrowed the strike zone, to stimulate hitting; and, as a way of accommodating the added expansion teams—but also as a competitive stimulus—they created two divisions in each league and added league playoffs at the end of the season. As the Stanford Research Institute study noted, competent and well-funded ownership was a necessity for a franchise to succeed. Daley, an active but substantially absentee owner, and Dewey Soriano, who operated the franchise day to day, were competent enough, but the club's funding was not robust. The inevitable missteps associated with an inaugural season combined with difficult financial circumstances stained the owners' ledger with far too much red ink. As Soriano set the Pilots' course, he understood both the advantage and the strategies of selling a novel product, but he bet too heavily on Seattleites' willingness to pay top dollar for a losing and constantly changing team. Seattle City Hall made things even more perilous (discussed in chapter 7).[2]

Emmett Watson had supreme confidence in his longtime friend. Watson rejoiced not only in his beloved Seattle finally becoming big league but in the Horatio Alger story of Dewey Soriano, the boy who sold programs at old Civic Field and grew up to operate a major league team. Admiring the spring training complex in Tempe, Watson observed, "Everything about this Seattle operation is top drawer." Seattle is no longer far off the beaten track, he exulted. Others agreed. A number of commentators rated the Seattle franchise tops among the expansion class of 1969—exceeding San Diego, Montreal, and Kansas City.[3]

As operations manager, Soriano tended to concessions, oversaw promotional events, negotiated with the city on Sicks' Stadium, and represented team interests to the stadium committee as it looked for a site. For playing personnel decisions, the club needed a general manager. Two months before the formal announcement, Hy Zimmerman correctly predicted it would be Marvin Milkes. The short, stocky forty-five-year-old was a baseball lifer. According to the *Seattle Times*, he had served as a clubhouse boy for the Rainiers in the early 1940s. As a teenager, he produced his own sports page, the "Milkey Way." After a stint in the army during the Second World War, he became the youngest general manager in baseball at twenty-three, taking the position with Fresno, a Saint Louis farm team. Cardinals owner Sam Breadon had asked the young Milkes if he wanted to work fourteen hours a day and take all the heat for losing. When Milkes said that he did, Breadon told him, "If you're that much of an idiot, you're hired." He joined the Los Angeles Angels in 1961 and helped assemble their expansion franchise. Milkes served as Seattle Angels general manager in 1966 and was a California Angels vice president and probable successor to Angels general manager Fred Haney when Soriano hired him in February 1968.[4]

Virtually everyone who knew Milkes described him as intense and hard driving. Other less complimentary descriptions included words like "restless," "complex," "tough," "aggressive," "uptight," "controlling," "volatile," "abrasive," "rude," "unwittingly cruel," and "a wild man." An article in early editions of the *Pilots Scorebook*, almost surely written by Harold Parrott, Milkes's own pick for public relations head, portrayed the general manager as burning up the phone wires, tranquilizers, and Rolaids. The apparently admiring article noted that even his wife, Patti, was not sure if Marvin was married to her or to baseball. Milkes's temperament was not really suited for an expansion franchise. Losses ate away at him. He expected more from marginal players than they were able to give. Before the season began, manager Joe Schultz, in an off-hand comment, told reporters that he thought the team could finish as high as third in the Western Division. The manager's optimism evolved into a demand from the general manager . . . and an albatross around the neck of the franchise. Milkes stormed at employees and players who acted too casually for his taste. He could work for Dewey Soriano because both were strong-minded men, but Soriano put him on a leash and frequently called Milkes into his office when he strained too hard at the tether. Milkes's self-perception was not far from the observations of others. He described himself as someone who moved fast and expected subordinates to keep up. Every game, every day, Milkes said, was a crisis. "I'm very candid. I like to win. I get a little impatient sometimes and I don't smile all the time when we lose. . . . This is not a buddy-buddy organization. I believe in results." Into the office at 8:30 a.m. on home game days and not out until midnight, he drove himself hard.[5]

Milkes rapidly moved players in and out of the organization. Some said he was a good judge of talent. Others thought his trades and shuttling of players between the club and the minor league teams reflected his personality more than baseball acumen. The April *Pilots Scorebook* article stated, "Of one thing you can be sure: Marvin Milkes won't sit still. Let the Pilots team lose a few games in a row, and he'll be on the phone looking to trade for a back-up shortstop or a left-handed pinch hitter." Even if the Pilots won, the article went on, Milkes would likely still be scowling, already fretting over future losses. Hy Zimmerman (almost as type A as Milkes) observed, "He has splendid mental furniture, but it may need re-arranging." If Milkes was a bit off, it manifested in an obsession with winning in a situation in which something less than third place in a weak division was entirely respectable. Years later, Seattle bull-pen coach Eddie O'Brien met Milkes and described him as pleasant, even-tempered, and no longer frazzled. Nonetheless, O'Brien would not quarrel with Lenny Anderson, the baseball beat writer for the *Seattle Post-Intelligencer*. Anderson considered Milkes the weakest link in the organization, scoffing that he could not have scouted Joe DiMaggio. English professor and Seattle historian Roger Sale was even more disdainful. Perhaps thinking of Willie Loman or George Babbitt, he wrote that Milkes was "one of those perennial losers who keeps getting jobs by learning how to get along with people with money or influence." Hard-driving or wild man, pursuing high goals or out of touch with reality, Milkes might have been one of Soriano's missteps. At any rate, he was the one who would assemble the team.[6]

The list of potential field managers was relatively short. Milkes complained that it was impossible to get a top-flight man because there was little glory in managing an expansion team. Former Houston manager Grady Hatton, ex–Minnesota skipper Sam Mele, and onetime Braves slugger and Seattle Angels manager Joe Adcock were in the running, but it was Joe Schultz who got the call. Schultz had been a journeyman catcher for the St. Louis Browns and had just won the World Series as third base coach with the St. Louis Cardinals in 1967. Schultz had coached in the majors and managed extensively in the minor leagues, including a term in 1957 at San Antonio, where he met Milkes. He was the general manager's choice. It is likely that Dewey Soriano knew Schultz only by reputation before the hire.[7]

The consistent compliment offered by those who knew Schultz is that he was a sound baseball man; he was easy to get along with, though he was not particularly polished. Rod Belcher, who served as a liaison between the manager and the press, remembered that "he was as rough as his gnarled fingers." Reporters found him grandfatherly but uncomfortable in their presence and not a particularly good source for quotations. One began a description, "Joe Schultz, whose command of time-tested cliches is vast. . . . " All thought him affable, greeting friend and foe with a "Howzit goin', buddy?" Players remembered him as easygoing and a players' manager, although he expected his team to hustle. Cardinals pitcher Ray Washburn warned his counterparts in Seattle not to dog it with Schultz. Some players were unimpressed with his intellect; the always hard-to-please pitcher Mike Marshall disdained him.[8]

Most baseball fans remember Joe Schultz through the eyes of relief pitcher Jim Bouton. In *Ball Four*, Bouton compared him physically to Nikita Khrushchev (there was a general resemblance). In his most memorable portrayal of the manager, Bouton described a Schultz pep talk: "Attaway to stomp 'em. Stomp the piss out of 'em. Stomp 'em when they're down. Kick 'em and stomp 'em. Attaway to go, boys. Pound that ol' Budweiser into you and go get them tomorrow." Schultz claimed that he never read the book, but he was hurt by Bouton's caricature. Bouton thought it was sympathetic. Joe Schultz—bumbling, kindly, inarticulate, wise in the ways of baseball—probably had an ideal temperament for managing an expansion team of less-than-confident, often struggling players through a losing season, unlike the intense and ever-striving Milkes.[9]

When Bouton turns to the coaches, what he says contains much truth but reveals his resistance to authority. (It is hard to say whether *Ball Four* is more a description of the Seattle Pilots or a revelation of Bouton's personality. Probably it's both.) He writes, "We decided jobs as coaches were really a kind of political patronage. They're dispensed for former favors. There's not much to do. Being a coach requires only showing up at the ball park, hollering cliches and being able to play false sorrow when you lose. It's a boring job. But people who become coaches are not easily bored." Bouton thought coaches were masters of the obvious and enforcers of minutiae.[10]

Joe Schultz got to pick one of his coaches, Ron Plaza, who oversaw conditioning. Milkes hired two coaches with an eye toward luring fans— if coaches can possibly have an impact on ticket sales. Longtime Yankee coach Frankie Crosetti was one pick. He had played sixteen seasons with the Yanks and coached for twenty-nine more. He signed on with Seattle to be closer to home and family in Stockton, California. He asked two favors: he no longer wanted to chase baseballs during batting practice and infield, as he had all those years with the Yankees, and, unfortunately for public relations purposes, he begged off the banquet circuit.[11]

The other drawing card was pitching coach Sal Maglie. "Sal the Barber" had pitched for the New York Giants and Brooklyn Dodgers. Most recently, he had been the Boston Red Sox pitching coach through the 1967 World Series. He and manager Dick Williams disagreed over the use of Jim Lonborg in the final game. At the close of the season, Maglie was informed that he had been let go. He was humiliated. In 1968, he became pitching coach for Seattle's farm team, the Newark Co-Pilots, a New York team located near his Niagara Falls home. Despite Williams's claim that he gave Maglie the boot because he wanted someone who could work with the young pitchers, Maglie's skill with tutoring youngsters had been the attraction for Milkes (besides name recognition). Pitchers Steve Barber, John Gelnar, Marty Pattin, and Diego Segui credited Maglie with improving their pitching, but he rubbed Bouton and Marshall the wrong way. Maglie was not much interested in helping Bouton perfect his knuckleball, which Maglie felt was beyond his expertise. More significantly, if Bouton can be trusted, Joe Schultz did not seem to esteem Maglie. Bouton quotes him saying at one point, "Listen, don't worry about Sal. I let a lot of the stuff Sal says go in one ear and out the other."[12]

Eddie O'Brien, one of the renowned O'Brien twins who had starred as basketball players at Seattle University in the late 1940s and early 1950s, rounded out the quartet of coaches. (Brother John was a county commissioner, a member of the stadium committee, and among the group of Seattle sports boosters.) Both brothers went on to play baseball for the Pittsburgh Pirates. Eddie was a major league infielder and pitcher for Branch Rickey's club. When he retired from the Pirates in 1958, he had four years and four months toward the five years he needed for a baseball pension. Dewey Soriano telephoned O'Brien in his office at Seattle University, where he served as athletic director for his alma mater, and invited him to earn the last year as bull-pen coach. Having worked at the university for seven years, O'Brien was eligible for a sabbatical and got approval from the National Collegiate Athletic Association (NCAA) to work in professional sports while at an NCAA institution. It was a friendly gesture by Soriano, and maybe some would come out to catch a glimpse or a wave from a hometown hero. The post was more honorific than substantive—his main job was to get relievers up and signal when they were ready—but O'Brien was hardly the baseball naïf Bouton depicts in Ball Four.[13]

As soon as Milkes was in place in February 1968, he and Soriano began to assemble the front office. They recruited more well-known locals. Bill Sears became director of press relations. Besides directing public relations for the Rainiers and the Seattle Angels, Sears had worked with the Greater Seattle business organization, and assisted in the stadium campaigns. Former major leaguer Earl Torgeson of Snohomish, Washington, managed a rookie-league team and served as roving batting instructor. The club named Edo Vanni group sales and team ambassador. Vanni was a Seattle baseball fixture, always good for a quotation, and was probably underused by a franchise that came up short in the areas of attendance and public relations. Perhaps Soriano was determined to be Mr. Baseball in Seattle and feared that the personable Vanni could steal the limelight.[14]

Most of the higher-level appointees had extensive experience in organized baseball. Gabe Paul, Jr., minor league executive of the year at Tulsa, was traveling secretary, charged with handling air travel for the team that would log the most air miles in the major leagues as well as a multitude of other logistics when the team went on the road. A thirteen-year baseball veteran, ticket manager Harry McCarthy had been assistant ticket manager for the San Francisco Giants. Ray Swallow was lifted from the A's to direct scouting. Milkes tapped Bobby Mattick as his special assistant. Mattick, an accomplished scout who had signed the likes of Vada Pinson and Frank Robinson, pursued free agents and hunted hidden gems on other major league and minor league rosters. Former Seattle Rainiers manager Bill Skiff served as a special assignment scout. The team employed at least seventeen other full-time scouts around the country and one in Latin America. Art Parrack, also from the A's, headed up the farm system, though Milkes took responsibility for player movement, especially between the major league team and the minors. Under Parrack, Bob Lemon managed the Triple-A Vancouver Mounties, which the Pilots owned along with the Montreal Expos. Lemon, striving to become a major league manager, quit his job as Angels pitching coach and took on the task of guiding a team that was an amalgam of the top minor leaguers from the two expansion franchises. The Pilots had working agreements with three A league teams. New York's Newark Co-Pilots, started up in 1968 with Sibi Sisti—a Boston and Milwaukee Braves veteran—as manager. In 1969, Sisti moved on to the Clinton, Iowa, farm team, and Torgeson took over Newark. Longtime scout and minor-league manager Bobby Mavis guided the third A-league team, Billings, Montana.[15]

Seattle had put together a solid front office—locals who knew the region mixed with veterans from around major league baseball. Most were longtime acquaintances of Soriano's or Milkes's. Harold Parrott deserves some special attention. Parrott, whose career began in 1927 as a reporter with the *Brooklyn Eagle*, had served in the Dodger organization many years and came to Seattle from a short stint with the California Angels as promotions and sales director. Parrott took the same position in Seattle, where his son was on the Seattle University tennis team. Milkes, with Dewey Soriano begrudgingly acquiescing, recruited him at double his Dodgers salary. Parrott brought as much major league experience as anyone to the Seattle front office. He took credit for negotiating a lucrative radio deal with Golden West Broadcasters (his former employer with the Angels, Gene Autry, owned the company). He put together the scorecards and programs and sold the associated ads. On the downside, sportswriter John Owen remembers being solicited, probably by Parrott, to write a feature story for the program on Seattle reaching the "Bigs." When it came out, it seemed almost nonsensical to Owen. It did not resemble his submission but carried his byline. The article contained Owen-like humor but often digressed and rambled . . . much in the style of other articles in the *Pilots Scorebook* by Harold Parrott.[16]

A month into the season, Parrott was gone. It was one of the first signs of a franchise in trouble. Bill Sears thought Parrott did not work very hard, but Max Soriano said the promotions director was fired because the club did not have the luxury of keeping someone as qualified, or as confident, as Parrott—a telling admission. Cash flow was already a concern, and Parrott's salary was high. But the expansion team could ill afford to scrimp on promotions when attendance was lagging and the national popularity of baseball was in the doldrums. Looking back, several commentators cited poor promotions along with underfunding as the main contributors to the failure of the Pilots. After the promotions director left, the Pilots staged few special events. The bitter Parrott, stuck with a lease on a pricey Mercer Island home, "began to wonder whether [American League owners] had even bothered to meet Soriano, much less research his ballpark and his ratings in Seattle."[17]

Even as the Pilots were assembling a leadership team and putting one together on the field, there was plenty of other work to do. As an expansion club, Pacific Northwest Sports, Inc., was starting from scratch and had just one year to get everything in order. The staff gathered in May 1968 at the Olympic Hotel to get to know one another and make decisions. Through the summer, they could be found in six trailers strung along the right field wall of Sicks' Stadium. The trailers were sealed together, three wide and two long, with paneled walls, carpets, desks, office machines, and telephones and were connected to the stadium by two doors. Giant puddles accumulated around the stairs leading into the trailers during steady rains. The complex was not up to code, but the city provided a variance.[18]

The staff's priority was to raise Northwesterners' awareness that a new major league baseball team would take the field in spring 1969. Throughout 1968, employees answered a flurry of requests for caps, balls, pennants, and other souvenirs. Bill Sears issued a cascade of press releases to get the team into the spotlight. PNSI held a name-the-team contest to pique fan interest. In March 1968, fans began submitting their ideas, with a supporting statement of twenty-five words or less, to Edo Vanni. As the competition got under way, Royal Brougham, knowing his son-in-law Dewey Soriano was a licensed harbor pilot, wrote, "In this city of giant freighters sailing the seven seas and world famous airplanes, somebody is pretty sure to suggest Seattle Pilots." Among the 21,252 names submitted were Green Sox, Rainiers, Kings, Mariners, and . . . Pilots. Sears, who pointed out that he had not gone to school just to eat his lunch, selected Donald J. Nelson's first-day entry on the basis of "originality." The team would be called the "Seattle Pilots."[19]

A batboy contest also helped build anticipation. Each contestant, age fifteen to eighteen, wrote a one-hundred-word essay on why he wanted to be a batboy. The winning entry got a $1,000 scholarship, two season tickets to Pilots games, and a chance to accompany the team on a road trip. Every boy (it was 1968, and the idea of a batgirl did not enter the minds of these baseball men) would get a game ticket.

Distinctive uniforms, worn for the first time on opening day, sparked interest. The foundation colors were blue and gold. Four gold stripes— insignia of a captain—marked the socks and the sleeves. (Some worried that the multitude of stripes on the sleeves of the pitchers might distract batters. It did not become an issue.) The cap was blue with a gold S. The player's number and the word "pilots" in lowercase letters were emblazoned on the chest. The home uniforms were traditional white; the road uniforms were azure blue with a lowercase "seattle" across the front. Most memorably a captain's "scrambled eggs" in gold adorned the bill of the dark blue cap. Although Bouton denounced the uniforms as gaudy, the rest of the players found them "different," liked them, or did not care one way or the other. *Post-Intelligencer* graphic artist Stuart Moldren won a nationwide contest for his Pilots logo, which also appeared on the uniforms. It was a good deal sportier than the white and red nautical flag ("pilot on board") the Pilots had been using up to that time on their stationery. Moldren's design was a ship's wheel in red with a baseball inside the wheel and a royal blue "Pilots" printed over the ball. Small yellow wings, like angel wings, protruded from the sides of the wheel. As one writer said, "You can hardly be more pilot-y than that." Despite a number of allusions to the airplane variety of pilots in the uniform and logo, references to the team were consistently nautical.[20]

Finally, the Pilots decided a team song would foster awareness. Milkes asked Harry Ruby, who cowrote the Kalmar and Ruby hits "Three Little Words" and " Who's Sorry Now" and had written a theme for the Angels, to do the same for the Pilots. Milkes waxed rhapsodic at the thought: "I can just hear the hum of motors from those big Boeing jets. I can visualize [*sic*] the sound of horns of the tug boats." Instead, Rod Belcher, who worked for the team and whose ad agency had a contract with the Pilots, wrote "Go, Go, You Pilots." Belcher had written song parodies for the Sportswriters and Sportscasters banquet but had never composed a commercial song. Dewey Soriano liked it, a musical group recorded it in Los Angeles, and by spring training, 2,500 copies were ready for sale on the Pilotune label, forever preserving these undying words:

Go, go, you Pilots. You proud Seattle team.
Go, go, you Pilots, go out and build a dream.
You brought the majors to the evergreen Northwest;
now Go, go, you Pilots, you're going to be the best!
Go, go, you Pilots, Go, go, you Pilots, when the umpire hollers play.

Through contests, colorful images, and catchy tunes, the Seattle Pilots were being impressed upon the popular culture consciousness of the city.[21]

But selling a baseball team is about more than creating good feelings. Relatively affluent fans must be persuaded that their entertainment dollars are well spent on season tickets. Season-ticket holders for the 1968 Seattle Angels got first crack at Pilots seats. The team staged orientation luncheons where it introduced itself to business leaders. Then Milkes and Parrott met in the trailers with members of the Seattle establishment and hosted phone conversations with players during spring training. Parrott tells a disquieting story. At some point in the process of ingratiating the team with Seattleites, James Douglas came to Parrott to confide that he and Ed Carlson were worried that the franchise was going to flop and embarrass the city. Douglas said that Carlson was ready to convene one of his breakfast meetings at the Olympic Hotel and bring Schultz and some players to meet with civic leaders so that they could encourage the city to get behind the ticket drive. According to Parrott, Soriano rejected the plan out of hand, insisting that the club did not need their help. Max Soriano, not so sanguine—or stubborn—as his brother, worried that members of the local business community were not getting behind the team. He supposed that it might take two or three years for them to warm up to the Pilots.[22]

Attendance surveys showed that the team was more successful attracting those who had to travel greater distances to see a game. The team worked at enticing fans outside the immediate vicinity. Schultz, several players, the radio broadcasters, and the publicity department made winter tours of the hinterland in early 1968 and again before spring training in 1969, busing from Aberdeen in southwest Washington to Vancouver, British Columbia; Spokane; Bremerton; and a number of points in between.[23]

Services at the stadium were set up. Ushers were hired at eleven dollars per game from a slew of applications. On the West Coast, Disneyland represented the height of customer service, so the Magic Kingdom's training manual for hosts, hostesses, and ticket sellers provided the basis for training. One of Dewey Soriano's biggest responsibilities was looking after the concessions contract. In February 1969, after some hard bargaining, PNSI struck a deal with Sportservice, concessionaire for half the major league baseball teams. PNSI granted the concessionaire an exclusive services contract for twenty-five years, the second-longest contract the company held. This meant that wherever the franchise went—to the King County Stadium, for example—Sportservice would be the concessionaire for baseball and, presumably, any other activities in the arena. The problem was that King County, not PNSI, had the authority to determine the concessionaire in the new stadium. In return for this somewhat dubious guarantee, PNSI got about one-third of all concession sales and a veto on prices. More significantly, in May, Sportservice tendered PNSI a $2 million loan at 0.5 percent above prime. Since Sportservice could borrow at 1 percent above prime, it cost the concessionaire $10,000 a year to service the transaction—apparently well worth it for the exclusive services guarantee. Sportservice gained a very vested interest in the franchise.[24]

Television had been a staple of baseball for many years by 1969. In the words of sports media expert David Quentin Voigt, it "was the most important of all the forces that molded major league baseball in the expansion era." By 1970, broadcasting contributed about 28 percent to each team's revenue. Altogether, local TV broadcasts provided $22 million yearly to all major league teams. In 1969, each team reaped $1.27 million per year from local and national broadcasting contracts.[25]

Unhappily, the Pilots were left in the dark. The expansion franchises did not get a share of the lucrative national television pot for three years, and the Pilots failed to secure a local deal after negotiations extended into May 1969. Dewey Soriano sought to sell broadcast rights at a rate that would yield profit and cover the expensive line fees for transmission of away games. Reportedly, the Pilots asked for as much as $20,000 per game, which was what the Angels charged in a significantly larger market. Even when the team reduced the price to $10,000 a game, channel 11 (a non-network outlet) insisted that all advertising slots be filled before televising. "Don't worry," Soriano assured channel 11 salesman John Upham in April, "I'll get everything fixed up in California [with the sponsors], and I'll call you back in a couple of hours." Upham was still waiting for the call three weeks later. The station owners were also nervous that most of the fans, being Seattleites, would be outdoors hiking and boating in the extended daylight of summer rather than sitting in front of their sets watching expansion team baseball. The Sorianos feared or rationalized that televising games, whether home or away, might sap attendance, even though the 1955 Rainiers televised their home games and fared well. The upshot was that the Pilots were not televised locally during their one-year season. NBC did come to Seattle to televise the Pilots against the Detroit Tigers in a late May Game of the Week.[26]

The radio contract was a different story. Gene Autry's Golden West Broadcasting signed a contract for $850,000 for the year, one of the most remunerative deals in the league. The Pilots were on KVI in Seattle and about fifty other stations from Fairbanks, Alaska, to Williston, North Dakota, to Elko, Nevada. The radio deal was surely one of the top "good news" stories for a tenuous franchise. Jimmy Dudley and Bill Schonely teamed up to provide play-by-play. Dudley, fifty-five, had been a Cleveland Indians broadcaster for the past twenty years but had reportedly fallen out with his co-announcers in Cleveland and was available. He was a small man and presented himself as dapper. Originally from Virginia, he still had a soft mid-South accent that, for some listeners, was reminiscent of Red Barber. That was the image the Pilots sought to conjure up. A *Pilots Scorebook* profile extolled Dudley's southern charm, quoting his signature greetings and sign-offs. "Good evening, sports fans, wherevah you ah," and concluding, "So lawng, and lots of good luck, do yuh heah." Schonely was best known as the Seattle Totems hockey team announcer and had done Husky football and Seattle Angels games. He went on to become the voice of the Portland Trail Blazers. Though he was entirely capable, many, especially those who knew him well, could detect that his heart was drawn to sports other than baseball.[27]

Seeking a way to make a decent profit, Dewey Soriano thought that higher ticket prices would make up for the smaller fan base. Field box seats were set at $6. The rest of the tickets ranged from $4.50 a seat in the "loge," as the old grandstand at Sicks' Stadium was now called, to $3.50 for bleacher seats, and $2.50 for new backless seats beyond the outfielders. The ticket prices set off a wave of complaints. John Owen pointed out that the ticket scale was the highest in the majors overall and observed that "big league" described the prices more than the brand of baseball that would be offered. Georg Meyers exclaimed, "Great Soriano! Where are the cheap seats?" noting that even the Yankees charged no more than $4, and other clubs went as low as 75¢. In all of major league baseball, only the San Francisco Giants sold seats at $6, and they had only a few at that price. The *Times* quoted Cincinnati president Francis Dale, who had worried, "We can't continually be raising the price of a ticket, say until it eventually climbs to $5. We would be pricing ourselves out of the market." Charlie Finley warned Soriano before the season began that the ticket prices were way out of line and that seats without backs cannot be priced so high. A fan wrote to Senator Magnuson that he was astounded to pay $4.50 for his grandson, thinking there would be some kind of discount for youngsters.[28]

Concessions were expensive as well. Hot dogs were 50¢, a cup of coffee and soft drinks cost 15¢ and 25¢, and beer 75¢. To compare, a loaf of bread cost 33¢, a movie $2, the daily newspaper was 10¢, and it was possible to purchase a man's suit at J. C. Penney for $3. Earl Luebker crowed in the

Tacoma News Tribune that fans coming to a Tacoma Cubs game would have to get used to $2 for the best seat in the stadium, 25¢ hot dogs, and 45¢ for beer.[29]

Bill Sears defended the prices. The $6 ticket was a little deceptive, he explained, because when sold as season tickets, the discounted average cost to the season-ticket holder was only $4.32 per game—and the entire supply of seats sold out as season tickets. The two were friends, but Owen's column on the $6 ticket irked Sears because Owen had not checked the story with the Pilots media relations officer. Sears complained that the column created an image of the Pilots as gougers that they could not live down. Moreover, Sears, perhaps a little disingenuously, charged that the Puget Sound area needed to get out of its minor league mentality about ticket prices. The higher prices were probably predictable. Western Management Consultants, in its study of Seattle as a sports market, expected tickets to be higher because of a lack of nearby competition. Charlie Finley said that Dewey Soriano had told him Seattleites were hungry for baseball and would pay anything to see it. Team management also argued that the ticket scale was not so different from the Sonics and Husky football or a stage show (Bill Cosby tickets cost $4.50 to $6.50), and that with such a small capacity at Sicks', the prices had to be scaled to fit the park, as Jimmy Dudley delicately phrased it. Harold Parrott and Soriano argued over a youth promotion. Parrott wanted to charge $2 for each young person and give the youngster a "co-Pilots" cap. The idea, of course, was that the whole family would attend the game with the youngster, and the team would make a nice profit. Soriano held out for a $5 charge, saying that kids were making good money. Parrott upped his bid to $3. Soriano kept it at $5, arguing that it was easier for a dad to tender a $5 bill than dig out three $1 bills. Clearly, the Sorianos, who set the prices and held a veto on concessions, were aiming at maximizing margins and hoping that volume would hold up. But by bringing together the highest prices in the league and expensive concessions with a fan base that included thousands of blue-collar workers who had demonstrated ambivalence about baseball in the stadium vote, Pilots ownership was taking a real chance.[30]

Only half of the hoped-for season tickets were sold. By February 1969, as sales were clearly lagging, Soriano alerted department heads that expenses were exceeding revenue and cautioned everyone to limit long-distance calls and conserve supplies. Anxieties over ticket sales emerged in a lengthy memo from Milkes to his staff before the general manager left for Arizona and spring training. He urged them to work long days, seven days a week, through opening day. He ordered Parrott to gather leads and meet with business leaders, as well as handle public relations. He pushed Vanni to cajole those who had turned down season tickets to reconsider. Milkes told ticket manager Harry McCarthy to keep the office open every day, admonishing him, "I will be most anxious to see our progress." Milkes topped off the exhortations by asserting, "Glib tongues *must* be used during March to finalize sales." Attendance of more than 1 million was expected, but just over 670,000 came out to Sicks'. Ticket revenue generated $2.05 million, about a million dollars short of expectations. Looking at it another way, American League rules required the home team to share 20 percent of after-tax game receipts with the visiting team. The visitors took a total of $415,088 from their trips to Seattle. When the Pilots went on the road, they received $467,964 from the opposing teams. As attendance lagged, it became clear that the Pilots had made the poorer choice between high margins and high volume.[31]

Another key to success, or survival, is player personnel decisions. Lenny Anderson's low estimate of Milkes's judgment notwithstanding, the Pilots made a good showing in this area, although the general manager's itchiness to pull off trades meant that the bottom part of the roster would never achieve name recognition with fans and the team was perpetually unsettled. Even before the expansion draft, the scouts had identified crucial players to purchase from other organizations. The key early signing, in June 1968, was Mike Hegan, who was languishing in the Yankees organization. The first baseman/outfielder had hit only .136 with the Yankees in 1967 and less than .300 with Triple-A Syracuse in the first part of 1968. After they purchased Hegan's contract for $20,000, the Pilots left him with the Yankees farm club, where he ended the season with a .304 average. He was one of the club's best investments. A few days later, the Pilots bought another Yankee who would arguably become their most famous player, Jim Bouton. Bouton had suffered arm trouble and was working his way back to the majors by perfecting a knuckleball. The Pilots picked him off for $12,000—$8,000 under the waiver price—and assigned him to the Seattle Angels for the rest of the 1968 season. There were other "name" pickups who did not play such a central role. Jose Vidal, purchased from Cleveland for $30,000, was traded to the Yankees soon after the 1969 season began. Pitchers Marv Staehle and Bill Stafford did not make the team. But John Kennedy, whom the Pilots picked up from the Yankees after the expansion draft, became a regular infielder.

Negotiating with other teams helped build the roster, but the event that would define the team was the expansion draft. Milkes, Soriano, farm director Art Parrack, scouting department head Ray Swallow, and Milkes's assistants Bobby Mattick, Bill Skiff, and scout Bob Clemens labored for months preparing for October 15, 1968, draft day in Boston. The ten established American League clubs would each protect fifteen players on their forty-man rosters. Then the two expansion teams, Kansas City and Seattle, would take turns selecting a player from those that were left unprotected. When a team lost a player, it froze three of its remaining unprotected players. No established team could lose more than one man per round. By the end of the sixth round, both Kansas City and the Pilots had drafted thirty players (major and minor leaguers), five each in each round. A special provision for the first round was that the team that selected second got two consecutive choices. The team that won the coin flip could decide if it wanted first choice or the next two selections. The Pilots won the toss and chose second and third. The expansion teams paid the established clubs $175,000 for each player. (The National League charged $200,000 per player in its expansion draft.) The draft served as an admissions fee for the expansion clubs, as the Royals and Pilots each paid $5.25 million, and each American League club received $1.05 million for the six players it lost.[32]

There was a good deal of debate among the Pilots' brain trust about draft day strategy. Initially, Milkes said that he was intent on finding young prospects and building for the future. Two weeks later, he told the *Post-Intelligencer* that he was going to select established players in order to create an immediate contender. Dewey Soriano was apparently behind the strategy change. Accusations of ticket price gouging were generating bad publicity. Season tickets, which had been on sale for two or three months by the mid-October draft, were going slowly. The box office needed a boost. Name players, even those who may have seen better days, would help. A team official, probably Milkes or Soriano, told the *New York Times*, "We felt we needed a product people could understand right now." So the Pilots went with veterans. Milkes commented that Seattleites had seen minor league baseball; he wanted "to give them the real thing."[33]

After Kansas City selected pitcher Roger Nelson with the first choice, the Pilots took Don Mincher from the Angels. Hard-throwing Sam McDowell of Cleveland had beaned Mincher in early 1968, leaving him with blurred vision and headaches. The Angels were not sure the slugging first baseman would fully recover and left him unprotected. Next, Seattle selected outfielder/infielder Tommy Harper of Cleveland. Bobby Mattick had originally signed the fleet Harper and now thought the twenty-eight-year-old could be an effective second baseman. When Mattick was in town, the scout helped Harper polish his skills. Harper was not a consistent hitter—he had batted .217 for Cleveland the previous season, and his best average, .278, came with Cincinnati in 1966. But he was fast and a skilled base runner. The Pilots would use him well. Joe Schultz gave him the green light to steal, telling him, "Go make yourself some money." Schultz could have been speaking to Dewey Soriano. Harper's stolen base totals rivaled Ty Cobb's for awhile. The *Pilots Scorebook* proclaimed him the most exciting player in Seattle since "Jungle Jim" Rivera, and his exploits drew fans who otherwise had written the team off as an expansion loser.[34]

Good-field-no-hit Ray Oyler, shortstop from Detroit, was next. He had batted .135 with the American League champion Tigers in 1967 and not gotten a hit after July. Bob Hardwick's Ray Oyler fan club reaped good publicity for the Pilots and Oyler, who was the only Pilot to continue to live in Seattle after the team moved. He would suffer a fatal heart attack in 1981, passing away at age forty-two. Sturdy catcher Jerry McNertney of the White Sox and pitcher Louis Robert "Buzz" Stephen of Minnesota, whose very brief major league playing career had already come and gone, completed the Pilots' first-round choices.[35]

Of the twenty-five other players the Pilots came away with, only nine spent any significant time with Seattle. Pitcher Diego Segui, whose career lasted long enough for him to become a Seattle Mariner, worked effectively from the bull pen and occasionally as a starter. Drafted from the A's, Segui had switched from being a southpaw to pitching right-handed as a boy in Cuba. He looked forward to playing in Seattle, where he could fish, but remembered his minor league night games in Sicks' as pretty chilly. Tommy Davis had been a star with the Los Angeles Dodgers, winning back-to-back batting titles and two-thirds of the triple crown in 1962 (batting average and RBIs). His career almost ended in 1965 with a broken ankle. Davis, a gifted hitter, was still slowed by the injury when the Pilots selected him from the Chicago White Sox, where his .268 average led the team. He played left field, started slow, and then hit with authority as the season went on. He did not contribute much to the Pilots cause off the field. Depending on whom one asked, he was competitive, prickly, moody, or disdainful. In short, he was a tough interview and not a likely service club speaker. Steve Barber was a name pitcher, and Soriano expected him to draw fans, but he came with a sore arm that never really healed. So it was Marty Pattin who got the opening-day start and became a rotation mainstay. Another gimpy player, Rich Rollins came to the Pilots with a bad knee that got worse as the season went on, but the ex-Twin showed that he could still hit, the few times he was reasonably healthy. The Pilots drafted Steve Hovley from the Angels, Wayne Comer from Detroit, and Jim Gosger from Oakland. The three young outfielders showed talent and gave fans hope for the future. Mike Marshall would one day win a Cy Young Award, but with Seattle, he only occasionally showed that kind of talent and spent much of his time commiserating with Bouton about the vagaries of the world of baseball.[36]

One player who did not stick could have been one of Seattle's favorites. Chico Salmon was a stalwart on the Pilots' winter tour and worked diligently with the front office. Newspapers explained to Northwesterners that his name was pronounced "suh MONE." A journeyman utility player for Cleveland, he was eager for a starting job as a shortstop or second baseman. Unlike several players who were disappointed to come to an expansion franchise, Salmon was ecstatic to be in Seattle. Speaking of his youth, he told stories of his fear of evil spirits but said that now he was "afraid of only one thing, that Seattle might trade me. I hope they do not do that. I have made up my mind for Seattle." He was with the wrong general manager. Just before the season started, Milkes informed the heartbroken infielder that he had been traded to Baltimore for pitcher Gene Brabender and a couple of minor leaguers. Despite losing what would have been a drawing card, the trade was a good one for the Pilots. Once he got into shape, Brabender became the ace of the staff.[37]

A player of note was left undrafted—Tony Conigliaro. Until a horrific beaning, Conigliaro had been a leading hitter for the Boston Red Sox. There was serious question about whether he would play again, but he started off 1969 hitting over .300 for the Red Sox and won the Comeback Player of the Year Award. Dewey Soriano kicked himself for skipping over someone who had been headed to the Hall of Fame at one time. Unfortunately for Conigliaro, the 1969 and 1970 seasons were a last flash of brilliance before the end. His appearance on the unprotected list illustrates the nature of the draft. Each selection was a gamble. Mincher, Davis, Rollins, and Barber were top caliber players . . . if they were healthy. Oyler was the best defensive shortstop in the league but could not hit. Harper had been through two down years. Comer, Marshall, and Gosger were young, promising, but substantially untried. No matter how much the American League owners may have congratulated themselves on giving their new partners a fighting chance, the rosters of the two teams were brimming with question marks. The Royals risked taking unproven players; the Pilots decided to take a chance on familiar names, in hopes that some would show a little of the old pizzazz and not break down before the end of the season.

Initial reactions to the team were positive. Seattle observers correctly predicted that the team would have some punch but could be thin in pitching. Barber, Gary Bell, and Pattin were the mainstays of the pitching staff, and that did not seem promising. With Barber hurting and Bell gone in a trade by June (and out of baseball by the end of the season), it was even worse than it first appeared. The *New York Times* and others rated Kansas City's draft better than Seattle's, despite the Royals' emphasis on young, untried talent. The expansion draft contributed many starters to the Pilots' first-year roster, but Milkes would tinker the whole season, molding a team he was more satisfied with. Altogether, fifty-three players circulated through the Pilots' twenty-five-man roster over that first season. Only the 1915 Philadelphia A's and the 1967 New York Mets had ever had that kind of turnover. Milkes told the press that other general managers began contacting him as soon as the draft was over. He made the point that he would seek only quality players in any transaction, but, in retrospect, trader Milkes must have felt a little shudder of anticipation every time his phone rang.[38]

The minor league draft and the amateur draft were two other ways of stocking the club. The new franchises had last pick, so they were out of the running for the top prospects. In midsummer 1969, the Pilots introduced their first-round amateur draft choice, a shortstop named James G. Thomas. After a day or two of interviews, the strapping young man revealed that he preferred being called by his middle name, Gorman. As an outfielder, Gorman Thomas would one day lead the American League in home runs with the Milwaukee Brewers.[39]

Getting the players under contract and ensuring they got to spring training on time was the next step. Milkes fretted over players in winter ball. He did not put pressure on the Latino players such as Segui, Vidal, and Gus Gil, who were essentially playing at home, but he did summon Mike Marshall and Jack Aker out of winter ball to get them ready for the season. Milkes also made it clear that no player should take his golf clubs to Arizona. He cautioned Hovley, who was finishing some college credits, that if he were interested in a major league job, he would make spring training before March 22. Hovley, who played baseball because he was good at it, not because he liked it, said that he did not believe he was ready for the majors anyway and shrugged off Milkes's threat. Hovley's independent attitude was a new aspect of the world of organized baseball and was beginning to be reflected in contract negotiations.[40]

The reserve clause, which bound each player to his team in perpetuity, was still in effect in 1969. There were true believers in its efficacy. Schultz told the team, "Boys, the reserve clause is the one thing you can't fool with. It's the foundation of the game. If you get rid of it, we're all out of business. And I'm serious." Most players had taken the same outlook as Schultz for years. The reserve clause restrained players from offering their services on a free market, but it was protected by baseball's longstanding exemption from antitrust laws. That the Pilots manager felt he had to make the statement, and that Bouton thought it was worth recording in *Ball Four*, indicate that the reserve clause was under some pressure in 1969 as the Major League Baseball Players Association (MLBPA) was strengthening.[41]

By 1966, all but one major league player was affiliated with the MLBPA, and some members sought to make it a more active organization. After some jockeying, the players elected Marvin Miller as their head and gave him a mandate to work on pensions, the minimum wage, and the grievance procedure and study the reserve clause. Miller was a union man who had served as a labor economist for the United Steel Workers. By 1968, the players had a new basic agreement that included a minimum salary of $10,000, a grievance procedure (an appeal to the commissioner), and an agreement to study the reserve clause. It was not much, but it ushered in collective bargaining. The power of the MLBPA became more evident before 1969 spring training, when Miller asked his members to delay signing their yearly contracts until owners had agreed to pension plan reform. The owners acceded by adding $45 million to the pension fund and agreed to begin four-year, rather than five-year, vesting.[42]

Milkes seemed to understand the emerging contractual relationship between player and team. He promised no salary cuts and acknowledged that some signings might be useful public relations events. He did note that the younger players had an inflated view of their value because they had cost $175,000 in the expansion draft. Several Pilots players heeded Miller's demand to hold out, but the club had signed everyone well before the start of the season. Newspaper reports suggested that Tommy Davis got $60,000–70,000, Mincher $40,000, and Barber and Rollins something in the $25,000 range.[43]

By 1969, racial consciousness had become a part of sports, but there is little evidence that the Pilots either shunned or sought African American or Latino players. Milkes had stated as he assembled his coaching staff that he was not contemplating a Negro for any of the positions but would be open to the possibility in the future. The Pilots were slightly less integrated than the average team in 1969. Tommy Davis, Tommy Harper, and Dick Simpson, who came to the Pilots in a trade, were the only African Americans on the team, putting Seattle at the major league average of 16 percent blacks. The two Tommys, especially Harper, were featured figures on the team. Bouton mentioned that the three African Americans generally went their own way, not regularly joining their other teammates after games, but *Ball Four* does not reveal any locker room friction or even hints of aloofness on the part of either white or black players. Six different Spanish-speaking players were a part of the Seattle roster at one time or another, but only two, Segui and Gil, spent significant time with the team. That would put the Pilots just under the 10 percent Latino average on major league rosters in the early 1970s. In short, the Pilots were substantially Caucasian, and both the team and the fans seemed to embrace players for their athletic prowess, making no ostensible issue of their race or ethnicity.[44]

As the season drew near, the mounting euphoria of Seattle sportswriters revolved mainly around their city's new status. Georg Meyers proclaimed, "Seattle has joined the exclusive lodge." A *Post-Intelligencer* editorial hailed opening day in Seattle as the emergence of the city as major league. Royal Brougham was relieved that now there would not be as much turnover in players as in the minor league days. (Milkes's itchy trading finger would dim that happy thought.) As for the team, manager Joe Schultz had ventured his incautious prediction of third place in the six-team Western Division. Hy Zimmerman was as hard-eyed as any Seattle sportswriter, but even he thought the Pilots veterans would outshine the Kansas City youngsters as well as the feeble Chicago White Sox, furthered weakened by the loss of Davis and McNertney to the Pilots.[45]

The Angels general manager, Fred Haney, put further pressure on the Pilots by pointing out that the Seattle club had a larger draft pool than his expansion club. The *Post-Intelligencer* dutifully reviewed the other teams in the division and came up with the same general assessment as its rival paper. The A's had strong pitching with Jim Hunter, John Odom, and Lew Krausse. The infield was solid, and the outfield and bull pen were filled with talented youngsters like Reggie Jackson, Rick Monday, and Vida Blue. The Twins depended on pitchers Jim Kaat and Dean Chance, combined with adept hitting from Rod Carew, the aging Harmon Killebrew, Tony Oliva, and Bob Allison. The Angels' strength was their outfield, and it was none too strong with Rick Reichardt, Roger Repoz, and Vic Davalillo. Tommy John and Joel Horlen gave the White Sox some pitching hope, but they were not distinguished as a team. Kansas City pinned its hopes on first expansion draft choice pitcher Roger Nelson along with Wally Bunker. Ed Kirkpatrick and Lou Piniella could provide some sock in the outfield. Fourth was a real possibility, the *Post-Intelligencer* thought, even if third place was a reach.[46]

The Pilots had assembled an adequate club both on the field and in the front office. But the team would finish last in the division and make some errors in management. Ticket prices were too high for blue-collar Seattleites, relations with the Seattle business community were oddly lukewarm, and Marvin Milkes churned the roster so much that fans had trouble identifying "their" Pilots. Those poor decisions, which alienated rather than cultivated the fan base, could have been overcome, but other circumstances pressed down on the club as well. Unending difficulties with the stadium and less than helpful city officials made life excruciating for Soriano. All of this, coupled with the tight financial position, sent the 1969 season careening toward disaster.

William Daley, from Cleveland, was the Pilots owner with the deepest pockets. He refused to underwrite team operations for 1970, and the team left for Milwaukee. (Cleveland Public Library)

Dewey Soriano (left), Pilots owner, made most of the business decisions. Marvin Milkes (right) was the general manager in charge of player decisions and on-field operations. (Collection of David Eskenazi)

Max Soriano (left), part-owner of the Pilots, and Mayor Dorm Braman unveil the Pilots' new logo in fall 1968 when relations were still relatively cordial between Pacific Northwest Sports, Inc., and the city. (By permission of Hearst Communications, Inc./Hearst Newspapers, LLC/Seattlepi.com)

There were no bobble-head night promotions, but Pilots bobblehead dolls were available in 1969. They were a very good buy: a pair of these sold for $500 in 2011. (Collection of Merwood "Johnny" Johnson; author's photograph)

Youngsters could add to their savings with this plastic Pilots coin bank. (Collection of Tim Jenkins; author's photograph)

A 45 RPM record of Rod Belcher's "Go, Go, You Pilots" sung by an artist identified as Doris Doubleday was available to fans. (Collection of David Eskenazi)

Fans! DON'T MISS THESE GREAT AUGUST EVENTS

HELMET NIGHT
MONDAY, AUG. 18

FREE Batting Helmet
for every youngster (16 & under) attending
plus the
PILOTS vs BALTIMORE'S
League Leading Orioles

KIDS vs FATHER'S GAME
SUNDAY, AUG. 17

See the Pilots play their
children before the
SEATTLE-BALTIMORE GAME

'TOMMY HARPER NIGHT'

Saluting Seattle's
Most Exciting Player
also
SEATTLE vs CLEVELAND
Friday, August 22

SPECIAL: 'RADIO APPRECIATION NIGHT' Saturday, Aug. 23

A poster enticed fans to the ballpark in August with an array of promotions. (Collection of David Eskenazi)

An unused ticket to the home opener against the Chicago White Sox on April 11, 1969. (Collection of David Eskenazi)

Opening day at Sicks' Stadium. Workers labored until shortly before game time to finish as much of the stadium renovations as they could. The Pilots argued that the stadium never met American League standards. (Collection of David Eskenazi)

Bridget Hanley, who starred in the TV series *Here Come the Brides*, gives manager Joe Schultz a smack on the cheek for good luck at the opening day ceremonies. (Robert H. Miller Collection, MOHAI, 2002.46.32 fr 35A)

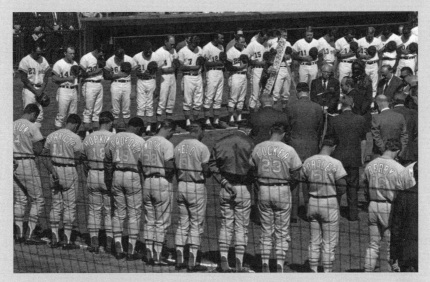

The Chicago White Sox (foreground) and the Pilots, along the third base line, take their places for the pregame invocation during the home opener. (Cary Tolman Collection, MOHAI, 2002.68.7)

Play gets under way for the sunny first game of the Pilots' only season in Seattle. (Cary Tolman Collection, MOHAI, 2002.68.7 fr 17/17A)

The Pilots' front office applied stickers with ticket prices to this picture of Sicks' Stadium as they developed their admission fee structure for the never-to-be-played 1970 season. The ticket prices were notably lower than they were for the 1969 season, when the Pilots opted for higher prices and higher margins and drew heavy criticism. (Collection of David Eskenazi; underlying photo copyright *The News Tribune* [Tacoma, WA] 1969, reprinted by permission)

Outfielder Jose Vidal (25) and infielder John Kennedy (11) join other players to listen to coach Ron Plaza (kneeling) at spring training in Tempe, Arizona. Coach Frankie Crosetti faces the camera at far left in the background. Manager Joe Schultz and Triple-A Vancouver manager Bob Lemon, also facing the camera, are to the left of Plaza, and pitching coach Sal Maglie (arms folded) is in the foreground at right. (*Seattle Post-Intelligencer* Collection, MOHAI, 1986.5.52269.1)

The kids versus fathers game on August 17, 1969. John Kennedy and son (11) are in the background. Jim Bouton's son (56) is in the foreground, in front of Tommy Harper. On the right, Diego Segui leans over his son, and future Mariner, David Segui. (Collection of David Eskenazi)

Pitcher Diego Segui (left) and manager Joe Schultz confer during spring training, 1969. Segui would become one of the Pilots' steadiest pitchers. Everybody said that field manager Joe Schultz was a baseball man, but he was probably too easygoing for Marvin Milkes and was fired at the end of the Pilots' only season. (*Seattle Post-Intelligencer* Collection, MOHAI, 1986.5.52269.2)

Tommy Harper was one of the most popular Pilots. The infielder stole seventy-three bases and was honored as Seattle Sports Man of the Year by the *Seattle Post-Intelligencer*. (*Seattle Post-Intelligencer* Collection, MOHAI, 1986.5/56053)

Don Mincher, the Pilots' first choice in the expansion draft, led the team in home runs. Here he slides in safe against the California Angels. (*Seattle Times* photo by Richard S. Heyza)

Chapter 7

NOT ENOUGH SEATS, NOT ENOUGH FANS

S PRING training is usually a harbinger of how the team will shape up on the field. In the case of the Pilots, it was also a foreshadowing of the future of the front office. In March 1968, the club went shopping for a spring training home. Indio, in California's Coachella Valley, and Tempe, Arizona, near Phoenix, bid for the Pilots. E. B. Smith, a Tempe land developer and baseball fan, formed a company called Baseball Facilities, Inc. (BFI). The city of Tempe agreed to sell Smith's company 115 acres of land for a dollar a year for ninety-nine years if he could attract a baseball team for spring training. Smith struck a deal with Pacific Northwest Sports, Inc., to build a baseball and resort complex. BFI and PNSI formed Pilot Properties, with 60 percent owned by PNSI and 40 percent by BFI. By the time exhibition games began in 1969, the six thousand-seat stadium had been completed. The main field was 360 feet down the lines and 425 feet to center, bordered by a blue wall. There were three practice diamonds, clubhouses that rivaled the Astrodome's, and separate shower rooms for the major and minor leaguers. *Los Angeles Times* sports columnist John Hall wrote, "It is splendor in the wilds—beauty by the buttes—easily the best organized, best equipped and most impressive training camp in the Cactus League, if not all baseball."[1]

But there was conflict. Dewey Soriano maintained that his organization had fulfilled its commitment by finishing the baseball facilities and announced that the fate of the rest of the complex—a motel, a dorm, and some road paving—was in the hands of the lawyers. Smith charged breach of contract and threatened to block spring training. He relented on impeding the ball playing, but filed a $6 million suit against PNSI. The contention over the complex lingered for the rest of the season and was resolved only as the Pilots expired in 1970. Max Soriano remembered, "Mr. E. B. Smith was very difficult, very difficult to deal with." Though it did not affect baseball in Seattle, it was another black eye, along with the high ticket prices, for the Sorianos. Eyebrows were being raised over the quality of ownership.[2]

In the best of all possible worlds, the batteries—pitchers and catchers—should have arrived in Tempe on February 20, 1969, and the rest of the squad on February 24, although major league baseball would not consider players to be holdouts until March 1. It was not the best of all possible worlds for the Pilots, because the Major League Baseball Players Association, led by Marvin Miller, was staging a brief holdout. Marvin Milkes, who sometimes had problems contacting other front offices because his name was similar to the name of the MLBPA head, pressed his players to report because the team needed the extra time to evaluate the new personnel. A few veterans showed up, but most obeyed the union. Jim Bouton, who had signed a contract before Miller put out the word to hold off, reluctantly decided to wait. It was only a brief delay. Miller gave the go-ahead to sign on February 25, and most of the new Pilots were in uniform a day later. Only Rich Rollins was absent on March 1.[3]

Milkes, Schultz, and his coaches were all business. Ron Plaza ran daily calisthenics. The players worked on fundamentals and played a few intrasquad games. Bouton's knuckleball was the talk of the camp. Steve Barber's arm felt good, but Chico Salmon's knee was stiff, and broadcaster Bill Schonely jammed his finger playing catch. By edict, after training there was to be no golfing and no swimming. The unmarried players, housed in a nearby motel, watched TV or lounged around the pool watching the girls (which might have struck a general manager as riskier than swimming). The married players found rental accommodations for their families around town.[4]

A local booster group, the Diablos, sold tickets and helped round up advertising for the game programs. Despite their efforts, a good number of seats went begging each game—an omen for the regular season. As of mid-January, only ten thousand of the expected twenty thousand tickets had been sold for games in Tempe. KVI broadcast selected games from Arizona but aired only eleven altogether, thereby limiting preseason exposure for the team and fan anticipation in Seattle. Yet, after the bumpy start, spring training went along smoothly. Tempe was rainy and windy early on, but by the end of March, the sun was beaming and the most optimistic time of the baseball season was at hand. The regular season records were spotless. The players who had made the roster had only promise ahead of them—the promise of a rejuvenated career, a step up to the majors, or a strengthened knee or arm. Though Schultz mentioned third place and Milkes demanded it, the players were not quite so euphoric or driven; still, they were heartened by what they had seen from their teammates and felt within their own bodies. They ventured that fourth place in the Western Division, out of six teams, was a realistic goal.[5]

Meanwhile, back in Seattle, opening day of the regular season was becoming more a threat than a hope. A long, drawn-out fight over the Sicks' Stadium lease and then over the nature of the refurbishment was pushing renovations right into the season. Sicks' was only a stopgap until the multipurpose stadium could be built, so it should not have been a test of what it would take to attract a new franchise. Mayor Dorm Braman and many on the city council clearly believed that the city was merely furnishing a facility, not luring a franchise. Any special subsidy for the Pilots should be left up to the county, which was building the permanent stadium. The city had gone far enough in its negotiations in 1967 with Charlie Finley to offer him a five-year lease on Sicks' Stadium at $165,000 a year and $1.61 million of city-financed renovations for the ballpark. Both sides drew on the Finley negotiation as the framework as they made their cases for a lease agreement for the Pilots.[6]

Negotiations between Braman and Dewey Soriano began in April 1968, a year before opening day. Soriano proposed a remodeling cost of $1.175 million to bring Sicks' up to American League standards, including seating for thirty thousand. The Pilots offered to pay rent of $165,000 a year for four years, suggesting that salvage plus the admissions tax should be sufficient for the city to break even on stadium improvements. Soriano also asked for all parking and concessions revenue. Braman rejected the offer and pressed for more rent. The two sides held meetings through the summer without coming to an agreement. Soriano offered to pay for a fifth year on the lease—an additional $165,000—even though the Pilots anticipated moving into the new stadium after four years. That seemed to help, but now the two could not agree on whether the admissions tax, estimated at $450,000 over five years, would be added to the $1.175 million to increase the renovation budgets or would go into city coffers. In August, Braman handed the issue over to the city council, telling Soriano, in essence, to leave him alone and talk with council president Floyd Miller. Soriano complained bitterly that local ownership should get at least as good a deal as Charles Finley and the A's, but the city offered to appropriate a half million less and continued to press PNSI for more concessions. The final lease agreement was for a five-year lease at $165,000 a year, yielding $825,000. The city promised to spend $1.175 million to bring the stadium to American League specifications (which were never specified) and expand the seating to twenty-eight thousand. PNSI would get parking and concessions income, pay the utilities, and keep the stadium in good repair. In addition, it had to put up a surety bond of $1 million against its rental commitment.[7]

All this did not get through the city council easily. Councilman Tim Hill asked for a delay on the vote, complaining that the city would not get parking or concession money. Much of the council was absent, and Hill's motion passed 3–2. Soriano fumed. If the lease was not finalized soon so that renovations could begin, he explained, the stadium would not be ready for play. The American League had made it clear that without an interim stadium, there would be no franchise. Hill pressed it further. He offered a motion to recoup the lost interest it would have received on the $1.175 million used to renovate the park. Floyd Miller carefully explained to Hill and Phyllis Lamphere, the other recalcitrant, that the terms of the contract were the city's and that, because the city would retain the admissions tax on tickets, it should come out $300,000 or $400,000 ahead. In mid-September, the lease contract finally passed 6–2, with Hill and Lamphere dissenting. Hill later said he thought the renovation money would be better used at the Broadview Library near Ballard, in northwest Seattle.[8]

Fallout over the final days of negotiations fell along the classic lines of debate over public expenditures on stadiums. The *Argus* praised Hill and Lamphere for standing up to the sportswriters on behalf of the taxpayers. If the Pilots want the stadium done on time, wrote the editor, the franchise should contribute some of its own money. He went on to castigate other council members as gutless. The *Argus* could have predicted the reactions of the *Seattle Times* and *Seattle Post-Intelligencer* sportswriters. The *Post-Intelligencer* found it incredible that the council could put the franchise in jeopardy. Hy Zimmerman thought that the businessmen and political leaders of Seattle were slowly maturing but still had not learned how to act like they were in a big-league city. Emmett Watson marveled at this performance and wondered whether Seattle was ready for the major leagues. For those who believed a city needs major sports in order to be major league, the taunts were on target. Braman never attended a Pilots game. Councilman Ted Best remembered, "On opening day I sat and explained to Tim Hill how baseball was played." Obviously, a person's priorities affect his or her opinions about how a community might attain status—and for the Choose an Effective City Council contingent, baseball was a low priority.[9]

Sicks' Stadium was a first-rate minor league ballpark well into the 1960s. Emil Sick had built it in 1938 for his Seattle Rainiers. By 1965, Alan Ferguson, president of Sicks' Rainier Brewery, was ready to sell. It was too costly to maintain for a minor league franchise, so, before turning the property into a shopping center, Ferguson contacted the city to see if it was interested in the facility. He offered the stadium for what he said the land alone would bring, $1.15 million. The city agreed and promised to pay off the amount in five years. An appraisal indicated that the city got a bargain, and there was some hope that the U.S. Department of Housing and Urban Development might provide a grant for 50 percent of the purchase price. The real impetus for the deal was that the planned, but never built, R. H. Thomson Expressway would run right through a corner of the stadium. If the city owned the land, it could avoid costly condemnation purchases of the commercial buildings that would be there if Ferguson built his shopping center. In the meantime, the minor league club or a major league team could use the facility. Braman told the city council that the stadium could be used to entice a major league baseball team to the city, but a new franchise would have to make "costly and temporary improvements."[10]

Milkes, on behalf of the minor league Seattle Angels, agreed to a $20,000-a-year lease for 1966—just $2,500 more than the team had paid to Sicks' the previous year. The mayor noted that the rent would make up for tax revenue lost by converting Sicks' to municipal property. In January 1966, after the sale to the city, Braman sent Hy Zimmerman a slightly misleading note attached to a telegram from the Seattle Angels congratulating the city for buying the stadium and keeping the Angels in Seattle. The note began, "Inasmuch that you do not appear to ever believe anything we do is beneficial to sports in the city of Seattle . . . " and neglected to mention the city's interest in the right-of-way for the expressway. And

Milkes was pleased. Citing the courage of the mayor and city council, he lauded the Seattle politicians for the purchase, "which enabled us to have the finest minor league plant to play in."[11]

So the city had a stadium. And by February 1968, it had secured a major league baseball franchise. But it had a capacity problem. The stadium was not major league, with 11,000 to 16,000 seats, depending on who did the estimating. The American League expected a capacity of 30,000. Ferguson and Paul Anson, the stadium administrator, had looked into expanding Sicks' over the past half decade. Their estimates ranged from about $350,000 to upgrade to 24,000 seats, using cheap bleachers, to as much as $7 million to create a capacity of 34,000 by adding a second concrete deck. In May 1968, the Narramore consulting firm had estimated it would cost a minimum of $778,000 to expand to 28,500 seats and install major league lighting. That turned out to be well off the mark, but this was the figure Braman had used as he began negotiations with Dewey Soriano that spring. There would be no city appropriations for improvements until the city and PNSI reached accord, and without an appropriation, there could be no architectural work. Construction should have begun in September 1968, but agreement was not reached until the middle of that month, so the architectural and consulting firm Narramore and Bain was not on the job until October 23.[12]

With time running out, not only the negotiations, but now the remodeling process grew tense. The budget was $1.175 million, and it was firm. After they reached a lease agreement, PNSI (usually represented by Dewey Soriano, Milkes, or Lew Matlin, director of stadium operations) and the city (represented by Don Johnston, director of Seattle Center, which oversaw the stadium) met and corresponded frequently. Johnston prophesied accurately as he penned a cordial note to Soriano in October 1968. "We know the next few months are going to be difficult ones. There will surely be unexpected problems and frustrations. However, we are as determined as you to make the April 1 deadline so that we can join the rest of Seattle in hearing that wonderful cry—'play ball'—with a major league ring."[13]

Things started out well. PNSI asked if Pilot Construction (Charles Soriano, vice president and general manager) could construct a home clubhouse and a stadium club in Sicks'. Johnston approved as long as it met code. Out of the $1.175 million refurbishment budget, the architects budgeted $270,000 for bleachers, $150,000 for restrooms, $112,000 for improved field lighting, $94,000 for press box work, including an elevator, and $75,000 for concession stands. As soon as bids came in, both sides knew that the project was in deep trouble. There were three bids, ranging from $1.064 million to $1.2 million—but none included seating. As he totaled the entire project, Don Johnston figured that the bids were about 65 percent above budget.[14]

The parties sat down at a meeting on December 19 to see what could be done. Johnston acknowledged the excruciating fact that they were up against an almost unreachable deadline, yet they still might have to redesign the project and rebid before any work started. In a meeting the day before, city council members reiterated that the city would allocate nothing more on the project, so Johnston pleaded with PNSI to find some way to work within the constraints. Milkes could only respond, "We do have quite a problem with the American League." The league front office had been asking why construction had not begun and reiterating that certain undelineated major league standards for the ballpark must be met. Johnston, invoking the time constraints, urged some alternatives. Maybe they could start with a target of 16,000 seats; then the city could rework the specifications, rebid, and install more seats as the season went along. Milkes rolled his eyes. "I can just see their [the American League owners'] reaction." Johnston tried again. What about an unpainted perimeter fence? Lesser quality of pipe in the ground? Eliminate turnstiles? Milkes retorted that the American League demanded a turnstile count so that it could compare this to the club's ticket count. On it went through the meeting. Considering Milkes's intense personality, the tension generated by the dire situation, and the civil, but adversarial exchanges, it ended on a good note. Milkes apologized: "I know we may not have been too helpful to you today. . . . I think those items are very minute which we cut. . . . We gave it a try." Johnston was equally gracious and apologetic. "It's not a pleasant situation," he observed diplomatically, "but it is better to have sight of the gravity of the problem." The writer covering the Pilots in the *Sporting News*, probably Hy Zimmerman, was not so gracious: "It is felt inconceivable that a governmental entity the size of Seattle cannot readily dig up the additional funds for a project of such import to the city."[15]

City councilman Ted Best spoke for both sides in early January 1969, declaring, "At the moment we are in real trouble." The city was inflexible—there were no more funds for the project. PNSI would not budge about meeting American League standards. Even in the toughest negotiations, however, there is wiggle room, if the sides choose to find it. The money to renovate Sicks' Stadium came out of the city's Cumulative Reserve Fund, a municipal savings account of sorts that could be used for capital improvements. The fund was composed of savings from unspent appropriations and held "ample amounts." The city was suffering serious budgetary pain, and officials might have argued that other projects had priority, but the city conceivably could have found more dollars for renovation. Seattle was adamantly unwilling to spend anything to win, or keep, a baseball team. Mayor Braman later emphasized that he was determined to lay out no more than the city could recover from the lease, salvage, and admissions tax.[16]

Staying in the good graces of the American League was PNSI's negotiating lever. Across the continent, the National League was contemplating withdrawing its expansion franchise from Montreal because of an inadequate stadium. Despite the portentous events in Montreal, the threat of the American League withdrawing the franchise from Seattle was exaggerated. The league had not actually specified what "adequate stadium" meant, so the Sorianos could only speculate (or bluff). The local owners' assumptions were not unreasonable—the league grew progressively dissatisfied with the physical state of the stadium as the season went on. But PNSI could not speak with authority about what would or would not push their fellow owners to rescind the franchise. Councilman Best, who firmly supported baseball in Seattle, asked for a list of standards. Soriano bandied about several numbers, Best said, yet never gave him a firm answer. The councilman hypothesized that the league would settle for twenty-five thousand seats, permanent restrooms in the bleachers, adequate lighting, and an expanded press box, all of which were included in the final negotiated agreement.[17]

The city won the negotiation. Braman could empathize with the Pilots' position. "The city was offering an interim facility brought up to certain standards," he said, "which they wanted at one level and we were willing to supply at another." But he was firm. Had the ball club not accepted a lower seat total, Braman said the deal would have been "down the drain." In a letter of understanding that Don Johnston sent to Dewey Soriano on January 10, 1969, the seating had decreased from twenty-eight thousand to twenty-five thousand, less costly lighting would be installed, restrooms would now be the smallest that would pass code, interior walls that needed no soundproofing would be plywood, and there would be no built-in utilities for concession stands. Soriano, despairing of having the stadium ready for opening day, responded by saying that he thought he could persuade the American League to accept the revisions and signed the agreement. The cranes rumbled into Rainier Valley to begin work with thirteen weeks to go before the first pitch. As it turned out, the deal was not quite so one-sided in favor of the city. Seattle spent almost $1.5 million on the upgrade and contributed additional resources in city-worker time to the project. But the stadium was well short of Soriano's expectation when he had begun dickering with the city.[18]

Once construction began, it went anything but smoothly, impeded by imagined and real problems. Johnston warned that general contractors would be skittish about working near the inner-city Central Area and hoped the Pilots would furnish a night watchman. In late January, snow and record-setting frigid temperatures set in for a week and a half. The bleacher installation caused numerous headaches. First, G & D Dozing brought in fill dirt that was the wrong consistency for drainage and compaction. The bleacher contractor, Sky-Hi Equipment Company, complained. G & D decided to remove part of the dirt but inadvertently trucked it all out and replaced it. A couple of months later, beginning on March 19, twenty-seven truckers staged a park-in at the site, complaining that they had not been paid for hauling in the dirt and removing it. They threatened to haul away the new dirt if they were not reimbursed the $53,000 owed them. Opening day was three weeks away. Dorm Braman had accepted the office of undersecretary of transportation in the Nixon administration, so Floyd Miller was now mayor. Miller sought to negotiate, but superior court judge Story Birdseye granted a restraining order after the protesting truckers had carted away six loads of dirt. G & D brought back the dirt, and all parties agreed to postpone litigation until the stadium was done.[19]

The stadium was not close to being finished. As of March 17, the press box was 60 percent complete and the bleachers were only half finished. Dewey Soriano complained to the *Seattle Times*, "People come here and want to buy tickets and I can't even show them where they're going to sit. When I look out there it scares me. I think the whole thing has been handled in a disgraceful way. We have had a lot of talk but no action, nothing but promises." Don Johnston was cautiously optimistic. Sky-Hi's Kenneth Hazelton said that he was grimly determined. A week later, the Pilots' stadium director, Lew Matlin, quantified the problem. "It is frightening," Matlin wrote to Johnston, "to think that we only have seventy-five-hundred seats available as of this writing." There were eighteen days to go until the opener, Matlin moaned, and sales were being lost every day because the team did not know if it would actually have the seats to sell. Johnston did not have to be reminded. Ten days earlier, he had warned Hazelton to accelerate his work schedule or the city would file damage claims.[20]

As opening day, April 11, drew closer and closer, the crews worked harder and longer. By March 26, there were almost 11,000 seats ready for the fans. Two days before the first game, the workers were putting in a new seat every five minutes and had begun to work around the clock. The left field bleachers were almost finished, but in right field, Sky-Hi had gotten only the concrete footings installed, and no one knew how long it would take to assemble the stands. Early comers to the home opener heard the banging of carpenters hammering more seats into place. Estimates varied on how many seats were actually available by game time out of the 25,000 promised. Some said there were as few as 16,000; Best said more than 18,000 but less than 25,000. The most accurate estimate was probably around 19,500. Attendance was 15,014, a low number for the first major league baseball game in Seattle history. Matlin believed 3,000 unpaid admissions poured through a hole in a fence that had not been properly installed. The nearby Stadium Vista Apartments lived up to its name, as several people sat on their porches watching the game and listened to Jimmy Dudley describe the action on their portable radios. Gilbert Braida of Narramore and Associates, the architects, had reported the day before the opener that aside from the seating situation, two restrooms were only partially complete, although the outfield portable toilets seemed sufficient. The press box elevator controls were not in, the press box needed glass, and the paint in two of the new sections was mismatched. The concession stands were open but not serving at full capacity. Beer ran out on the left field side. Edo Vanni joked, "I think the city just planned to send over one of the soup kitchens and a couple of trustees from the jail."[21]

Evaluations of what had been accomplished at the stadium by the first pitch of the inaugural season varied. Mayor Miller went out to take a look and was pleased to see the intimate quality of the park, with so many seats close to the field. He was confident that any shortfall could be remedied during the Pilots' next road trip. In later testimony, Braman admitted that the stadium was incomplete but felt that what had been done was adequate—after all, the teams played ball there. By comparison, in other expansion cities, San Diego finished construction on its stadium a month before the season, but Montreal was still anxious in the days before the opener that its team might not have a place to play (it did). Henry Berg, the city's construction supervisor on the project, noted with some frustration that "the city has cooperated in its effort to bring Sicks' Stadium up to whatever so-called American League standards are in existence." John Owen wryly commented in the *Post-Intelligencer*'s special opening-day insert that Seattle had at last become major league—"Not bad for a bunch of brash amateurs. Even if they did get caught with a few of their bleachers down."[22]

Whether one was a baseball booster like Owen or blasé about Seattle entering the majors, the Sicks' saga had anything but "big league" written all over it. Gabe Paul visited Seattle in March, perhaps to give a boost to his friend William Daley's enterprise. When briefed about the stadium situation, he made it clear what owners were thinking: "In no way do I want this to be misunderstood as a threat. I'm stating a fact. Seattle could lose its franchise to a city whose leaders are most desirous of it, who better understand its terrific impact." About the same time, Frank Lane, assistant to Orioles owner Jerry Hoffberger, found the situation in Seattle "unbelievable. . . . It is a big city in a big league and can't do better than that?" Lane went on, "So, with all that going for it, the town can't even get a park ready for its major league opener? Seattle could be the laughingstock of the country." Lane was a notorious loose cannon in baseball circles, but Seattleites must have cringed as they saw that acquiring a baseball franchise, supposedly a step toward greater renown, was bringing them scorn nationally. The disdain was enduring. Almost a decade later, Washington Senators owner Bob Short recalled thinking at the time that the city could not have spent more than about $200,000 on the upgrade and noted that the box seats were nothing more than the tin chairs an undertaker might provide. Bud Selig, who would purchase the franchise and move it to Milwaukee (and later become baseball commissioner) thought that the field was the most deplorable he had ever seen. Two decades later, former commissioner Bowie Kuhn called Sicks' "anything but major league." More quietly, but probably more significantly, the American League office was keeping a wary eye on the situation in Seattle. Joe Cronin sent his aide, Charlie Berry, to check out the situation in April. Cronin reported that Berry "was having cat fits" about the dirt controversy and the uncompleted bleachers.[23]

Berry, who made subsequent inspections, was never satisfied with the stadium. There was good reason. The Pilots went out on the road, returned, went out again, and returned again on May 6. The last of the repairs was still not complete. On May 2, Berg did the punch list on the press box, elevator, and two restrooms and promised to give the Pilots a couple of gallons of paint to finish the hitters' background in center field. On May 12, Matlin gave Johnston a list of twenty-six items that were incomplete, in need of repair, or required inspection. The list included completion of the park's perimeter fence, repair of several stairways and leaks in the grandstand roof, plumbing repairs, and replacement of a burned-out transformer. The right field bleachers were now installed, but not all were well secured. Several fans who attended the May 6 game complained to Pilot management that their clothes had smears of blue primer from the not-yet-dry bleachers they had sat in. (The Pilots sent the dry cleaning bills to the city, and Sky-Hi finally paid for the damages.) By the end of the season, even the city admitted that the decking, which was already warping, and the seats, which were coming loose, were substandard. But in May, Johnston had become defensive. He felt "constant pressure from Pacific Northwest Sports, Inc., for new improvements, replacement of present structures, repair and refurbishing of existing facilities." In short, he believed that PNSI's list (the first of a steady stream of lists he received during the season) was made up of change orders and further requests. He was out of money for the project and out of patience with the ownership, who in turn believed that the city was not living up to its agreement to furnish a big-league ballpark.[24]

With all the turmoil surrounding the stadium, how was it for baseball? For the team on the field, not bad. The renovations had shortened the fences, so what had been thought of as a pitcher's park now became a hitter's venue. The short porch in left field was only 305 feet. Then the field dropped off to 405 in center. Right field was 320 feet down the line. On warmer days and midsummer evenings, the ball tended to sail over walls that the Pilots had lowered from Pacific Coast League days. For Bouton, the beautiful setting outweighed the stadium's short fences. "That's the great thing about our ballpark," he reminisced. "When a home run hit off you disappears over the fence your eye catches a glimpse of the majesty of Mt. Rainier and some of the bad feeling [of giving up a home run] goes away." Left fielder Tommy Davis also seemed to find some solace even in opponents' home runs. As he turned to watch a ball arc into the stands, he enjoyed catching a glimpse of the people viewing the game from their apartments across the street. Both infielders and outfielders remarked on the perils of the ball field's longish wet grass, and a few found the poorly drained outfield dangerously spongy. Most players felt that the stadium had a minor league ambience and complained about tight quarters in the clubhouse.[25]

For some fans, the band-box dimensions made up for higher ticket prices. On the one hand, outfield seats were closer to the action than some box seats in other major league cities. On the other hand, the right field bleachers were no more than wooden planks and not too comfortable. Parking was almost nonexistent. The lots held maybe six hundred cars, and the rest of the parking spaces were on the street. It was usually a bit of a hike to the ballpark, and during well-attended games, cars cruised the neighborhood of Rainier Valley looking in vain for a spot. Many fans found it easier to take the bus. Some neighborhood business owners saw the Pilots as a boon. Gil Centioli, Ray Ferrari, and Frank Liberio added a motel to their Spin Drift Restaurant near the park. Service station owners were optimistic, undoubtedly contemplating the parking situation. But Rainier Valley was in transition, and, despite advantages for commercial enterprises, the flood of visitors that converged on the neighborhood seventy to eighty times that summer did nothing to stabilize the area or make it more desirable as a residential neighborhood.[26]

The battle between the city and PNSI continued into the season and beyond. Matlin wrote memo after pleading memo to Don Johnston; his replacement, Ed Johnson; Robert Lavoie, the mayor's chief administrative officer; and Mayor Floyd Miller himself. The seating problem was unending. The old bleachers in right field, constructed in 1938, were rotting away, and the new bleachers were warping. Sky-Hi pointed out that it had used construction-grade lumber, as specified in the contract, and maintained that warping should have been expected. The company agreed to refasten the seating that had come loose. The city supplied the press box with heating and ventilation, but the promised refrigeration had not been installed by June. Only when sportswriters and broadcasters threatened to make their grievances public did the city give the go-ahead to finish the project. Public address amplifiers were damaged in June when a sump pump failed and an electrical vault flooded. The

Pilots and the city argued over who was responsible for the damage for the rest of the season. In September, firefighters were called to the stadium twice after a night watchman discovered an electrical short in the vault. Ultimately, the city determined—or admitted—a design fault that allowed volcanic sand from the warning track to clog the pump. Matlin complained about dim lighting along third base, and every night, someone had to climb to the top of each of the poles and activate the stadium lights.[27]

Seating, public address problems, and lights paled in comparison with the park's low water pressure. From the first game, it was apparent that something was wrong. Whenever attendance exceeded eight thousand, the water pressure dropped. Toilets would not flush, and the press box was without water after the seventh inning. Although Henry Berg, city maintenance supervisor overseeing Sicks' Stadium, had written a memo in June and another in July, Ed Johnson claimed he was not aware of the problem until it was brought dramatically to everyone's attention in August by Yankee first baseman Joe Pepitone. As Berg described it in a city memo, "Out of the Yankee dressing room came Joe Pepitone covered with suds from head to toe across vacant lobby & into Pilots Restaurant demanding to know what happened to water for showers. Mr. Houk Yankee manager gave interview to press on water situation." Berg had it figured out in June—the water main was too small. An engineer's report confirmed this in late August and estimated a replacement cost of $28,000. Not until February 1970 did the city, using its own workers for a savings of $16,000, install a new pipe.[28]

By the end of the season, everyone was exasperated. Mayor Miller wrote to Matlin, "In the future, when problems such as this occur . . . please contact Mr. Edward J. Johnson's office." Matlin had already explained to the mayor that Johnson was unreachable. Johnson, for his part, seemed unreliable or incompetent. In a later deposition, he seemed to be able to recall little or nothing of the 1969 season, except that Matlin "complains about everything." In September 1969, the American League's Berry once again refused to certify the park as adequate and the city's own architects did not sign off on the stadium renovations until December 1969. Estimates of how much it would take to bring the stadium up to standard ranged from $25,000 for "musts" to $380,000 for both repair and upgrade to twenty-eight thousand seats. It was never clear who would pay for the work.[29]

Meanwhile, disagreement over carrying out the stadium lease was pushing the already tense relationship to the breaking point. Beginning in June, PNSI withheld rent for several days and then declared that it would not put up the $1 million surety bond required by the concession agreement (i.e., the lease) until the city had refurbished Sicks' Stadium to the satisfaction of the American League. The first year's rental payment of $165,000 was due on June 1, 1969. On June 5, Dewey Soriano wrote to Don Johnston, "We affirmatively state that there has been substantial non-compliance with that [concession] agreement on the part of the city." Soriano told the newspapers that Sicks' was like a "house without a door . . . inadequate by American League standards." He vowed not to pay the rent until the city finished the job. At the same time, Berry had taken another look at the upgrade and, on behalf of the league, declared it deficient, especially in terms of seating and restroom quality. Mayor Miller refused to speak to Soriano and then purportedly threatened the team with eviction. He asserted that the city had gone beyond its agreement and moved heaven and earth to get the project finished by opening day. On June 8, Soriano sent the rent check to the city with a note to Miller complaining that the mayor's remarks were "greatly unfair" and excoriating Johnston and Johnson for their lack of cooperation and deficient knowledge of stadium construction. Still, the Pilots had not posted the surety bond.[30]

The mayor and the owner remained at loggerheads through September. Soriano had countered the demand for the $1 million surety bond with an offer to provide a $660,000 letter of credit, which would cover the remainder of the rent, and a $150,000 performance bond. On August 1, Miller accepted those terms. Then Soriano insisted that the city complete the stadium work (he specifically mentioned the seating and the water pressure problems) before he would comply with his own offer. Miller gave him two weeks to come up with the financial pledges and renewed his threat to evict (or, at best, negotiate a new, day-to-day lease) at the end of the grace period. On August 20, Dewey Soriano and Floyd Miller had a shouting match in the mayor's office. Soriano was under a great deal of financial pressure, and, on the day Miller gave the two-week ultimatum, Soriano's maritime pilot's license had been suspended for a year because of a September 1967 collision in Puget Sound. Tempers were high. When Ed Johnson reminded the Pilots owner that the January 10, 1969, agreement limited the city's responsibilities, Soriano suggested where Johnson could file the agreement. Soriano spluttered to Johnson, "You guys from the Center have been disgraceful. There has been no help from you or Don Johnston." No wonder one of the few things Ed Johnson could recall was that "the mayor told Mr. Soriano to quit bitching."[31]

Emmett Watson reported, "Meanwhile, Mayor Floyd and Dewey the Pilot aren't speaking at all following a little cussing out session." Relations between the city and PNSI had collapsed. Once again, the big-league franchise had brought embarrassment to Seattle. Leonard Koppett's observation in the *New York Times* could not have been more galling, attributing the situation to "clannish feelings in an essentially 'small town' atmosphere in which the local 'establishment' had not warmed up to a baseball operation run by the Sorianos." Max Soriano was perplexed. "We just had a difficult time with the city," he remembered later, "the reason for that I can't answer." Miller maintained it was because the Sorianos did not live up to their agreement. William Daley and Joe Cronin stepped in to pinch-hit for Dewey Soriano with the mayor and had a cordial conversation. Miller relented on his eviction threat (there had been some talk about a late-season move to Dallas–Fort Worth if the Pilots were ousted from Sicks') but called again for the surety bond. Dewey Soriano responded in writing that nothing would be forthcoming until the stadium was in acceptable condition.[32]

A change in administration in late 1969 offered only marginally greater hope. Mayoral candidate Mort Frayn sounded much like Miller in his responses to questions about the Pilots: ticket prices were too high, the city did not have the money for more refurbishment, and PNSI needed to honor its obligation. Wes Uhlman was a bit more conciliatory as he cast some blame on the Miller administration, but he could not see spending city funds for renovating a temporary structure. Once elected, he carped that his inspection tour of the stadium "was in response to some very pickerunish complaints, that was the thing that struck me throughout, was most of the complaints were very nit-picky." The debate lingered into the spring of 1970. Uhlman reluctantly promised to try to finance the rest of the upgrade but made it clear that he wanted the surety bond first. The franchise would move before the matter could be resolved.[33]

The season-long bickering over Sicks' Stadium was a disaster for both PNSI and the City of Seattle. A lukewarm city administration took on the project as a duty, impelled by civic leaders who insisted that a major league baseball franchise would advance the cause of Seattle. Mayor Braman and most of the city council were willing to accede, but the city was not flush, and several found renovation of a baseball stadium a low priority. When budgeted funds fell short, the city made no effort to locate more money—which probably could have been found by a more motivated administration. The park never met reasonable standards. The Sorianos made a serious mistake in publicizing their grievances and then, like a player negotiating a raise, holding out on the surety bond until the city came up with a better deal. By detailing the deficiencies of the stadium in the press, they effectively persuaded fans to reject the opportunity to pay top dollar for uncomfortable seats and inadequate restrooms. In retrospect, it is clear that the club was in a desperate financial position. Wes Uhlman understood this almost as soon as he took office. He asked the American League to put up the surety bond guaranteeing that the Pilots would pay their rent, because he was pretty sure PNSI could not produce it.[34]

By the end of the season, any idea of the Pilots bringing big-league credibility to a city on the rise was turning to ashes. The Sorianos appeared petty and unwilling to meet their obligations (it was a letter of credit and a bond, not a payment, after all). The mayor appeared unreasonable to Seattleites who wanted a major league team, enjoyed sports, and could not understand why the city would evict a big-league franchise. Didn't cities fight for teams rather than try to drive them away? Hadn't Kansas City's Jackson County amicably sorted out cost overruns with the Royals and the Chiefs football team while planning two new stadiums side by side? Seattle was becoming an object of wonderment, if not derision. It was a city that could not even fix up a minor league park to keep its franchise. It would get worse.[35]

The 1969 baseball season was supposed to be a holding action—the first of three or four years until the domed stadium was built. *Then* there would be enough seats, and comfortable ones at that. *Then* there would be something more than an expansion team on the field. *Then* there would be a stadium worthy of calling major league. But until that time, the Pilots needed to be well marketed. Unfortunately, according to a knowledgeable anonymous Seattle source, the Sorianos, who had fired veteran publicist Harold Parrot early on, were not well versed in promotion. Bill Sears, the team's press liaison, and Dewey Soriano sought to fill the gap, but introducing expansion baseball to Seattleites, who had not-so-secretly hoped to snag an established franchise, was a challenging task. All of major league baseball was in the doldrums in 1969. With four new expansion teams, the national pastime drew more fans overall, but per-game attendance declined, with the American League West falling off the most. A third or more of major league teams ended the 1969 season in the red. Even though the American League owners were drooling over the Seattle market, it was a small market, almost too small if Tacoma were excluded.[36]

But the PNSI franchise owners should have had reason to hope. The San Diego Padres thought they could break even with an attendance of 800,000, and Finley's A's had turned a profit in Oakland in 1968 with just a few more than that. Before the season began, predictions for the Pilots' season ranged from 1.6 million fans (with a good stadium) to Emmett Watson's possible 800,000. Watson was casting a bit of a jaundiced eye on a Pilots official who said that he would bet $100 that attendance would reach a million. There was reason for optimism. New franchises typically multiplied minor league attendance in a city by 400 to 800 percent. Seattle regularly drew more than 130,000 in the early 1960s. Moreover, the recent track record of cities new to major league baseball boded well. Oakland and Houston had provided meager support for their first-year franchises, yet their numbers were better than break-even. In their inaugural seasons, more than 900,000 fans came out to sweltering Harris County Stadium to watch the Houston Colt .45s, and 837,000 turned out for the A's in the team's debut season in Oakland.[37]

If the fourth- and fifth-graders the *Post-Intelligencer* had interviewed at the beginning of the season were any indication, the Pilots would do well if they would only furnish autographs, win a championship, score a lot, and, above all, win. They also needed to find a reason for the girls to come to the park, since most of them found baseball games boring. In 1967, a national poll of adults also indicated that high-scoring games (the fences had been moved in and were low), as well as jazzy uniforms (Pilots' scrambled eggs on the hats and gold stripes on the sleeves), stricter security (Sicks' was in an iffy neighborhood), and a new park (oops) would increase the games' appeal. There was nothing that would get promoter Bill Veeck's pulse racing, but the Pilots did work at the basics to draw customers. Fans could purchase tickets almost anywhere around the Puget Sound area, from the Bank of California, to Bon Marche department stores, to restaurants. A fan could pick up a bouquet and a game ticket at a florist's shop, or purchase a carpet roll and a bleacher seat at one of the outlets.[38]

A big part of the Pilots' first-year strategy was aimed at drawing crowds to see American League stars in person for the first time. Twenty-one chartered buses brought Seattleites, fans from across the state, and Oregon residents to the opener. When the Yankees came to town, twelve buses transported supporters from central Washington to see the "Mabton Flash," hometown hero Mel Stottlemeyer, pitch a game. Payette sent buses when western Idaho hero Harmon Killebrew of the Twins came to play. As various teams came to town, the Pilots bestowed the Fred Hutchinson Award on a Hall of Famer or a future inductee associated with that franchise. Carl Yastrzemski of the Red Sox, Joe DiMaggio of the A's front office, and Ted Williams, manager of the Washington Senators, were all honored with an eye toward the turnstiles. Special nights, a staple of organized baseball, was the front office's favorite promotion. There were giveaways: helmets, hosiery on ladies' nights, and two Little League bat days. Bill Sears, who took a risk by staging one of the bat days on the Sunday of the Seafair hydroplane races, exulted that it drew more than twenty-three thousand, the top attendance day of the season. In fact, the Pilots had to give out three thousand coupons because the crowd outran the supply of bats on hand. Player portrait day was another draw. Movie studio artist John Wheeldon did several portraits of Pilots, including Don Mincher and Tommy Harper, that the team gave away at selected games. Leftover pictures were later sold at concession stands for a quarter.[39]

There were special nights for Kiwanis Clubs, senior citizens, and Boeing employees and a fund-raiser for the Boys' Clubs. Boeing representatives complained that they had to contact the team to set up their special days, and even then did not receive much cooperation. The City of Seattle, tight-fisted as ever, resisted a petition from the Boys' Clubs to donate the admission tax on the tickets to the organization. Just after midseason, the team staged a Tommy Harper Night in honor of its top attraction, who was stealing bases at a near-record pace. Olympian Jesse Owens came out to honor the second baseman. The team gave Harper and his wife a trip to Hawaii, several gifts, and Wheeldon's original portrait. Harper's mother was also at Sicks' to honor her son; Harper later discovered that he had been billed for her airfare. A disappointing 6,720 came out to honor "Tailwind Tommy." The team did not promote any of its other players very hard, outside of the Ray Oyler fan club. Oyler also served as the 1969 Seafair parade co–grand marshal with Lawrence Welk. Players complained that local businesses offered few endorsement deals. Toward the end of the season, the Seattle Chamber of Commerce became alarmed and embarrassed about the Pilots' sagging attendance. It decided, with the Pilots, to sponsor three Family Nights before the season concluded, offering general admission tickets at $1 for each member of a family group. By the time this could be arranged and advertised, school had started—and the Pilots had scheduled the nights for midweek. The result was disappointing attendance. Six major promotions (two bat days, a helmet give-away, and days for Boeing, Kiwanis, and the Elks) were successes, generating an average attendance of 17,924, compared to a season average of 9,161. Special nights worked; there simply were not enough of them.[40]

Despite the absence of television coverage, radio broadcasts were probably the highlight of the season. The first Yankees series purportedly pulled in more than 56 percent of the Puget Sound radio audience, and the Pilots nightly drew a large radio audience throughout the northwest quadrant of the United States. Listeners got to play Home Run for the Money, sending in postcards to win if a designated player hit a home run for a selected listener. Pitcher Fred Talbot hit a grand slam and won $27,000 for a lucky Oregon listener. The game was discontinued at the end of the season because of a strict Washington Supreme Court ruling against any kind of gaming in the state.[41]

If one of the Pilots' purposes was to win fans to major league baseball during the season, the rhythms of an expansion franchise combined with the frenetic habits of Marvin Milkes did not do the job. Movement of players was continuous. Even an admiring article in the *Pilots Scorebook* suggested that Milkes aspired more to the image of general manager Frank "Trader" Lane, a notorious shifter of personnel, than the legendary Branch Rickey. (Ironically, when the Milwaukee Brewers fired Milkes at the end of the 1970 season, Lane replaced him.) The near-record fifty-three players who joined the Pilots for parts of the 1969 season created an image of a minor league franchise operating at the whim of its major league owners. It was not so much that the trades were poor, though some were eminently regrettable. It was just hard to get attached to a favorite player. A fan was afraid to get too well acquainted with a player lest he be gone the next day. Salmon, Aker, Bell, and Davis, along with a number of lesser lights, were shipped off before the end of the season.[42]

John Owen grew worried about attendance the first week of the season. His concern continued into May as the numbers averaged about 8,000 a game. That projected to a season total of 700,000. The Pilots not only trailed the other expansion teams but were drawing just half as many as Montreal and Kansas City. Owen hoped that once summer arrived, vacationers from throughout the Northwest would come to Seattle to watch major league baseball. He was right. A stadium survey found that 75 percent of attendees at an August game were from outside Seattle city limits, more than half were from outside the greater Seattle area, and 19 percent lived outside the state. The far-ranging radio broadcasts probably fueled out-of-town interest. Max Soriano was not so hopeful. He thought the writing was on the wall in May when only 7,000 showed up on a pleasant evening to see the Boston Red Sox. Dave Cohn later said he had heard rumors as early as June that the Pilots might move if attendance did not pick up. Such a report was premature, since the Pilots owners discussed adding a Bridge Restaurant to Sicks' Stadium for the second season at about that time. The facility would generate more than $100,000 in profit each year through skyboxes and food sales and provide a venue for sales presentations to potential season-ticket buyers. Plans were afoot to more than double the 2,000 season-ticket holders for the 1970 season. Later in the summer, however, the average attendance was still a dismal 8,400, and the team was laying off ticket takers and ushers. With eleven games to go, the Pilots had to average an impossible 20,000 a game to break even. Joe Schultz put it to the team in homely terms. "Boys," he exhorted, "I guess you know we're not drawing as well at home as we should. If we don't draw fans we're not going to be making the old cabbage. . . . I'm going to lay it right out on the barrelhead. We got to win some games so we can draw some people." The team ultimately drew 677,944, considerably below the probable break-even mark of 800,000.[43]

The schadenfreude crowd noted that, at least, the attendance figure bettered the final count for the Chicago White Sox, Cleveland Indians, Philadelphia Phillies, and San Diego Padres. Ironically, the Pilots' high ticket prices may have allowed the team to generate more revenue than an additional four teams: Pittsburgh, Oakland, San Francisco, and California. The visiting team received 20 percent of the game receipts, and even though the Pilots drew 889,578 on the road, they paid out more than they took home from three or four of their opponents (e.g., more people came to see the Orioles in Seattle than came to see the Pilots in Baltimore). Baltimore, New York (both in six games), and Chicago came away from Seattle with the most revenue, because they drew the most Northwest fans. At the bottom of the list were Cleveland, California, and Kansas City, even though each of these teams played at least nine games at Sicks'.[44]

Why did Seattleites not come out to see their major league team? Gerald Scully in *The Business of Major League Baseball* concludes that the two primary factors in determining attendance are wins and ticket prices. The Pilots failed on both counts. With the highest overall prices in baseball and the worst record in the American League, the team finished last in value. Other factors that breed success at the box office created the cruel realities of 1969: a larger population base, a large stadium, and a new arena to play in. Local observers could figure it out without economic studies. Paying major league prices to watch an expansion team play in a minor league ballpark aggravated attorney Jerry McNaul. Max Soriano agreed, pointing his finger at the city for not bringing Sicks' anywhere close to major league standards. Dewey Soriano thought weather contributed to the problems. "You have to get dressed as though you were going duck hunting," he lamented. "It's that cold." The longtime Seattleite knew better, or perhaps he was longing for the controlled environment of a domed stadium. The 1969 Seattle summer (June 1 through August 31) was actually above average. There were five rainouts, and, based on the average high temperature and days of rain, 1969 was the nineteenth-best out of sixty-one summers from 1948 to 2008—the warmer and drier, the higher the rating. If anything, the weather was too nice, enticing potential fans away from the ballpark to their boats and the hiking trails.[45]

Race entered into the analysis. Several sociological studies assert that white attendance trends lower in black neighborhoods than in other locations. Sicks' Stadium was in a neighborhood in transition from European ethnic (mainly Italian) to African American. Consciousness of this cropped up in security concerns during the renovation of the stadium. Despite Seattle's self-image of racial sensitivity and tolerance, fans likely took the neighborhood demographics into account as they parked their cars along the streets. If such a concern was indeed a factor, the Pilots did little to counterbalance it by reaching out to the black population. The only notice of the team in the *Facts*, Seattle's African American newspaper, was a mention of the Boys' Club promotion. The team officials seemed relatively color-blind. Players were not drafted with much reference to race. An African American or two could often be found on the Pilots bench at a time when few nonstarting black players took up roster spots. Tommy Harper surmised that the Pilots, and most major league clubs, did not promote much among the black community because many African Americans were perceived as predominantly low-income. On a more sinister note, John Owen speculated that the high ticket prices might have been a method of keeping neighborhood blacks from attending games.[46]

A major reason for low attendance was that Seattleites were simply not that interested. Looking back, those close to Seattle sports still wonder if it was really a major league baseball town in the late 1960s. The fans had to be educated to appreciate (and pay more to see) the advanced skills of major league baseball players. Seattle was, and continued to be, a college sports town. Despite its awful record in the late 1960s, Husky football was still the top draw. Seattleites also spent their sports dollars on Seattle University basketball. The issue was not limited to the single-ticket, walk-up fan. The Pilots also failed to sell enough big blocs of tickets. The business community bought out the highest-priced season tickets, but downtown and beyond offered little support. Dewey Soriano, comparing his situation to Kansas City, complained, "Here in Seattle we do not have the intense interest in our business community." Some thought the Sorianos were not sufficiently of the "in" crowd; others speculated that the Pilots were just a poor value. Finally, the devastating Boeing recession of the early 1970s was beginning to emerge. By July 1969, the unemployment rate, which had hovered around 3 percent since 1966, had edged up to 3.6 percent. Much of this increase owed to the transportation manufacturing sector (read Boeing and its suppliers), which lost 88,000 jobs between January and August of the Pilots' single season. Even though the rest of the Seattle metro economy had seen jobs added in the spring and summer of 1969, the Boeing layoffs, which would accelerate in 1970, were problematical. Aircraft workers and others—whether out of work or merely anxious—were surely keeping a close eye on discretionary spending by summer 1969.[47]

All these were contributing factors, but the closest observers of the situation consistently returned to the same conclusion as Gerald Scully: a poor stadium combined with high ticket prices and run-of-the-mill promotions spelled disaster. Emmett Watson summed it up for the general observer. "The point is not whether Seattle is a major league city," he wrote in late August. "The point is that you can't come into any city, not in this day and age, and throw open the gates, charge a heavy tariff and say 'come and get major league baseball.' Imaginative promotion, lower prices, and a something for everybody atmosphere are what's needed."

But outside observers were not aware that PNSI was not just suffering a first-year loss. It was in economic trouble. By June, its accountants projected a $2.2 million shortfall after loans were paid off. Not only was cash flow a problem, but the franchise was not ready to absorb a loss of that size. At one time, the Sorianos and Daley could hope to hold on until the domed stadium was finished. Now there was some question as to whether there would be a stadium to offer deliverance. [48]

Play-by-Play

JUNE AND JULY

WELL into the middle of the season, it appeared that Joe Schultz's bold prediction of third place might just pan out. In June, the Pilots managed to play a bit under .500, but the rest of the division was equally undistinguished. Seattle was in and out of third place several times during the month even while the team lost ground against first-place contenders Oakland and Minnesota. The first of June was a Sunday game, winding up a series at home against Detroit. A Sunday game usually meant plenty of runs, a slew of home runs, and a Pilots loss. To the fans' delight, only the first two occurred. There were five home runs, the teams scored in seven of the eight complete innings, and Seattle prevailed 8–7. Diego Segui, now pitching almost every day in relief, won his sixth game against two losses. Don Mincher, Tommy Harper, Steve Whitaker, and Wayne Comer hit home runs for the home team. The next night against the Indians, Whitaker hit another homer and Mike Hegan slammed two. Steve Barber, still a question mark, pitched five effective innings for the win. Referring to Whitaker's contributions, Schultz caught the spirit of a winning ball club, proclaiming, "It's somebody different every time."[1]

Then came a four-game skid. Gary Bell, bouncing between the starting rotation and the bull pen, got a start against Baltimore, went three and two-thirds innings, and took the loss. The next night, Jim Palmer handed the Pilots their first shutout of the season , 10–0.

After Bell's outing, Schultz told writers that the right-hander, now two and six, would go back to the bull pen, but the next day, Milkes announced that he would go to the Chicago White Sox for reliever

Bob Locker. Especially before free agency, the life of a major leaguer's spouse could be tough. Bell had to leave his wife in Seattle, where she would pack up their goods for the move east. Locker's wife had recently given birth to twins and had seen him for the first time since April just before the trade. In the meantime, the June 15 trading deadline was approaching, and the general manager sought a last opportunity to mold the team. He was looking for right-handed hitting to stymie the left-handed pitching that was dominating the Pilots. Curt Motton, Dave May, Cap Peterson, Ken McMullen, and pitcher Frank Bertaina were the names bandied about. There was talk of Ray Oyler, Merritt Ranew, or even Segui being on the Pilots' trading block. But before the deadline, only catcher Larry Haney went to Oakland for infielder John Donaldson. Perhaps to make up for the lack of action, the team sent Jim Gosger to Vancouver and called up pitcher Gary Timberlake on June 15.[2]

The Pilots salvaged the last game against the Orioles, going three and seven in their last ten games. Nonetheless, they ascended to third place with the win. The team moved on to Detroit where the Tigers' Mickey Lolich struck out sixteen but lost the game 3–2. Marty Pattin, who had been pitching in similar tough luck, got the win, giving him six wins and four losses. Fred Talbot now became the fourth starter, with Pattin, Gene Brabender, and, usually, Barber. The bull pen was tiring. Segui had hurt his finger on a garage door in late April but was still gutting it out and getting plenty of work. O'Donoghue was pitching often as the lefty mainstay in relief. Brabender gave the pen a break in New York, besting Mel Stottlemeyer 2–1 in a complete game. It was clear that the towering right-hander had established himself as a key part of the rotation. Brabender was motivated by a story he had read in the New York papers. Looking forward to the matchup, the sportswriter had said that Stottlemeyer would be going for his tenth victory of the season, "and Gene Brabender will be trying for whatever the Gene Brabenders of this world are after."[3]

The next night, Seattle took a second game from the Yanks, coming from behind to win 5–4. Comer, who a week earlier had crashed hard into the outfield fence in Baltimore to rob Brooks Robinson of an extra-base hit, filled in as catcher in the final inning. Comer was hitting only .251 and had experienced some adventures in the field, but both Schultz and Milkes were impressed with his grit. Drafted from the Detroit Tigers, Comer was having the career year of his brief major league tenure. The *Pilots Scorebook* praised him in midseason as a hard-nosed player and claimed he was a major reason the Pilots might finish third. Before the season was done, he had hit fifteen homers, second behind Mincher, and batted .245. If there were factions in the clubhouse, Comer seems to have been the leader of the anti-Bouton group. He regularly demanded that Bouton be dumped, and Schultz's and Milkes's admiration for him probably did not win him friends among the Bouton contingent. The other position player who was looking very good into the middle of June was Hegan, who was hitting .305.[4]

The next day was bat day at Yankee Stadium and rainy. Play was suspended twice, and kids ran onto the field to slip, slide, and seek autographs. The Pilots lost, but Schultz filed a protest, claiming that the juvenile chaos had made the field unplayable. Maybe both Schultz and the Yankees were reflecting on the contrast between New York stadium security and the overeager Burns detective agency men who had sprinted onto the field in Seattle to break up a players' brawl. At any rate, even with the loss, the team had held its own against the American League East. Only the Pilots, at eighteen wins and sixteen losses, and Oakland, one game above even, had managed a .500 or better record against the stronger division.[5]

It felt good to be decent, even if the team was not over .500. The clubhouse continued to be loose. Bouton asks his readers to "think of a ballplayer as a fifteen-year-old in a twenty-five-year-old body." His stories and those of others confirm the image. The clubhouse tape recorders boomed out the music of the majority (no diversity or even earphones here). It was country and western. Oyler enjoyed Johnny Cash, for Ranew it was Charley Pride, and Brabender was happy with anything with a country flavor. Even Harper said that the music began to sound good to him.[6]

Bouton concocted a fake letter from a fan who had won $27,000 when Fred Talbot hit a grand-slam home run. The letter promised Talbot $5,000. When Talbot was flown down to Gladstone, Oregon, to meet the fan and be interviewed, there were thanks but no offer of a cut, much to his chagrin and his teammates' glee. In *Ball Four*, Bouton famously reveals the middle school sensibilities, shenanigans, sex escapades, and general rowdiness of young athletic men, especially when they are on the road. Some of the milder manifestations showed up during the Baltimore series. Gene Brabender and John O'Donoghue put the Oriole bull-pen benches on the bull-pen roof. In retaliation, Baltimore pitcher Pete Richert put a goldfish in the Pilots bull-pen's watercooler and hid the benches behind the scoreboard. For good measure, the Orioles' Eddie Watt cut the buttons off the two offending Pilots' uniforms. Bouton was also one of the first to make known a baseball drug culture, writing of "greenies"—amphetamines that seemingly sped up reactions and sharpened concentration. John O'Donoghue received a shipment of five hundred in early June, which he shared with, or sold to, his teammates. Bouton claimed that most of the Seattle players partook.[7]

The Pilots moved on to play the White Sox, but the first game of the series was in Milwaukee's County Stadium. The White Sox had a deal to play one game in Milwaukee against every American League opponent. The Milwaukee Brewers Inc., the group that was working to bring a team to Milwaukee permanently, made sure the trip was worth the Sox' time. A crowd of 13,133 turned out. Had fans been told that they were watching next year's Milwaukee Brewers play that night, virtually everyone in the stands would have guessed the White Sox would be the team that was moving. Mike Marshall started, and the Sox cuffed him around. He gave up five runs in less than three innings, and after the game, Schultz banished him to the bull pen. Harper committed three errors, and the future Brewer declared that he hoped he never had to come back because the stadium seemed to have put a hex on him. The Pilots lost 6–4. Returning to Chicago, the teams were rained out and then split a doubleheader the next day.[8]

Over the next week, in the last game in Chicago and the ensuing home stand against Kansas City and Chicago, several players began to distinguish themselves. Gary Timberlake got his first start since being called up and allowed only one earned run in four and one-third innings. Brabender continued to establish himself as the anchor of the rotation, with a complete-game 1–0 win over Kansas City. The native of Black Earth, Wisconsin, went into the seventh with a perfect game and wound up with a three-hitter. He cited good control as the key. Harper continued his stolen base tear. After his multi-error game in Milwaukee, Schultz moved him to center field. It seemed to take pressure off Harper, who revved up his base running, and it made room for newly acquired John Donaldson to play second. Tommy Davis, who had lingered around .200 most of the season, began to hit with authority.

As he raised his batting average thirty points in a week or so, Davis carried the team to most of its victories. He thought he had been trying too hard and was now beginning to relax at the plate. On the downside, injuries began to eat away at the lineup. Besides pulls and strains that sidelined Mincher, Kennedy, and Oyler for a few days, Barber finally went on the disabled list, Rich Rollins's knee continued to act up, and Dick Simpson went on the disabled list with a pulled hamstring.

The Pilots were greeted by a Kiwanis Night doubleheader crowd of 18,413 when they returned to Sicks' Stadium. The Kiwanians watched their team split with Kansas City. A rainout required another doubleheader against the White Sox. This time, it was Talbot and Timberlake who took the mound. The former went into the fifth allowing four runs; the latter gave up four runs in less than two innings. Chicago swept the twin bill, which lasted past midnight, dampening the spirits of the handful of fans who stayed the course out of the 7,417 who were (fool) hardy enough to come out to a drizzly doubleheader in the first place. The next night, John Gelnar pitched into the seventh inning, allowing Chicago only one run, and the Pilots won 3–1. This illustrates the chancy quality of expansion team pitching. If the pitchers were consistent, or wily enough, to get hitters out even when they did not have command of their pitches, they would not have been available in the expansion draft, even for $175,000. Some Pilots pitchers could zip a fastball, or break off a curve, or tantalize with a slider as well as anyone, but they could not consistently marshal their talents on the mound. One appearance would make it seem as though the hurler had finally found his groove; the next time out could be a disaster. Only Brabender had started to dominate appearance after appearance. Pattin had it some days, got by other days, and, sometimes could not get anyone out. By the end of June, Talbot and Gelnar were the best guesses Schultz and pitching coach Sal Maglie had about who should fill out the rotation, mainly because they had looked good in their previous outings. The team had just bought Gary Roggenburk from Boston. Schultz gave him a start in still another doubleheader against the Angels, and he pitched well to win 5–2. Maybe a five-man rotation was the answer.

By the end of June, the Pilots were still clinging to third place, seven and one-half games out of first and only five games under .500. The pitching was still a weak point, but with Brabender dominating and Locker the ace of the bull pen, there was hope. The Pilots had become a running club. Harper was the main reason, of course. He had forty-three stolen bases as July dawned. Comer chipped in with eleven, and even Mincher had seven. Comer also had ten homers, as did Mincher, whose home run bat had grown quiet in June. Harper was now being tried at third base, allowing Davis, Comer, and Hegan to play the outfield and Donaldson to continue at second. Edo Vanni once again came out of the front office to show Donaldson how to choke up to get base hits, and it was working. The infield defense was probably more solid with Harper out of the middle, but it was still not adept. In so many ways, the Pilots were the patchwork team they should have been as an expansion entry, but it was working well enough. Visions of third place were still reasonable, but every player had to perform up to his often limited ability, Schultz needed to push the right buttons as he subbed for regulars who fell into slumps, and the team could not afford injuries to its mainstays.

In July, the Pilots continued to match the record of all but two of their American League Western Division foes. As Oakland and Minnesota fought for first, the rest of the division staggered along behind. Through the month, the Pilots lost more than ten games to .500 yet were still contending for third. Injuries played a large part in the slide, especially weakening hitting, the team's strength. Oyler and Rollins had been hobbled by knee injuries but played occasionally. John Kennedy hurt his knee on July 1 and was put on the sixty-day disabled list. Four days later, the team called up Gordy Lund to play shortstop. Milkes traded Darrell Brandon, who was now in the minors, for minor league third baseman Ron Clark. Clark was soon to take up the slack in the infield. Harper played some third base but then injured his groin. A broken toe took down second baseman John Donaldson; Hegan pulled his hamstring and sat out for ten days. While the outfielders were out, Steve Hovley began to play regularly and got hot, hitting over .300 for the rest of the month. This was Hovley's debut in the majors, and he made the most of it, establishing himself as a regular. In the clubhouse, the Stanford-educated Hovley easily fell in with the Bouton group and may have been fully the nonconformist Bouton portrays in *Ball Four*. On July 10, Rollins gave up on his knee and had season-ending surgery. Milkes was upset because he thought Rollins should have put off surgery and made himself available for pinch-hitting until some of the other players healed. The Pilots seemed to make do when their recognizable name veterans played, but now a progressively larger contingent of starters were journeymen or worse.

The Pilots were usually outmanned if they had to play the class of the division, and July started in Oakland. Brabender continued his quality pitching with a 7–1 win. But the next night, Reggie Jackson launched the Pilots on a five-game losing streak with three home runs, and John "Blue Moon" Odom pitched a shutout. As the streak lengthened in Kansas City, the Pilots began to take on the look of a losing team. Talbot mastered the Royals into the seventh inning; then Davis misplayed a fly ball with two outs. Before the inning was over, the home team had scored six. The Royals added five in the eighth and won 13–2. The next night, Marshall got a rare start against the Royals and lost 7–3. After the game, he was ticketed for Vancouver but balked. The Pilots made arrangements to send him to Toledo, closer to his Michigan home. He had asked to be traded, but Schultz told him he had cleared waivers, and Milkes did not want to just release a $175,000 expansion draft player. Brabender proved he was a stopper in the fourth game of the series, winning 9–3. Mincher was sitting out against the Royals' left-hander Bill Butler when Hegan pulled his hamstring in the first inning. The big first baseman came into the game, went three for four, and hit two home runs. Joe Schultz mentioned several times over the next several days that he thought Mincher was swinging better against the Royals than at any time during the season. When the Pilots drafted Mincher first in the expansion draft, he was projected to supply power and average. He came through with the former, leading the club with twenty-five home runs on the season. Mincher had been a crucial cog in the Twins' pennant-winning 1965 team and then went to the Angels. Because of the McDowell beaning, Mincher had some trepidation about playing in July heat, fearing he might be struck by dizziness. But his strong performance in hot and humid Kansas City put those fears to rest, and the first baseman went on to have a solid midsummer.[9]

Roggenburk seemed on the verge of joining Brabender as a dependable starter. The former Boston minor leaguer, who had undergone elbow surgery, pitched a 3–1 complete game against the Angels. That was followed by a Talbot shutout. The shutout was fine with Talbot, but all he wanted to talk about after the game was his grand-slam home run off an Eddie Fisher knuckleball. Outside of Talbot, the offense seemed powered only by the hot-hitting Hovley and by Mincher, who had hit a three-run home run in the Roggenburk game. It was his fourth homer in five days.

The offense continued to sputter as the Pilots plodded through their second-longest losing streak of the season, eight in a row. Even Brabender lost twice. Roggenburk was no longer the promising pitcher. He lost his start and his spot in the rotation, giving up four runs in four innings against the unbeatable (for the Pilots) Twins. Both Harper and Hegan returned to the lineup and were reinjured. Hegan went out indefinitely. Talbot almost ended the losing streak at five. On July 13, he went seven shutout innings against the Twins, but they came from behind to win in the ninth.

The losing streak was at eight games, and the Twins were coming to Seattle for a four-game series. Schultz was typically philosophical, but down. On the hitting, he observed, "No, we're not hitting much right now. And we can't worry about injuries because you're paid on what you do with what you have." On July 18, Schultz pressed his workhorse Segui into action starting the first half of a doubleheader. The Cuban limited the Pilots' nemesis to one run and immediately joined the starting rotation. Talbot came on in the nightcap and won 3–2. Hovley provided most of the firepower with a two-run home run, but it was Talbot, who had singled, who scored the winning run. The Pilots may have been playing less than mediocre ball, but 14,134 came out to Sicks' to welcome them home, and, amazingly, the team was still clinging to third place.[10]

The series, which preceded the break for the All Star Game, ended on a bizarre note. The Twins and Pilots played a sixteen-inning game on Saturday night that ran into the American League curfew. It resumed on Sunday afternoon and went two more innings before Minnesota prevailed. In the regularly scheduled game, John Gelnar went seven innings to lose 3–0. That was after he pitched one and one-third innings of the suspended game. He told the press it was the first time he had lost two games in one day. During the All Star break, Marvin Milkes was cranky. His team was not playing particularly well, though it was only one-half game out of third place. He told the press he was upset at the pitching and the general quality of play, ignoring the fact that the Pilots were still scrapping to hold their own with the established franchises. Putting untoward pressure on Schultz and the team, Milkes avowed, "And let's stop that expansion excuse business. This is a representative ball club, it better start playing representative ball. . . . It will be third place or else."[11]

Mike Hegan was Seattle's All Star representative in Washington, D.C., but his hamstring was hurting. Jerry McNertney had finished third in the American League catcher voting, but the American League team had enough catchers. So Mincher took Hegan's place. He struck out pinch-hitting for Denny McLain in the fourth inning. Immediately after the All Star break, there was a sense of rejuvenation. Donaldson tried out his toe and found that he could play, though it was prone to swell. Harper had healed enough to get back in the regular lineup and stole two bases, his forty-sixth and forty-seventh, in the July 24 game, which the Pilots won 8–6 at home against Boston. To replace Hegan, whose leg was sore and who had to fulfill a reserve obligation, the Pilots brought up Greg Goossen. Seattle split the next two with the Red Sox.

After an 8–5 Pilots victory, the teams played a Sunday epic. On July 27, Pattin started and went eight innings, giving up only one run, a home run to Reggie Smith. (It was Pattin's twenty-fourth gopher ball of the season.) But Boston's Ray Culp went ten innings, also giving up only one run. It was tied 1–1 going into the nineteenth. Barber, pitching for the first time since June 8, went five innings but gave up a run in the nineteenth on a looper to left by Carl Yastrzemski that Greg Goossen lost in the setting sun. In the bottom of the inning, Jim Pagliaroni singled Hovley home to tie it up again. The Red Sox then went ahead for the win in the top of the twentieth. They scored three runs, featuring a two-run home run by Joe Lahoud off Bob Locker. Everyone but Diego Segui played for the Pilots, and he was warming up in the bull pen. Boston pitchers struck out eighteen, and the Pilots turned five double plays. Schultz summed it up for the 9,670 fans who watched the five-hour fifty-two-minute contest. "If people don't like this kind of baseball, I don't know what the hell we can give them. They [the Pilots] really stay in there, don't they?"[12]

The month ended with the Pilots twenty games out of first place, sixteen games under .500 . . . but still clinging to third. Roggenburk had quit, saying he was tired of baseball and would go back home to seek another profession. Goossen stayed hot, hitting two home runs on July 30 to win a game for Segui. It was a good thing, since Mincher had joined the injured, with a sore shoulder. Seattle purchased George Brunet, now at the end of his pitching career, from the Angels as they sought to put together a rotation before the end of the season. Had the season concluded at the end of July, even Marvin Milkes may have been satisfied. But a team thin in talent had to survive another two months.

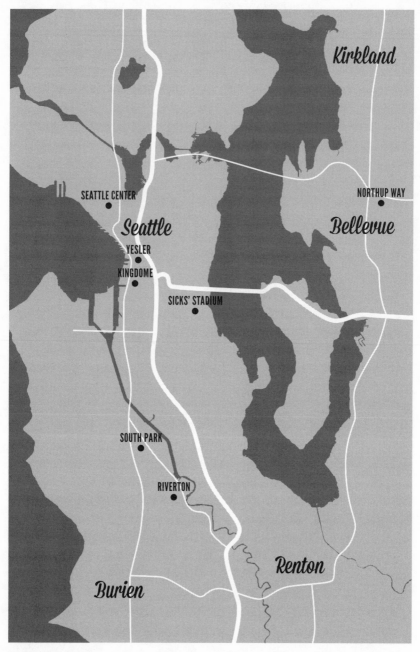

Map of the Seattle area showing the five sites Western Management Consultants recommended to the original Washington State Stadium Commission. Also shown are the locations of Sicks' Stadium and the Kingdome.

"STORM CLOUDS GATHER OVER PILOTS' PORT"

A s soon as the King County Stadium, popularly known as the King-dome, was built, attendance was sure to soar—maybe as high as 1.2 million. The travails of the Pilots ownership would come to an end. Seattle would finally be secure as a big-league sports town. After voters approved the bonds in the February 1968 Forward Thrust election, all that was left was finding an acceptable site. But deciding would be a tussle, and, once again, striving to become big league would cause Seattleites a good deal of chagrin.[1]

Through much of 1968 and all of 1969, while Pacific Northwest Sports, Inc., was assembling a team, as the Pilots played out the season, and while Dewey Soriano quarreled with the city over Sicks' Stadium, the city fathers were encountering their own problems siting the new arena. John Spellman and John O'Brien, representing King County; city councilmen Floyd Miller and Charles M. Carroll; and Joe Gandy and Dave Cohn continued the work of the Washington State Stadium Commission. Each had his ideas about the five sites Western Management Consultants had winnowed out: Fifth Avenue and Yesler Way, in the Pioneer Square area of downtown Seattle; the Seattle Center vicinity; Northup Way on the east side of Lake Washington; and Riverton and South Park, both near West Marginal Way along the Duwamish Waterway in the industrial area south of the city (see map). Spellman promised to pay close attention to the consultants' recommendations; Cohn said he would personally inspect every site; Carroll leaned toward a suburban location; and Miller was inclined to favor a site within the city limits. John Owen slyly suggested that Gandy, the commission chairman, had established some priorities of his own. Owen visualized Gandy saying, "Some day before long our various experts will tell us . . . one certain site is better than the others." The sportswriter added, "And if it's the Duwamish tide flats, he'll go straight out the window."[2]

The committee members were determined to be active decision makers. They made local field trips to eyeball each of the sites and inspected stadiums around the nation, from San Francisco, to Washington, D.C., to Houston. On their cross-country junkets, they learned about building configurations and stadium operation but discovered little new information about where to build one. Mainly, they returned with the disturbing sense that there was no such a thing as a true multipurpose stadium—a separate convention center might be necessary. Their trips around the Puget Sound area only confirmed how much commission members differed on stadium location.[3]

Spring 1968 was the season of lobbying. Seattle's civic leaders had always pressed for preserving downtown as the city's hub, but as they campaigned for a centrally located domed stadium, they defended their turf much more vociferously than they had when choosing a location for the world's fair or deliberating over the Forward Thrust slate of issues. The Seattle Area Industrial Council and the Central Association (the downtown interest group) argued that the stadium could fulfill its multipurpose functions only in a downtown location. They pointed out that conventions require nearby hotels and restaurants, which downtown supplied in abundance. Because sporting events would rarely occur at heavy traffic times, major transportation routes would facilitate access to a downtown arena. Both the *Seattle Times* and the *Seattle Post-Intelligencer* chimed in, calling on stadium commission members to "get their heads down out of the clouds of big league sports and keep faith with the electorate" by asserting that the building must be a genuinely multipurpose facility and, by inference, be built downtown.[4]

Mayor Braman, forever tepid about a major league franchise in his city, could get heated about where to build an already-paid-for stadium. "You could play football or baseball out in the sticks," he said, but a multipurpose building had to go downtown. Downtown is where the people are. Pragmatically, Braman supported the Fifth and Yesler location because it was the only site "we had even a forlorn chance of getting past the commission." He pictured a crescent of development—starting at Seattle Center, extending through the Pike Place remodel project along the waterfront, and curving back east toward the freeway and the stadium—uniting the downtown area. Warming to his vision, he extolled the view from the new stadium out over the Sound toward the Olympics. Earl Luebker of the *Tacoma News Tribune* reminded the mayor that the dome would substantially obscure the vista. Many congratulated the mayor on his fervent advocacy. His tart ripostes to those with different opinions showed his passion, for example, stating that a person who disagreed with him was "wrong on all premises," that a letter was "preposterous and insulting," that a correspondent did not have "much regard for the facts" or was "totally uninformed."[5]

Not all the critics of the Fifth and Yesler location could be disparaged or easily dismissed. The Model Cities environmental task force, for example, pointed out that no one had considered the impact of such a huge project on the neighborhood. Architect Frank Hope, one of the commission's consultants, explained that the Yesler site was up against a hill, and it would be impossible to construct a stadium there that did not partially extend into a slide area.[6]

The mayors of Bellevue and Renton, while acknowledging that suburban locations would necessitate new hotels, urged Western Management Consultants not to cave in to pressure from downtown Seattle as it made its final rankings. The Bellevue Chamber of Commerce argued that infrastructure costs would be lower in the suburbs because downtown locations would require building large parking garages. Braman retorted that a suburban location would necessitate highway construction, driving associated costs higher. James Ellis declared that he understood the public's frustration with the wrangling and told voters that his attention would be on securing a second Forward Thrust election. He also understood that taking any stand on what many voters, after all, perceived as "his stadium" would just make enemies.[7]

As spring verged on summer in 1968, the consultants inched toward revealing their final rankings. Their site selection scorecard was based on eleven weighted criteria—market area (proximity to population), accessibility, and utilities topped the list. At the same time, Western Management Consultants announced that the multipurpose aspect of the stadium would cause the cost to exceed the $40 million budget. Either a single building would need two floors and a costly concrete slab to rest on or an adjacent structure was needed to accommodate smaller events and conventions. On June 12, Western Management Consultants announced its top pick. It was the South Park location, along the Duwamish Waterway, west of Boeing Field. The stadium would straddle City of Seattle and King County jurisdictions. A major advantage was that the flat land surrounding the stadium facilitated a large parking lot. The consultants rated Riverton, in the same general area, second to South Park only because the site was hampered by soft soils. Suburban Northup Way was third. The Seattle Center and Fifth and Yesler locations finished fourth and fifth. Western Management Consultants estimated that it would take $39 million to construct a stadium, complete with parking, at the winning site.[8]

South Park was easily accessible—within a fifteen-minute drive for a substantial number of residents. The main drawback was that a small number of residents would lose their homes. The consultants rather spitefully reported that the Fifth and Yesler site was among the final choices only because of political pressure. But the stadium commission, not Western Management Consultants, would make the final selection. The game was not yet up. For the downtown contingent, Seattle Center was the best hope. The consultants had rated the center lower for several reasons. Mainly, building at Seattle Center would likely cost $53 million, making it the costliest of the five locations. Access was a difficulty. Say "Mercer Mess" to a Seattleite, and stories of traffic congestion pour forth. The proposed Bay Freeway, crossing town near the center from I-5 to the waterfront, could have helped but was not a solution in the eyes of the consulting team. Parking was another major impediment. The city, or a private party, would have to build one or more garages.[9]

Downtown leaders took the announcement neither well nor lying down. Frank Ruano, who had never known the mayor to swear, was taken aback to overhear Braman excoriate the consultants: "Those damn stupid people from San Diego didn't know what the hell they were doing." The *Times* reported, "The mayor, his voice charged with emotion, said he was 'astounded at some of the statements' in the consultants' report." Not everything can be measured by "graphs and charts," he went on. "I think that in the proper forum we could refute many of these statements relative to the 5th and Yesler site." *Post-Intelligencer* managing editor Lou Guzzo complained that the consultants had failed to genuinely consider Seattle Center architect Paul Thiry's plan for a stadium. And a *Post-Intelligencer* editorial labeled the consultants "not truly qualified" because they refused to consider the advantages of a multipurpose stadium, perhaps the key selling point that put the bond vote over the top. The editorial concluded, "The comedy has gone on long enough. On the strength of the inadequate unimaginative report made yesterday by its consultants, the state Stadium Commission should dismiss them and start over. And the waste of funds isn't funny." The *Times* was not nearly as adamant as the *Post-Intelligencer* but agreed that the consultants had betrayed the voters. The promise of a multipurpose stadium, the *Times* editorialized, was a "snow job" that dated back to the stadium vote of 1966. Finally, the Central Association prepared a twenty-one-page retort that raised 103 points of disagreement.[10]

The stadium commission was scrambling. It appeared that a majority was ready to endorse South Park. As members stewed over when to vote, pressure from downtown escalated. Braman, of course, wrote a letter counseling delay. Another letter from twenty prominent Seattle businessmen called for further deliberation. Commission members John O'Brien and Charles Carroll still leaned toward endorsing the South Park site. John Spellman worried that the legislature would revoke the room tax for the stadium if the committee delayed. It was Dewey Soriano's note asking the commission to hold off that convinced Charles Carroll to wait. (Carroll was justifiably surprised by the letter. Soriano surely preferred South Park and its parking over Seattle Center. He also could not have been expected to advocate slowing the process, since the American League was breathing down his neck about getting construction under way by the end of 1970.) Amid the cacophony, the stadium commission voted unanimously in late June to put off a decision until August. The *Times* condemned the commission for bowing to the pressure to delay and called for all commission members to resign. An editorial expressed the fear that dawdling would engender cost overruns but offered no advice on site selection. The mayor, who had astutely transferred his allegiance from the Fifth and Yesler site to Seattle Center, offered soothing advice. He suggested that Ed Carlson could be persuaded to help resolve the impasse.[11]

The creation of the Ad Hoc Committee for the Seattle Center Stadium Site, chaired by Carlson, demonstrated that there were times when even the wisest Seattle civic leaders could allow blatant self-interest to control their vision for a better Seattle. A stadium would bring major league sports, rouse admiration for the city, and generate income for the entire region. At the same time, a stadium was a jewel that the downtown interests could not fumble away. It ratified their district as the center of the region. It would stimulate construction activity in the relatively underdeveloped northern portion of downtown and bring dollars to the restaurants, hotels, and shops up and down the downtown corridor. The sole task of the Ad Hoc Committee was to demonstrate to the stadium commission, not the best location for the arena, but why it should be located at Seattle Center, or, as *Times* sportswriter Georg Meyers put it, "to dredge up the pure McCoy on the Seattle Center as a stadium site." Besides Carlson, a host of notables populated the committee's ranks. James Douglas (Northgate Shopping Center) was vice chairman, and members included developer Henry Broderick, jeweler Leo Weisfield, arts patron Paul Friedlander, department store operator Lloyd Nordstrom, head of Alaska Steamship Ned Skinner, and venerable banker Joshua Green.[12]

Carlson, accurately representing his committee's position, declared that the logic was irrefutable. It had to be at Seattle Center. The report worked backward from there in order to prove that contention. The committee recommended purchasing the Seattle Transit barn and repair yard next to the center as a building site. The main sticking points were parking and access. Building multistory garages would take $8–13 million beyond the cost of the stadium, but the city could issue councilmanic bonds for the purpose. (This meant that the city council could issue a limited number of bonds based on property valuations, simply by decree, without a citizens' vote. There was never any hint of using this ploy a year later when it came to finding funds to finish the renovation of Sicks' Stadium.) The committee argued that parking fees and admission taxes on stadium and Seattle Center events could help fund these and any additional revenue bonds, if needed. The east-west Bay Freeway (never to be completed) was already in the works, so there would be little extra cost involved in providing access to the arena. In fact, committee members claimed that the freeway made access less onerous for this site compared to the suburban locations. Redesigning the off- and on-ramps to the stadium would be the only hurdle. Plus a stadium at the center would automatically be a multipurpose site, because existing buildings could be used for non-sports purposes—and a multipurpose stadium is what voters had been promised. The Seattle Center location was convenient for everyone and would group entertainment facilities in one spot. It was on many bus routes, so people would take public transportation. In short, the committee's report was more sales document than objective analysis.[13]

On August 7, 1968, the Washington State Stadium Commission announced that it had selected Seattle Center as the site for the domed stadium, if nine conditions could be met by mid-November. The conditions involved parking and access, including the appropriation of the $8 million of councilmanic bonds by the city, the go-ahead for the Bay Freeway, and acquisition of parking rights and land for the stadium. By November, it was announced that all conditions had been fulfilled, although in several cases only expressions of goodwill or memos of agreement rather than contracts had been collected. Saving face while making a point, Western Management Consultants endorsed the choice, explaining that Seattle Center would have topped its list if cost had not been a consideration. It predicted that the entire project, including the parking garages, would cost $53–55 million, excluding the Bay Freeway and the newly designed off-ramps needed to accommodate stadium traffic. The *Post-Intelligencer* rejoiced at the news, disdaining the consultants as "outlanders." An editorial thanked architect Thiry, Braman, and, most of all, Seattle businessmen who had revived the Seattle Spirit of 1962. Dewey Soriano, who would be the prime tenant of the new building, stated that he would stay out of the argument, but those attending the commission's announcement thought he looked "stricken," "stunned," and "disgusted." Hy Zimmerman, writing with insight if not inside knowledge, explained that Soriano went along with the delay and accepted the Seattle Center site, but, in reality, "no sane baseball owner would wish that congestion and lack of parking on himself." John Spaeth, the Seattle city planning director, was another skeptic. Somehow his department had not participated in the deliberations of either the Ad Hoc Committee or the Washington State Stadium Commission.[14]

Planning got under way immediately. The county purchased the transit center barn and bus parking for just under $5 million, a little less than expected. Narramore, Skilling, Praeger, the architects, drew up a square field within an octagonal building that looked something like the Seattle Coliseum, located across the Seattle Center from the stadium site. The proposed arena would seat fifty-three thousand and could be built for $30 million. The sketches showed cars whizzing by on the as-yet-unbuilt nearby Bay Freeway. The architects thought construction could begin by December 1970, the American League deadline.[15]

There was still a tumult of criticism. The *Argus* wondered why the stadium commission did not stick with the $40 million authorized by voters. Seattle Democrat Gordon Herr held hearings in the state legislature. Witnesses, mainly from south King County, attacked Gandy as high-handed for ignoring the consultants. A later *Fortune* magazine article saw the arm-twisting done on behalf of the Seattle Center location as a Seattle Chamber of Commerce plot. Angry letters from constituents poured into Mayor Braman's office. Ronna Smith wrote a blistering indictment of Seattle's efforts at achieving status, complaining, "Locating a huge domed stadium in an inaccessible part of a traffic jam—merely to satisfy the money kings—seems to be a Chicago or New York trick. It is sincerely too bad our scenic naive little town—which happens to have a million residents—has now 'grown up.'" Joe Empens derided Braman in a letter, writing, "By the time you and the Seattle Business Men get through it will be $100,000,000. . . . Apparently you feel the average tax payer can not add or is stupid." Jack Waidman, an underwriter for Penn Mutual Insurance, thought the stadium was a snow job and wrote, "It seems to me you either were very stupid or promoting a lie, either way this city can not afford your type of government." Salty as ever, Braman wrote back the next day, "I thought you should know some idiot is writing me letters using your stationery and signing your name," explaining sardonically that no businessman would make the "asinine statements" that Waidman had.[16]

"Storm Clouds Gather over Pilots' Port" read the headline in the *Sporting News* in mid-December 1968. The domed stadium was under attack, and by something more than angry letter writers. Tony F. Ferrucci, South Park property owner, almost immediately brought suit against the stadium commission for ignoring the consultants' recommendations. Within nine months, Frank Ruano had organized the Committee to Save the Seattle Center (which it intended to do by blocking the stadium at that site). Ruano and his associates began circulating an initiative petition to stop the stadium. The Progressive tradition of placing political power in the hands of the people was once again being practiced, and by mid-1969—midseason for the Pilots—the county and the petitioners were in a race.[17]

If the project was far enough along, John Spellman, who had assumed the newly created post of King County Executive (something like the mayor of the county) in May, could claim that the county had too much work and money invested in the project for the petition or even a vote to have any legal effect. James Ellis understood this and had already urged in February 1969 that building commence without delay lest the chance be lost. Ruano also understood the game and filed a suit to stop expenditures on the stadium. The court rejected it. In October, Spellman proclaimed the project on schedule and had sold $10 million worth of bonds. He pressed the architects to finish the design work by November 1969. The architects responded that bids would be let no later than December 1969. In early 1970, they had finished phase 1 of the planning process, which cost $250,000. In February, the county signed a contract for phase 2, for $780,000. The "storm clouds" had complicated life for Pacific Northwest Sports, Inc. If there was a vote and it went against the Seattle Center location, the start date might be delayed beyond the American League's mandated December 1970 deadline. But if it was built at Seattle Center, the Pilots would get no revenue from the parking. That, low attendance, a thin pocketbook, and contention over Sicks' Stadium were all cascading down on Pilots ownership. The prospect of a domed stadium had once been the redeeming hope for the franchise; now it was just another problem. The upshot was that the Pilots became a complicating factor in constructing the dome. Off and on from October 1969 to April 1970, the team teetered on the verge of leaving town. County council chairman John O'Brien had spoken for most observers when he declared in October 1969 that without the Pilots, the county should not even consider building.[18]

Amidst all this, Ruano had collected forty thousand signatures, more than twice the number needed to put the stadium location on the ballot. The Committee to Save the Seattle Center had tapped into a vein of voter discontent. While some might have actually wanted to save the world's fair site from a huge arena, it is likely that most King County voters were miffed at the process by which the location had been chosen. To them, the stadium commission had been coerced by (or were in league with) the downtown powers, and the project was going to cost more than the advertised $40 million. It left the bitter taste of politics in the mouths of many citizens.[19]

In early January 1970, the King County Council set the vote on the stadium initiative for May 19, the day Forward Thrust had selected to give voters a second chance at endorsing the issues that had failed in 1968. Ellis was uneasy, hoping voters would be able to separate the stadium from Forward Thrust. Immediately, legal action commenced. Alfred Schweppe, former dean of the University of Washington law school and just as much a gadfly as Ruano, sought an injunction, arguing that voters could not halt the stadium, a project that had already started. The county had bought the transit property and spent more than $9 million on architectural fees, the suit claimed. Ruano fired back that because Schweppe was a prominent member of Forward Thrust, the Committee to Save the Seattle Center would consider Forward Thrust a co-instigator of the injunction and oppose its second campaign. He called on Ellis to force Schweppe to drop the suit. (Ruano was also put out because Ellis had not invited him to participate in the Forward Thrust effort.) A King County Superior Court granted the injunction against the vote, but the state supreme court overturned the ruling. The vote would be held, and the supreme court would rule later on the question of whether the vote had any force to relocate the stadium, if that were the wish of the voters. So the campaign was on.[20]

Supporters of the Seattle Center site argued that a vote against the site (a "yes" on the initiative) was tantamount to ending the hopes of a stadium anywhere. Ed Carlson asserted that Seattle was genuinely major league, and with a stadium, the city would have major league baseball, the National Football League, and a multipurpose facility. If the voters rejected the Seattle Center location, the city would not see a stadium for twenty-five years. Others argued that the center was the only place a multipurpose stadium could be built for $40 million, conveniently ignoring the fact that someone had to pay for parking garages and the Bay Freeway off-ramps. Those who owned up to these realities cleverly—probably too cleverly—maintained that $40 million was the amount voters had authorized to be added to the bonded debt, but it was not necessarily the limit of all expenditures. In February 1970, while the Pilots were still hanging on, John Owen warned that vetoing the stadium at Seattle Center would send major league baseball packing and be the end of a stadium for years to come. (In May, with the Pilots gone, he would argue that building a stadium would allow the city to call the shots and probably draw a National League team to Seattle.) Both daily newspapers recommended a "no" vote. The *Post-Intelligencer* agreed with many that the initiative would kill any stadium if it passed; the *Times* warned against wasting the money already spent and just wanted to get on with it. Those supporting the initiative said that they cared for the little guy, unlike the Pilots with their high ticket prices. Others worried about clogged traffic at Seattle Center. Some said a stadium could be built within the budget at another location. Bumper stickers read "Vote Yes for No Stadium." Ruano denied that his group was trying to kill a stadium project regardless of location.[21]

It was a disaster at the polls for Forward Thrust and stadium proponents. In the midst of the Boeing recession in Seattle, all the Forward Thrust issues fell short of the necessary 60 percent, and only one, a health and safety measure, got even 50 percent. The initiative to reject the Seattle Center site received over 60 percent approval, 149,592 to 96,526. Outside of Seattle, voters endorsed the stadium initiative 83,000 to 32,000. Even in the city, voters rejected the Seattle Center site by 66,500 to 64,600. In September, the state supreme court made its final ruling, saying that because the transit property had not yet been paid for and "irrevocable preparations" for the stadium had not yet been made, the vote would stand. The civic leaders, whose vision usually encompassed the entire region, had focused too narrowly on their own interests—the well-being of downtown. They had not made a particularly persuasive argument for building the stadium at Seattle Center, and they fudged the expenditure figures for the project as a whole. The initiative process could be troublesome, but it demonstrated that if the city fathers, including even Carlson and Gandy, strayed off course, the people still controlled their city's destiny. Once again, irony afflicted Seattle. For most of the downtown leaders, building a stadium for major league sports was part of becoming big league, but pushing hard to locate the arena at the Seattle Center alienated the populace, bringing embarrassment to the striving city.[22]

Some were bitter. "The story has not had a happy ending. . . . We were defeated in an off-beat election," Gandy lamented. He did not see how a stadium could be built anywhere. Georg Meyers seemed to hold out hope. "It is never too late for a new start," he began brightly. "The first thing is to pick a new site." But his conclusion gave away his frustration. "You pick the site, I'll circulate the petitions." Apparently focusing on the petitioners and missing the magnitude of the vote at the May election, the *Post-Intelligencer* claimed that a small group had thwarted the stadium, the Bay Freeway, and Forward Thrust. Mayor Wes Uhlman agreed that a stadium, anywhere, seemed dead. A few people were still believers. Spellman thought that it could be done for $40 million, even including the lost expenditures for drawing up plans for the Seattle Center project. Another optimist was Ruano. He did not have a site in mind but advised the county to get going on it right away.[23]

John O'Brien had once warned that it would be Seattle Center or no stadium, but he was now ready to join Spellman in identifying a new site. When reminded that the new arena would be without a team because the Pilots had left town, O'Brien argued that a stadium was the only way to attract one. Spellman acknowledged that his was an "if we build it, they will come" strategy and argued that he was still after a multipurpose facility. Envisioning mainly a sports stadium, he believed that conventions—even national political conventions—or a Billy Graham crusade could be staged there. Spellman had an eye on the office of governor but denied that pushing the stadium through would enhance his stock with voters. Privately, his campaign staff was sure it would be an asset. The stadium had suffered a reversal, but the local political landscape had changed. In Spellman, sports boosters now had an important politician on their side. In June, the new Washington State Stadium Commission was in place. Dr. James L. Wilson, an M.D. from Bellevue, was chairman. Arnie Weinmeister of the Joint Labor Council, city councilmen Ted Best and Wayne Larkin, and county councilmen Ed Munro and William Reams made up the rest of the board.[24]

Their mandate was to find a location that could provide good parking, that was easily accessible, and that was central to the King County population base. The stadium commission contracted with a new group of consultants. It considered a wider range of options than the original commission had. An open stadium with an adjacent convention center joined the domed multipurpose stadium as a possibility. Also under consideration were the options of using Husky Stadium for football, upgrading Sicks' Stadium for baseball, and building a convention facility at Seattle Center, or some combination of these options. By August, the commission and its technical staff had pared down the choices from 150 to 17, and then to 5. At that point, things slowed down. Dr. Wilson pointedly remarked, "We inherited a basket of snakes," as he explained why the second stadium commission would be very deliberate in arriving at its final decision. The five choices were Seattle Center (unaccountably, considering the basket of snakes), the Riverton site, a location east of Longacres racetrack in Renton, just south of Seattle, King Street Station downtown, and south Seattle on Dearborn Street east of the interchange between I-5 and I-90. Despite Ruano's plea for South Park, it did not make the cut due to perceived difficulties in acquiring property. Ruano promised to block any downtown site.[25]

The possibility of upgrading Sicks' Stadium, which came up at one of the later hearings, appealed to the commission. A study indicated that the stadium could be enlarged to thirty-two thousand permanent seats, but any more than that would require purchasing additional property. Parking would also have to be built. Deliberations concluded in January 1971. (Had the Pilots still been in town, this would have been a month after the American League deadline for the initiation of construction.) The consultants chose the King Street location, just south of downtown, and the stadium commissioners agreed. King Street was the most accessible of all the options, and with help from the city, parking would be adequate or better. The Riverton site was plagued by soft soil; flood control was needed at the Longacres location in Renton; insufficient acres and acquisition headaches were problems for the Dearborn option; and Seattle Center somehow did not seem like a wise choice. The commission called for $9 million of councilmanic bonds to bolster the funds left from the $40 million bond issue after the Seattle Center fiasco. Just in case, it also recommended that if the King Street site did not work out, upgrading Sicks' and using Husky Stadium for football was a strong backup option. Ruano now threatened to overturn the original vote on the $40 million bonds.[26]

The county council accepted the recommendation. The arena would still be domed. Spellman claimed that it would still be multipurpose, but that was merely because it would be domed, affording protection from the weather for conventions and shows. There would be no separate meeting halls or smaller rooms—all events would have to take place on the main floor of the arena. Some hoped that the federal government might contribute to a separate nearby convention center. By December, county officials were making it clear that the new building would be austere. The plan was to build the stadium for $31 million and acquire the land, add parking, and pay taxes with $18 million. Despite Ruano's promise to sue if costs exceeded $40 million, the second try at locating the stadium had gone smoothly. Even without a team to occupy the structure, most leaders and regular citizens seemed satisfied . . . and it was still going to be downtown, in the same general area as Braman's Fifth and Yesler site and, most ironically, almost atop the location Ruano had originally suggested.[27]

Norris Poulson, mayor of Los Angeles when the Dodgers came to town, once commented, "Los Angeles is probably America's softest touch for a guy clutching a petition . . . [anyone] putting his mind to it could gather enough signatures in the city to outlaw orange juice." Seattleites, especially political leaders, could well believe that had Poulson met Frank Ruano, he would have included their city in his observation. Since 1966, Ruano had been almost as much a constant in Seattle stadium politics as Joe Gandy. But Ruano was forever the outsider, and that peeved him. Remembering the reception his suggestion for a stadium above the train tracks had received, Ruano said, "They gave me the brush-off. Just kicked me away. I said to myself, 'I'll just see what the hell I can do.'" These feelings intensified as Forward Thrust rejected his offers to serve. "My nose just got outta joint, I guess," Ruano recalled. Though bitterness marked his motives, Ruano also seemed intent on assuring that taxpayers got what they wanted for their money. The 1970 vote on the Seattle Center location demonstrated that his initiative drive overwhelmingly expressed the feelings of the voters. He claimed that he was a stadium proponent before and after the election, but after the vote, as he fancied himself a watchdog over expenditures, Ruano fell into the role of obstructionist. At least one official guessed that Ruano ended up costing taxpayers a million dollars.[28]

In late 1971, Ruano formed Citizens against Stadium Hoax. He was ready to circulate a petition to revoke the Forward Thrust vote on the stadium. By the end of December, he had the required twenty thousand signatures. Further, he asked that all work on the project halt until September 1972—voting day on the initiative. Echoing Norris Poulson, Spellman retorted that you just cannot stop governmental processes every time you get twenty thousand signatures on a petition. Ruano was not a bad guy, Spellman thought, but he was probably too tenacious for his own good. Ruano was not so politic toward Spellman, accusing him of hiding cost overruns from the public. The two were in another heated race. Spellman was trying to push the project far enough along so that a court could not halt what was already under way; Ruano wanted to keep the plans confined, literally, to the drawing board. King County Superior Court judge George R. Stuntz agreed with Spellman and dismissed Ruano's call for an injunction. Ruano gained a hearing in nearby Kitsap County Superior Court. Judge Olaf Johnson also agreed with King County and threw out the suit. Ruano appealed to the state supreme court, which put off a hearing until November 1972. In the meantime, the work on the stadium could go on, and there would be no September vote. When the state court ruled in favor of Spellman and King County in early 1973, Ruano's initiative was dead.[29]

Because Ruano lost at every turn, it might seem that these later suits were frivolous. But it did not seem so to those in the midst of all this. A letter writer told Spellman that Ruano's efforts made him a traitor to the community on the scale of Brutus, Judas, Aaron Burr, and Rudolph Hess. County officials took Ruano quite seriously, worrying that he was a major threat to getting the stadium done. At one point, Spellman sought to strike a compromise by setting up an independent watchdog commission to monitor expenditures. In return, Ruano would drop his suit. Ruano declined. He was not done. In late 1972, he circulated another petition opposing a city building permit for the stadium. A court ruled that he had not submitted enough signatures by the deadline. In 1974, when it was clear that the project was going to incur cost overruns, Ruano circulated one more petition, essentially to bar the county from using councilmanic bonds to fund the extra amount. The petition fell well short of the required number of signatures. When the stadium was completed in spring 1976, the "old" Frank Ruano, the man eager to see an arena built, emerged. Let's make the stadium work, he proclaimed. He declared that he had had his day in court and would support the operation of the Kingdome. "Sports is getting to be a sizable segment of our community," he observed. "Our city is growing up."[30]

Play-by-Play

AUGUST AND SEPTEMBER

BOTH hope and luck ran out in August. The Pilots played the worst baseball of the season, and by the end of the month, they had sunk to last in the Western Division. On the first of August, the Pilots, despite Milkes's angst, had been the star of the expansion crop with a record of forty-three wins and fifty-eight losses. The Kansas City Royals were close, at forty-two wins and sixty losses, but Montreal and San Diego were thirty-six and thirty-seven games under .500 respectively. For a while, the team played near its season's pace; then, in mid-August, the wheels came off.

As the month started at home, the shaky pitching got shakier. Marty Pattin could get only one out in the second inning before he left the game and the rotation. The Yankees completed a three-game series sweep on August 3 with a 5–3 win, scoring all their runs off Steve Barber in the first. It was Seafair race day. As the hydroplanes tooled around Lake Washington, the Pilots drew their largest crowd of the season, 23,657, with a shrewdly scheduled bat day. Although the club slipped to fourth place, they were not done yet. The team made some personnel adjustments as it went out on the road. Steve Whitaker (acquired in the Lou Piniella trade) went to Vancouver. Dick Simpson came off the disabled list as Mike Hegan prepared to leave for military reserve duty. Between the reserves and leg aches, Hegan had only eleven at bats from July 6 to August 6.

Out on the road, the Pilots opened in fine form against the Red Sox. Gene Brabender pitched a complete game, Tommy Harper stole bases fifty and fifty one, and Tommy Davis was getting hotter. He went three for five and added to his team-leading total of sixty-two runs batted in for

the Pilots' 9–2 win. The second game in Boston was one of the most grati-
fying of the season. Down 4–2 in the seventh inning, the Pilots staged
a comeback to tie and then win 6–5 in the tenth. Joe Schultz exulted
that Wayne Comer, Davis, Jerry McNertney, and Hegan just "never know
when they're whipped." The Sox turned the tables the next night for what
the *Seattle Post-Intelligencer*'s Lenny Anderson called the "most agonizing
reversal" of the season.[1]

Moving on to Washington, D.C., the Pilots lost two out of three to
the team they usually beat up on. Injuries once again plagued the Seattle team. Ray Oyler went out with a knee injury for a couple of weeks,
and Simpson reinjured his leg. Milkes sold infielder Gordy Lund to the
Angels. The road trip ended in Cleveland, where the Pilots won two of
three games. The team clung tenaciously to third. They had won five out
of nine games on the road, Davis had an eighteen-game hitting streak,
and Harper was at fifty-six stolen bases.

Then home and the deluge. Without playing really miserable baseball,
and continuing to strive as they had all season, the Pilots nonetheless
suffered a ten-game losing streak. The home stand started with one of
the season's best human interest stories. Billy Williams (not the Cub
outfielder, but a minor league journeyman) had just been called up. Williams, an African American, had grown up in the hardscrabble mining
town (he described it as just a camp) of Clincho, Virginia. He had labored
for seventeen years in the minors, stuck at the Triple-A level for the last
eight. He was asked to manage a minor league club in 1967 but turned it
down because it was in the South and he did not want to risk encountering racial problems. There were tears in the eyes of the thirty-five-year-
old as he signed his first major league contract. When asked if he was
nervous, he replied, "Nervous. You be scared to death." Williams, whose
fall-back job was a clothing store partnership in Berkeley, California, had
achieved his lifelong goal. This was not just an expansion team courtesy,
not with Marvin Milkes at the helm. Williams had earned the call-up. He
was leading the Pacific Coast League in RBIs and gave the Pilots a needed
right-handed hitter.[2]

Though he was released after only ten days and went hitless in
twelve plate appearances, Williams was in the mix right away. Schultz
brought him into the first Baltimore game as a pinch runner in the seventh inning. Williams was on third base when Harper laid down a bunt.
Baltimore pitcher Mike Cuellar shoveled the ball with his glove hand to

catcher Ellie Hendricks. Umpire Frank Umont called Williams out. Williams trotted to the dugout and then was astounded to see that the clubs were changing sides. He was sure that he had been safe, and so were most of the Pilots. Even sportswriters from Baltimore differed with Umont. The run would have tied the score 2–2, but the Orioles hung on to win 2–1. The loss turned out to be the beginning of the end. The next night saw the Orioles ring up Diego Segui and Pattin 15–3. On August 17, the Pilots were still in third place. It would be the last time. Don Mincher hit his twenty-first home run, Harper stole his fifty-eighth base, and Fred Talbot went into the seventh inning having given up only two runs. It was not enough—Orioles 4, Pilots 1. The Baltimore club completed the sweep against George Brunet 12–3.[3]

Brabender started against Detroit and again pitched like the stopper he was, giving up only four earned runs into the ninth. Mickey Lolich pitched better. He struck out fourteen Pilots and picked off three base runners. The next night, Seattle staged one of its frequent come-from-behind performances to tie the Tigers 6–6. Then, in the eighth, trying to avoid a walk, knuckleballer Jim Bouton fed Mickey Stanley a 3–2 fastball. Stanley hit it out of the park for the winning run. It was the Pilots' seventh loss in a row.

Next in was Cleveland. August 22 was Tommy Harper Night, honoring the team's top attraction, who had now stolen sixty-one bases. Harper went two for four, and Tommy Davis had three hits, but to no avail, as the pitching and defense broke down. Cleveland won 9–8. The home stand ended with two more losses, to bring the streak to ten. The home team had been out-homered sixteen to six. They were winless in thirteen home games in August.

Marvin Milkes added a testy exclamation point to the streak as the home stand concluded on August 24. Reporters queried him about the state of the team, including Schultz's future. Milkes provided anything but a ringing endorsement for his manager, saying, "No, I haven't made up my mind on Joe's contract but I do want something done about our 1970 manager before the World Series." Milkes went on about the third-place prediction. "Sure, some people say Schultz is under undue pressure on the statement attributed to me that the Pilots could finish third in their division. But remember, Joe made the prediction first. . . . Yes, I will be a little sick if we don't end up third or fourth, because I feel we have built a club capable of this. If we don't go that high, I won't jump off any bridges in this city, either." But he was pointed about Schultz. "I feel Joe's made some mistakes, but so have I. Some maintain a manager who is loved—presumably by players and fans alike—should be retained. Well, I'm not conducting a 'Love-In.' I'm running a major league baseball team." His pique extended to the team, or at least the pitching. "I'm very perturbed about our pitching staff," Milkes declared. "This club has not collapsed, but most of our pitchers have. The biggest disappointment is we have experienced pitchers—admittedly not the top ones in baseball—who continue to make mistakes." Finally, he gave some insight into the pressure to win. "If we draw only six to seven hundred thousand on a budget geared to a million attendance, that makes a tougher operation too." Clearly, Milkes and the Sorianos had been discussing something more than third place all season. From the beginning, attendance had not matched expectations, and the situation was growing worse. The losing streak had dragged attendance down to 6,000 a game during the last week of the home stand. That projected to 670,000 for the season (just 7,000 less than the final actual total), and that was not enough to break even or, as it turned out, even stay afloat.[4]

Reaction was immediate. Georg Meyers pointed out that players do not perform well when they feel insecure, and that is precisely the atmosphere Milkes had created. Moreover, the finger could be pointed at the general manager. "Joe's job is to manage the players the general manager provides," Meyers observed. "Given a pitcher who can get a batter out, Schultz may win another game sometime." He concluded his column by reminding Milkes that the woeful 1962 Mets drew well because the franchise had given the fans ownership of their team. "Now THAT was a love in," Meyers concluded. Hy Zimmerman quoted Bob Locker at length. The relief pitcher thought that "Schultz got the best out of everyone, had the club playing without pressure." Zimmerman hoped Milkes would be wise enough to soften his rhetoric in the face of comments like Locker's but knew that the general manager did not like to be pushed. The *Post-Intelligencer* began to poll the fans on Schultz's fate. They voted overwhelmingly, 3,227 to 53, to keep the manager. Several commented that it was not the skipper who threw the gopher balls and lauded Schultz for turning Tommy Harper loose on the bases and keeping the team scrapping to the end of every game.[5]

Brabender finally brought the losing streak to an end on August 26 with a complete-game victory in the first tilt on the road. The Pilots defeated Baltimore 2–1 on a Tommy Davis home run and run-scoring single. After the game, the players made it clear that they knew what, or whom, they were playing for.

Gene Brabender: "This one was for the skipper. . . . Through the streak, Joe tried his hardest to keep us up, to keep us plugging. And we kept fighting."[6]

Don Mincher: "Yes, the [pregame] meeting was about Joe Schultz. All these words about his being too nice a guy as a manager bugged us. We are 110 percent for Joe—and not because he is a nice guy, because he has been a man through everything, through victory and defeat."[7]

Jim Pagliaroni: "I never saw 25 guys pull so hard for a man as these for Joe Schultz."[8]

Tommy Davis: "I'm really grateful to Joe for letting me stay in the lineup and work it out. He's one of the best managers I ever played under. He's a real good guy."[9]

After the breath of fresh air, the team started another losing streak that stretched to six games and into the first of September. That made it sixteen losses out of seventeen games played and sent the Pilots plummeting into the cellar, where they landed on August 29. They would be looking up from sixth place, and briefly from fifth, the rest of the year. It was time to deal for 1970 and beyond. The team called up reliever Skip Lockwood from Elmira and released Williams. Bouton went to Houston in exchange for right-hander Dooley Womack and pitching prospect Roric Harrison. The Pilots shipped Talbot to Oakland for minor league pitcher Bob Meyer and right-hand power prospect Pete Koegel. Then it was Tommy Davis's turn. He had raised his average to .275 and had a team-leading eighty RBIs as he kept his team in games even as they lost, but Milkes saw a good opportunity for the future. It was a good trade for the team. Houston sent infielder Sandy Valdespino and hard-hitting minor leaguer Danny Walton to Seattle in exchange.

August had been a disaster. The Seattle club went from third place to sixth. Its August record was six wins and twenty-two losses, with no home wins. Injuries played a big part, but, with the exception of Brabender, the pitching was atrocious. Pattin lost his command and probably wore out. Talbot shone for a bit and then fell on hard times. Even Segui was inconsistent. The Pilots' spirit seemed intact into September, but the thin line of talent that typifies expansion teams (especially those loaded with veterans whose talents and durability are suspect) gave way, and there were few reserves (Steve Hovley, Greg Goossen, perhaps John Gelnar) who could take up the slack that the injuries and slumps had created.

The beginning of September saw some of the new Pilots in the lineup alongside year-end call-ups. The pitching strengthened toward the end of the season as well. After a 6–1 loss to Mel Stottlemeyer in the first game of a doubleheader in New York, Meyer pitched nine innings in the second game and gave up only one run. Segui, then Womack, held the Yankees for three more innings, and Seattle won 5–1 on a three-run home run in the twelfth by Mike Hegan, who had returned to the lineup. The next day, the Pilots were vexed by umpire Larry Barnett's crucial obstruction call against Brabender, who was pitching in relief. Brabender had caught Horace Clarke in a rundown between third base and home plate in the fourteenth. Barnett called obstruction and sent Clarke home with the tying run. Seattle lost 5–4 and was mathematically eliminated from winning the division. Brabender's heated comments after the game were telling. "We're an expansion club and we go out there and break our backs trying to win and they do things like this to us," he complained. "It happens all the time. It's happened all season long."[10]

Close games would hound the club throughout September. The team came home on September 4 and lost to Kansas City but then beat them the next day 5–4. It was the first home victory since July 30, a fifteen-game streak. Brabender was once again the streak breaker, pitching a seven-hitter. The other big news was that for the first time in Seattle baseball history, attendance topped 600,000. Only 4,744 fans came out to the game, but it pushed the season mark to 604,089. After a four-game split with the Royals, the Pilots swept a doubleheader with the White Sox. Miguel Fuentes, up from the Clinton farm club, promised, through interpreter Sandy Valdespino, to throw strikes. He did. Fuentes pitched a complete-game seven-hitter and won 5–1. Schultz, feeling no need for a translator, congratulated the twenty-year-old, "Atta boy, Miguel. No base-o on balls." The Pilots then traveled to Oakland and split a two-game series. Brabender picked up his twelfth win, but the Seattle club was now mathematically eliminated from second.[11]

Back at home, the team peeked out of the cellar for a day, then fell back with a thud as they split with the Angels. Segui won the game in relief, 6–4, for his eleventh victory of the season. The team then went on a string of mainly one-run games that were mostly losses. The rotation, outside of Brabender, was not really set, but starters and relievers did some of their best work of the year. Brabender set the record for expansion team wins by a pitcher with thirteen as he beat the Royals at Kansas City 3–2 on September 15. Three of the next four games were 2–1, each a loss for the Pilots. Then it was Brabender, relieved by Segui—the Pilots' best pitching combination—losing 3–2 to Minnesota's Jim Perry on September 20. A 4–3 win in Minnesota, a 5–4 win at Anaheim, and a 5–4 loss to the Angels rounded out the streak of eight one-run games out of nine played. The loss to the Angels extinguished the Pilots' last hopes of taking third place. It also marked the end of Walton's debut with the team when he dislocated his knee. He batted only .228 but hit some smashes that promised more in future seasons. Brabender made a bid to extend his expansion franchise streak with a five-hitter, but the Angels prevailed 3–1. During the series in Southern California, a chain saw company "honored" Ray Oyler with an enormous bat. It was, the company said, the biggest bat for the smallest batting average (.156 at the time) for a regular major leaguer. Oyler, perhaps buoyed by his Seattle fan club experience, accepted the award with good humor.

A seven-game home stand rounded out the season. The strong pitching continued. Steve Barber had what was probably his best outing of the year. He struck out ten over eight innings to defeat the Western Division champion Twins 5–1 but still complained of pain in his arm. The next night, the teams used a record forty-four players in fourteen innings. The Pilots came out on top when Comer blasted a game-winning home run. Gelnar, who had not won since June 25, was ecstatic about ending his nine-game losing streak. The next day, the two teams split. The loss eliminated the Pilots from fourth place. (Milkes, true to his word, did not plunge from a bridge.) Mincher got his twenty-fifth home run in the second game, which saw him drive in three for his career-best 79 RBIs on the season. On September 30, the Pilots lost 8–4 to Oakland—even though Brabender was striving for his fourteenth win—-and clinched sole occupancy of the Western Division cellar. On October 1, Segui got his twelfth win in relief and nailed down the team's best winning percentage at twelve wins to six losses. Thursday night, October 2, the Pilots played their last regular season game, a loss. Only 5,473 came out on a cool evening to see Barber give up three in the third inning and Whitaker homer in a 3–1 loss to Oakland.

Seattle stabilized in the last month and couple of days of the season, with fifteen wins and seventeen losses, compiling a final record of sixty-four and ninety-eight, a .395 winning percentage for the year. The Pilots finished thirty-three games behind first-place Minnesota. Their record was better than the average expansion team, and it would tie the 1977 mark of the Seattle Mariners. Tommy Harper was the standout of the Pilots' season with a league-leading seventy-three stolen bases. Greg Goossen hit .309 and Mike Hegan .292. Don Mincher's twenty-five home runs added up to a robust total. Bob Locker posted a 2.49 ERA over seventy-six innings, but Diego Segui was an innings eater with 142 innings and a winner at twelve wins and six losses. The other workhorse was Gene Brabender, with 202 innings and thirteen wins. In comparison, there were a dozen twenty-game winners in the majors in 1969. Harmon Killebrew hit forty-nine home runs. The Pilots won the season series against the Washington Senators and split with the Red Sox and Angels. They could manage only five wins in twenty-four games against Detroit and Baltimore combined. They played fifty-eight one-run games and won twenty-six. Despite the horrific August at home, the Pilots had a better home winning percentage (.420) than road record (.370). More than anything, pitching was a drag on the record. The staff gave up 172 home runs, only 20 less than the 1962 Mets, who played in the Polo Grounds—at least as accommodating as Sicks' Stadium to round-trippers. Opponents scored in double digits sixteen times, and the team lost by five or more runs twenty-six times.[12]

Joe Schultz's review of the season substantially reflects this array of statistics, but his memories bring some emotion to the numbers. When asked about his highs and lows, Schultz talked about opening day in Seattle and Gary Bell's shutout. He especially savored the 16–13 comeback win against the Senators in May and the first road trip east, when the Pilots won three series. It was fitting that he cited Harper's base running, since he was the one who had urged the player to steal as many as he could. Schultz's lows were all lodged in August. Series with Baltimore and Detroit took up almost all of the second half of the month. It was a tough schedule and, as it turned out, an insurmountable hurdle as the club went one and twelve. The other disappointment, which fed into the first, was the injuries, especially those that took out Hegan, Kennedy, Rollins, and Barber. As easily as a sabermetrician might solve an equation, the baseball man had succinctly explained, to Marvin Milkes or any questioning fan, why the Seattle Pilots had failed to finish in third place.[13]

Chapter 9

THE CIVIC LEADERS STRIKE OUT

URING the 1969–70 off-season, the American League dithered over the fate of the Pilots. Team owners viscerally exult in being number one, yet each understands that exerting dominance over a long period is harmful to the rest of the league and to his own team's finances. A perpetual loser is an even greater threat to the rest of the league's economic well-being. Early on, major league baseball parlayed this understanding into an exemption from antitrust laws, specifically the Sherman Antitrust Act of 1890. Baseball, alone among professional sports, runs its business and plants its franchises without fear of interference from the federal government. Most recently, in the 1953 Toolson decision, the Supreme Court tossed the matter of extending or limiting the antitrust exemption into the lap of Congress. Though baseball has always been particularly solicitous of congressmen, especially U.S. senators who represent the areas where franchises operate, owners exercised substantial power in the age of expansion and franchise transfers. Cities compete for a limited supply of teams. The result? Each owner has a good deal of leverage. If attendance flags, if the local government refuses to provide a decent—or better than decent—stadium, an owner can threaten to leave. The major leagues have been careful to leave a few markets open. Cities without a franchise sing the siren song of promises that lures owners dissatisfied with their current situation or wait patiently for the ripe fruit of a franchise on the move to drop into what is often an empty and available arena. Cities at risk have a few defenses. A better stadium or more favorable lease can be an enticement to stay. The threat of a suit against the franchise owner or the entire league might make both parties think twice before relocation. Such suits, however, almost necessarily revolve around the very antitrust laws to which baseball is immune.[1]

None of this should have had any bearing on the Pilots' situation in 1970. The team had not drawn well, but home receipts were only $180,000 less than those of the pennant-winning Baltimore Orioles. Relations with City Hall were not good, but there was a new mayor. At the time, baseball had moved a team after one season only once in its history (when, ironically, the Milwaukee Brewers left for Saint Louis to become the Browns). Two of the most powerful men in the United States Senate represented Washington: Warren Magnuson and Henry Jackson. If the Pilots left, they could make the rage of Missouri senator Stuart Symington, whose wrath had swayed the owners in 1967, look like a zephyr. Moreover, St. Louis outfielder Curt Flood's ultimately unsuccessful legal attack on the reserve clause, which began in January 1970, made the owners more than a little sensitive to the status of their precious exemption. Baseball had plenty of motivation to see that its wayward new franchise in the Northwest got its act together and stayed put. But that did not happen, and many share the blame. The record of Pacific Northwest Sports, Inc., had been spotty. American League owners did a poor job of studying the Seattle market and evaluating the Pilots ownership. The owners set themselves up for a dilemma and then, during the 1969–70 off-season, demonstrated timid and ineffective leadership as they tried to escape it. Finally, though the top leaders of Seattle expended a good deal of effort to save the team, the final months of the Seattle Pilots' tenure in the city once again brought Seattle chagrin.[2]

Rumors of the impossible, a move from Seattle after one season, began to circulate at the end of August 1969. *Houston Chronicle* sportswriter John Wilson reported that William Daley had made a tacit agreement to sell the Pilots to Lamar Hunt, Dallas oil and football magnate, and Tommy Mercer, Fort Worth baseball man. The *Seattle Post-Intelligencer* asked Dewey Soriano about the report. Soriano, whose patience with the mayor, the city, and the press had long since evaporated, replied snappishly, "I know nothing about it . . . I thought the *P-I* would have it figured out. They have been experts on everything else about the Pilots." A week later, when Mayor Floyd Miller's talk of eviction grew serious, Hunt and Mercer sent a telegram to the Pilots inviting them to finish the 1969 season at their Turnpike Stadium in Arlington, Texas. American League offices were already getting an earful. Orioles owner Jerry Hoffberger had warned league president Joe Cronin in mid-August that the domed stadium was in trouble. Costs would exceed the budgeted $40 million, Frank Ruano's initiative efforts might kill the stadium, and the follow-the-club contract with Sportservice, the concessionaire, might not be enforceable in the new stadium. Hoffberger's source for all this was Alan Ferguson, the head of Rainier Brewery. Cronin sent out aide Andrew Williams to ascertain whether the new stadium would be built in a timely manner, check on the concessions contract, and determine whether the Pilots could move if a suitable stadium could not be completed.[3]

As the 1969 season was in its final month, bickering between the ownership and sportswriters began to mirror the squabble between Pilots officials and the city. In an interview, Daley reviewed his grievances over the Sicks' Stadium lease and his concerns about starting the domed stadium in time and then lit into the local leadership: "We don't seem to be getting support from the Seattle business people. If I continue to get the brush-off I'm going to lose interest too."[4]

Hy Zimmerman had no use for this kind of talk, especially from someone he considered an outsider. Zimmerman's favorite sport was boxing, and it fit his personality. He was intense, willingly combative, and even described himself as "brusque," "abrupt," and liable to stomp on toes. Fellow journalist Don Duncan observed, "You'd swear Damon Runyon invented [Hy]." In early September, Zimmerman was fed up with both the city administration and PNSI and wrote a column condemning the bickering between the two parties as childish. Zimmerman thought that the city and the Pilots could still work it out, but criticized Mayor Miller for embarrassing the city and blamed Dewey Soriano's constant carping and high ticket prices for alienating the fans. After venting his rage, he held out a bit of hope for a situation that he described as a mess. "The public," he optimistically observed, "is bigger than its leaders."[5]

Neither Daley nor Zimmerman was through. In late September 1969, the press asked Daley about his plans for the team. (No one but American League insiders seemed to know that Daley had promised to underwrite the Pilots for $8 million during hard times, and the league never held him to his pledge.) Daley now admitted that he had met with interests from Dallas–Fort Worth but allowed that he would give Seattle one more year to prove itself. Joe Cronin remembered the scene. Cronin and Daley were eating in the ballpark press room where a reporter (Zimmerman?) kept pestering Daley about how long he might keep the team in the Northwest, and Daley was becoming upset. Cronin thought that Daley may have responded, "Yes," to the query "Will you stay one more year?" Cronin, the better politician, kept his poise under pressure. He was asked about the schedule for the new stadium, since, by this time, the decision to locate it at Seattle Center had come under attack. He mumbled generalities about a slow start and that people downtown wanted it downtown.[6]

Zimmerman went on the warpath against Daley. In a column titled "Won't You Go Home, Bill Daley?" he led off with his layman's definition of public relations: "Getting the customer and the public on your side, getting them to respect and like you, to feel a kinship of sorts with you." He then compared Daley's comments with the comments of fellow expansion owner Buzzie Bavasi of San Diego. On the one hand, Zimmerman said, Bavasi held out carrots, assuring interviewers that he understood why people in San Diego were reluctant to come out to see a losing team and promising that the franchise would do better by its fans. Daley, on the other hand, went for the stick, suggesting that Dallas–Fort Worth might be a possibility after one more season. Zimmerman concluded, "The area's baseball fans, considering the circumstances in which they watched the Pilots, at no small outlay, deserve a salute, not a slap. . . . Rudely we say to our baseball caliph from Cleveland, 'Take your ball club.'" Zimmerman's less volatile colleague Georg Meyers also responded to Daley's semi-ultimatum, writing, "That's upside-down, isn't it? What we're really doing is giving Daley one more chance" to market his team better, cease the wrangling, and avoid ultimatums in the future.[7]

There was speculation about whether Daley was willing to wait even a year. A week after Zimmerman's column, the *Post-Intelligencer* reported that "harsh criticism from Seattle has not brightened [Daley's] view of the situation." Bowie Kuhn later stated, without being specific about the timing, that Daley had become disillusioned and decided to sell. Interestingly, the *Post-Intelligencer*'s Lenny Anderson, as easygoing as Zimmerman was explosive, found a good deal of significance in Cronin's noncommittal comments about the construction of the new stadium. Usually, Anderson noted, Cronin was the ebullient optimist. His lack of enthusiasm about the prospects for the domed stadium made Anderson think that the Pilots were in jeopardy. Others were more optimistic even if they considered immediate circumstances troubling. Earl Luebker of the *Tacoma News Tribune* and John Owen both predicted that the American League would back off any threats when Senators Magnuson and Jackson reminded them not to put their antitrust status in jeopardy.[8]

All of this was a backdrop to the actuality: the Pilots were for sale. When the Pilots played the Chicago White Sox in Milwaukee in mid-June, Lenny Anderson had poked around to get a story on the Milwaukee Brewers group that had formed to bring major league baseball back to its city. He found a well-funded, hardworking body that had unsuccessfully courted franchise after franchise after the Braves left. When Anderson wrote his story, the group was after the White Sox. At its head was Bud Selig, whom Anderson described as "a young, aggressive, total baseball fan and owner of an automobile sales and leasing agency." It had money and a stadium, along with a track record of 1.5 million in average attendance during the Braves' sojourn. In August, when relations with the City of Seattle began to deteriorate into enmity and threats of eviction filled the air, American League owners urged Selig to contact the Sorianos. Serious negotiations began around September 8, when Selig came to Seattle and continued—even while Daley was promising (or threatening) one more year—into October. In the meantime, on September 24, the Bank of California called in its $3.5 million loan "because of losses and apparent insolvency of the borrower." The Pilots owners and Brewers representatives met in the Bird Feed Room in Baltimore on October 11 during the first game of the World Series. Soriano had asked $13.5 million for the franchise, and Selig had countered with $9 million. They made a handshake deal for $10.8 million.[9]

As soon as the deal was made, everyone went into full denial. Daley claimed that he was happy with the Puget Sound region but asserted that, with the concerns over Sicks' and whether the new stadium would be built in a timely manner—or at all—the league would have to decide whether to keep the franchise in Seattle. After a meeting among Cronin, Dewey Soriano, and other league officials, which everyone denied had taken place, Max Soriano announced that it was all in the league's hands. Dewey Soriano also spoke pessimistically. He expected the league owners to declare that the city had failed to meet their agreement, especially in regard to Sicks'. Cronin's private note to Daley during the World Series indicated that neither he nor the league would be the fall guy for a franchise shift, even though the Pilots consistently insisted that any decision was up to the league. "I don't think," Cronin wrote, "there's a Chinaman's chance of anybody wanting to move out of Seattle." Cronin scheduled an American League meeting for October 20 in which a number of the owners would discuss the Seattle situation with a Northwest contingent representing the city, county, and private interests.[10]

In the interim, Seattleites wrung their hands. In an October 1969 editorial, Lloyd Cooney, executive vice president of KIRO TV, caught the real significance of losing the franchise, whether one was a sports fan or not. If the Pilots left, it would jeopardize the stadium, which in turn would have a negative impact on next May's second Forward Thrust vote, particularly the transit issue. Cooney thought residents expected their civic leaders to maintain Seattle's sense of vigor, which had started with the world's fair, led to Forward Thrust, and brought the baseball team. If the team left, momentum would reverse, and Seattle would likely take a step backward that would go beyond merely the loss of major league baseball. The *Seattle Times* agreed, and the *Tacoma News Tribune* thought the loss of the Pilots would be "a severe blot on the Northwest's image as a major league territory."[11]

Dewey Soriano and John Owen got into a spat. Owen was not sympathetic to PNSI's complaints about financial losses. The *Post-Intelligencer* sports editor pointed out that Charlie Finley made money with lower prices and only 100,000 more in attendance. He noted that Seattle outdrew the expansion San Diego Padres, which were not for sale, and that the other National League expansion team, Montreal, made do with only a few more seats than Sicks' but drew 1.2 million fans. Pressing his point, Owen concluded that the reason for the threatened move was that a $13 million purchase price yielded a nice return on an investment of $5 million. Soriano fired back that it was Owen who had played up the seat prices early on, giving the team a black eye. Owen retorted, "The Pilot management has incurred the displeasure of a lot of Seattle sports fans, and if you don't believe that come look at my mail someday."[12]

The *Argus* was even more critical. Characterizing Pilots ownership as "panhandlers," it asked rhetorically, what does Seattle have to prove? That it can enlarge Daley's bank account while overlooking his bad manners? For his part, Daley spoke to the two Milwaukee newspapers, expressing admiration for their city and slamming Seattle. He set forth the usual complaints: lack of support among the business community, lack of seats at Sicks' Stadium, and lack of hot water in the showers.[13]

The waters were roiling by the October 20 American League meeting in Chicago. PNSI had its not-entirely-secret handshake deal with the Brewers, and Daley openly told the *Milwaukee Journal* that he "would be happy to come to Milwaukee, if we could get permission from the American League and the commissioner." He also told the *Journal* that he had a solid offer from Dallas–Fort Worth. Seattle's delegation to the meeting included Charles Carroll, Dave Cohn, Joe Gandy, John Spellman, and representatives from Senators Magnuson and Jackson. Floyd Miller was attending a conference of U.S. and Japanese mayors but let it be known that, in his opinion, "the plight of the Pilots is due to poor management." Commenting on the ongoing initiative campaign to relocate the domed stadium from Seattle Center, the mayor warned, "The league is in a poor position to second guess what might or might not happen in an election which may not be held." The messages from Magnuson and Jackson to Cronin and Commissioner Bowie Kuhn went well beyond the mayor's mere admonitions. On October 8, they wrote, "We feel that there is *no* good reason for the threatened move." On October 16, Magnuson spelled it out. "If the people who control major league baseball, will allow franchises to move from city to city 'willy nilly for purely commercial reasons,'" they are transgressing the ruling that theirs is a sport, not a business. Magnuson promised to press Congress to repeal baseball's antitrust exemption if the Pilots left Seattle. Despite all the threats, Charles Carroll admitted to the *Milwaukee Sentinel*, "It is mostly a show for the home folks. I think that [the move] is inevitable." Daley was not so sure but revealed his hopes for a move, saying, "I know there are some owners in favor of a move but I wouldn't know if *we* had enough votes" (emphasis added).[14]

So when the Seattle delegation met with Cronin and six owners— Bob Reynolds of the Angels, Jerry Hoffberger of the Orioles, the Senators' Bob Short, Twins owner Cal Griffith, Gabe Paul of the Indians, and the Tigers' John Fetzer—it was like going to the principal's office. Short and Hoffberger were skeptical at best and, at worst, ready to recommend a transfer. Cronin assured the delegation that the league had no meetings scheduled to consider shifting the Pilots, but everyone knew Seattle was battling for its baseball club. The Seattle spokesmen rather weakly defended the condition of Sicks' Stadium, but the central message was that the new stadium was on track and would be built, despite Ruano's petition. Hoffberger was doubtful, based on the city's failed promises on Sicks' and his understanding that the county could not finish the new stadium for $40 million. Everyone agreed that if the domed stadium were not completed, the American League had every right to remove the franchise. Spellman then revealed that Seattleite Fred Danz was willing to buy the franchise. It is not clear what swayed the group (Fetzer had called a franchise shift "morally wrong," and Cronin was keenly aware of the position of the two senators from Washington), but by the end of the meeting, the Pilots were still docked in Seattle. Cronin reiterated that the terms of the original franchise agreement must be met but denied that he was issuing an ultimatum. Sicks' must be improved, the new stadium had to be under way by the end of 1970, and, now, new owners had to come forth by the end of the month. Cronin was done with Dewey Soriano. He later remarked that Soriano's disagreements with City Hall were as vexing as the actual status of Sicks'. In October 1969, Cronin thought the Pilots had a chance to stay if Soriano would leave. Cronin added that the "league did not want to welsh on a commitment," but "Seattle was on thin ice." Seattle would have to work hard and work fast. The *Milwaukee Journal* did some hopeful nose counting around the American League after the meeting. The Angels and Tigers wanted the Pilots to stay in Seattle, the Red Sox and Yankees were neutral, and although the seven other owners were for a move, it required nine votes.[15]

The day after the Chicago meeting, Daley announced that he would comply with the league's desires and give a Seattle buyer a chance at ownership. He would also reduce the price for a local owner. The names of potential owners other than Danz were also floating around. Dave Cohn was excited but frustrated. He yearned to be a baseball owner but had no idea where to come up with the money. Tacoma's Ben Cheney, a lumberman who owned a partial stake in the San Francisco Giants, was a possibility, but he preferred to continue to assist Tacoma's minor league operations. Mystery man Fred Ruge said he was ready and able to pay $11.5 million for the Pilots. Besides his claim that he was from Alaska, not much was known about him, and the local papers did not seem to know that Dewey Soriano had formally accepted his offer to buy as of October 28. (The Pilots soon rejected the offer because Ruge could not come up with the money.) The *Times* caught up with Ruge in early November, labeling him a possible buyer who could even build a stadium. Two weeks later, the *Post-Intelligencer* gleefully revealed that Ruge had turned himself in for grand larceny. He owed the Roosevelt Hotel $900 for lodging in May and June. The Fred Ruge initiative appeared over.[16]

Facing an almost impossible nine-day deadline, pondering the domino effect of the Pilots' demise on the stadium, on the second Forward Thrust vote, and on Seattle's image, and knowing that there would be little leadership from City Hall, Seattle's civic leaders galvanized for action. The fifty-one-year-old Danz, who would lead the effort, was the head of Sterling Recreation Organization, which his father, John Danz, had founded. It owned fifty theaters, several bowling alleys, some radio stations, and a racetrack. He was not excited to be a prominent actor in civic affairs and had attended only one Pilots game, but he was willing to spearhead the campaign to save the team. He later remembered, "It was important for the greater Seattle area to emerge as one of the top cities in the country." Danz, his attorney Charles Burdell, and Zollie Volchok, Northwest Releasing impresario and future general manager of the Sonics, had already met with Daley in Chicago, where they had sounded out purchase possibilities. Daley reiterated his antipathy toward the press and the community but assured the group that he was willing to sell, even at a discount, to a Seattle contingent.[17]

On October 23, Ed Carlson, who publicly deferred to Danz but seems to have been the instigator of the effort, sent out a letter to a group of "good friends," asking them to meet him in the Pacific Evergreen Room of Carlson's Olympic Hotel for a meaningful civic effort—to save the Pilots. The letter went to an army of familiar civic notables. James Ellis, Joe Gandy, and Dave Cohn would be there. Carlson invited Paul Friedlander, a leader of Seattle's cultural community. Business owners and leaders such as James Douglas (Northgate), M. Lamont Bean (Pay 'n' Save drugstores), Leo Weisfield (jewelry), Lloyd Nordstrom (department stores), D. E. Skinner (Alaska Steamship), Walter Schoenfeld (furniture stores), Thomas Bolger (Pacific Northwest Bell), W. G. Campbell (Bank of California, which held the $3.5 million loan to PNSI), and Mechlin Moore (Central Association) were on the list. Carlson invited media leaders Ross Cunningham of the *Times*, Lou Guzzo of the *Post-Intelligencer*, and KIRO's Lloyd Cooney. From Seattle were Councilman Charles M. Carroll and mayor's aides Ed Devine and Robert Lavoie; John Spellman and John O'Brien represented King County.[18]

Ever conscious of his invitees' busy schedules, Carlson outlined the agenda and allotted five to fifteen minutes to each speaker. The entire meeting was to last no more than an hour and a quarter. There would be an explanation of the gathering, a report on the Chicago meeting with the American League, and news on the stadium project (not yet begun and under the threat of Ruano's initiative campaign), and then Danz would speak on financial costs and prospects for the purchase. Ellis was responsible for explaining the public implications of losing the franchise. Carlson jotted down the gist of Ellis's remarks on his agenda sheet: "Public confidence in community leadership will be seriously threatened if we lose the ball club and fail to deliver on the promise of the multi-purpose stadium." Privately, Ellis put it even more personally. He and Carlson had promised the people that a stadium would bring major league sports; they would have egg on their faces if they lost the Pilots. Ellis continued his presentation by underlining the threat to Forward Thrust and, particularly, rapid transit. If listeners did not pick up on that message, Carlson, after relaying assurances of support from Magnuson and Jackson, rammed home the message. In order to keep the club in Seattle, the team needed to sell 800,000–1,000,000 tickets. The Pilots and, directly connected to them, the domed stadium and Forward Thrust needed community and business support. "The group present at this meeting," reads Carlson's notes for his speech, "can decide whether Seattle is or is not a Major League City!"[19]

The next day, Carlson wired Daley that more than sixty businessmen had attended the meeting, extended their appreciation for Daley's purchase of the Pilots, and expressed their willingness to work with him, since Daley would be one of the partners in the Danz deal. Carlson ended by saying that they looked forward to "many years of pleasant association" with Daley. This was someone who understood just how problematic Zimmerman's "Won't You Go Home, Bill Daley?" column could be. On the same day, he wrote to Joe Cronin, assuring him of wide civic support for Danz's bid. Within two days, the *Times* made the customary proclamation that the Seattle Spirit was alive. Emmett Watson defended public expenditure on baseball, or a multipurpose stadium, by reminding his readers that "the argument is for a 'total city' where we can have opera, arts, symphony, and sports." Baseball just made it a better summer, he concluded.[20]

Meanwhile, Danz was in the midst of complicated negotiations. The structure of the group would be a limited partnership, which offered the best tax advantages. PNSI would be liquidated, as the Danz group proceeded to buy it out and assume its loans. The total package would come to approximately $10.3 million, a small discount off the Brewers' bid. Daley would remain a 25 percent owner, and the Sorianos would be cashed out. The new ownership not only had to purchase the team; it also had to fund operating expenses, come up with $300,000 or more to complete renovations at Sicks' Stadium if the city would not pitch in, and solve the property dispute in Tempe with E. B. Smith. The trick was to find enough partners. Carlson, who joined the partnership, was candid about the prospects. Saving the Pilots would be a civic effort, he said, because the financial opportunities were not very attractive. Carlson was good for $50,000, and his Western International Hotels put up $400,000. Danz was also good for $400,000. Other investors included Douglas, Skinner, Friedlander, Burdell, and several PNSI limited partners who contributed up to $100,000 each. It was a hard road, Danz remembered. "We didn't find much support in the fund-raising effort." The plan was to raise $4.8 million and combine that with the $4 million Bank of California loan, the $2 million Sportservice loan, and an additional bank loan for $1 million. That would provide enough to buy out the Soriano interests, pay off the Soriano and Daley loans, and give the Danz group $1.7 million of operating capital that was supposed to carry the franchise through the next three years until the club could play in the new stadium. The league had postponed the October 30 deadline a couple of times, and the Danz group had to put up a $261,875 advance to run the club through December. But on November 18, at the top of the front page, the *Post-Intelligencer* declared, "It's the SEATTLE Pilots."[21]

For a month, there was rejoicing and speculation on the success of the new team ownership. Surely someone with Danz's experience in the entertainment industry would do a better job of promoting the Pilots. Accolades went to the Sorianos for bringing baseball to Seattle, but the consensus was that the Pilots would be better off without them. In early December, the league gave its approval to the sale but retained its provisions. The city or the new ownership would have to bring Sicks' Stadium up to major league standards. The multipurpose stadium still had to break ground by the end of 1970.

Then, on December 17, Danz announced, "I felt I should tell the public there is trouble in Paradise." The Danz syndicate was struggling to make the two payments that would complete the sale. The first had been scheduled for December 5 but then moved to December 15. In the meantime, Price Waterhouse, reviewing the PNSI records for the transfer of ownership, came across a note indicating that the Bank of California loan was in default. According to Danz, his group believed that this was just a technical default and could be worked out once the sale was complete. Interpretations diverge widely at this point. Danz maintained that he was caught by surprise by Bank of California's assertion that the loan was actually due and payable. W. G. Campbell, senior vice president of the bank, argued that Danz was aware of the condition of the loan very early in the game. Campbell, in fact, had informed the Sorianos when they began talking about a sale of the club in September that the loan must be paid off upon transfer of ownership. In their first meeting on November 13, Campbell let Danz know that he was disillusioned with baseball in Seattle. Nonetheless, Danz maintained that he had no reason to assume that Campbell really meant that he "expected immediate payment and would not transfer the loan."[22]

According to a lengthy memo titled "Pilot Purchase Activities," probably written by Danz, Danz and Carlson called together major Seattle bankers on November 21 to ask them to collectively furnish a $1 million line of credit and a $4 million loan that would be interest-only for three years. The latter was to cover the Bank of California loan. Nowhere does the memo suggest that the money was being solicited to cover a loan in default, but Campbell argued reasonably that concern over the loan's status must have been the reason for bringing the bankers together. Bank of California volunteered to put up $750,000, which was twice its proportionate share, but the other banks declined to participate. On December 12, Campbell wrote a formal "due and payable" letter to PNSI, with the proviso that he would delay the demand for thirty days so that the Danz group could finish its financing. Danz argued that this was the first time the bank had actually demanded its money, implying that he had always been confident that with new ownership, the Bank of California would feel more secure about its loan and would allow it to be assumed. In fact, Danz referred several times to assuming the loan as part of the sale. Campbell again emphasized that Bank of California wanted to be cashed out no later than the first part of 1970 no matter who owned the club. As conversations with Danz took place, Campbell or his assistant made at least two telephone calls to Bud Selig. Selig assured Campbell and the Sorianos that the Brewers group, with a term loan from Northwestern Mutual Life Insurance and equity funding from other sources, had sufficient resources to cash out all parties.[23]

Danz now felt thoroughly torpedoed by the bank. The campaign to find financing for the purchase was flagging, Danz needed more investors, and without the loan, it would be impossible to recruit them. He prepared a couple of press releases that spelled out his frustration, especially his feeling of being betrayed by the Bank of California, but Campbell was able to persuade him that blaming the bank was consummately unfair. Charles Burdell, Danz's attorney, agreed after a meeting with recently elected mayor Wes Uhlman to issue a statement that merely reported that the parties were endeavoring to find solutions. When asked for his approval, Danz replied dejectedly, "I suppose that is all right if that is what you want."[24]

Meanwhile, the Danz group, having missed the first of two payments on the sale, missed the extended deadline. The group pressed on. During the first week of January 1970, Danz finally issued a press release expressing surprise that Bank of California had called the loan. He let Seattleites know that he had rounded up $5.3 million toward the purchase (he did not mention that this included $1.5 million from Daley and the $2 million Sportservice loan, which had the follow-the-club strings attached). So even if the $3.5 million loan, now in default, had been in place, the group needed $7 million more to keep the Pilots operating in Seattle. A substantial part of that would have to come from Seattle banks, which wanted proof that the fans would support the ball club. In response, Danz, calling it a "last ditch" effort, launched a two-week ticket-selling campaign to raise $1 million in advance sales. Fans could show support by purchasing season tickets for one, two, or three seasons or by buying single-game tickets. He pointed out that the average ticket for the 1969 season had cost $3.05, but the new, or prospective, ownership was selling them at an average price of $2.87.[25]

Uhlman, who was not much more of a fan than his predecessors, saw the Pilots as "just really a pimple on an awful lot of serious problems." But, more than Braman or Miller, he sought to be of active assistance. During the mayoral campaign, he had promised $300,000 for further improvements at Sicks'. Now he met with Danz, Max Soriano, and Campbell and called on the public to buy tickets. In a *Post-Intelligencer* column, John Owen wondered why the banks needed convincing, since sports franchises were proven collateral. The newspaper asked both residents and financiers to show their support. The *Argus* thought that the American League (and maybe the civic leaders who had launched the campaign to save the Pilots) was playing Seattle as rubes. The weekly paper blamed the two dailies, especially the *Post-Intelligencer*, for the needless commotion and asserted that Danz, in over his head, should have checked on the loan. The editor did not deny that the team might be good for the city but was emphatic that it was not worthy of taxpayer dollars. Meanwhile, there were rumors of new investors. Three more leading businessmen had pitched in. Bill DeWitt, former Cincinnati executive, was interested; then he was not. An airline executive had expressed interest. Halfway through the ticket drive, Kuhn, Cronin, American League counsel Sandy Hadden, Kansas City Royals owner Ewing Kauffman, and Bob Reynolds of the Angels visited the city. This time, it was not to support the ticket drive or sell Cronin's "fresh fish." The two owners were among the strongest supporters of having the franchise stay put. Kauffman enunciated their hopes and concerns. "I think the area will come through," he told reporters. "There are some new people getting behind it." But he went on to warn, "We do not want another shortstop operation here like last year." The Danz group set a deadline of January 22 for completion of the sale. Several days after his visit, Commissioner Kuhn told Milwaukee baseball writers that the Seattle franchise had serious problems and might have to move. But he still offered Puget Sound interests a thread of hope, encouraging Milwaukee not to give up on getting a franchise if it did not snare the Pilots.[26]

A few days beyond the ticket campaign deadline, the trustees of the account reported that $310,000 of the hoped-for $1 million had been raised. Undaunted, Danz and his investors went back to the banks, seeking to form a consortium that would proffer a $4–5 million loan. On January 15, 1970, bankers and businessmen met one last time to discuss the problems. William Jenkins, president of Seattle First National Bank, agreed with Carlson that it was "a crummy loan" but a civic duty and promised to take his bank's share. W. G. Campbell said he was still good for $750,000 if the others helped out. Then Maxwell Carlson of the National Bank of Commerce stated that his bank would not participate and walked out of the meeting. He seemed to represent the attitude of most of his fellow financiers. The bank loan idea was dead.[27]

As the January 22 deadline approached, then passed, Danz was still working hard, figuring he had until the next league meeting, which was scheduled for January 26 and 27 in Berkeley, California. Meanwhile, Mayor Uhlman thought that the situation was bleak, and, as the deadline passed, the Angels' Reynolds was disconcerted. "I'm frustrated," Reyn-

olds told the *Times*. "It defies my comprehension. It appalls me." Kauffman, the other owner in Seattle's corner, was equally put out, saying, "I
don't understand that town. In Kansas City four different groups would
come up with the money if I wanted to sell the Royals." The *Milwaukee
Sentinel*, which had been irritated for some time at Seattle's second and
third chances, wrote, "In all fairness, Seattle hasn't earned another year
of membership, even on a probationary basis. Yet, Seattle's chances can't
be kissed off too lightly." Bud Selig was at the meeting, taking up his
usual inconspicuous position behind the potted plants. (Cronin, Selig
recalled, would always move away from him as fast as he ever moved in
his shortstop days.) Daley said that the Pilots were now "up for grabs." A
rumor had Daley and Dewey Soriano in Dallas, speaking to Lamar Hunt
and Tommy Mercer, even though the October 30 deadline for invading
Texas League territory had long since passed. Soriano's secretary told
callers to his office that he was out piloting, despite the fact that his
license was suspended.[28]

The Danz initiative was as good as dead. Seattle would send its A-team
to the meeting in Berkeley to plead for more time, but the city's political
powers were planning a different strategy. They would give the American
League owners a whiff of grapeshot. Uhlman told the press, "Seattle is
truly a major league city in every sense of the word and shall be given
time to prove it," while he asked the city corporation counsel to seek an
injunction against any relocation of the Pilots. The suit, against PNSI,
cited the loss of the $1.4 million the city had spent on Sicks' Stadium,
breach of performance in regard to the lease, and the $10 million worth
of multipurpose stadium bonds King County had already sold. Uhlman knew that this would be merely a delaying tactic, but it would get
the league's attention. Washington attorney general Slade Gorton and
private attorney William Dwyer, whom the state would soon retain to
lead its cause in court, began to develop a suit on behalf of the state.
They would file it in state court, where the case would get a sympathetic
hearing and where they could invoke state antitrust laws. Further, they
would claim that the American League had restrained trade with other
commercial interests, specifically the concessionaire, Sportservice, and
the Pilots' broadcaster, Golden West. For their part, Senators Magnuson
and Jackson endorsed the actions and once again threatened to pursue
legislation removing baseball's antitrust exemption.[29]

There were many reasons Fred Danz was stumbling. For one, he was probably out of his depth. He did not seem to have the clout to recruit partners from a city that lacked either the financial resources or the will, or both, to support a major league franchise. And there was a bit of a subversive element to the story, as well. Bank of California had seemed relatively cooperative when Danz solicited the city's financial institutions to help rework the loan. It was reasonable, then, for Danz to assume that Seattle leaders could convince Campbell that his bank's stature in the community would rise if it rolled over the loan. But the bank was actually working against Danz all the while. Campbell desperately wanted to be free of the burden of the Pilots and was convinced that Milwaukee was the most responsible purchaser. The bank hired attorneys and a public relations firm to persuade Seattle politicians and business leaders that conditions for major league baseball in Seattle were impossible; then it later sought to charge PNSI for these efforts. When Jerry McNaul, one of the state's attorneys in the ultimate suit brought by the state of Washington against the American League, asked Campbell why he tried to pull the rug out from under the group campaigning to keep the franchise in the Northwest, he answered smugly, "Mr. McNaul, we're following the old banker's adage that he who has the gold makes the rules."[30]

Further, Danz tried to work with Sportservice, which was willing to extend its $2 million loan. He hoped he could persuade the concessionaire to advance another million to help with the purchase of the Pilots. But Danz was either unwilling to grant, or unaware of, Sportservice's demand to have its concession contract honored when the Pilots moved into the domed stadium. He offered the company only the opportunity to bid on the contract along with others. Since the privilege of following the franchise was the reason for the $2 million loan, the concessionaire turned down his request for $1 million more. Sportservice would later add a million to its $2 million loan to help Selig buy the Pilots. Finally, Uhlman learned that Danz had become persona non grata with one or more American League owners. If Seattle was going to have a chance of keeping the franchise, someone new had to head the attempt. Just before the Berkeley league meeting, Ed Carlson contacted James Ellis with an idea.[31]

Carlson proposed running the ball club as a public trust. He was confident that he could enlarge the consortium of supporters he and Danz had put together if the partnership were sold, in part, as a nonprofit corporation. When the club got on its feet, Carlson suggested, then anything left over from operating expenses would be donated to community organizations such as United Good Neighbors (United Way), Children's Hospital, educational institutions, and amateur sports groups. This was civic duty at its best, and Carlson knew it. Now the call could be to save the Pilots and contribute to the community. If the Seattle Spirit were really alive, it would be hard for leading citizens to turn down this appeal. Plus it could work to save not only the stadium but also any hopes of passing the second Forward Thrust bonds. As the American League owners met in Berkeley, they might have had antitrust on their minds. Magnuson and Jackson had sent another telegram laced with references to the difference between business and sport. They praised Ewing Kaufman's wisdom in declaring that the current ownership of the Pilots should not realize a profit from its sale of the team. The telegram foresaw lawsuits, legislation, and bad publicity for the league if it made poor decisions and not so subtly suggested, "If you want baseball to be a sport, make your case by seeing that the franchise stays in Seattle." The grapeshot was whizzing ever closer.[32]

Carlson stepped in for Danz and spoke to the league about the novel ownership structure. The owners were flabbergasted. Joe Cronin observed at the end of the meetings, "I think we are dealing with a different breed of cat." The owners did not know what to think. They did not like the nonprofit idea at all, if they understood it. Negotiations between Carlson and his group and the league lasted hours. Afterward, the owners were still wary but set the sale price at $9 million and gave Seattle leaders until February 6 to put it all together. When Carlson left the room, Senators owner Bob Short made a motion to approve the sale to Milwaukee. Short was a perpetual detractor of ownership in Seattle and ever fearful that a fellow owner would impinge on his privilege to sell his club for whatever he could get or make him run an organization that would limit his profits. Frank Cashen, representing Baltimore, advised a Machiavellian patience, counseling, "By going along with them, all we are doing is giving them enough rope to hang themselves because they just can't make it." Joe Cronin echoed the sentiment as he spoke to Short, who now agreed with Cashen. "Bob, is it your suggestion that we let them run and if they fall on their face, let them fall on their face?" Short answered, "Yes."[33]

Carlson came back to Seattle and started work immediately. There would be a limited partnership. Daley, happy to work with Ed Carlson, would contribute $1.5 million. Twenty-two other firms and individuals supplied just under $2 million. The nonprofit general partner would be called the Northwest Sports and Community Service Foundation, the organization that would pull in the extra financial support by making the project a badge of community involvement. More than sixty businesses, labor organizations, and individuals contributed. Ned Skinner took the job of recruiting the well-off to get involved in saving the Pilots. His answer to one respondent who had no interest in baseball illustrates the campaign's appeal. Good, he responded, then you can do your civic duty. Altogether, the group needed just over $9.4 million to purchase the Pilots plus $2 million more for operations. Carlson worked on accommodations with Sportservice and Bank of California to round out the financing. He appealed over Campbell's head to the president of the bank, who was willing to continue the loan on an interest-only basis for a year if Carlson's financing was sufficient. The latter proviso probably meant that Carlson's group had to pare down the loan by $1 million or else place $3.5 million in a bank account as collateral. At any rate, the two parties were close enough to agreement for bank vice president Campbell to tell the *Post-Intelligencer*, "I can see where something might be worked out." The Sportservice loan would continue at $2 million, and Carlson had a verbal understanding with the concessionaire that the new owners could cancel the loan and buy out the contract at a later date—a deal that might solve the follow-the-club provision. Discussions were still going on as the next meeting, in Chicago, loomed, and Carlson asked Jack Zander, the Sportservice head, to meet with him there. Zander protested that he could not get a room at that late date. Carlson replied that he owned the hotel and thought he could find Zander a place. Zander stayed as Carlson's guest.[34]

The league had pushed the February 6 deadline back to February 10. Everyone was to assemble in Chicago for the final decision. As the meeting approached, praise came from Seattle, but there were rumblings among the owners. The Seattle sports and editorial pages were filled with the by-now obligatory references to the Seattle Spirit and the world's fair. Ellis noted that the community raised more money for the Pilots in ten days than it had raised for the fair in six months. Even Dewey Soriano, who by this time was feeling completely dejected, endorsed the Carlson plan, saying, "I want what is good for Seattle. I want our city to keep the club if it is possible." Daley saw the proposal as thin but was hopeful that it would carry the day.[35]

Not all were celebrating the prospect of a second season. While the *Times* thought that the campaign had united the suburbs and the central city, Emmett Watson was skeptical. He noted that the moneyed interests were having their way. Marvin Milkes awaited concrete evidence that Carlson had saved the day. Milkes knew that season-ticket sales were lagging badly, and the club had missed its February 1 payroll. Golden West Broadcasting told Danz on February 5 that it was expecting to renegotiate the radio contract downward. Charles Finley and Bob Short, expecting Seattle to fail, concocted similar schemes. Move the Pilots to Milwaukee; then, when the dome was completed, put a team back in Seattle (which is what would finally happen). Finley thought it was the Pilots who should return. Bud Selig thought Finley must have had a bad dream. Angels general manager Dick Walsh's attitude was undoubtedly common to all the owners. He wanted to see the money, not just a batch of promises.[36]

Even with the grousing of some of the owners, the Seattle delegation, which included Carlson, Daley, Danz, Ellis, Milkes, and the Sorianos, felt confident as it arrived in Chicago. The group's members had raised enough money and financial pledges, the Bank of California would work with them, and the Sportservice loan was still in place. Commissioner Kuhn and the counsel for the American League had both assured members of the Seattle group that their managing scheme was a better alternative than moving the team. Then, shortly before the meeting, one of the key supporters who had guaranteed $200,000 said that he wanted to be the managing partner. Carlson told him that they were going to hire a professional manager. The supporter replied that he was qualified. When Carlson continued to deny his request, he withdrew from the partnership and took his money with him. About then, James Ryan called and asked if there was anything the group back in Seattle could do to help. Do you need more money? Carlson told his story, and Ryan responded that the group had $200,000. Carlson replied, "Ryan, if you were here right now, we'd kiss you." It appeared to be a good omen.[37]

The night before the meeting, a committee led by Ewing Kauffman interviewed the group. What Carlson thought would be a perfunctory review turned into an intense grilling. Nonetheless, the Kauffman delegation reported that there were a number of reasons to approve the new Seattle ownership. Carlson had raised enough capital to meet, even exceed, the league's financial demands. The general partner had been changed from a nonprofit corporation into a business corporation whose stock was totally owned by a nonprofit corporation. This meant that those who had objected to the nonprofit angle in the Berkeley meeting had been heard but not really attended to. Kauffman reminded his colleagues that it was the American League that had wooed Seattle. Joe Cronin, after all, had promised the city that the league was here to stay, given a place to play, and the domed stadium was still on track. Finally, Kauffman warned, "possibly the most important is the consideration of a lawsuit." In sum, the Kauffman committee recommended approval.[38]

Carlson was aware that the league feared a pinchpenny operation. When he went before the owners the next day, he assured them that he and the others understood how important it was to develop players in order to have a successful franchise and promised not to disburse the club's revenue until the ownership had funded operations that were of major league quality. He went on to remind the league that the community was behind this effort and maintained that the enterprise would be financially viable over the three years it would take to build the domed stadium.[39]

Then the conversation started. The owners could not get comfortable with the nonprofit idea. Jerry Hoffberger, almost pleadingly, asked why Seattle could not do private finance like other communities. Carlson explained that his approach had succeeded in financing the world's fair. It was a way of harnessing the credit of the community for civic progress. Seattle did not have deep pockets to turn to—at least none were available for baseball. But this way, a number of community-minded Seattleites could offer up credit, not cash, and in smaller, more affordable amounts. Then Carlson made a strategic error. Underlining how hard it was to raise money in Seattle for baseball, he told his interrogators that it would have been a snap to do this for a football team, that he could have gotten $15 million with a couple of phone calls. His comment may not have killed the deal, but several owners were not pleased. The large size of the potential ownership group provoked another question. An owner asked, "Who gets stuck if all the bills are not paid?" In the business plan, Carlson was the spokesman for the club, but the short answer was that this would most likely be William Daley. Though the organizational chart was evident, the bankroll of last resort was not clear.[40]

After they had finished interviewing Carlson and ushered him out of the conference room, the American League owners debated approval.

Michael Burke, president of the Yankees, outlined the dilemma, as he warned his associates of "the frightful public relations rap that we have to buy if we [reject] the proposal that these fellows have come up with—they have met all of our conditions, financial conditions, I would say, and they are simply being excluded from baseball because we, as profiteers, do not want a nonprofit member." Charles Finley eschewed all rational argument, rejecting the Carlson plan out of hand. "Never would I vote," Finley ranted, "for any group of people that was approaching baseball in that idiotic manner." Finley also worried that when word of a nonprofit baseball club reached Oakland, "the fans would say 'well my gosh, why can't Finley be magnanimous as Carlson and his group in Seattle?'" Senators owner Bob Short did not think the club would ever make any money to distribute to charity and never wearied of labeling the whole idea "a fraud and a hoax." He and Hoffberger were also concerned that the idea of a nonprofit franchise might ruin their opportunities to take their tax write-offs or sell their clubs at a profit. While the nonprofit approach was the most discussed aspect of the proposed ownership, the league also worried about the financial viability of the prospective owners. Cronin did not think that $2 million for operations would carry the club through the 1972 season (i.e., until the dome opened). John Allyn of the Chicago White Sox could not ascertain who would come forward if the franchise needed an infusion of cash. After the meeting, Allyn observed that the Carlson group "wanted to give baseball to Seattle as a sport; but baseball has to be a business." Daley had promised to be good for $8 million when the league approved PNSI but had not come through, and now he was the most likely financial savior for the Carlson group. Short put it succinctly, "Where is the money?"[41]

Before they adjourned on February 10, Cronin wearily told the press, "We took nine million votes." It was actually nine, but the league could not reach agreement. The owners considered a move to Milwaukee, but only Short and Allyn supported that. Cronin took straw votes on the Carlson group with several variations on financial help from the league. They all failed. The league considered keeping the same ownership but could not muster the necessary nine votes for that. Financially, the obvious answer was the well-heeled Milwaukee Brewers, but the owners were spooked by the threat of a lawsuit and a public relations fiasco. In two weeks of hard work, the Carlson group had pretty well matched the league's demands—they had not hung themselves, as expected. But the owners were entirely put off by the idea of community ownership, much less a nonprofit operation, and wondered if the group was any better funded than the original owners. The final, formal ballot on the Carlson ownership plan was eight in favor and four against, one vote short of approval. Allyn (Chicago), Finley (Oakland), Hoffberger (Baltimore), and Short (Washington) voted "no." There was no acceptable solution, and the owners came to exactly that conclusion.[42]

On February 11, the second day of meetings, the American League voted nine to zero, with three abstaining, to hand the franchise back to PNSI and give the group $650,000 to make it to spring training. Publicly, Cronin was obscure about what the league had in mind, beyond keeping the team in Seattle. Privately, the owners were seeking to buy time. Initially, the proposal was to grant the team $2 million to get it through 1970, but that was voted down. Because the stipend was stingy, the owners purchased only a few weeks in which to find their way out of their dilemma. The hope was to continue to negotiate with Carlson, find another group, or negotiate among themselves to increase the loan. When the owners spoke to Ed Carlson to tell him that they had rejected his plan but would not move the team, he thanked them and told them that since he had achieved his purpose of keeping the team in Seattle, he would disband his group. Within a few days, the money and pledges were back in the hands of his supporters. Several owners advised their colleagues that their organizations would furnish no more money beyond the $650,000 loan. Cleveland's bank agreements prohibited it from making any contribution at all. The entire, insufficient sum ultimately came out of the league treasury.[43]

Even before the Chicago meeting adjourned, the owners suspected that their life raft was not seaworthy. The original motion, made by the Yankees' Lee MacPhail, read: "I move that the Seattle Club stay in Seattle in 1970, the league advance $650,000 to be spent with the approval of the league. . . ." A delegation then went off to inform Carlson that his proposal had been rejected but that the team was staying put. But as the owners began to have second thoughts, they realized that the resolution had not yet been released to the press and could be changed. Jack Hayes, counsel for the Boston Red Sox, asked, "Can't we doctor that resolution and make it read so that there won't be any commitment to stay if circumstances make it unfeasible?" League attorney Sandy Hadden agreed, adding, "That is right. I think we ought to tidy it up a little bit." After discussion, Lee MacPhail agreed to have the resolution rewritten. It now read: "RESOLVED that it is the *intention* of the American League to retain the Seattle Club in the City of Seattle . . ." (emphasis added). It passed unanimously. It is hard to tell what the league was thinking. The owners' words and actions seem to indicate that they were genuinely scrambling and saw their decision as a stopgap. But Jerry McNaul, attorney in the ensuing suit against the American League, believed that at this point, the league had given up on Seattle.[44]

It was Seattle's turn to set off skyrockets. The theme of a John Owen column was "Can the owners really be this stupid?" Owen marveled that they had rejected the most influential business leader in Seattle and his financially sound plan, which would have cost the league nothing, and then paid out $650,000 to put the team back in the hands of the old owners, who had charged too much and promoted too little. Emmett Watson promised a cold shoulder for the Pilots. He believed that the league had chosen a cynical alternative that promised failure in order to avoid an antitrust suit. "They haven't done a damned thing to help baseball here," Watson raged, "and you don't owe them a damned thing." Warren Magnuson was saying the same thing, but because it was, after all, Warren Magnuson, the language was more than an echo of newspaper columns. The *Post-Intelligencer* quoted the senator, "They threw peanuts and handed the franchise back to the same people who fouled it up in the first place. How do they expect any support after that?" There was plenty of suspicion that the owners were setting Seattle up for a fall so that they could get out in 1971. Whether the Pilots would survive the 1970 season in Seattle was an open question.[45]

The last-minute efforts to retain major league baseball in Seattle represented the pinnacle of civic leadership on behalf of sports. For about seven years, it had been Gandy, Cohn, and the Sorianos who had strived to bring major league sports to the Puget Sound area. At the other end of the spectrum, the city's political leadership had been mostly recalcitrant. Mayors Braman and Miller were admirable in their stewardship of the taxpayers' money but could not, or would not, make Sicks' an acceptable venue for major league baseball.

As Ellis decided to roll a multipurpose domed sports stadium into the Forward Thrust package in hopes of attracting more voters, the civic leaders had come to the aid of the Gandys and Sorianos of the city. But they almost lost their credibility, along with the stadium, by trying to force the Seattle Center option. Then, when the stadium and Forward Thrust were threatened by the sudden flight of the Pilots, it was not only Carlson, Ellis, and the others who pitched in. Now there was significant assistance from the politicians. Mayor Wes Uhlman, King County Executive John Spellman, and, especially, Senators Warren Magnuson and Henry Jackson came forward to save the team and preserve the prestige of the city. But Seattle's best group was composed of too many small investors and no major players, besides Daley, who could assure the league that the new ownership could avoid the headaches of 1969. Seattle would later have financial angels like Paul Allen of Microsoft and even Howard Schultz of Starbucks (who ended up demonized for selling the Sonics to Oklahoman Clay Bennett), but Boeing, the local giant in 1970, shunned leadership in any city-building projects. The nonprofit approach Carlson used to attract enough supporters was too novel for the league owners. Seattle's inability to conduct finance like other cities signaled that, despite the best efforts of the pillars of the community, the city was still not quite major league.

BIG LEAGUE CITY
or small time town

YOUR OPPORTUNITY
TO BRING MAJOR
LEAGUE BASEBALL
TO SEATTLE

This brochure from the 1966 stadium bond campaign promises major league baseball as a reward for supporting an arena. Seattle voters rejected the measure as they had in 1960. (Collection of David Eskenazi)

Joe Gandy, instrumental in bringing the 1962 world's fair to Seattle, was a prominent Seattle booster and civic leader. Especially eager to build a major league stadium for his city, he headed the failed 1966 campaign and subsequently played a key part in the successful Forward Thrust drive for a stadium in 1968. (*Seattle Post-Intelligencer* Collection, MOHAI, 1986.5.25901 fr. 12)

Ed Carlson, speaking on behalf of the Century 21 Exposition at the Waldorf Astoria, was one of the key civic leaders in the 1960s and early 1970s in Seattle. After teaming with Joe Gandy to put on the Seattle World's Fair in 1962, he would figure prominently in stadium politics and the effort to keep the Pilots in Seattle. (University of Washington Libraries, Special Collections, UW 32295)

James Ellis, another civic leader who got involved in stadium politics, inspired and led the Forward Thrust bond initiative of 1968, which included a successful appeal for a $40 million multipurpose stadium, the Kingdome. (*Seattle Post-Intelligencer* Collection, MOHAI, 1986.5.55884)

Mayor Dorm Braman was unenthusiastic about the prospects of baseball in Seattle. As a steward of the city's budget, he did not see much point in spending anything extra on the refurbishment of Sicks' Stadium. (*Seattle Post-Intelligencer* Collection, MOHAI, 1986.5.56021)

The Washington State Stadium Commission appointed by Governor Evans meets in June 1968 to consider the recommendations of Western Management Consultants. Two months later, it selected Western Management's fourth pick out of five: Seattle Center. From left to right: Restaurateur Dave Cohn, city councilman (later mayor) Floyd Miller, county commissioner John O'Brien, Ford dealer and commission chairman Joe Gandy, county commissioner (later county executive) John Spellman, and city councilman Charles M. Carroll. (By permission of Hearst Communications, Inc./Hearst Newspapers, LLC/Seattlepi.com)

seat gives you preferential seating in the Super-Colossal Indoor Stadium

The Pilots promised a "Super-Colossal Indoor Stadium" for fans, tantalizing them with this artist's rendering of the stadium at Seattle Center. It was not to be. The voters rejected the Washington State Stadium Commission's choice of location in an initiative election in May 1970. (Collection of Tim Jenkins)

Gadfly Frank Ruano led the successful petition drive against the Seattle Center location. Ruano later launched several unsuccessful petitions against stadium building and cost overruns. (*Seattle Post-Intelligencer* Collection, MOHAI, 1986.5.55813 fr16/16A)

Fred Danz headed the first effort to purchase the Pilots and keep them in town, but he came up short. Here he stands alongside Joe Cronin (foreground), president of the American League. (University of Washington Libraries, Special Collections, UW 28708z)

When the Danz initiative foundered, Ed Carlson put together a consortium of Seattle investors and others to save the Pilots. Carlson addresses the media in January or February 1970 about his effort to keep the team in Seattle. Seated, left to right, are Westin Hotels executive Henry Henke III, James Ellis, and president of Northgate Shopping Center James Douglas, a close ally of Carlson's. (*Seattle Post-Intelligencer* Collection, MOHAI, 1986.5.51821)

Even as the civic leaders worked to save Seattle's baseball team, the state, county, and city initiated litigation against the American League. Mayor Wes Uhlman announces the legal action in early 1970. (*Seattle Post-Intelligencer* Collection, MOHAI, 1986.5.51719 fr8A)

Attorney William Dwyer was an active player in Seattle stadium politics. He won King County's case against Drake Construction, bringing $13 million to the county, and led the state's, county's, and city's suit against the American League, which brought the expansion Mariners to Seattle. (University of Washington Press)

King County Executive John Spellman kicks a football through goalposts at groundbreaking ceremonies for the Kingdome, a few moments after installing a golden home plate. Spellman and the dignitaries were later bombarded by mud balls hurled by protesters seeking to draw attention to the impact the stadium would make on the fragile local neighborhoods. (County Executive Photograph Files 1968–1979, Record group 137, series 413, box 1, King County Archives, Seattle, Washington)

Falsework holds up four of the beams for the Kingdome roof. Once the concrete was poured, Drake Construction claimed that it could not move the falsework without imperiling the beams. The ensuing conflict between Drake and the county led to the replacement of the contractor and, ultimately, a successful suit against Drake. (Office of Resource Management, Kingdome visual materials, Accession 10–011, box 2, King County Archives, Seattle)

After eight years of wrangling and a false start, the Kingdome was completed in 1976. (Office of Resource Management, Kingdome visual materials, Accession 10–011, box 3, King County Archives, Seattle)

Chapter 10

DROPPING THE PILOTS

EWEY was in a dream world. He had no money. I swear to God, the whole franchise was being run on a Visa card." That's how *Seattle Times* reporter Dick Rockne remembered it. The fall and winter of 1969–70 was a scramble to find a new owner, while Marvin Milkes, operating on a frayed shoestring, tried to remold the team, from the front office down to the field, into an outfit that could reach that elusive third-place finish.[1]

At the end of the season, as the players scattered to all parts of the country or to winter ball, Milkes began his alterations. Cost saving led to layoffs in the trailers. Bob Lemon, who had managed Vancouver, moved to Kansas City to become the Royals' pitching coach. In fact, problems with Vancouver caused the Pilots to move their Triple-A franchise to Portland, Oregon. They also dropped the class-A Billings, Montana, club. On the field, Milkes had replaced the entire coaching staff by spring training. Sal Maglie was let go and left major league baseball behind, though he did a stint as a minor league general manager. Ron Plaza was ousted, and Eddie O'Brien went back to Seattle University. Milkes kept Frankie Crosetti and Joe Schultz dangling for months. Seattle sports fans would debate Schultz's future from August, when Milkes refused to firmly back his manager, into November. For his part, Schultz was typically innocuous. "I just hope I'll be invited back next year to see what I can do to help it along," he shrugged. "I'm in limbo," the manager responded when a *Times* writer asked about his status. The writer observed, "Schultz continues to wander about at the World Series like a lost soul." The erstwhile manager wondered if the Pilots, who had given him permission to speak to other clubs—a pretty big hint—were waiting for him to resign. Finally, the verdict was in. The easygoing Schultz, who may have been too permissive with the players, was out. After interviewing the distinctly not-easygoing Billy Martin and Dick Williams for the position, the hard-driving Marvin Milkes hired hard-driving Dave Bristol. Crosetti heard about his fate on the radio the same day as Schultz.[2]

The front office also underwent extensive reshaping. Ray Swallow, director of scouting, and Art Parrack, farm director, were out. Jim Kittilsby became secretary of scouting, and Bobby Mattick moved to director of player procurement and development. He was joined by Lew Matlin, who undoubtedly welcomed the move from stadium operations (chief correspondent with the city about Sicks' Stadium problems) to secretary of the minor league system. Milkes was placing those closest to him in positions of greater responsibility. It was likely that Dewey Soriano pressed for certain of these changes. For example, Gabe Paul, Jr., son of the influential part owner of the Cleveland Indians, took over the job of stadium operations. The Pilots were furnishing the American League with a personal window on their battle with the city. Bill Sears, who privately thought that Milkes had made Schultz his fall guy, moved from press liaison to the crucial post of promotions and publicity director. On the field, Milkes hired new manager Bristol's coaches. Roy McMillan, first base coach, and local product Wes Stock, pitching coach, came from the Mets. Cal Ermer moved from the Twins to coach third base, and Jackie Moore of the Red Sox became bull-pen coach.[3]

Milkes remade the team on the field as well. He traded Don Mincher to the A's for pitcher Lew Krausse, who had gone seven and seven in 1969. Oakland included catcher Phil Roof and outfielder Mike Hershberger in the deal. Diego Segui and Ray Oyler also went to Oakland for pitcher George Lauzerique and shortstop Ted Kubiak, whose .249 batting average added more than one hundred points to the position. Power pitcher Bob Bolin (also seven and seven in 1969) came from the Giants for Steve Whitaker and Dick Simpson. Milkes was trying to shore up the Pilots' pitching, though the loss of the versatile Segui would hurt. Bristol proclaimed that "pitching and defense will keep you in a lot more games than if you rely on power hitters." If Bolin and Krausse could reach the potential that the baseball analysts had seen in them when they debuted in the majors, Bristol's hopes would be rewarded. Miguel Fuentes, a September call-up, would have added even more punch to the pitching staff for 1970 or 1971. Fuentes had pitched a complete game in his short stint.

But in late January, he got into a dispute in his hometown of Loiza Aldea, Puerto Rico, and was murdered.

The off-season caravan was not as extensive as the 1969 trip, but Mike Hegan, John Kennedy, Wes Stock, Jimmy Dudley, and Sears bused to southeastern and central Washington and also publicized the Pilots in Bremerton. Tommy Harper generated good news and goodwill. Two voters ranked him among the top ten American League most valuable players, and the *Post-Intelligencer* named him Man of the Year at its annual January sports banquet.

Once the American League had made its decision to retain Pacific Northwest Sports, Inc., as owner, lines of power had to be established. The league installed Roy Hamey, former general manager of the Phillies and Yankees, as "overseer," working under the aegis of the commissioner. The Sorianos knew that they were as good as out and volunteered to be advisers. When the league owners at the Chicago meeting discussed contracting with Bill DeWitt to run the club for two years, Milkes exploded. They took the hint. Milkes became the vice president and general manager of the club, with full control over baseball operations.[4]

Milkes and Hamey immediately set about mending fences. As Milkes informed Joe Cronin, "We are taking a better role of appeasement to date than the late Neville Chamberlain." He went on to talk of the necessity of "window dressing," putting up a "bold front," and acting "sort of like missionaries" in order to win fans and sell tickets. They talked to Russ Cunningham of the *Times,* which seemed sympathetic, and to the *Post-Intelligencer,* which seemed wary, although Emmett Watson promised to be supportive. The team and the City of Seattle were still at an impasse, but relations were civil. Mayor Uhlman continued to call for a performance bond from the league before discussing repairs to the stadium. Ticket prices were reduced. The $6 field-box ticket now went for $4.50. Loge boxes fell a dollar to $3.50. And the team knocked 50¢ off reserved and general admission seats, which now sold for $3 and $2 respectively. The Milkes-Hamey team took the message to service clubs throughout the Puget Sound area and believed that they "had them pretty well quieted down." Nonetheless, by March 10, less than a month before opening day, season tickets were off considerably. Compared to 1969, field-box tickets had declined from 1,571 to 1,246; loge sales were off 394 to 258; and reserved season tickets sank to 3 from 22. The financial picture was dim. The Bank of California, which knew enough not to foreclose, asked about collateral for its loan, which had bulged to more than $4 million with interest. Attendance of 750,000, an increase over 1969, projected a loss of about $900,000 for the 1970 season, not including the customary depreciation of players.[5]

Gene Autry's Golden West Broadcasting had been warning since January that something had to be done about the radio contract. The company had signed a generous $850,000 agreement with the Pilots for 1969 but had sold only three-quarters of the advertising time. Golden West wanted to renegotiate the multiyear pact. The uncertainty about ownership impeded its ability to sell ads for 1970, and, for several months, it was impossible to identify anyone who could negotiate the contract. Though Daley thought the advertising was entirely Golden West's problem, Milkes and Hamey accepted a renegotiated broadcast contract of only $212,500, which would double if all ads were sold. Golden West would also be reimbursed pro rata for any games not broadcast if the Pilots moved away from Seattle. Stadium and program ad sales were taking a hit as well. Valu-Mart expressed its displeasure with promotions and the general operation of the club. Cudahy Bar-S meatpacking had the same concerns and chose not to renew. As March went on, Milkes evaded the key question, saying that he knew only what he read in the papers and assumed the season would start in Sicks'. But he had already talked to player representative Bob Locker about who might pay moving expenses to Wisconsin for the players' families. Hamey, a shred more optimistic, said, "I haven't given up that the club will stay in Seattle."[6]

Meanwhile, in Tempe, spring training had started just a few days after the Chicago meeting. There were problems in Arizona as well. E. B. Smith still pressed Pacific Northwest Sports, Inc., to build the promised accommodations and do some extensive paving around the complex. Smith worried that PNSI's instability imperiled his own investment. He threatened to block the team from its spring training facilities. Milkes, apparently a personal friend of Smith's, saw to it that the access road got paved. That mollified the Arizona developer for the time being.[7]

On the field, the optimism that seizes every team in March was a good counterpoint to the front office trials. Gene Brabender and Harper were among the late signers. Milkes thought that he did not bargain as hard as he could have with them but desperately wanted his best players to get to spring training. Hegan, Danny Walton, Steve Hovley, and John Kennedy, eager to impress Bristol, got to camp early. The new manager ran a structured spring training, emphasizing conditioning and fundamentals. He impressed Lenny Anderson, who likened him to Fred Hutchinson—high praise indeed from a Seattleite. Krausse made his mark early and was soon slotted as the opening-day starter. Steve Barber came to camp saying that he had not felt so well in a long time but was released before the season began. The Pilots knew they needed some punch at the plate and eagerly awaited Rich Rollins, who was still working on his master's degree. To shore up the infield, Milkes traded Roy Foster to Cleveland for Max Alvis and Russ Snyder.[8]

By late March, conversation in camp was as much about the fate of the franchise as about the players. Hegan, after Eddie O'Brien had assured him that the team would remain in Seattle, had bought a home and moved his family from Massachusetts to the Northwest. Uncertainty weighed on everyone's mind. Players asked sportswriters daily if they had heard anything. Milkes told reporters, "I'm Little Orphan Annie looking for Daddy Warbucks." By the end of spring training, word had come. A sign on Tempe's main street still read "Welcome Seattle Pilots," but the public address announcer did not miss a beat as he gave the lineup for "your Milwaukee Brewers."[9]

Back in Seattle, things continued bleak during the final month of the Pilots' existence. The American League scheduled another meeting for March 11 in Tampa. The purpose of the meeting depended on whom one asked. Hamey reiterated that the season would start in Seattle "and go as far as we can." The meeting was just a financial report, which, Hamey granted, would not be a very good one. The $650,000 was almost gone, and much more would be required. Joe Cronin avowed that the final determination had been made—there would be no move. In an article in the *Milwaukee Sentinel*, he waffled a bit, saying, "We're going to do our best unless the bottom falls out." He then added with resignation, "We love Milwaukee, but we're in Seattle." William Daley considered the meeting another referendum on moving. "I am quite disturbed by the Seattle situation," he warned. "It is a bad one. I think we have the votes [to move]." The *New York Times* and Milt Richmond of United Press International (UPI) predicted a move to Milwaukee, even as Ewing Kauffman and Bob Reynolds sought two more votes to block a transfer. Then Cronin announced that the March 11 meeting was postponed. William Daley had entered the hospital and was not even able to communicate with the league by telephone. Daley soon communicated with the press by telephone to let them know that he was just in for a checkup. "I wouldn't have gone into the hospital if I thought it would result in postponement," he said. "I thought they were going to reach a decision and I thought the decision was to be to move the team to Milwaukee."[10]

"For years troubled officials had faced east and prayed to Maggie from whom all blessing flowed," regional historian Murray Morgan once wrote. Joe Durso of the *New York Times* thought that Warren Magnuson's renewed threat to attack major league baseball's antitrust exemption was more likely the reason for postponement. Magnuson said that he was not sure but hoped that the letter he and Henry Jackson had sent had something to do with it. This time, they promised Senate hearings and legislation. The senators followed through on their threat, though only after the move was complete. In April 1970, Magnuson, Jackson, and six other senators submitted a brief bill that added baseball to the Sherman Act. Hearings were scheduled for the fall. They delivered speeches on the Senate floor reviewing the exemption from 1922 through the Toolson case of 1953 and suggested that it was only legislative inertia that protected the owners. They issued press releases explaining that though they could not save the Pilots, perhaps their actions would forestall the business of baseball from harming another city. Though some constituents asked Magnuson to work on more important matters or accused him of blackmail, most endorsed his efforts to end baseball's exemption. He and Jackson never succeeded in getting their legislation passed, but, along with the Curt Flood case challenging the reserve clause, their efforts got the attention of baseball for several years and made the owners more pliable about granting Seattle a new franchise.[11]

To the last, the Pilots kept baseball in a dilemma. Without more American League financial assistance, the franchise in Seattle was defunct. If it were sold to outside investors who moved it, baseball was in for tough times in Congress and the courts. Bowie Kuhn thought he saw a way out. About the time of the postponed Tampa meeting, he contacted Ed Carlson to ask if he would renew his bid. Carlson's answer was both diplomatic and adroit. He told Kuhn that since the American League had assured him that the Pilots would stay another year, he had returned the underwriting agreements and the money he had raised, disbanded the consortium, and could not reassemble the group. Carlson, with the advice of James Ellis and James Douglas, advised Kuhn that the owners must "carry out their financial responsibility which they assumed for the full franchise operation" and keep the team in Seattle. He added that poor ticket sales and the renegotiated radio contract meant raising more operating capital, which he did not think he could do. It was not clear whether Kuhn was acting on his own as commissioner—in the best interests of baseball—or if he had the approval of the owners. Although Kuhn assured Carlson that he could find the votes, the nay voters, once again citing the nonprofit aspect of the plan, denied that they had ever considered changing their minds. Kuhn came to a conclusion about his effort to woo Carlson and, perhaps, about baseball in Seattle: "When Carlson told me it was dead, I knew it was; he was very reliable."[12]

The last days of March—the latter days of spring training—were the final days of the Seattle Pilots. The handshake deal at the 1969 World Series became a formal agreement to sell the franchise to the Milwaukee Brewers on March 8, 1970. All that was needed was the American League's OK, and that was supposed to come at the Tampa meeting, rescheduled for March 17. Daley would not appear at the postponed meeting either. He and the Sorianos had given their proxy to Bud Selig. Northwestern officials made good on their last-ditch threats. Washington attorney general Slade Gorton had already made the terms of the state's suit clear in a letter to Cronin, Daley, the Sorianos, and American League attorney Sandy Hadden. If the league approved the sale and move, the state would claim false promises, financial damage including the loss of $25 million of revenue on the state hotel/motel tax devoted to the stadium bonds, loss of business revenue, and fraud. The state would also charge the American League with violation of Washington antitrust law. The city claimed a loss of $3 million on the purchase and refurbishing of Sicks' Stadium. King County warned that it would join the suit in the likely event that the move would affect the construction of the stadium. The state claimed that the violations had been willful and sought treble damages. That added up to $82.5 million. On March 16, superior court judge Solie Ringold issued a restraining order against a move. A day or two later, Seattle attorney Al Schweppe joined the litigation. Schweppe was a season-ticket holder who claimed he was in danger of losing his investment. He successfully filed for an injunction in King County Superior Court and in Tampa, Florida, to restrain the league from voting on a transfer. Part of Schweppe's actual motivation was his belief that the loss of the team, if it did not kill the stadium entirely, would certainly imperil the Seattle Center site, which was inching toward a vote in May 1970.[13]

The owners were concerned, and some felt a bit guilty. Ewing Kauff-man told his colleagues, "Number one, you get a girl pregnant. You have to stand responsible, and we have wooed and seduced Seattle. We made a mistake in our original franchise people financially. This we know today . . . and this is the price you have to pay." Another league front office official agreed that "the American League is doing something serious to reject Seattle." But the league and Seattle had parted ways. Most reports indicated that the sale to Milwaukee had the necessary nine votes when-ever the owners were allowed to make a decision. The Bank of Califor-nia joined the league in seeking to dissolve the two restraining orders. Apparently to demonstrate resolve, Cronin threatened the impossible: if the team could not move, the American League might play the 1970 season with just eleven teams. In the meantime, Milwaukee was ready to host major league baseball on a moment's notice. County Stadium, with twenty-two thousand more seats than Sicks', had been kept in good repair with the expenditure of more than $500,000 over the previous four years. The employees who had worked the occasional White Sox games in Milwaukee were ready to go. The county was prepared to rent out the stadium on a sliding scale, topping out at 10 percent of ticket sales if the Brewers attracted 2 million or more fans during the year.[14]

Back in Washington, on March 19, PNSI executed a cagey flanking maneuver to get around the injunctions. It filed for chapter 11 bank-ruptcy in federal court. If PNSI was found bankrupt, the remedy would be a sale to a qualified buyer. The league and the courts would have no choice but to permit the Milwaukee Brewers to purchase the franchise in order to liquidate the debts. During the last half of March, King County Superior Court heard the suits to keep the Pilots in Seattle in the morn-ing. In the afternoon, Judge Sidney Volinn convened his federal bank-ruptcy court. For several days, the fate of the franchise was lobbed and volleyed through the courtrooms of Seattle. Ellis told the superior court that Jerry Hoffberger assured him that the $650,000 was just the begin-ning of American League support to keep the team in Seattle for the 1970 season. Cronin testified in bankruptcy court that the "American League has done everything within its power" to carry out its obligation to Seat-tle. If Judge James Mifflin—who was hearing Schweppe's Washington suit—was any indication, a bankruptcy ruling would put all sides out of their misery. Mifflin declared that he did not see any reason for the franchise to stick around. He observed that there was nobody to operate the franchise and nobody to attend the games. "I've listened to comment after comment," he concluded, "and they don't want the bloody ball team here." On March 24, bankruptcy judge Volinn summoned the state, city, and Schweppe to his court to show cause why he should not enjoin them from their suits to preserve the assets of PNSI (i.e., he was prepared to suspend their legal actions against PNSI and the league). On March 25, the bankruptcy court did stay the suits. It was now all up to Volinn.[15]

In the bankruptcy proceedings, PNSI asked to sell the Pilots and pay off all creditors, claiming that it was currently unable to pay its debts as they matured but was solvent. Because operating costs were running $250,000 a month, it was an emergency situation. PNSI claimed to have lost almost $2.3 million in 1969. Although the court agreed to this figure in its ultimate finding, the number is misleading. A substantial portion of the loss came in the form of depreciation of assets (players) and in interest payments on loans supplied by the corporation's investors, Daley and the Sorianos. A tax accountant for the Danz group projected player depreciation in 1970 at $1.3 million. That would cover all but $1 million of the loss. Toronto vice president Paul Beeston's later explanation of base-ball accounting is relevant here. "Anyone who quotes profits of a baseball club is missing the point," he writes. "Under generally accepted account-ing principles, I can turn a $4 million profit into a $2 million loss, and I can get every national accounting firm to agree with me." The Pilots lost money, but given the rules of depreciation and operating costs, it is hard to say how much. Pilots publicist Bill Sears estimated that it was as low as $250,000 in cash operations. (He added that William Daley could have paid that out of petty cash.) Accounting firm Peat Marwick's later esti-mate of a loss (not including depreciation of player contracts) of $636,750 was probably closer to the mark. The court was surely impressed that PNSI projected a more devastating loss of $1.5 million, before deprecia-tion and interest, for the coming year.[16]

The main problem was the debt load, since the $3.5 million loan from Bank of California had grown to more than $4 million, including unpaid interest, and was in default. That automatically triggered default on the $2 million loan from Sportservice. In addition, PNSI had to reimburse Danz $261,000 for the loan his group had made in mid-negotiation, and it owed several hundred thousand on the loans from Daley and the Soria-nos. The ledger showed lesser debts owed to players and $2,233 to Jimmy Piersall for promoting the Forward Thrust stadium bond. On a more personal level, Edo Vanni discovered that he was being pursued by a collection agency. He had signed for a credit card on behalf of PNSI and was liable for the bill if the Pilots could not pay. Altogether, PNSI declared that it was $7.4 million in debt and had no way to pay it off. As the hearing continued, Bank of California once again campaigned hard for a ruling and the sale of the team. "There is no chance any lender in his right mind would loan any money to this corporation," Campbell declared. The bank's attorney Orlo Kellogg lobbied Volinn, dangling the prospect of a sale to the Brewers. "Ten million dollars, judge, think of it. Ten million dollars would pay everybody, including my client . . . and what do they have to offer? Only hopes." "They" was the City of Seattle, which argued that bankruptcy and sale would prevent PNSI from carrying out its lease for Sicks' Stadium and would rob the city of $61,000 of estimated tax revenue from ticket sales. More persuasively, the state argued that if Volinn declared PNSI bankrupt, which he was surely going to do, the American League by its own constitution had an obligation to take over the club and run it. Perhaps the clincher for PNSI's plea was Max Soriano's testimony that if the players were not paid within ten days of their scheduled pay date, they could become free agents. The team's most crucial asset was in jeopardy.[17]

There was one more interlude before Volinn made his determination. Fred Ruge briefly reappeared to ask the court for a chance to buy the Pilots. He said he could put up $1.5 million in April and a second $1.5 million in June and then complete the sale, which would take $11 million, in October. In fact, Ruge claimed, he could borrow $100 million, buy the team, and build a stadium. The court rejected Ruge and the offer out of hand.[18]

Volinn agreed that it was an emergency situation. PNSI was in default on its loans, it had to pay its players, it had incurred a severe loss in 1969, it faced another significant loss in 1970, and its shareholders would supply no more funds. (Again, no one spoke of Daley's pledge to provide up to $8 million to keep the franchise afloat.) This evidence, Volinn ruled, "graphically demonstrates" that the debtor is in an "extremely depressed financial condition" and its franchise and properties are a "wasting asset." He continued, "The fact that the debtor is simply incapable of carrying on is beyond question." He was intrigued by the state's argument that the American League constitution mandated that the league take over the team, but he rejected this remedy in a statement that captured the predicament of both the league and the city. "It would be most inequitable," he determined, "to require . . . that the American League be burdened with operating an enterprise promising economic loss of major magnitude with only the hope that the building of a domed stadium, itself the subject of litigation, might make major league baseball a profitable operation in Seattle." It was not an issue of how the situation came into being or how it could theoretically be remedied. "What mattered most," Volinn later asserted, "was the future, and they didn't have it." On the basis of his findings, he declared PNSI in bankruptcy and authorized the sale of the Pilots to the Milwaukee Brewers. The Bank of California would be cashed out, the Brewers would pay the interest on the Sportservice loan and then assume it, and Golden West Broadcasting would be paid out of the proceeds of the sale to terminate its contract. The judge's ruling granting the sale also lifted the bar that prohibited a suit against the league and the owners but continued the court's protection of the bankrupt PNSI. The *Post-Intelligencer* noted that the formal papers were signed at 4:52 p.m. on April 2, 1970.[19]

The Milwaukee Brewers partnership had formed in 1965, when the Braves announced their move to Atlanta. It was made up of several prominent Wisconsin businessmen—firms like Schlitz, Northwest Mutual Life Insurance, Evinrude, and Oscar Mayer were represented. Local auto dealer Bud Selig was head of the consortium. The Milwaukee group had a number of assets: credibility, money, a stadium, a generous lease deal, and a certain measure of guilt on the part of baseball officials, which grew deeper every time Selig's partnership missed out on a replacement team for the Braves. The $10.8 million Selig and his partners paid for the Pilots was comparable to other sales that took place around the same time. The Washington Senators sold for $11 million, the Yankees for $10 million, and the National League expansion teams also cost $10 million. The loan from Northwest Mutual for $3.5 million, an increase in the Sportservice loan from $2 million to $3 million, and Daley continuing as a partner for $1 million helped the Brewers with the purchase.[20]

Volinn made his decision only a week before opening day. Marvin Milkes called traveling secretary Tommy Ferguson to finally give him the word that the equipment truck should head for Milwaukee. Milkes stayed on as general manager and joined the team in Milwaukee. Eight thousand fans greeted the team at the airport. More than thirty-seven thousand, including Lenny Anderson, turned out on opening day to watch ballplayers in Pilots uniforms restitched to read "Brewers" across the chests. In their first year, the Brewers finished fourth in the West, tied with Kansas City, and finished ahead of Chicago, with a record of sixty-five wins and ninety-seven losses. Attendance was 933,690, about 40 percent better than the Pilots'. By 1972, Brewers attendance had sunk to 600,000. Selig and Milkes did not get along well, and Frank Lane replaced Milkes in January 1971. Milkes eventually returned to the West Coast, set up a sports administration school, and helped run a major league soccer team.[21]

In Seattle, the bon voyage to the Pilots ranged from sardonic to wistful. The luncheon to launch the Pilots' 1970 season went on, though not quite as planned. Twenty showed up at the hotel dining room for what was essentially a wake. Pilots souvenirs went on sale. Few in 1970 had dreamed they would become collectors' items. A $3 cap sold for 88¢ at the Osborn & Ulland sporting goods stores. The ad read "Non-opener specials for Pilot fans. . . . These buys will remind you of 'Big League' days in old Seattle." "Sentimental fans" could get a Pilots poster for free. In columns over several days, Lenny Anderson found it "incredible," "impossible," and "unbelievable" and remarked how hard it was to no longer see "Seattle" sewn on major league uniforms. Even hard-boiled Hy Zimmerman felt twinges of melancholy. When he saw *Milwaukee Sentinel* writer Lou Chapman at spring training after the sale, he mused, "It was like watching someone else out with your girl." Zimmerman wrote only one more article on the Brewers after opening day. On April 21, he did note opening night for the Tacoma Cubs, the only game in town. The *Tacoma News Tribune*, in fact, found it ironic that it was the Pilots who left town, not the nearby minor league franchise. It probably caused "a number of Tacomans to laugh up their sleeves," the *Tribune* added. Earl Luebker rejected the possibility that the "T-Cubs" play some games in Seattle. It would not be fair to season-ticket holders, he observed, and Seattleites could always travel to Tacoma to see some baseball.[22]

The recriminations started before the team left and continued at least until the Mariners arrived in 1977. The accusations of failure were reminiscent of the nineteenth-century Thomas Nast cartoon showing the Tweed Ring boodlers standing in a circle, each pointing a finger at the person next to him. The politicians blamed the American League, the league denounced Seattle, Seattle faulted the ownership, and the ownership said it was the fans. Observers as diverse as Al Schweppe and Arthur Daley of the *New York Times* bashed the league owners. "They're a bunch of bush leaguers," Schweppe railed, "who don't have the faintest idea that contracts have to be performed. They think they are above the law. . . ." Daley was sweeping in his condemnation, writing, "The American League blunderers have made a frightful mess of the disposition of the franchise. It was a mistake from the start." Mayor Uhlman agreed, saying, "What has happened to Seattle in this whole mess should not be perpetrated on any other cities." He continued, perhaps with an eye to a future suit, "Baseball is too much of a civic activity and a public endeavor to permit a few franchise owners to make a substantial amount of money by transferring these monopolies." Hy Zimmerman and John Owen complained that the American League selected an underfunded ownership for the Seattle franchise. Zimmerman considered the whole fiasco worse than the Black Sox scandal. Georg Meyers echoed Zimmerman, lashing out against league duplicity and stupidity. A KIRO on-air editorial wondered at the mess the American League had made of the situation. The editorial writer questioned whether the league owners had ever grasped the innovative quality of Carlson's proposal enough to give it a chance. After giving Ed Carlson, Seattle's hero, two weeks to come up with funding, then repudiating his admittedly unconventional plan after he had satisfied their demands, the owners could be nothing other than reprehensible in the eyes of Seattleites.[23]

Dick Rockne of the *Times* complained that the loss of the Pilots had consigned Seattle to territory even beyond the bush leagues, into the weeds. There were others who thought the fate was deserved. New York sportswriter Red Smith blamed the city for not keeping its promises and foot-dragging on the new stadium. Residents of Auburn and Kent charged Seattle officials with handling the domed stadium decision poorly and derided the Pilots as a special interest of downtown groups. Several years after the move, Dewey Soriano expressed his frustration with both political and business leaders: "If we had received the help the city turned loose a couple of years earlier trying to land the Cleveland franchise or if we had gotten any appreciable help from the business community or chamber of commerce, [or from] a mayor who remained idle when it came to helping the ball club or something like substantial aid from the county officials we would have wound up respectable." Leonard Koppett of the *New York Times* agreed that Seattle politicians had been neither cordial nor interested in providing an adequate interim stadium. Anderson thought Dewey Soriano's problem with the business set was that he could never overcome the handicap of being from the wrong side of the tracks.[24]

Wisconsin native Brabender, the Pilots' ace pitcher in 1969, blamed the Seattle fans: "It's a crying shame. The people of Seattle wouldn't support this club and you can't expect to keep a man up there and make him lose a million dollars. It's not fair to the ballplayers." Seattleites associated with the team, such as Bill Sears, coach Eddie O'Brien, and prospective owner John Danz, concurred that Seattle had not embraced major league baseball as they had expected. Sears insisted that the fans needed to understand that they had to pay a premium for a better class of ball. O'Brien believed that Seattle had yet to grow into being a baseball town. To the Seattle University athletic director, Husky football and Seattle University basketball were still the preeminent sports in the city.[25]

But it was the ownership that bore the brunt of the blame. Someone hung a six-foot dummy from a noose at the Westlake entrance to the monorail. The sign appended to the effigy read "Thanks Max and Dewey." PNSI office staffer Mary Soriano thought Dewey's next step would be to join brother Milton's law firm after he passed the bar exam. She then made the telling comment, "Who would be his clients since he is so unpopular in Seattle?"[26]

The analysis of Dick Young of the New York Daily News was more complex and disdainful of all. Young wrote, "[The Lords of Baseball] had sold a franchise to a hick town that had outslickered them. Seattle didn't have any money. It had bought its franchise on a promissory note, and after one year needed money to meet the bills. . . . [The owners] emptied their pockets on the table and came up with $650,000. Then they went home and the pained truth struck them. 'What have I done? I have been outslickered by the sucker.'" Bowie Kuhn, Jerry Hoffberger, and Lee McPhail, particular targets of Young's critique, agreed: the American League erred by not paying attention to the new owners' funding. Numerous observers, some defensively, some objectively, recited a familiar litany of poor decisions. High ticket and concession prices, inadequate promotions, a poor stadium compounded by self-defeating complaints about its inadequacies, and Daley's late-season finger-pointing marked an operation that Earl Luebker believed had "oversubscribed its quota of goofs." All this made the franchise and, to a degree, the city an object of scorn. Emmett

Watson, who quoted Dick Young in his column, agreed with the condemnation of PNSI but took umbrage at the phrase "hick town." A constituent's letter to Warren Magnuson asked the senator to urge Watson to write an article for *Sports Illustrated* assuring the nation that, despite the Pilots debacle, Seattle was not bush league. Speaking about expansion sometime later, National League president Bill White must have had the Pilots in mind when he declared, "One thing we don't want to do is put in a franchise that's in trouble two years down the road." The Seattle Pilots are forever a candidate for lists of failed ownership. In 1991, the commissioner's office enumerated the desirable attributes of franchise owners. Maybe the qualities are mere common sense, but a number of the criteria seem drawn from major league baseball's experience in Seattle: the owner should be local, have a net worth of $100 million, have the support of the local government, and have a yearly guarantee of 10,000 season tickets for five years. While some of his mates were relieved to get out of Sicks' Stadium, outfielder Steve Hovley characteristically saw the whole story a little differently. "The way I like to think about the Pilots," he told Jim Bouton, "it's like the upside-down postage stamp. The most important one is the one they screwed up."[27]

There is blame enough to go around. The American League was in a bind and behaved disingenuously, if not duplicitously, in the final month of negotiations with Seattle. Danz was beyond his expertise, and Carlson did some fancy shuffling so that he could claim he had a viable package. He probably met the league's terms technically, but the Pilots would still have been underfunded. In 1969, Seattle was not a strong major league baseball city. Ample natural attractions kept too many people away from the ballpark. The smallish population base provided too few fans to sustain the franchise. The stadium was inadequate and ticket prices high. A better-financed ownership could have overcome these impediments. The Pilots could have played another year in Seattle had the funds and willingness to spend them been available. William Daley had pledged up to $8 million to keep the ship afloat. Dewey Soriano was perplexed by his partner: "I thought he was going to [provide the additional capital]. I told him we were going to need more money for the club. I don't know whether I may have made him unhappy there." But Daley reneged, and the Pilots left for Milwaukee. Bill Dwyer, who prosecuted the American League in a subsequent suit, concluded that the failure was "out of a kind of pal-ship among owners when they just didn't want to ask each other

. . . fellow businessmen, to come up with additional funds. Rather than that, they would accommodate each other by moving a team somewhere else."[28]

Bill Sears remembered that it was hard to read Dewey Soriano, but Sears knew that "he was hurt deeply." Soriano wanted to bring baseball to Seattle and was not in it for the money. "He felt in some ways personally to blame," Sears continued, and was brokenhearted. Max Soriano echoed the sentiment, saying, "It was like the dream of youth ending up in a nightmare." Dewey resumed his career as a harbor pilot. Neither brother ever went back into baseball.[29]

As the sale was completed, Milkes made a mildly surprising remark about his former bosses. "The crummy thing," he told a Seattle reporter, "is that those jokers [the Sorianos] will make a profit." He was correct. The profit was a good one. But despite the difference between the purchase price of $5.35 million and the sale price of $10.8 million, it was not the financial killing many people in the Northwest assumed. The estate of Pacific Northwest Sports, Inc., had to go through liquidation first. The substantial part of this process took about eight months. Receiver Richard T. Saunders asked other creditors to allow him to reimburse ticket holders first. Altogether, almost $274,000 was disbursed to cover the unused tickets. Other creditors received their money back, plus 6 percent interest if they had to wait for payment. The Bank of California was paid off directly by the Brewers, which also assumed the Sportservice loan. The City of Seattle claimed $660,000 in lost rent for Sicks' Stadium. The parties settled on $525,000. In addition, the city obtained the scoreboard, the stadium reader board, and the PNSI trailers, equipment worth an estimated $60,000.[30]

In Arizona, the Sorianos gave up their 60 percent ownership of Pilot Properties, and, after extended litigation in Arizona and Washington, the Brewers and E. B. Smith came to a settlement on the spring training complex. The PNSI estate paid back the Danz group loan plus interest and settled the receiver's and attorneys' fees. The only serious matter left was the indemnity to the Pacific Coast League, which had finally been established at $300,000. PNSI still owed $150,000 plus interest. Negotiations lasted into 1972, when the league accepted $158,000.[31]

Early in 1971, the receiver announced that shareholders would get back all their investment and there would be between $387,000 and $637,000 in profit. A firm final figure was contingent on the resolution of the PCL indemnity and a few other smaller claims. Many years later, Max Soriano claimed that the profit was about $200,000 after the costs of the bankruptcy proceeding were factored in. Whatever the final number, it was distributed proportionately among the ownership group. The group had put up a total of $1 million, which it received back. Even at the lowest of the three profit figures, the investment of three to four years (from the first payment to the league to the completion of liquidation) yielded a decent return on a supposedly losing proposition. Interestingly, the *Post-Intelligencer* reported that Dewey Soriano did not have an ownership stake by the time of the final disbursement. [32]

By the middle of 1970, the Seattle sports community was down in the dumps. The Pilots were gone. The voters had rejected the Seattle Center as the new stadium location, so now the stadium itself was in limbo. The Husky football team, wracked by dissension and racial tension, had gone one and nine in 1969. The Sonics front office was turning over at a rapid rate. A labor dispute shut down Longacres racetrack. But all that was of little significance in the face of a declining economy.

Jerry Hoffberger told of the time he ran into Ed Carlson years later. Carlson told him that the owners had done him a real favor by rejecting his bid for the Pilots. Fred Danz felt the same. When asked about his failure to purchase the franchise, he almost whooped, "Oh, golly, it's one of the luckiest things that ever happened to me. No, I didn't really want to own a baseball team." There was good reason for their relief and joy. The Boeing recession and an unemployment rate of 9.5 percent would have made the 1970 season a trial for the Carlson group, with its barely sufficient funding. Had the American League granted the franchise to Carlson, it might have been the Pilots who turned out the lights as they moved from a city suffering a big-league recession. [33]

Sicks' Stadium went from major league to afterthought during the 1970s. The Seattle Rainiers, a Northwest League class-A team, played there from 1972 to 1976. Jimi Hendrix, Janis Joplin, the Youngbloods, and the Steve Miller Band performed at Sicks' during the decade. After an effort to sell the stadium failed, it was demolished in 1979. Today a home plate inside a home improvement store marks the location of the field.

There was a curious and significant sideshow to the saga of the Seattle Pilots. During the season, only a couple of players noticed Jim Bouton writing in a notebook. John Owen saw his journal and offered to publish excerpts in the *Post-Intelligencer*. Bill Sears mainly remembers Bouton "bird-dogging" his secretary. But *Ball Four* is the lens through which most fans recall the Pilots, if they think about the team at all. Excerpts appeared in *Look* magazine in June 1970, and the book was published later that summer. *Ball Four* dwells extensively on Bouton's career with the New York Yankees but centers on his tenure with the Pilots and then the Houston Astros. [34]

Bouton had been a star pitcher with the Yankees, winning a combined total of thirty-nine games in 1963 and 1964. He injured his arm and never approached that level again but developed a knuckleball that kept him in and out of the majors through 1970. The Pilots acquired him from the Yankees in 1968, and he pitched most of 1969 with the Seattle club until he was traded to the Astros near the end of the season. Bouton soon retired and spent some time as a sportscaster in New York. From the end of the 1970s, Bouton has been content to build a cozy enterprise around writing and his celebrity.

Jim Bouton disdained authority. His conversation drifted from ironic to sarcastic. He read books and played chess. The knuckleball pitcher thought of himself as anything but an organization man and relished being unpredictable. When he visited the University of California, Berkeley, he felt an affinity with the sandal-wearing Vietnam War protesters. Bouton acted on his principles as a compassionate political liberal. He and his wife Bobbie extended themselves financially to adopt a Korean orphan, and Bouton led the New Jersey delegation to the 1972 Democratic National Convention, which nominated George McGovern. In the world of baseball, all this made him a threat to owners and an oddball to his fellow players. It is no surprise that, when he was with the Pilots, he hung around with Steve Hovley, a Stanford graduate, and Mike Marshall, who would earn a Ph.D. He thrilled young sportswriters who were ushering in an era of skepticism. To venerable writer Dick Young, he was a "social leper."[35]

In 1968, writer Leonard (Lenny) Schecter, who had done an article on Bouton and found him a decent fellow, asked the pitcher if he would be interested in compiling a journal of his experiences during a season. Bouton had already been keeping notes and readily agreed. Schecter had been a sportswriter for the *New York Post* and then a freelancer. Bouton and others have characterized Schecter's style as cynical, humorous, and skeptical. He was a fan of Muhammad Ali, suspicious of jocks, and ready to expose greed, racism, and hypocrisy. Although he and Bouton shared similar outlooks, Schecter probably influenced Bouton, at least in *Ball Four*, toward a more sardonic style and pushed him to cull the more head-shaking stories as grist for the book. Over the course of the 1969 season, Bouton took notes, told his stories into a tape recorder, and sent the tape to New York to be transcribed. He ended up with 1,500 pages of material that he and Schecter edited down to 520. The book resonated with a society suspicious of heroes and fed up with phoniness. It quickly sold 250,000 copies. The first edition ultimately sold 500,000 hardbacks and 5 million paperbacks.[36]

Ball Four was not the first tell-all book on baseball. In 1959, pitcher Jim Brosnan wrote *The Long Season* about his stint with the Cincinnati Reds. It poked fun at the human foibles of players and the ironies of the game in a relatively sanitized manner. Overt sex, drugs, and profanity were still taboo in Brosnan's literary world and did not show up in his book, unlike Bouton's. Nonetheless, broadcaster Joe Garagiola feared its impact on baseball's image and characterized Brosnan as a kookie beatnik.[37]

Bouton has always been a bit defensive about his book, probably because it has elicited so many attacks from those who felt that he betrayed a trust—the confidences of friends, the sanctity of the locker room, or the unspoken pledge to preserve the image of baseball. A regular point Bouton makes when asked is that he just wanted to "share the fun" he'd had in baseball. It is the guys who are funny, Bouton maintains, not him. Schecter, in the introduction to the book, offers a defense that sounds suspiciously like a sales pitch. He writes that the book was created "to illuminate the game as it never had been before. We resolved to reveal baseball as it is viewed by the men who play it, the frustrations and the meanness as well as the joy and the extraordinary fun. The difficulty is that to tell the truth is often, unfortunately, to offend. Bouton never flinched. It was not our purpose to offend, of course, but if in the process of telling the truth we did, so be it." The book is full of vignettes. Many are humorous, some are hackneyed, a number of them did offend, but most are interesting because they furnish an insider's view of professional baseball through Bouton's personal experiences. They are selected with an eye to shock, as though Bouton (prodded by Schecter) is a little boy using street language in an effort to get a rise out of the adults. The themes include sketches of personalities, the odder the better; needling; trainers as front-office spies; a manipulative authority structure (only Mike Marshall was more disdainful of someone in authority); life on the road, including episodes involving sex and booze; roommates (usually told in a friendly rather than derisive tone); the tenuousness of friendships; and ballplayers as anti-intellectuals.[38]

Bouton struck the same chord as Howard Cosell (who, perhaps threatened by Bouton as a sportscaster, despised him). Many Americans were attracted to someone who claimed to "tell it like it is." In short, *Ball Four* fit well with the general and ongoing challenge to the Establishment in 1970. Bouton was probably most criticized for portraying Mickey Mantle as a hard-drinking playboy, which Mantle later admitted to be true. The author launched a flurry of defenses for his accounts of the "Mick." Bouton asked, Can't our heroes have flaws? Anyhow, it would be better to idolize a Nobel Prize winner, or Allard Lowenstein, or Ralph Nader than an athlete. Bouton argued that kids needed to be fully acquainted with their heroes so that they would not be let down when their heroes failed as humans. The author, not sensitive to certain boundaries he was crossing, was surprised at the harshness of some of the responses to his book.[39]

Much of Bouton's defense rested on the fact that what was written was true, even if carefully edited to make it interesting. The profanity? Without it, the book would lose its realism. So "rate it 'X,'" said Schecter, "the only thing we left out was repetitiveness." The first revelations of drug use in baseball were included because it was a part of the game. Amphetamines? Don Mincher claimed that half the players took them. Bouton admitted that he'd taken greenies; they just make you think you are doing better. Why (in 1970) are there no black managers? Owners like to pal around with the manager, wrote Bouton, so race would be a barrier to that. The sanctity of the locker room? Everyone knew that he was writing a book, Bouton maintained (though they did not imagine what he might write). Besides, nothing really goes on in the clubhouse (which does not explain why people flocked to read the book). Sex? In perhaps his weakest defense, Bouton asserted that he did not mention any adulterous person by name, that what he wrote should not disturb a truly stable marriage, that a wife that naive should not read the book anyway, and that the book did not cause any divorces. These comments came in response to an accusation by sportswriter Joe Falls that he had

caused the divorce of former Pilot Gary Bell. Bouton and his wife Bobbie divorced in 1981. Bobbie Bouton's book *Home Games: Two Wives Speak
Out*, written with Nancy Marshall, former wife of Mike Marshall, was
not so demure about unfaithful baseball-playing husbands. [40]

Baseball was not amused. Commissioner Bowie Kuhn brought Bouton in for a meeting. Bouton arrived with Marvin Miller, head of the
Players Association. Kuhn told the writer-pitcher that he thought the
material in the book was not credible, that Joe Cronin found its content
unforgivable, and that it violated the confidentiality of the clubhouse.
The commissioner demanded an apology and suggested that Bouton
could claim that Schecter was at fault for the scurrilous parts. Bouton
said that the book was entirely true and he would take responsibility for
its content. Kuhn backed off, saying that no action would be taken but
Bouton should consider the meeting a warning. Miller asked what Kuhn
was warning against. The two finally hammered out a press release from
the commissioner that read, "I advised Mr. Bouton of my displeasure
with these writings and warned him against future writings of this character." Afterward, Bouton happily, and Kuhn grudgingly, agreed that the
whole episode had been excellent publicity for the book. Kuhn's memoirs
retold the story in less than a page. Bouton's account, in a sequel to *Ball
Four*, spanned thirteen pages.[41]

Most players did not take *Ball Four* well. Yankees were antagonized
by Bouton's comments about themselves and, especially, about Mantle.
Elston Howard never forgave his battery mate, and Bouton, remorse-
ful, thought that he might have brought better balance to his account of
Howard. The Pilots' Harold Parrott, who had had little time to become
acquainted with Bouton, dismissed the book as the work of a peep-and-
prattle writer. Manager Joe Schultz was probably the Pilot most at the
center of *Ball Four*. At first, he denied that he had read the book but soon
revealed a close working knowledge of Bouton's story of his one managerial season, complaining, "Jim Bouton in that book of his got some
of his effects by not finishing off some of those stories and by coloring
things. Did you ever hear me use some of those words he had me saying?"
Hy Zimmerman agreed that he had not heard Schultz say some of those
things. Others remembered that "pound down that Bud" was, indeed, a
common Schultz-ism. Bouton, for one, did not think that he had been
unkind to Schultz. In fact, Schultz was one of the pitcher's heroes because
the manager kept his perspective. Schultz later recovered his more typi-

cal long-suffering persona, conceding, "What the bleep. The more I think about it, it's not so bad." Other Pilots players were not so generous. Ray Oyler was blunt. "When I do see him," Oyler threatened, "I'm not going to say hello or anything. I'm just going to punch him in the nose." When the *Seattle Times* wanted to do a story on *Ball Four* around 1990, there was reluctance. Don Mincher told the reporter to leave him out. Frankie Crosetti had no desire to talk to Bouton. Rich Rollins remained upset that he had not realized that Bouton was writing about the team. The normally gregarious Eddie O'Brien told an interviewer, "When you see Bouton, tell him I didn't say hello." Yet, several years after *Ball Four* had come out, Marvin Milkes treated Bouton to dinner and joshed with him about one of the book's running jokes about the general manager.[42]

Many commentators found *Ball Four* transcendent. More than a baseball book, some said, it was representative of the times. David Halberstam stopped just short of calling it courageous. Robert Lipsyte, in the *New York Times*, asserted that whether Bouton was a bringer of truth or a tattletale, his insight as an author made the book shine. More than anything, critics called the book groundbreaking because it was a sports book that was revealing, iconoclastic, and frank—so much so that several reviewers accurately predicted the backlash to come. An example of that backash was Roger Kahn's complaint that Bouton's portraits, especially of those directly over him, looked more like caricatures. Dick Young winced at the petty cruelty Bouton displayed toward former teammates and, unlike most commentators, thought Bouton had shown disrespect for the game. Young's remark to Bouton when the two ran into each other became the title for the pitcher's sequel. "I hope you didn't take it personally," Young told Bouton, half-apologizing for his invective.[43]

Seattle sportswriters generally applauded *Ball Four*. Georg Meyers noted that Bouton was the same "tell it like it is" fellow in interviews that he revealed himself to be in the book. John Owen commented, pragmatically, that *Ball Four* was entertaining, provided you were not the one being skewered. Surprisingly, Seattle's' senior sportswriter, traditionalist Royal Brougham, praised the book as droll and honest. Hy Zimmerman wrote most extensively on the *Look* excerpts as they came out. He clearly admired Bouton, noting that he was in tune with youthful dissidence and had demonstrated against racism as a spectator at the 1968 Olympics in Mexico City. Bouton had a keen mind and could be a formidable adversary in discussions, Zimmerman allowed—a genuine accolade from him. Bouton's teammates seemed to shun him, maybe because he was too articulate. But Bouton also had an ego that made him overly conscious of his own statistics, and he was something of a publicity hound. One of Zimmerman's most perceptive points was that comments that are innocent or playful in conversation can turn harsh in cold print—it took more skill than one might think to be a writer. The veteran sportswriter concluded by suggesting that if his column sounded like an indictment, blame it on the cold print.[44]

Play-by-Play

SPRING TRAINING 1970

THE Seattle Pilots lasted through most of spring training 1970. The camp would be more unsettled than usual that year. The personnel were substantially new. There had been a major turnover among the players and the coaches. The Pilots, once a strong hitting team with questionable pitching, now would rely on pitching and defense. Hitting became the question mark.

The other unknown was where they would start the season. The question of the future of the team had ebbed and flowed all winter. Where would they play the 1970 season? How would they get their personal possessions from Seattle to Milwaukee? Who would pick up the tab? Where should their families go? For a few, it would be a question of selling a house they had just bought. It is no wonder that the players badgered the beat writers for the *Seattle Times* and *Seattle Post-Intelligencer* every day for the latest on the litigation.

Marvin Milkes, who was running the club with American League overseer Roy Hamey, was needed in Seattle. Jim Kittilsby, now secretary of scouting, handled matters in Tempe. Milkes had time to visit Arizona only once through the entire period of spring training. The whole operation had a tentative sense about it.[1]

On the field, manager Dave Bristol's style was a direct contrast with that of the easygoing Schultz. Bristol viewed spring training as a kind of boot camp. Players would get in shape. They would learn fundamentals. There would be calisthenics and drills. All would be organization and discipline. Even if the team was not the most talented, Bristol wanted it to be the best prepared.

As the exhibition games started, the main focus seemed to be the starting rotation. Gene Brabender had a sore arm, so he sat out the first two weeks of the spring season. The Cactus League games started with a 6–1 loss to Cleveland. Lew Krausse looked solid, and Bob Locker picked up where he left off in 1969 with an effective two innings of relief. But Skip Lockwood gave up five runs over three innings. Tommy Harper started at second base and began his successful campaign to stake it out as his opening-day position. The next day against the Indians, Mike Hegan commenced a springtime of effective hitting that won him the first base job for the regular season. Bob Bolin gave up two earned runs in three innings in his first bid to be in the rotation. Then George Lauzerique was perfect and Marty Pattin adequate as they helped shut down the Padres 4–2. Ted Kubiak, obtained for his hitting, was already impressing observers as a better fielder than Ray Oyler, John Kennedy, and other assorted occupants of the shortstop position in the inaugural season.

By the middle of March, Bolin had pretty much nailed down a starting spot. He was impressive in a five-inning shutout performance against the Padres. Krausse, Pattin, and Lauzerique were prime candidates for the rotation if the team went with five starters. Lauzerique elevated his stock when he pitched four scoreless innings against the Padres the day after Bolin had shut them down. Though it seemed unlikely, there was speculation about whether Brabender, who had not seen any game action by March 20, would make the starting four or five. Steve Barber was also in the running but was a bit less consistent than the others. Through March 22, Locker had not given up a run. Kubiak (shortstop), Harper (second base), and McNertney (catcher) had established themselves at their positions by the midpoint of spring training. Finally, on March 23, Brabender was ready to go and hurled three innings, giving up only one run. He told everyone not to worry about his arm, that it was just some adhesions (scar tissue that built up in the off-season) he had to tear loose.

The Pilots' dilemma was reflected in the daily reports of the games. On March 17, Lenny Anderson of the *Seattle Post-Intelligencer* wrote a game recap headlined "Last Rites?" and made it sound suitably funereal. On March 20, he was calling the team "Sea-Waukie." The judicial processes were winding down, but the box score continued to read "Seattle." At one point, E. B. Smith, the Arizona land developer who had partnered with the Sorianos in Pilot Properties, became concerned that the bankruptcy court was going to override his claim for unfinished improvements at the spring training complex. Smith, who had filed claims against his Pilot Properties partners, had promised not to do anything as drastic as lock the team out, but Kittilsby arrived one morning to find the entry-ways chained and secured with locks he had never seen before. It was all resolved before the workday began, but the situation was wearing on all the team administrators in Arizona. Kittilsby also had to communicate with the bankruptcy court daily. He was, after all, in possession of most of the assets—the players. The court advised him to shut down all bank accounts in the name of Pacific Northwest Sports, Inc., and establish new ones under the court's supervision. He did so and paid the bills with starter checks for several days.[2]

After an outbreak of nineteen runs against Cleveland, the Pilots scored less than three runs a game over the next eight games. (Even the Cleveland game was a bit suspect. It had been a windy day, and the teams were using a "juiced" ball that was 5 percent livelier. Cleveland scored fourteen.) Bristol told the press, "We may not score too many runs and we'll have to look for good defense." The matter of where the team landed entered in as well. If the outfielders were going to be patrolling the much more spacious County Stadium rather than Sicks', some skill would be needed. The outfield seemed to be a contest among Mike Hershberger (who came with Krausse in the deal for Don Mincher), Steve Hovley, Danny Walton, Roy Foster (a free agent purchased from the Mets' Tide-water club), and Wayne Comer. Walton had the most power, but he was a defensive liability. He also reinjured the knee he had damaged at the end of the 1969 season. He was back before spring training was over, but there was a question about his durability.[3]

Finally, the cuts began. Dick Baney, Skip Lockwood, and Gary Timber-lake went to the team's Portland Triple-A club. The Pilots released Bar-ber. Lauzerique was added to a five-man rotation. The Pilots played their last game ever, a 4–2 loss to the California Angels. Both Seattle papers printed the box score. The *Seattle Times* gave it only four lines, and the *Post-Intelligencer* described it in seventeen. The new Brewers team had three more games in the Cactus League; then it was off to Milwaukee.

It was not quite so easy as it sounded. The Brewers did not want Kit-tilsby to release any players until the transition had been made (again, he could not dispose of the assets). It presented a sticky situation. The minor league rosters were filled, so he could not assign the players to the Pilots', now Brewers', minor league teams pending notification of their release. In any case, the minor league teams had already left camp for their home cities. The players were housed in an almost-completed privately operated dorm near the Arizona State University campus where all the minor league players had been staying. Kittilsby understood that if they received their releases and then returned to the dorm, they might trash the rooms in frustration. So when he received the go-ahead from the court and the Brewers owners, he sent word for the players to bring all their gear with them. He met them at the diamond, gave them their airfare home, and got them on the bus to the airport. The operation ran without incident. There was more. On the last day of spring training, as Kittilsby waited with the Brewers ownership, a Maricopa County sheriff's deputy served papers for misappropriation of funds. It harked back to Kittilsby's closing the PNSI bank accounts at the court's request. Kittilsby explained the situation to the deputy, telling him that the plane to Milwaukee, along with the team and personnel, was waiting for him at Sky Harbor Airport. He pleaded with the deputy to call the bankruptcy court. The deputy relented and told him to go on and the sheriff's office would just work it out.[4]

The Brewers were welcomed by thousands of fans at the Milwaukee airport and, on April 7, by 37,237 in the stands. Lew Krausse started against the Angels' Andy Messersmith. Recent arrivals Max Alvis was at third base and Russ Snyder started in center field. The Brewers lost 12–0. In Seattle, the Sicks' Stadium reader board said, "Collectors Sale: Pilots Novelty Items at Cost." It was a good buy.[5]

Chapter 11

A STADIUM AT LAST

JOHN Spellman became the first King County Executive in May 1969. Spellman, forty-two, was a graduate of Seattle University and Georgetown Law School. He got his start in civic affairs with Forward Thrust and became one of three county commissioners in 1967. His father had been an assistant football coach at the University of Oregon and the University of Washington. He was a sports fan, and his family had attended several Pilots games. The *Bellevue American* described the perpetually pipe-smoking executive as a conciliator and diplomat—almost laid-back. But Spellman, who in the heat of the effort to save the Pilots insisted that the stadium could not be built without the prospect of a team, stiffened his and the county's resolve after the Pilots' departure. He saw to it that the Kingdome got built.[1]

Spellman's accomplishments in the newly created office, especially in regard to the stadium, impressed many observers. A UPI sportswriter lauded Spellman for getting the Kingdome completed despite "tangles of litigation, hard-nosed labor negotiations, spiraling inflationary costs, a dispute that saw the original prime contractor pull off the job and considerable dissatisfaction from some environmentalists, racial groups and disgruntled taxpayers." Recalling the days of Mayors Braman and Miller, Ross Cunningham of the *Seattle Times* wrote admiringly in 1972, "The City Hall zero progress philosophy is one of no growth, preservation of antiquities and to let Seattle become a self-contained and self-satisfied inward-looking community." In contrast, Cunningham continued, the county exhibits "prudent dynamism to accommodate a measured growth to encourage a thriving community with job growth." Though Spellman was not the only one who believed in the stadium project, his decision to go ahead tipped the balance. Throughout construction, plaudits rolled in. The *Post-Intelligencer* reported glowingly that Spellman stuck his neck out a mile to build the stadium and then guided the project through a maze so complex he became known as "Swivel Hips." Spellman was willing to take risks for several reasons. He knew the hotel/motel tax was steadily generating revenue that would help cover the bonds; a multiuse facility was a critical need for a growing population; the stadium could generate jobs and boost morale in a tough economy; and, though he denied it, that completing the project could help him win the governor's seat.[2]

By the beginning of Spellman's second year in office, the spring of 1970, Seattle had struck out based on the three essential criteria the Stanford Research Institute had identified in its 1960 study. First, support from the city had been insufficient: the fans had not turned out; the civic leaders appeared on the scene too late to save the team; and sports was nowhere near the top of most politicians' agendas. Second, ownership was inadequate: Pacific Northwest Sports, Inc., was underfunded, and no one in the region had the wherewithal or desire to buy the team. Third, prospects for a stadium were dim: the American League deadline went unmet; the arena could not break even without a team; and building costs were rapidly rising above the appropriated $40 million. Moreover, Seattle's economy was at its worst since the Great Depression. The Achilles heel of the city, dependence on Boeing, was taking its toll as the company edged toward possible bankruptcy. What happened over the next six years seems amazing given this context—and it was. So substantial credit goes to John Spellman, who picked up the pieces of the stadium siting controversy and combined leadership, determination, and good fortune to deliver a new stadium.

Seattle was changing. In December 1971, Ed Carlson left to become the CEO of UAL, the parent company of United Airlines and Western International Hotels. Joe Gandy had suffered a fatal heart attack in June 1971. James Ellis was still active, but he was more interested in preserving the hinterland from urban sprawl. (He would return to city affairs in the 1980s and assist a successful push to build a trade and convention center in Seattle.) A new mayor and a revamped city council were injecting vigor into Seattle government.

But for stadium boosters, the transformation of King County government was the significant event. In November 1968, over 60 percent of King County voters had approved remodeling their government to allow for a separation of powers, creating a single county executive and a nine-member council to serve as a legislative body.

Even with the Pilots long gone, the county council, in January 1971, approved the Washington State Stadium Commission's recommendation to build at King Street and assigned Narramore, Skilling, Praeger to design an arena that could be constructed for $30 million. In December 1971, King County concluded negotiations to purchase almost thirty-six acres for the Kingdome from Burlington Northern for $4.7 million. Though the Narramore firm would oversee the project, a stadium advisory executive committee would tend to the county's interests. The oversight committee included Spellman; county councilman John O'Brien, charged with finding prospective tenants; Gerald Schlatter, who would be the project manager for the county; and Norm Maleng, King County deputy prosecuting attorney, who monitored the contracts. The committee would spend ample time worrying over a new series of Frank Ruano challenges to the stadium, but it would also orchestrate city-county relations concerning parking, hire minority contractors, establish a no-strike no-lockout contract for the job, and trek to Hawaii to display a model of the domed stadium to major league baseball. The committee advised Narramore to put the design process on a "fast track," meaning construction would begin before all design aspects were complete.[3]

Original project estimates were now at least four years out of date in an inflationary economy. The executive committee ordered the design team to be cost-effective. Costs typically balloon during such large projects. The Louisiana Superdome cost three to five times more than projected. The price for Olympic Stadium in Montreal was seven to ten times higher than the original estimate. Frank Ruano constantly reminded King County that it was on a financial leash. Every expense must be spared in order to construct a utilitarian structure that met its budget. The designers decided to enclose the stadium in a cost-efficient "thin shell" concrete dome five inches thick. Some construction expenditures were moved into the operating budget. Donald B. Murphy of Tacoma, for example, would build the heating and cooling plant and lease it back to the county. The scoreboard technology was revised and its cost spread over fifteen years with an eye toward selling advertising to pay for it. The outside reader board was eliminated. The concessionaire would build the food-handling facilities. The stadium would have fewer restrooms than most its size. Seating would be mainly bench seats. The Kingdome was built economically and looked it. With its gray interior and exterior walls and its unpainted concrete roof, it appeared unfinished, although structurally it was complete.[4]

Site preparation got under way at King Street in the summer of 1972 as Spellman pulled up the ceremonial first railroad spike. The county awarded bids through the spring and summer. Bidding was done in two parts: the first bid was for the dome and a later one for the stadium proper. Donald Drake Construction won both bids and was required to finish the job in two years, by late 1974. The Portland, Oregon, construction company bid $28.9 million for the stadium, edging out Peter Kiewit's offer of $30.57 million. Kiewit submitted the low bid of $5.8 million for the dome but insisted on using its own design consultant. Drake Construction imposed no conditions and landed the project for $5.9 million.[5]

Spellman and other dignitaries gathered again on November 2, 1972, for groundbreaking ceremonies, two years after the now-moot American League deadline for the start of construction. The officials kicked a football through a goal post that had been set up for the occasion, and Spellman installed a golden home plate. Young Asian Americans hurling profanities and mud balls interrupted events. Concerns over the stadium's impact on Pioneer Square and the International District had been simmering for some time. Though the county and city both promised to address them, representatives of these nearby areas were not convinced. The mud-ball throwers were young leaders in the community. Roy J. Flores, a Filipino, was director of the University of Washington Ethnic Culture Center and principal spokesman for the group. Mike Castillano was from the university's office of minority affairs, Francisco Irigon was second vice president of the Associated Students of the University of Washington, and Fred Cordova was a member of the governor's Asian American Advisory Council. They had more or less spontaneously decided to demonstrate so that they could draw attention to the pressures that the stadium would exert on a neighborhood already under stress. Others came to launch their own protests. Tyree Scott represented minority contractors seeking inclusion in the project; Robert Maestas and Juan Bocanegra spoke for El Centro de la Raza; and Frank Ruano circulated a petition.[6]

There were advantages and disadvantages to locating the stadium in the midst of the city. Business interests saw it as a force for revitalizing an older, tired, impoverished area. Restaurants, entertainment centers, even hotels would spring up, giving a boost to south Seattle. Others were not so sure. Owners of small businesses feared displacement. Poorer residents worried that they might lose services or shelter. By the early 1970s, a keener consciousness of the latter group had developed. Students, activists, social workers, and others arose to give the poor and homeless a stronger voice in the councils of decision makers. By the day of the groundbreaking, the county and the city had been working for some time to mitigate the impact of the stadium on the nearby neighborhoods.[7]

Seattle's International District had been in decline since the Second World War. By 1970, the population had dropped 40 percent since 1950 to around 1,600. The stadium, no more than two home run blasts west of the edge of the district, presented a threat to the fragile neighborhood. Rising property values could squeeze out marginal businesses that catered to residents. Parking and traffic would make the streets chancy, especially for elderly pedestrians. More positively, the stadium drew attention to the already imperiled neighborhood, and with that notoriety came a chance to save it.[8]

To the north of the Kingdome lay Pioneer Square. In the nineteenth century, it was one of the commercial centers of Seattle. By the mid-twentieth century, it had declined and become the center of Skid Road. Hotels were closing or being condemned. The population was rapidly diminishing. Pioneer Square was not just fragile; it was decrepit and even more vulnerable than the International District to being overwhelmed by the new stadium.[9]

Typical of Seattle in the 1950s and 1960s, City Hall had not paid much attention to either district. The International District Improvement Organization had formed in 1968 and was probably the strongest advocate for the residents near the stadium site. The group supported the stadium but wisely used the issue to press for the needs of its constituents.[10]

Before the 1972 groundbreaking, under mild but mounting pressure, Mayor Uhlman and John Spellman had formed the Citizen Action Force to look at the situation and offer recommendations. Uhlman made it clear that the purpose of the committee was not to determine whether the stadium should be built but to develop policies for coping with the impact of the facility and devise programs that would assure the stability of the area's economy. In August 1972, early in the process, the committee lost a prominent member in a noisy resignation. Architect Victor

Steinbrueck, declaring that "this will be an urban disaster of colossal proportions—especially for the nearby areas," quit the group. Steinbrueck feared that he was being used to assuage the protests. He had reason to be concerned. The committee's recommendations were substantially ignored as the city issued the building permit.[11]

In addition, the recently formed Washington State Environmental Protection Agency required an impact statement for projects like the Kingdome. The preliminary document concluded that the stadium would have little overall effect on the area. Hurlon C. Ray, assistant regional director of the agency, condemned the impact statement as little more than a justification of the county's choice of the King Street site.[12]

Taking Ray's cue, city council members George Cooley and Jeanette Williams pressed the county to do more. They drew up a list of thirty questions for the county to consider as it, they hoped, expanded the impact statement. City and county staff worked together to produce 117 pages of responses in just a couple of weeks. Cooley and Williams, who had come under pressure from organized labor for impeding the start of construction, were satisfied. The Filipino community was not. The federally funded Legal Services Center of the International District, on behalf of a group of protesters, filed a suit asking for a six-month delay in construction after the final environmental impact statement was submitted. The suit was dismissed, but the writers of the final impact statement got the message. Although the conclusions were similar to the preliminary statement, the document was much more detailed, discussed methods for preserving low-income housing, and recommended a traffic control zone and a land-use review zone to protect areas adjacent to the stadium. Not satisfied, Lem Howell, head of the Central Seattle Community Council Federation, Victor Steinbrueck, and Frank Ruano circulated a last-ditch petition to stop construction in fall 1972, but a judge ruled that their final group of signatures had arrived too late to validate the initiative blocking the issuance of a building permit. The city authorized the building permit in October 1972, and the contested groundbreaking took place November 2.[13]

The Kingdome was on its way, but there were still tensions as late as 1975. Francisco Irigon lobbied for jobs at the stadium for International District residents, asked for free admission to events for elderly residents of the district, and argued that some of the ticket revenue should be used for community projects. In mid-February, Irigon arrived at Spellman's office with some two dozen young supporters demanding a hearing. Spellman refused to be pressured into a meeting. The group pushed past Spellman's secretary and staged a sit-in in the county executive's office. Spellman left through a back exit. Although the ceremonial spike from the King Street site went missing after the episode, the group left the office in only mild disarray.[14]

The effort to use the stadium as a consciousness-raiser for the area was reasonably successful. The International District and Pioneer Square were not transformed, but the neighborhoods improved. There were special review boards to guide change in both areas. Work started on an Asian cultural and community center within two years, and a shelter was completed in the Skid Road area. The Kingdome contractors worked at hiring minorities, reaching a level of 13 percent minority employment—a point of pride for Spellman. Contractors Harold Wright and Tyree Scott assisted the county in finding opportunities for minority contractors. A public corporation helped steer development in the International District. In 1970, the city, pushed by city council members Phyllis Lamphere, Sam Smith, and Tim Hill, had already made Pioneer Square into a historic district. Conditions improved, but rather than providing a haven for its residents, renovations led to gentrification.[15]

The thorniest issue dividing the city and county was traffic and parking. Although the preliminary impact statement predicted only 60 percent of the stadium crowd would drive, a planning consultant predicted it would be more like 75 percent. The best solution would have been to construct one or more parking garages, but funds could never be coaxed from the tight budget. Locals' primary concern was that Pioneer Square and the International District would become parking lots during events. The final plan was something of a stopgap. The county provided 217 bus spaces and 6,500 car spaces in lots surrounding the stadium. Metro bus shuttles transported fans for twenty-five cents, at least for a year. It was not ideal, but it would prove adequate.[16]

Although it was already overshadowed by larger undertakings such as the Louisiana Superdome, the Kingdome was a massive project. It would seat sixty thousand for baseball and sixty-five thousand for football. The structure resembled a hamburger bun or a low-lying mushroom. At its center, the dome was 250 feet high and 660 feet in diameter. At the time of its construction, it was the largest concrete roof in the world, covering 7.85 acres. The entire building took up about 9 acres. In the beginning, the project proceeded as expected. There were problems, and work fell behind, but passers-by could see the supports for the dome and the outlines of the superstructure taking shape.[17]

"King County Multipurpose Stadium," a newsletter sent to city leaders and others interested in the progress of the dome, proclaimed, "The lineup, supervisory and otherwise, represents as much talent as has ever been assembled for a Northwest building operation. They [Drake Construction] have backed their men with a vast amount of equipment." It is doubtful that project manager Schlatter would have been so effusive. Bundles of reinforcing steel were being driven into the ground. Concrete would be poured into forms around them to create the towers that would ultimately hold up the roof. Early in January 1973, one or two of these bundles bent at their bases, bringing down a total of six as they toppled like dominoes. Apparently, a turnbuckle on the supports had failed, and the tower collapsed, falling on a workman. Work continued, but by March, about three months into construction, the project was two months behind schedule. The December 1974 completion date would be hard to meet.[18]

By January 1974, the stadium was about 50 percent complete, but difficulties were in store. First, the Arab oil embargo slowed down delivery of materials. In February, the state emergency fuel board authorized sufficient gas and diesel fuel to keep the project going. In June, a construction workers' strike against selected contractors prompted a general lockout by the Associated General Contractors of Washington. The county asked Drake Construction to honor the no-strike no-lockout agreement, and it did until a court injunction shut down the job site for a month.[19]

By July, the stadium was 60 percent complete. Work would now extend into 1975. In one of the project's odder turns, Wes Uhlman had received a letter from Virginia Davis in March. Davis called for warnings about the ruin of man to be carved into tablets gracing the stadium. She asserted that civilization had "concreted His [God's] land in excess of our needs and that Seattle was the new Babylon." Uhlman passed the note along to Spellman, who was the one in charge of this particular parcel of concrete, after all, with the warning that "your problems . . . may be just beginning."[20]

Uhlman was right. Drake Construction was running into trouble. Perhaps, it was in over its head or, as an expanding company, had taken on too many projects at once. Whatever the cause, it had assigned insufficiently experienced managers to oversee a project of this size. Many of the supporting pilings were driven in at the wrong places, about a foot off. The contractor was making do with only one pile driver, slowing up the entire operation. Subcontractors were delivering late. The toppling towers may have been the result of a subcontractor's failure to deliver pouring forms in a timely manner. The carpenters' foreman charged that there was a shortage of tools on the job and that Drake's schematics were incomplete. Schlatter said that he tried to be publicly supportive but "personally, inside," thought the company was doing a poor job. Drake claimed that much of the fault lay with the county and the design team—there was an uncommon number of change orders as the team made constant alterations to the plans. The design team countercharged that Drake superintendents were unusually dependent on them for advice on construction matters. No provision for inflation had been built into the contract. As the project continued to lag and costs rapidly rose, subcontractors were not willing to stay on the job and lose money. Drake itself was looking at significant losses.[21]

Recognizing this, Schlatter offered Drake an extension in March 1974 and invited the company to submit claims for reimbursements that it thought were due from the county. At this point, the construction company changed managers. The new construction superintendent spent most of the next six months creating a list of repayments that Drake thought would lead to a new contract. Drake did not file its claim for $10.5 million and an extension from December 1974 to February 1976 until October. (The penalty for missing the December 1974 date was $1,500 per day. The county was willing to negotiate a finish date for late 1975.) The company asked for a response to its claims, which it had taken six months to prepare, in two weeks. Stuart Oles, Drake's attorney, claimed that so many changes had been made by the design team that many of the instructions were "vague, incomplete, or contradictory" and that subcontractors were delivering materials that now cost one and one-half times more than their bid price. He asserted that the best solution would be to rewrite the contract into a cost-plus agreement—that is, Drake would be guaranteed a certain percentage above what it would cost the company to complete the job. Spellman opposed the notion. For him, it was neither financially nor politically feasible.[22]

That is where things stood until November 1974, when the roof almost fell in . . . or didn't. The first step in forming the roof was to install forty concrete ribs extending from the edges of the dome up to its center. The ribs were made in sets of four by pouring concrete into forms, which rested in a massive wood-and-steel falsework that supported them until the concrete hardened. When the first four ribs had set, the falsework was to be lowered and rotated along a track to support the next set of forms. The problem was that when the falsework was lowered, the concrete ribs—long arches reaching from the outer walls to the top of the dome-to-be—settled a bit with them, and the falsework would not release from the ribs. Drake called on the design team, which had predicted that lowering the supports only one inch would be sufficient. The device being used to lower the structure was a sand jack, and there were two inches of sand between the two plates of each jack. As sand was blown out from between the plates, the jacks slowly dropped two inches as they were designed to do, but it was not enough.[23]

The designers decided that digging another four inches into the ground would safely release the falsework. Drake's construction managers wanted the county to take responsibility for the operation. The county refused. Spellman, on the advice of his engineers and deputy prosecuting attorney, pointed out that the contractor was responsible for the design of all the construction work, whether or not it had obtained advice from the building design team. A Drake official made his thoughts on the consequences of failure clear, declaring, "If this SOB falls down, Seattle is going to have an 80-year eyesore on its hands." He was correct, but the threat of outright collapse was not very large. Drake's engineers and the county's experts agreed. Digging down under the jacks would be cumbersome but workable. So Drake was holding the roof hostage as it negotiated with Spellman over a new contract. Declaring the county culpable, the contractor left the job site.[24]

All this time—as the engineers were working on how to get the falsework unstuck—Spellman and Drake representatives, including owner Franklin Drake and Stuart Oles, had been hashing out how much King County should pay the construction company and how much time Drake would have to finish the job. The county had initially offered to add $100,000 to cover the change orders and to extend the deadline for completion to January 1975 while strongly hinting that the end of 1975 would be acceptable. Drake found that unacceptable. The talks reached an impasse on November 22, and that is when Drake walked off the job. Oles told the press that the issue was assigning responsibility for the roof when the supports were removed, but the real problem was the contract.[25]

Privately, negotiations continued, with Drake demanding the cost-plus contract. Apparently, between November 22 and 24, Spellman agreed to pay an additional lump sum to Drake for work completed and then put the remainder of the job (about 20–30 percent of the project) on a cost-plus basis, if he could get an acceptable estimate from the company. Drake thought it had a deal and prepared its estimates. But the accord quickly unraveled. Spellman found the construction company's figures unacceptable. Drake thought Spellman had reneged on the deal when he determined that he could not get the county council to approve it. Franklin Drake had threatened to turn Oles loose to the press if the county would not come to an agreement, and he did. Oles essentially accused the county, specifically Spellman, of bad faith regarding the roof and the contract. Drake had returned to the job on November 24 when it thought it had struck a deal and then walked off again on November 27. Spellman was vulnerable to Oles's attack on two fronts. First, baseball's winter meetings were coming up, and another stadium controversy would dampen whatever enthusiasm owners might have to grant Seattle a franchise to play in the domed stadium by 1976. Second, Spellman planned on running for governor in 1976. If the stadium did not get finished or incurred enormous cost overruns, his political stock would plummet.[26]

Spellman demanded that Drake return to work on December 2 or be considered in default on the contract. He extended the deadline a week to December 10 as last-minute negotiations took place. They proved fruitless. The county put the remainder of the project out to bid immediately. With an eye toward future litigation, the county barred Drake from participating. Three firms submitted bids. King County selected Kiewit, even though it did not submit the low bid, because of its national reputation and the experience of Kiewit's key personnel assigned to the project and because the design commission was most comfortable with the company. Kiewit would finish the stadium for $10 million, plus a $500,000 profit and a profit of 4.5 percent on change orders.[27]

Reviews of Spellman's actions were mixed. The *Times* lauded him for keeping the project moving and suggested that Drake would have been better off staying on the job while negotiating. James Ellis wrote a note of encouragement. "It was a gutty move, John. If the new stadium is successfully completed and houses new professional football and baseball teams for the area, you will be vindicated." The *Post-Intelligencer* worried over the work stoppage, then criticized Spellman for awarding Kiewit the contract. Leaders of organized labor were sympathetic to Drake, which they considered a good contractor. And Frank Ruano warned that he would ensure that the county could not use general obligation or revenue bonds to augment the allotted $40 million worth of bonds the voters had approved.[28]

The first task for Kiewit was to lower the falsework. The method was already established, so it was mainly a matter of execution and gallows humor. On January 18, 1975, county councilman John O'Brien stood with John Spellman under one of the ribs as the support structures were lowered. As O'Brien intoned, "In the name of the Father, . . ." the foreman went over to a cautious bulldozer driver pulling the supports off the jacks and yelled, "Just pull it!" He did. The segment stayed in place. From that point onward, Kiewit worked swiftly. The roof was done by July, and the rest of the structure was virtually finished three months ahead of the March 1, 1976, deadline. The only glitch occurred when the Kiewit construction supervisor was discovered skimming off the proceeds of scrap metal sales. He was fired. Also, subcontractors demanded renegotiation, especially because they had not caused the delay and their expenses had risen steadily in the inflationary climate. Schlatter assured them that they would be accommodated so long as their demands were reasonable.[29]

King County voters had authorized $40 million in bonds to build a stadium that should have been completed by opening day of the 1972 baseball season. The Kingdome was completed by opening day . . . of 1976, and at a much higher cost. A false start at Seattle Center, which cost about $1.5 million, delays while inflation sent costs soaring, a change in construction companies, and the revision of agreements with the contractor and subcontractors added up to more than the voters had approved, even on a cost-saving, bare-bones concrete domed stadium. The final figure was $59.8 million. Including expenditures on the Seattle Center site, the county spent $61.3 million—a $20 million cost overrun.[30]

How could this be paid for? Besides the original $40 million of stadium bonds, there was $7.4 million in interest that the bonds had generated before they were spent. A federal grant provided almost a million dollars for the Astroturf surface of the arena. Spellman pondered the sale of surplus county land, but that would never cover the remaining $13 million. County commissioners rejected the idea of a lottery.

The Drake Construction imbroglio became a key piece to the puzzle of stadium finance. When asked about "firing" Drake, John Spellman quickly retorted that he did not fire the company; it walked off the job. This was an essential contention. King County sued Drake for more than $10 million for breach of contract, charging the company with failure to share information with the design team, failure to manage the project, and failure to negotiate in good faith. Drake launched a countersuit, claiming damages of $10.5 million because the county directed it not to proceed with the work (that is, as long as Drake would not take responsibility for the falsework removal). Essentially, the county maintained that Drake sought an enhanced contract while boycotting the job. Drake contended that the matter was a straightforward disagreement over liability for the roof. Norm Maleng brought in Bill Dwyer, a private attorney, to help him with the case. Maleng, defending the expense of hiring a private attorney, declared, "Bill Dwyer is the best and only lawyer for the job" and pointed out that Dwyer would take 60 percent of his normal fee. The *Bellevue American* was effusive, writing, "Bill Dwyer is, in legal circles, rather like God. The Seattle lawyer has won tough complex civil cases involving tons of documents and technical testimony." By the time the trial got under way in 1977, Dwyer was also known by area sports fans as the attorney who had defeated the American League.[31]

In early 1975, Spellman was able use the potential proceeds from the suit as security to recruit a consortium of seven banks that would loan the county $13.5 million for two years. If the county lost the suit, it promised to issue general obligation bonds to pay back the loan. The banks agreed to establish an interest rate at 65 percent of the prime rate. Even considering the taxing power of King County, getting the banks to help was a remarkable feat on the part of the county executive and an unusual act on the part of the banks. The finances were now in place.[32]

But the loan was due by March 31, 1977, and the trial would not even start until September of that year. As the March date grew nearer without an out-of-court settlement and with a $10 million countersuit in the offing, the county council had some work to do. On March 17, 1977, looking over their shoulders at Frank Ruano, who stood ready as always to circulate a petition barring expenditures, council members authorized $13.4 million of councilmanic general obligation bonds to pay back the bank loan. The motion declared that the county would collect this "as a part of the tax levy permitted to counties without a vote of the people upon all property of the county subject to taxation." It was politically risky to alienate residents by levying a property tax without their consent. In reality, the risk had been taken back in 1975. Once obligated to the banks, the council could not very well do anything *but* pass by fiat, as some saw it, bonds to redeem the loans.[33]

Settlement of the suit did not come until 1980, and King County's litigation expenses were high—about $1.6 million, $400,000 of which were attorney costs. But the wait and the costs were worth it. The county hired construction experts who judged the design team's documents entirely adequate and argued effectively that the delays in the project owed almost entirely to Drake's poor coordination with subcontractors, faulty workmanship, and a shortage of tools and equipment at the construction site. In July 1978, Judge Morell Sharp ruled that Drake's decision to walk off the job was "deliberate, intentional, and inexcusable." The roof, the judge decided, "was not an unusual engineering or safety problem." He agreed with the county that the reason for Drake's abandonment of the work site was the prospect of a huge financial loss. Drake Construction had breached its contract. Judge Sharp ordered the company to pay $10.9 million plus interest. Drake immediately appealed to the Ninth Circuit Court of Appeals, but in 1980, before the appeal could go to trial, Drake's liability insurers reached an out-of-court settlement with King County for $12.8 million, covering the ruling and interest. The county took $10 million of the payout and invested it in long-term federal securities to service, and then pay off, the councilmanic bonds. Property taxes, which had been used for three years to pay interest on the councilmanic bonds, would not be affected from that point onward. The county, especially John Spellman, had taken a risk, which even in the midst of the trial was looking rather foolhardy, but had stood firm in the face of financial and political pressure. The Kingdome had been completed, and Drake Construction had contributed to it in ways it surely had not anticipated. [34]

There was a bit more. Savings gained by leasing the heating and cooling energy plant, requiring the concessionaires to install their own facilities, and subsidizing the scoreboard through advertising reduced the final cost of the Kingdome by $6–7 million. In the end, the home owners of King County paid just a few more dollars in property taxes (interest on the councilmanic bonds from 1977 to 1980) than they had authorized in the Forward Thrust vote of 1968.

In January 1974, while the Kingdome was still under construction, the county council selected John O'Brien, who had just stepped down from his position as councilman, as the interim operations manager of the stadium. The council then conducted an extensive search for a permanent stadium director. Marvin Milkes applied and made the first cut, but the council chose former major league pitcher Ted Bowsfield. Bowsfield had been assistant director and then director of Anaheim Stadium. O'Brien became Bowsfield's assistant, bringing his experience with the Kingdome, from the first site selection committee through oversight of construction as council member, to the job.

One of the first duties of the new manager was to find a concessionaire. Conspicuous by its absence from the bidding process was Sportservice, which would have demanded to follow the Pilots to their new home. There were only two bidders: Alpine Food, which ran the concessions at the Pacific National Exposition in Vancouver, British Columbia, and Volume Services, a national concern. After a legal wrangle over the status of the bids, the county chose Alpine.[35]

In anticipation of the grand opening, pins proclaiming "Stadium 75" were sold for one dollar. Souvenir decanters in the shape of the stadium (more or less) were imprinted with "1975." Unfortunately, the building was not ready until March 1976, so the hoopla had to start over again. Opening night, March 27, 1976, was both a celebration and a relief. There was a gala show with something of an American history theme to honor the bicentennial. Tommy Walker, famed orchestrator of Disney extravaganzas, involved all manner of local talent for the show, along with Danny Kaye (who would help bring baseball back to Seattle), Bill Cosby, the Pointer Sisters, Paul Anka, Anne Murray, and Meredith Wilson of *Music Man* and "Seventy-Six Trombones" fame. The relief came when no traffic jams developed, and parking proved adequate for the 54,759 who showed up at the free event. "The Dome opens and it works," proclaimed the *Times*. The budget went immediately into the red when a concert scheduled to pay for the grand opening was canceled. But the deficit was made up when Pele and the New York Cosmos played the Sounders in a soccer match, the first sporting event in the Kingdome. Before that, Billy Graham held an eight-day crusade in the stadium. The Roman Catholic John Spellman had invited the Graham team eighteen months earlier, employing some religious-sounding language that probably did not particularly resonate with the Protestant minister. Spellman wrote that a Graham revival would be "an outstanding christening" for the arena.

Whatever the metaphor, it was a great success. The county charged Billy Graham Ministries $120,000 for the eight days. Graham paid it off in cash the second night. Police had to turn back as many as 10,000 at the gates the night Johnny Cash appeared with the evangelist.[36]

The arena was not all that the populace had voted for. Without separate meeting halls, it was not really the multipurpose stadium promised by Forward Thrust. Spellman could be accused of bowing to the demands of the major league sports establishment in pushing the Kingdome forward. But the Kingdome could and did host a number of events besides big-league sports. There were softball games; variety performances; recreational vehicle, auto, boat, gift, home, mobile home, and trade shows; and American Legion and restaurant conventions. Well-grounded fears that the Kingdome would operate in the red proved untrue. By 1977, when professional football and baseball arrived, the operating budget showed a profit almost every year. And the impact on the surrounding neighborhoods was moderate. In a follow-up three years after the opening, 70 percent of those polled in the neighborhoods near the stadium thought that traffic was a problem. But vacancies were down one-third overall, property assessments had not risen, and 85 percent of the respondents reported that crime had not gotten worse. Most evaluations concluded that the Kingdome had a significantly positive impact on Seattle economically.[37]

It was a remarkable and risky undertaking, building a stadium with no team in sight, working with an already partially spent budget that could not possibly match the rate of inflation. John Spellman was shrewd, lucky, and successful. He knew that inflation would furnish interest on the unspent bonds, which would, in turn, expand his budget. He turned Drake's untoward negotiating strategy into a windfall for the county. He convinced bankers to bridge part of the budget gap and challenged Frank Ruano to stop him from issuing bonds to finish the stadium. The state added almost a half million dollars a year from its lodging tax, which softened the impact on home owners. In a city where politicians had previously lacked much appetite for sports, Spellman worked aggressively, even heedlessly at times, to build an admittedly austere arena while burdening taxpayers with very little more than what they had authorized in the 1968 bond vote.

And it had paid off. The city put behind it the embarrassment of opening the Pilots' season in an uncompleted minor league stadium and the ignominy of losing a major league baseball team after one year. Seattle now had two of the three Stanford Research Institute criteria firmly in place. It had a major league–quality stadium, and the city—voters and elected leaders—had shown a recognizable interest in hosting big league sports. Even before the completion of the stadium, the *Argus* conceded, "The coming of the Domed Stadium has provided symbolic confirmation of the city's emergence." In what would have been music to Joe Gandy's ears, *Time* magazine proclaimed that the Kingdome "literally made Seattle a big league city." The Louisville *Times,* looking on enviously in 1978, noted, "Ten years ago Seattle was a minor league town. Now it is about to be the only city in the country with four major league teams [Mariners, Seahawks, Sonics, and Sounders] playing in the same stadium."[38]

Don Duncan of the *Seattle Times* put a bit of a damper on expectations, peering into his crystal ball in 1973 and reminding Seattleites what happens to big arenas. "So, if history repeats itself," he cautioned, "the domed stadium will need a complete refurbishing within 20 years, be the rag-tag town joke within 30 years, and be the subject of serious discussion for replacement before the mortgage is burned in 2015 A.D." He was not far off. Tiles fell from the ceiling in 1994, requiring a major renovation. On March 26, 2000, the Kingdome was imploded (it is still a day of mourning for John Spellman), making way for a new baseball stadium and a separate football arena. But that story is of another era.[39]

Chapter 12

OUT-OF-COURT SETTLEMENT: THE MARINERS

A CITY with a big-league stadium but no major league team is a laughingstock—or pitiable. The Kingdome needed permanent tenants. It was as though the Milwaukee Brewers group, relieved of the task of pursuing a team, had bequeathed the job to Seattle. The process began almost as soon as the Pilots left. Discussions about using Husky Stadium for pro football surfaced again. There were rumors about the Boston Patriots and the Buffalo Bills looking at Seattle, but the Pilots episode had soured both baseball and football owners on the Northwest for awhile. Once stadium construction was under way, John Spellman, Bill Sears, who had moved back from Milwaukee to become the Kingdome publicity director, and other King County representatives began showing up in Hawaii, or Houston, or Scottsdale—wherever major league baseball or the NFL was meeting—with scale models of the future arena. In 1973, Spellman formed the Major League Sports Committee, composed of "leading civic personalities from around the state," to recruit a team. Much like Bud Selig's group, the Puget Sound area lobbied for a team but mainly stood around waiting for a franchise to drop into its lap. Dave Cohn was also back and negotiating, with Spellman's approval, to lure the San Diego Padres north.[1]

John O'Brien, a former major league player and county councilman, was in charge of buttonholing Bowie Kuhn. O'Brien met with the baseball commissioner all over the country. He asked whether Seattle should pursue an established club or an expansion franchise. Kuhn countered, asking whether O'Brien had found local ownership. Neither had an answer. Stanford Research Institute's third requirement for major league status, deep-pocketed Northwesterners interested in baseball, was still missing. In 1974, pursuit of an owner reached as far as Japan. As the possibility of moving the Oakland A's was heating up, Kuhn came to Seattle to talk to Hidekazu Takuma, senior vice president of Mitsui Electric, and four other prospective owner groups. O'Brien reserved rooms for Kuhn and baseball attorney Sandy Hadden at the Olympic Hotel under the name "Dewey Soriano." Kuhn was intrigued by international ownership, but nothing came of the meeting. Another time, O'Brien and Kuhn met at a Chicago hotel to discuss progress on the stadium—at midnight to avoid publicity. When the meeting broke up, they walked out the door into a gaggle of waiting reporters.[2]

In the meantime, the suit that the state, county, and city had launched against the American League sat and simmered for seven years—a further reminder to major league baseball that Seattle was seeking a team for a stadium that was still under construction. The commissioner and a few of the owners were on good terms with Seattle representatives even while they were courtroom adversaries. Kansas City Royals owner Ewing Kauffman, a consistent defender of Seattle, dropped by to speak with local officials in July 1974. Kauffman was candid. He confided that Oakland could be for sale, Cleveland was hurting financially, and the Baltimore and Minnesota franchises might be looking to move. But his advice to the Northwest was to purchase an expansion team, which, at $10–12 million, would be cheaper than an established franchise. He cautioned Seattleites that baseball was a losing proposition, but a Seattle club might break even, including depreciation of the players, if it could draw a million each season. Kauffman suggested a stadium lease of $400,000 per year, with parking and concessions going to the team. He outlined a revenue-generating plan and strongly urged recruiting local ownership. He also admitted that the suit gave Seattle some leverage, but if the state actually went to trial and won, the city would not soon see major league baseball. Although this could have come across as intimidation from an owner—Spellman perceived that the Kansas City owner was in the game primarily for the money—his listeners judged Kauffman reliable and objective.[3]

In the winter and spring of 1974, all attention turned to the National Football League, which, pressured by the newly formed World Football League (WFL), was ready to expand. Spellman met with the NFL and suggested a lease deal for the stadium. The NFL calculated that Spellman's rent figure combined with other team expenses would equal 17–22 percent of a team's revenue—the highest in the league. It was doubtful a Seattle franchise owner could break even. The league granted a franchise to Tampa Bay but held off on a second team. Pete Rozelle declared that Seattle, Memphis, Phoenix, and even Honolulu were in the running. Some speculated that while the NFL was playing Memphis off against Seattle, Spellman was playing the WFL against the NFL. There was a WFL brochure in the county stadium files, but Spellman maintained that his lease figure was a negotiating point that he planned to ratchet down as discussions went on. The city was full of angst. In June 1974, Spellman tried again, lowering his lease figure to 10 percent of the gate, concessions, and parking. Though it was still one of the costliest leases in the NFL, the league granted Seattle a team. Estimates varied, but the county predicted it might receive $1 million or more per season from such a deal, and the city would get $350,000 from its admission tax.[4]

There were two viable groups seeking the franchise. The better publicized was the Seattle Kings, which was bankrolled by Wayne Field of Minnesota and had Husky football legend Hugh McElhenny as its public face. The entry price was too high for the group, and the NFL preferred local ownership. So it was a consortium of Seattle businessmen who became the owners of what would become the Seattle Seahawks. Lloyd Nordstrom was the lead partner, and Ned Skinner (head of Alaska Steamship), M. Lamont Bean (CEO of drugstore chain Pay 'n' Save), and builder and investor Herman Sarkowsky made up the rest of the partnership. Sounding typically Seattle-like, they maintained that they had bought the team for the good of the city—it was not a business investment but an investment in Seattle. The Seahawks sold twenty-four thousand season tickets in one day and fifty thousand in two weeks. The availability of local buyers and the rush for tickets underlined the results of a statewide poll revealing that 22 percent of Washingtonians preferred professional football, while 18 percent rated baseball number one, and 14.8 percent liked Husky football most. The Sorianos would not have been surprised to discover that Washington, and, by inference Seattle, was more a football market than a baseball region.[5]

Kingdome dates were beginning to fill. In December 1975, the Seattle Sounders soccer team announced that it would be playing its 1976 North American Soccer League games in the stadium. But there was still a yawning gap where seventy to eighty baseball games should fit. Both the suit against the American League and hopeful talks with baseball officials continued into 1976. Privately, Spellman favored a National League team, but he preferred an American League franchise to no team at all. He assured American League president Lee MacPhail that local ownership was available, writing that King County was ready to pursue the A's, Giants, Twins, or White Sox, all of which were rumored to be available. Senators Magnuson and Jackson pitched in with a telegram to the commissioner, telling him that "Seattle fans 'deserve another time at bat.'" Bowie Kuhn said he was enthusiastic about bringing baseball back to the Northwest. Spellman talked to baseball officials about a lease agreement that would yield the county 7 percent of the gate receipts (7.5 percent if attendance exceeded a million) plus one-third of the concessions. There was plenty of goodwill and negotiation, but no team, as the newest trial date for the suit, January 1976, drew closer.[6]

The original suit had been filed in the heat of the battle to keep the Pilots and elicited an injunction against the move. Bankruptcy court judge Sidney Volinn effectively put an end to this first suit by dissolving the injunction. But Volinn's final ruling that Pacific Northwest Sports, Inc., was permanently protected from suits did not preclude future action against the American League or major league baseball. In October 1970, the state of Washington and the City of Seattle added King County to the list of plaintiffs and sued the American League and all its constituent owners. The case bounced from King County Superior Court to federal courts and ultimately to Snohomish County Superior Court, in the county just north of King County. The process dragged on for six years.[7]

The state, county, and city lodged several claims, most of which had been part of the earlier suit (hereafter referred to collectively as "the state"). They sued for breach of contract, fraud, and breach of promise. Seattle had been promised a team; the city had remodeled Sicks' on the anticipation of three or four years' rent; the voters had voted for stadium bonds because a team would play in the new arena; and the league owners kept assuring everyone that the team would stay even though they were aware that a sale that would profit the Pilots' owners was in the works. Knowing that baseball was protected from antitrust litigation on the federal level, the plaintiffs charged violations of Washington State antitrust law. Moreover, since the Pilots controlled the concessions agreement and the radio contract, they would sue for restraint of trade in those industries. The state claimed that these were willful violations of the public trust and state law, so, again, it pressed for triple damages. A verdict for the plaintiffs in this suit could yield more than $30 million. State attorney general Slade Gorton remembered thinking that the state had a good chance because the owners were "a terrible bunch of people." He later observed, "My conclusion was that if any American League owner moved into your neighborhood, he would lower property values." Get them on the stand in front of a jury, Gorton figured, and the case would be won.[8]

The plaintiffs based their reimbursement demands on a whole slew of expenses and lost taxes over ten years: the state claimed more than $1 million in sales tax and business and occupation taxes, $800,000 in lost taxes on baseball, and in excess of $1 million lost from two years of paying the hotel/motel tax to King County for a no-longer-needed stadium. The county totaled unrealized income from the stadium, lost sales tax, and expenditures on design of the Seattle Center site for its claim of more than $3.7 million. The city wanted its outlays for renovating Sicks' Stadium reimbursed and asserted that $75,000 in rent was due even after the bankruptcy settlement. It cited an additional $1.3 million in the business activity taxes it would not collect. The total claim for an anticipated ten years without the Pilots added up to $9.7 million. Some of these figures were more or less cooked up. The attorneys made an assumption that the Pilots would average 900,000 fans a year (about 250,000 more than they drew in 1969) and that 25 percent of them would come from out of state and spend $4.44 on tickets. The latter two figures rested on no firm evidence.[9]

The American League's arguments centered around its antitrust exemption (it fought to move the case to federal court) and the fact that the bankruptcy ruling exempted PNSI from prosecution. In any case, its lawyers argued, it was all Seattle's fault. Sicks' was unacceptable. The multipurpose stadium was not built on time. Seattle's politicians, the business community, and the fans did not support the team. Danz had failed to come through on his promises, and Carlson knew the rules—he had to get nine votes and failed to do so.[10]

The lead attorney for the American League was David Wagoner of the prestigious Seattle firm Perkins, Coie, Stone, Olsen, and Williams. But the state was one up on the defendants. As attorney general, Slade Gorton headed the prosecution's legal team, but he hired Bill Dwyer to

conduct the trial for the state. Gorton once claimed that if he were innocent, Dwyer was the man he would want defending him. (He went on to
say that if he were guilty, John Ehrlichman would be his choice.) Dwyer
grew up in Seattle and worked his way through the University of Washington and then New York University law school. In 1987, the Republican
Gorton, as a United States senator, nominated Dwyer, a Democrat, for a
federal judgeship out of respect for the attorney. Dwyer was masterful.
He seemed to command every bit of evidence in the boxes and boxes of
trial materials scattered about his office. Once the actual trial began, a
reporter observed one of the league's attorneys, John Ferguson, searching in vain for a bit of testimony. Dwyer reached over and handed him
the court transcript, pointing out the section he was looking for. Another
time, Charles Finley came out of the courtroom, ran into Dwyer, and
blurted out, "You've done your homework, haven't you, pal?" The more
self-controlled Jerry Hoffberger said, "I don't want to go back in there—
this guy's ripping me apart."[11]

With Dwyer at the helm, the strategy of putting the owners on display was working. Dwyer was no flamboyant TV prosecutor. He was
calm, polite, and respectful. If a witness evaded his question, he would
simply state, "The question was . . ." as many times as necessary to get
a straight answer. At the end of the trial, a juror commented that Joe
Cronin seemed warm and friendly but thought the owners were high-
falutin, tended to leave out details, and seemed coached on what to
say. Dwyer, the juror also said, was "exceptional." Wagoner and Ferguson were "dippy." As would be the case in the later Drake Construction trial, there was concern about Dwyer's fees. When the state settled
out of court with codefendant Sportservice partway through the trial,
much of that pressure was alleviated by applying Sportservice's payment to the legal bill.[12]

The trial itself lasted only a few days in early 1976 before a settlement
was announced. But as one reads the boxes of documents churned out
in the six years leading up to the trial, it is almost possible to hear the
back-and-forth courtroom arguments that would have developed had
the trial run its course. Brief upon brief reviews the entire history of the
case. Depositions provide testimony and reveal the contours of the legal
strategies of both sides. Petitions for summary judgments preview final
summations.

Attorney Jerry McNaul, Dwyer's right hand, believed that the American League had "an obligation . . . to consider the public interest and to deal with the public in a candid and honest fashion." McNaul and his fellow attorneys were convinced that the league had fallen well short of its responsibility, and he sought to drive home the point that the league had breached its contracts and broken its promises. The plaintiffs touched on ancillary matters. Joe Cronin had told Hy Zimmerman that a team would bring jobs. Cronin, in his deposition, demurred at first, maintaining that he had been referring to the opportunity Zimmerman would have to be official scorer, and then admitted that he had meant that baseball would attract employers to the community. The prosecution also dwelt on more concrete issues. The state asserted that the city had refurbished Sicks' Stadium and the county began to build a new arena on the promise of the rental income and tax revenue that the new franchise would generate. Yet the league did not make a genuine effort to ensure that the team stayed in the city. It failed to hold William Daley to his obligation to underwrite the club for up to $8 million. Dwyer pulled this from Finley's deposition: "We inquired of Mr. Daley if he would be interested in carrying it all [as the Pilots floundered financially], and he said absolutely no." The plaintiffs questioned why a team that outdrew several other major league baseball clubs should have to leave a city after one year. Even if it was mismanaged, Dwyer noted, the American League constitution called for the league to take over a club that fell into bankruptcy.[13]

That line of reasoning, Dwyer knew, would lead to the league's rebuttal that the bankruptcy court had compelled the sale and the move. But in a careful sidestep, he argued that the league could have been more diligent in forestalling bankruptcy in the first place by giving more time to Danz to solve the bank loan problems or by approving Carlson. During those deliberations, Ewing Kauffman had clearly said that if Carlson fulfilled the terms—which he did—the American League would have to grant him the franchise. Charles Finley had gone further, predicting a lawsuit if Carlson were rejected. The Carlson bid was rejected because of its novel nonprofit feature, the plaintiffs argued, not because of any financial issues. The owners had not included a prohibition on a nonprofit arrangement in the criteria they required of Carlson. James Ellis recalled Jerry Hoffberger, after the Carlson group was voted down, promising that baseball would stay in Seattle with the help of the American League. Later in Seattle, Roy Hamey made the same promises. In the briefs, much was made of the "doctored" resolution as the league began to backtrack on its promises to keep the club in Seattle even before the mimeograph machine printing the press release had begun to turn.[14]

The defense countered mainly with protests that the Danz and Carlson offers were inadequate and that the league had not entered into a multiyear contract with the city, county, or state to maintain a ball club in Seattle. It was PNSI that held the contracts, and those were terminated by the bankruptcy ruling. If anyone had broken the contracts, it was the city, for failing to provide a proper stadium, and the county, which failed to start construction on the stadium on time.

One of the state's strongest points involved the Forward Thrust stadium vote. In the trial, James Ellis was the first to take the stand. He testified that the Forward Thrust committee had waited for the American League to promise a team before making the final decision to put the stadium on the ballot. Dwyer later awarded Ellis an autographed ball honoring "the best leadoff hitter in Snohomish County." Both Ellis and Spellman maintained that the league's promises of a team weighed heavily in their decision making. Ellis pointed out that the stadium bonds were behind in the polls until the American League emissaries campaigned for them. Dwyer was ready with Joe Cronin's words that his league was in Seattle to stay. On the stand, Cronin endeavored to be as opaque as possible—one observer was unsure whether Cronin always understood what he was being asked—as he argued that the American League did not have a contract with Seattle but with PNSI.[15]

The Sicks' Stadium issues mainly served the defense. According to the league, it was the city that had failed to honor its promises to provide a major league stadium and brought the loss of the Pilots upon itself. The state was fortunate that Pilots stadium director Lew Matlin's copious correspondence with the city, pointing out the deficiencies of Sicks', was not admitted as evidence (highly prejudicial, argued McNaul). The state was prepared, just in case, to offer pictures of deteriorating American League stadiums in Detroit and Cleveland as evidence that Sicks' was not such a bad place for baseball after all. The main advantage for the plaintiffs on the Sicks' issue was that the Pilots had run out on what improvements had been made and left their rent unpaid. Since neither offense had been redressed in the bankruptcy liquidation, contentions over Sicks' could have yielded some reimbursement for the city.

The antitrust charges died a quiet death midway through the suit. The plaintiffs argued in the basic terms of an antitrust grievance. Baseball was a business that engaged in "creating, selling and transferring franchises." Franchises were limited and, consequently, artificially inflated. Tickets prices were artificially fixed. Restraint of trade afflicted broadcasting with its exclusive contracts. There were only a few viable bidders for any concessions contract, and they often had tying contracts to follow the club wherever it went. These arguments were not new and had not been effective when Milwaukee sued to keep the Braves. But the state's attorneys decided that the Wisconsin precedents did not bind Washington courts. Dwyer made a major misstep by referring to the Sherman Antitrust Act in his background section as he tried to anticipate defense arguments. The reference opened the door to remanding the case to federal court. The Curt Flood case, which involved the reserve clause and, thus, antitrust issues, had an impact as well. After the U.S. Supreme Court ruled in favor of major league baseball in the Flood case, the defense in the Pilots case petitioned the court for a summary judgment regarding the antitrust issues, claiming that the Supreme Court had agreed that state antitrust laws were preempted by federal law. In February 1974, the antitrust portion of the state's suit was dismissed, but the judge saw fit to retain conspiracy charges along with questions about the concessionaire's exclusionary business practices.[16]

Probably the most viable argument supporting the claim of violation of antitrust laws involved Sportservice, the concessionaire. The state asserted that the guarantee that the concessionaire could follow the Pilots wherever the team went—that is, into the Kingdome—was illegal on the basis of *Twin Cities Sportservice v. Finley*. In that case, the court had ruled that the tying contract the A's had signed with Sportservice in Kansas City could not constrain Finley's choice of a concessionaire in Oakland. Further, Dwyer and his staff argued that a tying contract was an outright violation of free trade. Dwyer underlined this point, noting that at least once Dewey Soriano had told a Sportservice representative that "if we can't put you in that dome, then we recognize we [the Pilots] might have to go someplace else." Since King County deputy prosecutor Norm Maleng had ruled that competitive bidding must take place in the selection of the Kingdome concessions provider, did it mean that the Pilots would relocate to another city if Sportservice lost the bid? The defense had some ammunition in defending against the charges. It pointed out that John Spellman had been willing to negotiate with

Sportservice, and Ed Carlson had not seen the tying contract as much of an issue as he finalized his bid for the team. Though the plaintiffs were ready to make the argument that the concessions contract pushed the Pilots into the arms of an out-of-town buyer, it was not completely clear that matters were that stark.[17]

Nonetheless, the state argued that Sportservice had pressed owners to vote against the Carlson plan in order to save its contract with whoever owned the Pilots. The concessionaire provided Selig with an additional $1 million in loans. But, since it faced a competitive bidding process once the Kingdome was finished, it would not provide Danz or Carlson with an additional loan—proof of restraint of trade. Moreover, Sportservice had contracts with the four American League clubs that voted against Carlson, evidence that the company had pushed its partners in other cities to get it out of a jam in Seattle.[18]

It would be hard, the defense maintained, to prove that Sportservice had orchestrated a conspiracy of owners against Seattle. Clearly, Charles Finley did not have a positive relationship with Sportservice since he was suing them. Bob Short, owner of the Washington Senators, had been vociferous in his displeasure with the firm. A portion of a team's reputation, Short argued, rides on the quality of the food, and an owner had to be able to exercise control over that. Another Sportservice franchise, Detroit, had voted for Carlson. It may well have been difficult to prove, but the charge had enough weight to force an out-of-court settlement. In spring 1975, Sportservice agreed to pay more than $200,000 to the state. Attorney General Gorton had his eye on a baseball team as the ultimate out-of-court settlement, so the dollar payment was a welcome bonus that covered most of the attorney fees.[19]

The charges against Golden West Broadcasting had the flavor of "covering all the bases." Not much research went into the issue, and it did not get off the ground at the actual trial. The plaintiffs maintained that Pilots caretaker Roy Hamey had drastically pared down the radio contract from $850,000 to $212,500. The state argued that the action, done without negotiations, was "intended . . . to render the Seattle club's financial position untenable." The league's rebuttal was that it was necessary, because 1969 had been "disastrous" for KVI, and 1970 ad revenue had plummeted. And that was the extent of the arguments.[20]

The case moved with all the swiftness of a catcher running from second to third on a triple. The laborious task of gathering evidence, the arguments over jurisdiction, and the waxing and waning hopes of obtaining an established franchise, which stimulated continuances in hopes of a settlement, all bogged down the process. Attorneys for both sides traveled the country to obtain depositions. A trip to see Charlie Finley was an adventure. The A's owner was a loose cannon who might say or do anything, often to the advantage of the prosecution. Dwyer remarked, "Caution was not Mr. Finley's nature. He was a very enthusiastic, strong-minded and good-humored entrepreneur who didn't believe in beating around the bush." Jerry McNaul remembers going with Dwyer to Finley's office. Finley sought to provide them with call girls and an autographed baseball bat. They turned him down and got on with the interview. Dwyer also pushed hard on a very unwilling league to obtain documents, especially those relating to Cronin's visit in support of the Forward Thrust stadium vote and materials relating to the transfer of the Pilots. The clubs maintained that the documents could not be located. The pulling and tugging lasted until it was discovered in 1973 that the American League had word-for-word transcripts of the league meetings. They were to be the basis of sanitized minutes that would become the official documents, but the transcripts had not yet been destroyed. The state obtained access to them, after about three months of foot-dragging by the league, when the superior court ordered them produced and gained entrée to the deliberations of the owners. Besides these, the league had to provide studies of the economics of baseball in Seattle, documents concerning Finley's anticipated move to Seattle, and its records regarding PNSI. McNaul observed that this trove of information changed the complexion of the trial, allowing the state to put the owners' sometimes cynical deliberations on display.[21]

One of the reasons the discovery phase of the trial (i.e., the gathering of evidence) took so long was the prolonged litigation over jurisdiction. The American League immediately asked that the trial be transferred to federal court based on Dwyer's passing reference to the Sherman Act. The defense further argued that it was a federal case since the Pilots had moved out of the state, the bankruptcy court that ordered the move was a federal court, and baseball was an interstate enterprise. The case went first to U.S. District Court in 1971 and then on to the federal Ninth Circuit Court of Appeals. In May 1972, the circuit court ruled that although the claim involved interstate commerce, the law allowed for litigation to take place in state courts and that the claim itself was based on Washington's consumer protection act. So, the case returned to state superior court. That was not the end of the venue issues. In 1974, the superior court rejected the plaintiffs' antitrust arguments connected to the hotel/motel tax and the broadcast contract. The state then filed these grievances in federal court, where they would be heard after the case in superior court—now centered on concessions and the building of the stadium—came to a conclusion. One final change in venue was the move from King County Superior Court. The American League argued that inflammatory newspaper articles in the Seattle papers biased potential jurors. Further, King County residents had voted on the stadium in the Forward Thrust election and, as property-tax payers, had a direct stake in the stadium. King County jurors would also likely be favorable to prominent witnesses like Carlson and Ellis. Lee MacPhail, who had become American League president, was undoubtedly correct when he said that there was no place in the state where the league could get an unbiased jury. The trial was moved one county north to Everett and Snohomish County Superior Court.[22]

With no team in sight by December 1974, major league baseball, the state, and the county once again agreed to one last continuance, until January 1976. This time, the delay spurred tough negotiations between the state and the city. Corporate counsel John Harris informed Dwyer that the City of Seattle did not want to wait any longer and was prepared to go to trial alone to seek reimbursement for the improvements at Sicks' and lost tax revenue. Dwyer wrote to Mayor Uhlman urging him to stay calm. He told Uhlman that the threat of a trial had put Seattle ahead of Toronto and Washington, D.C., for a franchise and reminded Uhlman that the city would have to win the suit (probably without Dwyer's participation) if it were to obtain any compensation. Conversely, if the city backed off and obtained a team, it could reasonably expect to earn $203,000 a year in taxes, and the lost expenditures would soon be made up. The mayor chose not to disrupt the state's strategy and acquiesced to the delay.[23]

January 1976 came, and there was still no team. The trial began in the Snohomish County Superior Court of Frank Howard. Jury selection was biased toward those who knew little about baseball or the Pilots. Only one jury member had bought a ticket to a Pilots game. But the state's strategy of exposing jurors to the owners worked. Bob Short was combative. The *Times* wrote that Joe Cronin shadowboxed his way through his testimony and that every witness for the league needed his mind refreshed with a reading of the transcripts. The trial lasted only a few days before a settlement was reached. An interview with jurors after the trial revealed that one had favored the league, one had been undecided, and nine had sided with the state.[24]

Slade Gorton, John Spellman, and Bill Dwyer had been in serious negotiations with baseball since the summer of 1975. Both sides preferred to avoid actually going to trial. Specific local owners had been identified: Dave Cohn had a group; Bank of California represented a threesome of potential owners; and Les Smith and Danny Kaye were ready to buy a franchise. John Spellman guaranteed that the Kingdome would be ready for an April 1, 1976, opening or else the county would reimburse any lost revenue. Baseball officials were getting nervous. Their attorneys assured them that the case would eventually be won, but White Sox owner Bill Veeck, for one, thought he detected some doubts. Lee MacPhail put it most pragmatically: "There was going to be a jury trial in the state of Washington and I didn't think we were going to fare too well, so we gave them an expansion team." Two days into the trial, the American League awarded Seattle a franchise at its Phoenix meeting. The deal included an ironclad agreement that the team would stay in Seattle at least twenty years. Next, the league needed to settle on ownership. As the owners dawdled over finalizing the franchise award, the trial went on. Dwyer made sure they got the message that it was critical to act by issuing an ultimatum. If the league did not officially grant Seattle a team by January 31, just a few days away, the state would seek a franchise plus $1 million. Negotiations and paperwork extended the process a few extra days without repercussions, and by February 6, Seattle had a new major league baseball team.[25]

There were still some matters left over. The state wanted to be sure that the settlement was nailed down. The two sides agreed to a continuation of the trial until April 1977. Only after the new team had taken the field would the case be dismissed. The city, which had not really contributed much to the legal effort, balked again. Seattle, not so sure it was satisfied with just a new baseball team, threatened to derail the settlement. It still wanted compensation for the refurbishment of Sicks' Stadium and was ready to argue that the new team would cost the city $50,000 a year in game-day traffic control. The city estimated that the league still owed it at least $750,000 after subtracting one year's rent and accounting for its portion of the bankruptcy settlement. Dwyer was aghast. He launched one of his strongest arguments of the entire episode in a letter to the city. The state had paid for most of the trial. Continued litigation risked the loss of the franchise. The city did not have much prospect of winning damages. Asserting that the team would cost the city rather than benefit it would destroy a central contention of the plaintiffs. In short, if the city did not go along, the past six years could be wasted. The mayor and city council were persuaded. The council voted eight to one to accept the settlement. Only Tim Hill, who had argued from the beginning that the money for Sicks' could have been better used for a library, voted against it. John Spellman quickly worked out a contract with the new team. The lease for the Kingdome would last twenty years, with an option for five more. The county would get a 5 percent cut of all ticket revenue for three years, after which it would rise to 7 percent. The county would select a concessionaire, and the team would get 20 percent of sales.[26]

Warren Magnuson celebrated the second baseball franchise with a self-congratulatory press release. He announced with "sheer delight" that "we brought back major league baseball to the City of Seattle, the County of King, and the State of Washington where it belongs." There was no question that the lawsuit helped stimulate the decision, but he wanted his constituents to know that their congressional delegation had done its best to convince Bowie Kuhn that it was serious about the matter.[27]

The heroes, though, were Slade Gorton, Bill Dwyer, and, above all, John Spellman. Without the threat of a suit, the owners' resentment toward Seattle leadership and fans for putting them in a no-win situation in the winter and spring of 1970 might have endured for some time. The league could have easily put other worthy cities ahead of Seattle for one or more expansion cycles. The suit conjured by Gorton's and Dwyer's diligence and brilliance had moved Seattle to the top of the list. But it was Spellman's determination to get the Kingdome built and—with the help of John O'Brien, Kingdome publicist Bill Sears, and, yes, probably Dave Cohn—to hound major league baseball for a franchise that restored the game to the Puget Sound region in 1977.

The nautical figure may have changed from Pilots to Mariners, but many aspects of baseball in Seattle remained eerily familiar. Much of the ownership was local. Lester Smith owned Seattle radio station KJR. Walter Schoenfeld ran furniture stores. Stan Golub was in the jewelry business, Jim Stillwell construction, and Jim Walsh department stores. Dick Vertleib was associated with every Seattle professional team at one time. But, again, the only truly wealthy owner was from out of town: entertainer Danny Kaye was the managing general partner. They had bought the franchise for a total of $6.5 million, but the ownership group was undercapitalized. Because of the need to draw fans, the Mariners went after name veterans in the expansion draft. Attendance was more than 1 million the first year. But it took fifteen years for the Mariners to produce a .500 season, and the team failed to reach the million mark six out of the next seven years. During the 1980s, attendance figures were the lowest in major league baseball. There is something about Seattle that does not like a losing baseball team. To the credit of the new franchise, its "win/cost ratio" was in line with those of other major league teams. Seattle's average ticket price divided by its winning percentage stood at 11.5, just off the league average of 11.6.[28]

In 1981, with the five-year depreciation window closing, several owners wanted out. George Argyros, a California developer, bought the team for $13 million. In 1989, Argyros sold the Mariners to Indianapolis radio broadcasting executive Jeff Smulyan for $77.5 million plus $12 million in liabilities. Smulyan was lauded as the savior of baseball in Seattle, but by 1993, he was ready to sell the team to Tampa–Saint Petersburg. Again, echoing the plight of PNSI, Smulyan was afflicted with debt and pressed by the call of a loan by Security Pacific Bank. Smulyan claimed that he had lost $6 million in 1990 and $11.6 million in 1991. Sports business writer Andrew Zimbalist, reflecting Paul Beeston's comments on baseball accounting, reworked Smulyan's numbers and came up with a $2.3 million profit in 1990 and a profit of $1.3 million in 1991. Major league baseball required that Smulyan offer the team to local ownership first. Again, a prospective owner from Japan stepped forward. Commissioner Fay Vincent and major league baseball showed less enthusiasm for international ownership than Bowie Kuhn had in the 1970s. Nonetheless, Hiroshi Yamauchi of Nintendo joined a local group of buyers to purchase the team for $100 million. In September 1995, King County voters, displaying their characteristic reluctance to tax themselves for sports, turned down a .1 percent sales tax increase to fund a new baseball stadium. As it had before the 1968 Forward Thrust vote, the legislature then imposed its own tax on restaurant food and beverages, rental cars, and entertainment tickets in King County and added some lottery money to build the stadium. The total cost ended up being $517 million, 81 percent from the public coffers, for an arena with a retractable roof. The Mariners, now seemingly a stable franchise, moved into what was then baseball's most expensive single-purpose stadium in midseason 1999.[29]

EPILOGUE

THE BOX SCORE

MOST Seattleites still remember the Pilots, if only as the team that left Seattle after one year or as the forerunners of the Milwaukee Brewers. Long-term residents might recall the Virginia drawl of Jimmy Dudley as the background to an extended summer twilight. Others remember spending a day at Sicks' Stadium, or even making several visits: sitting in the broiling (for Seattle) sun watching Joe Sparma go eight innings before giving up a ringing double to Don Mincher or shivering in an evening drizzle just to be one of the hundred fans still in the park at the end of a doubleheader. Seattleites got their first taste of major league baseball in 1969. Their descriptions make clear that the Pilots' brand of baseball and its setting made it feel as though they were more on the cusp between the majors and minor league ball. It was a thrill to see the stars of other teams in person for the first time. With the stands so close to the field, almost anybody could strike up a conversation with a player before the game or even run onto the field and "kipe" a batting practice ball. A fan could heckle a preening Ken Harrelson and know that the Hawk heard the jibes. Even in a more restrained era, a kid knew that if he could screw up his courage, he was likely to get a major league autograph—though probably from a player he had never heard of. The sight of Ichiro Suzuki in a Pilots uniform on Turn Back the Clock Day in 2006 could be startling, invoking memories of another team in another Seattle.

The Seattle of the twenty-first century cannot help but bear a resemblance to the city of 1969. Though the urban sprawl that Jim Ellis urged his city to prepare for has arrived, it is still the mountains, trees (even though there are not as many of them), water, long stretches of cloudy days, and, of course, the rain that give the city its character. But there are more people in the Puget Sound area, over a million more. Traffic jams on stretches of I-5 now last twelve to fourteen hours. Downtown is still vital, but people go there more for entertainment than to shop. Condominiums sprout where single-family dwellings used to dominate. The Port of Seattle is bustling. Sea-Tac International Airport has a third runway and satellite terminals. The Seattle area is headquarters to Amazon.com, Costco, Microsoft, Nintendo of America, and Starbucks. Seattle is no longer a one-company town in the twenty-first century. And those new companies have not only furnished deep-pocketed ownership for sports teams in the city but underwritten cultural institutions, festivals, and charitable activities. Seattle has a national reputation now, one that does not rest solely on sports. It may still be tucked away in a mossy corner of the country, but that adds to the ambience. It is the epitome of coffee culture in the United States. Though the genre is now rather passé, Seattle was the home of grunge rock in the 1990s, and, consequently, it is watched for further contributions to popular culture. The city is far more cosmopolitan. Diversity is a deeply held value rather than a pleasant theoretical ideal. And, ironically, for a place that seemed indifferent to sports in the 1960s, Seattle was the greatest expansion team city in the nation for almost four decades. From the 1960s though the 1990s, it snared two expansion baseball teams, one NBA team, and an NFL team. All this points to Seattle as a major league city. Viewing the proposition through a sports lens, the fact that so little was made of the relocation of the city's first major league team, the Supersonics, to Oklahoma City indicates that Seattle has grown up. It is now a metropolis that can take that kind of loss without suffering status anxiety. Its place and self-perception are secure.

In the early 1960s, words like "careful," "restrained," and "prudent" best described the civic psyche. City Hall and much of the populace were comfortable with a caretaker government. Civic leaders chafed at the idea that their city appeared remote, or even quaint, to the rest of the nation, but only a few took action to change the perception. But during the 1960s and into the 1970s, the city began to take measures to put itself on the map. Seattle, typically, would take its time. There would be no quantum leaps or explosions of growth in the Northwest. But there were steps toward becoming big league.

The first step was the Century 21 Exposition, an early sign that civic leaders were ahead of the politicians. Ed Carlson, James Ellis, and Joe Gandy fully emerged as men who could make things happen and recruit others to advance the welfare of their city. These men and their friends became important players in bringing greater recognition to Seattle, first through the world's fair, then Forward Thrust, and then major league baseball.

But lacking enthusiasm from the mayor and the city council, the push for major league sports and a major league stadium sputtered for a time. When Gabe Paul and William Daley visited from Cleveland, Seattle's welcome was lukewarm. Charlie Finley felt he got the cold shoulder. Voters defeated two stadium bond issues. Only when Gandy and Ellis allied to put the stadium vote on the Forward Thrust ballot did things got rolling again. The positive stadium vote assured Seattle of a baseball team.

Most scholars writing about the business of sports find the advent of the Pilots atypical. It was not the city that bent over backward to acquire the team (Gandy and Dave Cohn notwithstanding). It was the American League owners who saw an untapped territory and rushed like a band of stampeders headed to the Klondike to get to Seattle before the National League. Even with a team at the door, Seattleites had to be heavily courted to do something they had never done—approve bonds for a stadium. It was at this point, according to the more skeptical sports scholars, that a team was supposed to blackmail the city to get a quality interim stadium and push the county into cost overruns to build a wondrous domed facility. Instead, it was the city that told the team, literally, to take or leave Sicks' Stadium as it had been prepared. When the Pilots decided to leave, the more vigorous civic leaders weighed in and almost saved the day, but without truly wealthy investors, even they fell short. The loss of the Pilots after only one year was a step backward for Seattle's reputation, at least in sports circles.

It was a change in political leadership that began to recoup the region's status. New mayor Wes Uhlman and CHECC changed the city's government into a more active force. King County Executive John Spellman exercised similarly dynamic leadership to bring major league sports to the Northwest. Spellman risked building a stadium without a tenant, waded through Frank Ruano's endless initiatives, called Drake Construction's bluff, and massaged both the project and the budget to bring forth the Kingdome—a spartan building—without incurring a significant additional burden beyond what taxpayers had authorized. With the stadium in place, and with legal pressure on organized baseball, Seattle was finally ready for the next step: major league sports.

Seattle had done a good deal of growing from 1962 to 1976. By the time the Kingdome was completed, both the city and its leadership had established a much stronger claim to major league status. The story of baseball in Seattle, reaching from the inception of the Pilots to the completion of the Kingdome, exemplifies something about professional sports and cities that declare themselves big league. The arrival of the Seahawks and the Mariners did not make Seattle big league. It reflected what the city had already become.

APPENDIX A

Pilots Team Statistics

WON 64   LOST 98

HOME 34–47   ROAD 30–51

versus

Baltimore	3–9
Boston	6–6
California	9–9
Chicago	8–10
Cleveland	5–7
Detroit	2–10
Kansas City	8–10
Minnesota	6–12
New York	5–7
Oakland	5–13
Washington	7–5

Team Batting and Rank among Twelve American League Teams

RUNS	HITS	HR	RBI	BB	K	BA	OBP	SLG	OPS	SB	E
639	1,276	125	583	626	1,015	.234	.316	.346	.662	167	167
7	9	7	9	4	1	11	7	8	8	1	1 (most)

HR = home runs; RBI = runs batted in; BB = bases on balls; K = strikeouts; BA = batting average; OBP=on base percentage (hits + base on balls + hit by pitch/at bats + base on balls + hit by pitch + sacrifice fly); SLG = slugging percentage (total bases/at bats); OPS = OBP + SLG; SB = stolen bases; E = errors (#1 rank means most errors)

Team Pitching and Rank among Twelve American League Teams

HITS	RUNS	ER	HR	BB	K	CG	SV	ERA	WHIP (BB+H/IP)
1490	799	707	172	653	963	21	33	4.35	1.464
12	12	12	12	9	3	12	7	12	12

ER = earned runs; HR = home runs allowed; BB = bases on balls allowed; K = strikeouts; CG = complete games; SV = saves; ERA = earned run average; WHIP = base on balls + hits/innings pitched

Sources: Data from Hogan, *The 1969 Seattle Pilots*;
SeattlePilots.com, http://www.seattlepilots.com/; and
Baseball-Reference.com, http://www.baseball-reference.com/

APPENDIX B

Pilots Batting Statistics

NAME	G	AB	H	R	AVG	OBP	SLG	OPS	HR	RBI	SB
Ron Clark	57	163	32	9	.196	.260	.227	.485	0	12	1
Wayne Comer	147	481	118	88	.245	.356	.380	.735	15	54	18
Tommy Davis	123	454	123	52	.271	.322	.379	.697	6	80	19
John Donaldson	95	338	79	22	.234	.307	.284	.591	1	19	6
Mike Ferraro	5	4	0	0	.000	.200	.000	.200	0	0	0
Gus Gil	92	221	49	20	.222	.272	.253	.525	0	17	2
Greg Goossen	52	139	43	19	.309	.385	.597	.982	10	24	1
Jim Gosger	39	55	6	4	.109	.197	.236	.433	1	1	2
Larry Haney	22	59	15	3	.254	.323	.407	.730	2	7	1
Tommy Harper	148	537	126	78	.235	.349	.311	.660	9	41	73
Mike Hegan	95	267	78	54	.292	.427	.461	.888	8	37	6
Steve Hovley	91	329	91	41	.277	.339	.365	.703	3	20	10
John Kennedy	61	128	30	18	.234	.315	.367	.682	4	14	4
Gordy Lund	20	38	10	4	.263	.349	.263	.612	0	1	1
Jerry McNertney	128	410	99	39	.241	.291	.349	.640	8	55	1
Don Mincher	140	427	105	53	.246	.366	.454	.821	25	78	10
Ray Oyler	106	255	42	24	.165	.260	.267	.526	7	22	1
Jim Pagliaroni	40	110	29	10	.264	.333	.455	.788	5	14	0
Merritt Ranew	54	81	20	11	.247	.330	.272	.601	0	4	0
Rich Rollins	58	187	42	15	.225	.270	.326	.596	4	21	2
Dick Simpson	26	51	9	8	.176	.236	.333	.570	2	5	3
Fred Stanley	17	43	12	2	.279	.319	.372	.691	0	4	1
Sandy Valdespino	20	38	8	3	.211	.250	.237	.487	0	2	0
Freddie Velazquez	6	16	2	1	.125	.176	.250	.426	0	2	0
Jose Vidal	18	26	5	7	.192	.323	.385	.707	1	2	1
Danny Walton	23	92	20	12	.217	.275	.370	.644	3	10	2
Steve Whitaker	69	116	29	15	.250	.323	.440	.763	6	13	2
Billy Williams	4	10	0	1	.000	.167	.000	.167	0	0	0

G = games played; AB = at bats; H = hits; R = runs; AVG = batting average; OBP = on base percentage (hits + base on balls + hit by pitch/at bats + base on balls + hit by pitch + sacrifice fly); SLG = slugging percentage (total bases/at bats); OPS = OBP + SLG; HR = home runs; RBI = runs batted in; SB = stolen bases

Sources: Data from SeattlePilots.com, http://seattlepilots.com/; and Baseball-Reference.com, http://www.baseball-reference.com/

APPENDIX C

Pilots Pitching Statistics

NAME	G	IP	GS	W	L	SV	HR	BB	K	ERA
Jack Aker	15	16.2	0	0	2	3	4	13	7	7.56
Dick Baney	9	18.2	1	1	0	0	2	7	9	3.86
Steve Barber	25	86.1	16	4	7	0	9	48	69	4.80
Dick Bates	1	1.2	0	0	0	0	1	3	3	27.00
Gary Bell	13	61.1	11	2	6	2	8	34	30	4.70
Jim Bouton	57	92.0	1	2	1	1	12	38	68	3.91
Gene Brabender	40	202.1	29	13	14	0	26	103	139	4.36
Darrell Brandon	8	15.0	1	0	1	0	4	16	10	8.40
George Brunet	12	63.2	11	2	5	0	11	28	37	5.37
Bill Edgerton	4	4.0	0	0	1	0	1	0	2	13.50
Miguel Fuentes	8	26.0	4	1	3	0	1	16	14	5.19
John Gelnar	39	108.2	10	3	10	3	7	26	69	3.31
Bob Locker	51	78.1	0	3	3	6	3	26	46	2.18
Skip Lockwood	6	23.0	3	0	1	0	3	6	10	3.52
Mike Marshall	20	87.2	14	3	10	0	8	35	47	5.13
Bob Meyer	6	32.2	5	0	3	0	4	10	17	3.31
John Morris	6	12.2	0	0	0	0	2	8	8	6.39
John O'Donoghue	55	70.0	0	2	2	6	5	37	48	2.96
Marty Pattin	34	158.2	27	7	12	0	29	71	126	5.62
Garry Roggenburk	7	24.1	4	2	2	0	6	11	11	4.44
Diego Segui	66	142.1	8	12	6	12	14	61	113	3.35
Jerry Stephenson	2	2.2	0	0	0	0	0	3	1	10.13
Fred Talbot	25	114.2	16	5	8	0	12	41	67	4.16
Gary Timberlake	2	6.0	0	0	0	0	0	9	4	7.50
Dooley Womack	9	14.1	0	2	1	0	0	3	8	2.51

G = games played; IP = innings pitched; GS = games started; W = wins; L = losses;
SV = saves; HR = home runs allowed; BB = bases on balls allowed; K = strikeouts;
ERA = earned run average

Source: Data from Baseball-Reference.com, http://www.baseball-reference.com/

ABBREVIATIONS USED IN NOTES

BL-SMA   Seattle Municipal Archives, City of Seattle Law Department Baseball Litigation Files

DEPC   David Eskenazi, Personal Collection

KCA   King County Archives

M-SMA   Seattle Municipal Archives, Office of the Mayor

UWSC   University of Washington Libraries Special Collections

WaNW   Washington State Archives, Northwest Regional Branch, Bellingham

WaPS   Washington State Archives, Puget Sound Regional Branch, Bellevue

NOTES

Introduction

1   *Seattle Times*, 8 March 1969.
2   Duckstad and Waybur, *Feasibility*, 6–9.

Chapter 1. Seattle

1   Duncan, *Meet Me at the Center*, 21.
2   A. T. Kearney and Company, Inc., "Economic Action Task Force," 12; Forward Thrust, "Developing a Capital Improvement Plan: Part IV," 27; Robert Gladstone and Associates, "Basic Economic Indicators," 43; A. T. Kearney and Company, Inc., "Economic Action Task Force," exhibit 3; and Forward Thrust, "Developing a Capital Improvement Plan: Part I," 172.
3   Findlay, *Magic Lands*, 11, 216; Griffith, "The Pacific Northwest," 47; and *Argus*, 27 June 1969.
4   Halpin, "Our Musty, Crusty City Council," 14; A. T. Kearney and Company, Inc., "Economic Action Task Force," IV-12; Thiel, *Out of Left Field*, 12; Study City Team, Northwestern University, *Seattle*, 25–26; and Sale, *Seattle*, 195, 214.
5   King County, Washington, "1970 Overall Economic Development Plan," II-C-2; Sale, *Seattle*, 197; and Sell, *Wings of Power*, 34.
6   Sell, *Wings of Power*, 14–15.
7   Allen, quoted in Rodgers, *Flying High*, 78; Serling, *Legend and Legacy*, 68; and Watson, *Once upon a Time in Seattle*, 150.
8   Dumovich, *The Boeing Logbook*, unpaginated; *Seattle Times*, 27 January 1976; Forward Thrust, "Developing a Capital Improvement Plan: Part I," 170; and King County, Washington, *Official Statement*, 4.
9   William Allen, speech, 23 September 1965, folder "Stadium 2," box 3, Ellis Collection, UWSC; Sell, *Wings of Power*, 54; young activist, quoted in Study City Team, Northwestern University, *Seattle*, 39; and Sell, *Wings of Power*, 55.
10 A. T. Kearny and Company, Inc., "Economic Action Task Force," III-14–17, IV-3; Sale, *Seattle*, 237; and Herrera, "Megalopolis," 121.
11 *Seattle Times*, 13 and 21 September 1960.
12 Watson, *Digressions of a Native Son*, 184; and Bunzel, "Antidisestablishmentarianism," 25.
13 Bunzel, "Antidisestablishmentarianism," 25; Slade Gorton, interview by author, Seattle, 17 January 2008; Cunningham, quoted in MacDonald, *Distant Neighbors*, 169, and Brewster, "The Good, Gray Times," 40; and Speidel, *Through the Eye of the Needle*, vii.
14 Ellis and professor, quoted in Study City Team, Northwestern University, *Seattle*, 30–31; Morgan, *Skid Road*, 281; and Banfield, *Big City Politics*, 146.
15 Banfield, *Big City Politics*, 134–35.

16 Brewster, "Floyd Miller," 24; and John Spellman, interview by author, Seattle, 30 July 2008.

17 LeSourd, "How a Slate Took Over"; *Argus*, 8 September 1967; and Morgan, *Skid Road*, 276.

18 *Argus*, 5 September, 7 November 1969; Crowley, "So Long, Wes"; and MacDonald, *Distant Neighbors*, 174.

19 Halpin, "The Auto's Terrible Tyranny," 45.

20 Peck, "Arts Activists and Seattle's Cultural Expansion," 88–89; and Park, "Prescriptive Plans," 110–11.

21 Bouton, *Ball Four*, 397; and Ross, quoted in Duncan, *Meet Me at the Center*, 97–99.

22 Hauberg, quoted in Michener, "The Growing Cultural Crisis," 19.

23 Brewster, "The Good, Gray Times," 34.

24 Crowley, *Rites of Passage*, 34; and Bunzel, quoted in Jones, *Seattle*, 261–62.

25 Study City Team, Northwestern University, *Seattle*, 79; Slade Gorton interview; John O'Brien, interview by author, Seattle, 22 August 2008; *Seattle Post-Intelligencer*, 18 February 1968; and John Owen, interview by author, 2 January 2008.

26 Van Lindt, *The Seattle Pilots Story*, 26.

27 Crowley, *Rites of Passage*, 11; Cowley, quoted in Sale, *Seattle*, 195–96; and *New York Times*, 13 April 1969.

28 Sale, *Seattle*, 196; and Abbott, "Regional City and Network City," 307, 316–17.

29 Watson, *Digressions of a Native Son*, 240–43; Watson, *My Life in Print*, 126; and Sale, *Seattle*, 223.

Chapter 2. The Seattle Spirit and a World's Fair

1 Speidel, *Through the Eye of the Needle*, 3–6.

2 Mansfield, *The Space Needle Story*, 28, 31; and Leffler, quoted in Noe, *Innocence Revisited*, 28.

3 *Seattle Times*, 13 September 1960; and Duckstad and Waybur, *Feasibility*, 59.

4 *Seattle Times*, 14 September 1960; and Resolution 21844, box 80, Series 124 Resolutions, Record Group 102 Commissioners, KCA.

5 *Seattle Post-Intelligencer*, 7 November 1960; *Seattle Times*, 11 September 1960; *Seattle Times*, 2 November 1960; and *Seattle Post-Intelligencer*, 21 September 1960.

6 *Tacoma News Tribune*, 9 November 1960.

7 *Seattle Times*, 6 November 1960.

8 "King County Resolutions," Superintendent of Elections Report, folder 1, box 4, Series 261 Bond Files, Record Group 102 Commissioners, KCA.

9 Findlay, *Magic Lands*, 264.

10 See Mullins, *Depression and the Urban West Coast*; Carlson, *Recollections of a Lucky Fellow*, 144–45; Kraeger, quoted in Fischer, "Seattle's Modern Day Vigilantes," 20; and Morgan, *Century 21*, 9, 81.

11 Morgan, *Century 21*, 42–43; and Duncan, *Meet Me at the Center*, 21.

12 Carlson, *Recollections of a Lucky Fellow*, 146; and Duncan, *Meet Me at the Center*, 45.

13 Skinner, *Annals of Century 21 Center*, unpaginated; and Carlson, *Recollections of a*

Lucky Fellow, 150.

14 Morgan, *Century 21*, 124–25.

15 Duncan, *Meet Me at the Center*, 35; and Findlay, *Magic Lands*, 230.

16 Morgan, *Century 21*, 152; and Findlay, *Magic Lands*, 228.

17 Gandy, quoted in *Seattle Post-Intelligencer*, 5 February 1966; Morgan, *Century 21*, 133; and Century 21 Exposition, "Final Report," unpaginated.

18 Seattle Municipal Reference Library, "Notes on Economic Effect," unpaginated; Findlay, *Magic Lands*, 239; and Noe, "Innocence Revisited," 32.

19 Carlson, *Recollections of a Lucky Fellow*, 174; and Skinner, *Annals of Century 21 Center*, unpaginated.

20 Findlay, "The Off-Center Seattle Center," 2; Noe, "Innocence Revisited," 32; Skinner, *Annals of Century 21 Center*, unpaginated; Wilson et al., *Whatever Happened?* 1; Gandy, quoted in Duncan, *Meet Me at the Center*, 51; and Skinner, *Annals of Century 21 Center*, unpaginated.

21 Citizens Committee for Major League Baseball, "Public Relations Final Report," folder 4, box 19, Gandy Collection, UWSC.

22 Poll, folder 6, box 20, Gandy Collection, UWSC.

23 Torry, *Endless Summers*, 93, 95.

24 *Seattle Times*, 13 October 1964.

25 Paul, Braman, and Devine, quoted in Angeloff, "Are We Ready?" 10, 14–15.

26 Wood and Lebovitz, quoted in Torry, *Endless Summers*, 96–97; and Citizens Committee for Major League Baseball, "Public Relations Final Report," folder 4, box 19, Gandy Collection, UWSC.

27 Cleveland Indians Directors Minutes, folder 2, box 5, BL-SMA.

28 Dewey Soriano, interview by Mike Fuller, August 1994, SeattlePilots.com, http://seattlepilots.com/dsoriano_int.html; and *Seattle Times*, 2 January 1966.

29 Paul, quoted in *Seattle Times*, 19 October 1967, and in Angeloff, "Are We Ready?" 14.

Chapter 3. For Want of a Stadium

1 Baim, *Sports Stadium as a Municipal Investment*, 1; Fort, *Sports Economics*, 300–301; Danielson, *Home Team*, 225; *Seattle Times*, 4 November 1965; *Seattle Post-Intelligencer*, 4 and 5 November 1965; and *Seattle Times*, 11 and 14 September 1966.

2 *Seattle Times*, 1 October 1966; *Seattle Post-Intelligencer*, 19 January 1966; and *Seattle Times*, 4 August 1966.

3 *Seattle Times*, 1 December 1965 and 24 April 1966.

4 *Seattle Post-Intelligencer*, 12 May 1966; and ibid., 18 and 19 May 1966.

5 *Seattle Post-Intelligencer*, 5 December and 5 November 1965.

6 *Seattle Times*, 5 January and 27 September 1966.

7 Robertson speech, folder 10, box 8, Series 261 Bond Files, Record Group 102 Commissioners, WaPS; Dorm Braman to Henry W. Maier, Mayor of Milwaukee, 5 November 1964, folder 5, box 41, M-SMA; and Braman to Jay Adams, 3 August 1965, folder 14, box 60, M-SMA.

8 Bill Sears, interview by Mike Fuller, 1 January 1994, Seattlepilots.com, http://www.seattlepilots.com/sears_int.html; Frank Ruano, interview by Mike Fuller, January 1994, SeattlePilots.com, http://www.seattlepilots.com/ruano_int.html; Gandy, quoted in *Seattle Times*, 1 February 1966; and *Seattle Times*, 17 April 1966.

9 Western Management Consultants, "Economic Feasibility of a Multi-purpose Stadium," IV-9, II-1.

10 Praeger-Kavanagh-Waterbury, "Engineering Study," 15; and Western Management Consultants, "Economic Feasibility of a Multi-purpose Stadium," VI-3.

11 Notes, folder 7, box 20, Gandy Collection, UWSC; and *Seattle Times*, 11 May 1966.

12 Resolution 32226, box 127, Series 124, Record Group 102, Commissioners, WaPS; and O'Brien, quoted in Angeloff, "Are We Ready?" 15.

13 *Seattle Post-Intelligencer*, 20 August 1966; ibid., 7 September 1966; and ibid., 19 August 1966.

14 *Seattle Post-Intelligencer*, 16 August 1966; and list of speakers, folder 16, box 20, Gandy Collection UWSC.

15 *Seattle Post-Intelligencer*, 20 September 1966; ibid., 31 August 1966; Braman, quoted in ibid., 7 September 1966; *Seattle Post-Intelligencer*, 24 August 1966; and *Seattle Times*, 14 September 1966.

16 Folder 18, box 20, and folder 3, box 22, Gandy Collection, UWSC; *Seattle Post-Intelligencer*, 10 September 1966; O'Brien, quoted in ibid., 15 September 1966; *Seattle Times*, 15 September 1966; and *Seattle Post-Intelligencer*, 20 September 1966.

17 *Seattle Times*, 23 September 1966; and folder 10, box 8, Series 261 Bond Files, Record Group 102 Commissioners, WaPS.

18 Schmechel, Chadwick, and Gandy, quoted in *Seattle Times*, 21 September 1966; *Tacoma News Tribune*, 23 September 1966; Brougham comment and Gandy, quoted in *Seattle Post-Intelligencer*, 21 September 1966; Dorm Braman to Joe Gandy, 21 September 1966, folder 12, box 3, BL-SMA; and *Seattle Times*, 6 August 1968.

19 *Seattle Post-Intelligencer*, 27 October 1966.

20 O'Neil, "You're a Good Man, Charlie O.," *Life*, 6 September 1968, 72–73; and *Seattle Times*, 10 October 1964.

21 Finley, quoted in *Seattle Times*, 7 August 1967; *Seattle Times*, 8 August 1967; and Demmert, *The Economics of Professional Team Sports*, 5.

22 Folder 14, box 2 of *Washington et al. v. American League*, WaNW; Peterson, *The Kansas City Athletics*, 258; Finley, quoted in *Seattle Times*, 9 August 1967; *Seattle Times*, 8 October 1967; and Finley deal, 8 September 1967, and Dorm Braman to Charles Finley, 15 September 1967, both in folder 6, box 2, BL-SMA.

23 *Seattle Times*, 16 January 1976; *Seattle Post-Intelligencer*, 4 September 1970; and folder 2, box 3 of *Washington et al. v. American League*, WaNW.

24 *Seattle Times*, 11 February 1968.

25 *Seattle Times*, 5 February 1967, 22 December 1966, and 28 December 1967.

Chapter 4. Come, and They Will Build It

1 Danielson, *Home Team*, 150, 191; and Voigt, *From Postwar Expansion*, 178.

2   Deposition of Charles O. Finley, folder 5, box 3, *Washington et al. v. American League*, WaNW; Minutes, American League Meeting, October 1967, folder 5, box 3, *Washington et al. v. American League*, WaNW; and Van Lindt, *The Seattle Pilots Story*, 11.

3   Minutes, American League Meeting, October 1967, folder 5, box 3, *Washington et al. v. American League*, WaNW.

4   Ibid.; *Seattle Times*, 19 October 1967; and folder 6, box 2, BL-SMA.

5   Quoted in *Seattle Times*, 19 October 1967.

6   Deposition of Dorm Braman, folder 3, box 3, *Washington et al. v. American League*, WaNW; and *Seattle Post-Intelligencer*, 31 October 1967.

7   *Seattle Times*, 19 October 1967.

8   Plaintiffs' Brief Opposing New Motion from *Washington et al. v. American League*, folder 9, box 5, BL-SMA.

9   *Seattle Times*, 16 November 1967; Buzzie Bavasi, telephone interview by Mike Fuller, 1994, SeattlePilots.com, http://seattlepilots.com/ bavasi_int.html; Braman, quoted in *Seattle Times*, 24 October 1967; *Tacoma News Tribune*, 24 October, 6 December 1967; *Milwaukee Journal*, 5 February 1970; and *Milwaukee Sentinel*, 17 September 1969.

10 For discussions of the dynamics of cities questing after sports franchises, see Curry, Schwirian, and Woldoff, *High Stakes*; Danielson, *Home Team*; Euchner, *Playing the Field*; and John Wilson, *Playing by the Rules*.

11 Western Management Consultants, "Economic Feasibility of a Multi-purpose Stadium," VII-2–5, IX-2–7.

12 *Seattle Times*, 19 October 1967; and *Seattle Post-Intelligencer*, 28 October 1967.

13 *Seattle Times*, 19 October 1967; *Seattle Post-Intelligencer*, 28 October 1967; and deposition of Joe Cronin, folder 4, box 3, *Washington et al. v. American League*, WaNW.

14 Danielson, *Home Team*, 65, 87–88.

15 Max Soriano, interview by Mike Fuller, January 1994, SeattlePilots.com, http://www.seattlepilots.com/msoriano_int.html; and *Tacoma News Tribune*, 31 October 1967.

16 *Seattle Post-Intelligencer*, 17 March 1969; *Seattle Times*, 10 April 1969; Brewster, "Joy Comes to Mudville," 16; *Seattle Times*, 6 December 1966; *Seattle Post-Intelligencer*, 6 January 1968; "History," SeattlePilots.com, http://seattlepilots.com/inthome.html; and *Seattle Times*, 24 October and 14 November 1967.

17 Bill Sears, "How the Dome Miracle Became Reality," *Kingdome Magazine*, 84, in Inventory folder, Gandy Collection, UWSC; and deposition of Charles Finley, folder 5, box 3, *Washington et al. v. American League*, WaNW.

18 Torry, *Endless Summers*, 62, 48, 64–65; Bowker, "Who's on First?" 34; Torry, *Endless Summers*, 89; SeattlePilots.com, http://seattlepilots.com/inthome.html; Torry, *Endless Summers*, 61; *Seattle Times*, 25 March 1969; and John Owen, telephone interview by author, 2 January 2008.

19 Affidavit of William Daley, folder 1, box 6, BL-SMA; folder 3, box 3, *Washington et al. v. American League*, WaNW; *Argus*, 3 January 1969; David Eskenazi, "Dwyer KO's American League," 25 October 2011, *Sportspress Northwest*, www.Sportspressnw.

com, http://sportspressnw.com/2011/10/wayback-machine-bill-dwyer-kos-ameri-can-league/; Owen interview; and Max Soriano interview.

20 Folder 9, box 5, BL-SMA; and folder 26, box D-1, Series 491 Director's Files, Record Group 502 Stadium Administration, KCA.

21 Affidavit of William Daley, folder 1, box 6, BL-SMA; deposition of Jack Zander, folder 12, box 3 *Washington et al. v. American League*, WaNW; and *Tri-City Herald*, 3 April 1970, in Jackson Papers, UWSC.

22 Hoffberger, in transcript of American League meeting, December 1967, in deposition of Charles Finley, folder 5, box 3 *Washington et al. v. American League*, WaNW.

23 SeattlePilots.com, http://seattlepilots.com/inthome.html; and Thiel, *Out of Left Field*, 10.

24 Max Soriano interview.

25 "Conditions for Expansion Franchise," November 1967, folder III, box 1, *Washington et al. v. American League*, WaNW; *Sporting News*, 21 December 1968; *Spokane Spokesman-Review*, 28 January 1969, DEPC; and Gerald Waring to Dewey Soriano, 23 January 1969, and Elten Schiller to Bowie Kuhn, 21 February 1969, both DEPC.

Play-by-Play: Spring Training, 1969

1 Len Monheimer to Sharon Switzer, 17 February 1969, DEPC; and *Seattle Times*, 11 March 1969.

2 *Seattle Post-Intelligencer*, 5 March 1969; and *Seattle Times*, 11 March 1969.

3 *Seattle Times*, 16 March 1969.

4 Ibid., 19 March 1969.

5 Bouton, *Ball Four*, 67; and *Seattle Times*, 19 March 1969.

6 *Seattle Post-Intelligencer*, 13 March 1969.

7 Ibid., 22 March 1969; and *Seattle Times*, 22 March 1969.

8 *Seattle Post-Intelligencer*, 23 March 1969.

9 *Seattle Times*, 23 March 1969; and *Seattle Post-Intelligencer*, 25 March 1969.

10 *Seattle Times*, 24 and 25 March 1969; and *Seattle Post-Intelligencer*, 25 March 1969.

11 *Seattle Times*, 31 March 1969.

12 Eddie O'Brien, interview by author, Seattle, 8 September 2008; and Hogan, *The 1969 Seattle Pilots*, 25.

13 *Seattle Post-Intelligencer*, 4 April 1969; and *Seattle Times*, 3 April 1969.

14 *Seattle Times*, 2, 3, and 7 April 1969; and *Seattle Post-Intelligencer*, 2, 3, and 7 April 1969.

15 Bouton, *Ball Four*, 88.

16 *Seattle Post-Intelligencer*, 11 April 1969.

Chapter 5. Build It, and They Will Come

1   Douglas, "Forward Thrust," 30; Fischer, "Seattle's Modern Day Vigilantes," 14; James R. Ellis, "Human Environment and Public Investment," 21 January 1966, in Forward Thrust, "Selected Speeches," 17; and James R. Ellis, "Remarks at the First Meeting," 28 July 1966, in Forward Thrust, "Selected Speeches," 29.

2   Study City Team, Northwestern University, Seattle, 34; Vandenbosch, "1968 Seattle Forward Thrust Election," 62–63; and Fischer, "Seattle's Modern Day Vigilantes," 14.

3   Seattle Times, 3 November 1965; and James R. Ellis, "Transportation and the Shape of the City," in Forward Thrust, "Selected Speeches," 8–9.

4   Ellis, "Transportation," 8–9.

5   Forward Thrust, Forward Thrust Work, 1968–1970, inside cover; and Forward Thrust, "Developing a Capital Improvement Plan: Part II," 51–56.

6   Study City Team, Northwestern University, Seattle, 35; Wilkinson, "Forward Thrust," 156; Vandenbosch, "1968 Seattle Forward Thrust Election," 21–23; and Wilkinson, "Forward Thrust," 66, 76–77.

7   Forward Thrust, "Developing a Capital Improvement Plan: Part I," 182–88.

8   Forward Thrust, "Developing a Capital Improvement Plan: Part II," 145.

9   Forward Thrust, "Developing a Capital Improvement Plan: Part I," 174; Forward Thrust, "Developing a Capital Improvement Plan: Part III," 59–60; Forward Thrust, "Developing a Capital Improvement Plan: Part I," 82–83.

10 Forward Thrust, "Developing a Capital Improvement Plan: Part II," 37.

11 James Ellis, telephone interview by author, 19 May 2008.

12 Curry, Schwirian, and Woldoff, High Stakes, 3–4; and Danielson, Home Team, 227, 280–83.

13 Seattle Post-Intelligencer, 21 and 23 August 1967.

14 John Kraft Survey of Seattle Bond Issue, 2 February 1968, folder III, box 1, Washington et al. v. American League, WaNW; and deposition of Jerald C. Hoffberger, folder 7, box 3, Washington et al. v. American League, WaNW.

15 Max Soriano to James Ellis, 9 January 1968, 1968 correspondence, box 1, James R. Ellis papers, UWSC; Seattle Post-Intelligencer, 19 January 1968; Seattle Times, 6 February 1968; and Seattle Post-Intelligencer, 2 February 1968.

16 Deposition of Joe Cronin, folder 4, box 3, Washington et al. v. American League, WaNW; Cronin, quoted in Seattle Times, 3 February 1968; Cronin quote, folder 1, box 1, Washington et al. v. American League, WaNW; Cronin, quoted in Seattle Times, 31 January 1968; and Seattle Post-Intelligencer, 15 February 1968.

17 Seattle Post-Intelligencer, 27 January 1968, 22 December 1967, and 29 January 1968; and Seattle Times, 8 February 1968.

18 Forward Thrust, "Developing a Capital Improvement Plan: Part II," 72; Seattle Post-Intelligencer, 13 June, 7 February, 2 February, and 6 February 1968; Smith, quoted in Seattle Post-Intelligencer, 29 January 1968; Seattle Post-Intelligencer, 13 February and 1 February 1968.

19 Seattle Post-Intelligencer, 13 February, 9 January, and 9 February 1968.

20 *Seattle Post-Intelligencer*, 25 January 1968; and Graham, quoted in *Seattle Post-Intelligencer*, 11 February 1968.

21 *Seattle Times*, 5 February 1968; *Seattle Post-Intelligencer*, 22 February 1967; *Seattle Times*, 30 August 1967; *Argus*, 22 September 1967; *Facts*, 7 September 1967; *Tacoma News Tribune*, 12 November 1967; and *Helix*, 1 February 1968.

22 *Seattle Times*, 20 October 1967; and Steven Chadwick to John O'Brien, 28 September 1967, folder "Stadium 1," box 3, James R. Ellis Papers, UWSC.

23 *Seattle Post-Intelligencer*, 4 October 1967.

24 *Seattle Times*, 2 November 1967; *Seattle Post-Intelligencer*, 3 November 1967; and *Tacoma News Tribune*, 8 and 12 November 1967.

25 *Seattle Post-Intelligencer*, 14 and 15 February 1968.

26 Vandenbosch, "1968 Seattle Forward Thrust Election," 85, 92.

27 *Seattle Post-Intelligencer*, 14 February 1968; and Cronin, quoted in Plaintiff's Brief, folder 14, box 2, *Washington et al. v. American League*, WaNW.

28 For comparisons, see Newhan, *Anaheim Angels*, 83–88; Peterson, *The Kansas City Athletics*, 187, 251; and Weiner, *Stadium Games*, 12–19, 36–37, 70–75, 86–105.

Play-by-Play: April and May

1 *Seattle Post-Intelligencer*, 9 and 10 April 1969; and *Seattle Times*, 9 April 1969.

2 Van Lindt, *The Seattle Pilots Story*, 59–60; *Seattle Post-Intelligencer*, 11 April 1969; and *Seattle Business*, 8 April 1969.

3 *Seattle Post-Intelligencer*, 11 and 12 April 1969

4 *Seattle Times*, 12 April 1969.

5 *Seattle Post-Intelligencer*, 26 April 1969; and *Seattle Times*, 18 April 1969.

6 *Seattle Times*, 26 April 1969; Van Lindt, *The Seattle Pilots*, 68–85 passim; and *Seattle Times*, 27 and 30 April 1969.

7 *Seattle Post-Intelligencer*, 24 April and 5 May 1969.

8 Ibid., 28 April 1969.

9 Ibid., 1 May 1969.

10 Bouton, *Ball Four*, 180, 144; *Seattle Post-Intelligencer*, 3 May 1969; and Dudley, quoted in *Seattle Post-Intelligencer*, 11 May 1969.

11 *Seattle Post-Intelligencer*, 11 May 1969; and *Seattle Times*, 12 May 1969. Cobb's American League record was subsequently surpassed by Rickey Henderson in 1980 (100 stolen bases) and 1982 (130).

12 *Seattle Post-Intelligencer*, 13 May 1969.

13 *Seattle Times*, 15 May 1969; *Seattle Post-Intelligencer*, 19 May 1969; and *New York Times*, 26 May 1969.

14 *Seattle Post-Intelligencer*, 5 May 1969; and Bouton, *Ball Four*, 163–64, 190.

15 Van Lindt, *The Seattle Pilots Story*, 90; and Bouton, *Ball Four*, 172–73.

16 *Seattle Times*, 25 May 1969; and *Seattle Post-Intelligencer*, 18 May 1969.

17 *Seattle Times*, 29 May 1969.

18 Ibid., 1 June 1969; and *Seattle Post-Intelligencer*, 1 June 1969.

Chapter 6. Setting the Course

1 Daley, quoted in *Pilots Scorebook*, DEPC.

2 *Forbes*, "Baseball Feels a Pinch," in Lineberry, *The Business of Sports*, 55–64.

3 *Seattle Post-Intelligencer*, 16 March 1969; and *Seattle Times*, 6 October 1968.

4 *Seattle Times*, 21 February 1968; and *Seattle Post-Intelligencer*, 23 March 1969.

5 Eddie O'Brien, interview by author, Seattle, 8 September 2008; Rod Belcher, telephone interview by author, 8 January 2008; John O'Brien, interview by author, Seattle, 22 August 2008; Bill Sears, interview by Mike Fuller, January 1994, Seattlepilots.com, http://www.seattlepilots.com/sears_int.html; *Pilots Scorebook*, April 1969, DEPC; *Seattle Times*, 20 December 1970; *Seattle Post-Intelligencer*, 23 March 1969; Milkes, quoted in *Milwaukee Journal*, 5 April 1970; and *Seattle Post-Intelligencer*, 3 September 1969.

6 *Pilots Scorebook*, April 1969, DEPC; *Seattle Times*, 20 December 1970; Eddie O'Brien interview; Schaefer, "Play Ball!" 17; and Sale, *Seattle*, 230.

7 *Seattle Times*, 23 August 1968.

8 Belcher interview; *Seattle Times*, 26 May 1969; Hogan, *The 1969 Seattle Pilots*, 159; and *Seattle Times*, 2 October 1968.

9 Bouton, *Ball Four*, 189.

10 Ibid., 287.

11 *Seattle Times*, 5 November 1968.

12 Testa, *Sal Maglie*, 374, 381–82; and Bouton, *Ball Four*, 204.

13 Eddie O'Brien interview; and Bouton, *Ball Four*, 75.

14 John Owen, interview by author, 2 January 2008.

15 *Seattle Post-Intelligencer*, 20 November 1968; D. Grant Johnson, *The Seattle Mariners*, 25; SeattlePilots.com, http://seattlepilots.com/minors.html; *Tacoma News Tribune*, 1 April 1969; and *Seattle Times*, 29 May 1969.

16 Parrott, *The Lords of Baseball*, 62; Sears interview by author, Edmonds, Washington, 31 May 2007; and Owen interview.

17 Sears interview by Fuller; Max Soriano, interview by Mike Fuller, January 1994, SeattlePilots.com, http://www.seattlepilots.com/msoriano_int.html; and Parrott, *The Lords of Baseball*, 60.

18 *Seattle Times*, 6 August 1968; and Paul Hansen to L. J. Gillis, 30 December 1970, folder 10, box 3, BL-SMA.

19 *Seattle Post-Intelligencer*, 10 March 1968; Hogan, *The 1969 Seattle Pilots*, 17; Sears interview by author; and *Seattle Times*, 30 March 1968.

20 Hogan, *The 1969 Seattle Pilots*, 145–77 passim; and Schaefer, "Play Ball!" 17.

21 Milkes, quoted in *Seattle Times*, 15 August 1968; *Seattle Post-Intelligencer*, 18 March 1970; Belcher interview; and *Seattle Times*, 10 April 1969.

22 Parrott, *The Lords of Baseball*, 61–62; and Max Soriano interview.

23 *Seattle Post-Intelligencer*, 12 January 1969.

24 Lew Matlin to Milt Albright, 21 January 1969, and Marvin Milkes to Joseph M. Shave, 5 February 1969, both DEPC; Plaintiff's Brief, folder 12, box 3, Series 491 Director's Files, Record Group 502 Stadium Administration, KCA; deposition of

Jack Zander, *Washington et al. v. American League*, WaNW; and deposition of Francis Gruene, folder 6, box 3, *Washington et al. v. American League*, WaNW.

25 Voigt, *From Postwar Expansion*, 314; Zimbalist, *Baseball and Billions*, 48; Riess, *City Games*, 249; and Ira Horowitz, "Sports Broadcasting," in Noll, *Government and the Sports Business*, 287.

26 *Seattle Post-Intelligencer*, 21 March 1969; and Soriano, quoted in ibid., 28 April 1969.

27 SeattlePilots.com, http://seattlepilots.com/radio.html; *Seattle Post-Intelligencer*, 11 April 1969; *Pilots Scorebook*, April 1969, DEPC; Owen interview; Eddie O'Brien interview; Belcher interview.

28 *Seattle Post-Intelligencer*, 11 April 1969 and 14 August 1968; *Seattle Times*, 21 July 1968; Dale, quoted in *Seattle Times*, 23 February 1969; deposition of Charles Finley, folder 5, box 3 *Washington et al. v. American League*, WaNW; and John E. Healy Jr. to Warren Magnuson, 24 October 1969, folder 5, box 197, Magnuson Papers, UWSC.

29 *Tacoma News Tribune*, 21 March 1969.

30 Summary of season tickets sold, folder 5, box 5, BL-SMA; *Seattle Post-Intelligencer*, 8 June 1969; and Parrott, *The Lords of Baseball*, 60–61.

31 Dewey Soriano to All Department Heads, 11 March and 18 March 1969, and Marvin Milkes to Parrott, McCarthy, et al., 20 February 1969, both DEPC; ticket tax summary, folder 5, box 5, BL-SMA; and "Report of Counsel on Seattle Franchise," folder 14, box 2, BL-SMA.

32 Van Lindt, *The Seattle Pilots Story*, 38–39; and *Seattle Times*, 7 August 1968.

33 *Seattle Post-Intelligencer*, 11 and 24 July, 29 September, and 13 October 1968; Sears interview; *New York Times*, 13 April 1969; and Milkes, quoted in Brewster, "Joy Comes to Mudville," 55.

34 Van Lindt, *The Seattle Pilots Story*, 39–40; *Seattle Times*, 3 November 1968; and Schultz, quoted in Rousso, "An Exhilarating Big League Bust," 119.

35 *Seattle Post-Intelligencer*, 8 November 1968; and Rousso, "An Exhilarating Big League Bust," 122.

36 *Seattle Post-Intelligencer*, 21 March 1969; *Seattle Times*, 28 October 1968; Eddie O'Brien interview; and Belcher interview.

37 *Seattle Post-Intelligencer*, 17 August 1969; and Salmon, quoted in *Seattle Times*, 30 October 1968.

38 *Seattle Post-Intelligencer*, 17 October 1968; *New York Times*, 16 February 1969; and Van Lindt, *The Seattle Pilots Story*, 181–82.

39 *Seattle Times*, 3 July 1969; and Van Lindt, *The Seattle Pilots Story*, 115.

40 *Sporting News*, 9 November 1968; and Hogan, *The 1969 Seattle Pilots*, 71.

41 Schultz, quoted in Bouton, *Ball Four*, 312–13; and Burk, *Much More Than a Game*, 121.

42 John Wilson, *Playing by the Rules*, 164; Voigt, *From Postwar Expansion*, 210–14; and Burk, *Much More Than a Game*, 159, 161.

43 *Seattle Post-Intelligencer*, 17 January 1969; and *Seattle Times*, 10 November 1968.

44 Richard E. Lapchick, "The Promised Land," in *Fractured Focus*, 123; Bouton, *Ball Four*, 334; and Voigt, *From Postwar Expansion*, 244.

45 *Seattle Times*, 7 and 8 April 1969; and *Seattle Post-Intelligencer*, 6 and 10 April 1969.

46 *Seattle Post-Intelligencer*, 11 April 1969.

7. Not Enough Seats, Not Enough Fans

1   Contract, file 6, Pacific Northwest Sports, Inc., Debtor, Case File 6682; Records of the District Courts of the United States, Record Group 21; Max Soriano, interview by Mike Fuller, January 1994, Seattlepilots.com, http://www.seattlepilots.com/msoriano_int.html; *Seattle Times*, 20 February 1969; and Hall, quoted in *Tacoma News Tribune*, 26 March 1968.

2   *Seattle Times*, 14 January 1969; and *Seattle Post-Intelligencer*, 14 December 1968.

3   *Seattle Post-Intelligencer*, 4 February 1969.

4   *Seattle Times*, 27 February 1969.

5   Jim Kittilsby to Marvin Milkes, 17 January 1969, DEPC; and *Seattle Times*, 1 April 1969.

6   "Concession Agreement," folder 8, box 2, BL-SMA.

7   Paul Anson to Files, "Sicks' Stadium Renovation," folder 7, box 1, BL-SMA; *Seattle Times*, 4 September 1968; *Tacoma News Tribune*, 9 April 1969; and Concession Agreement [Stadium Lease], file 1, Pacific Northwest Sports, Inc., Debtor, Case File 6682.

8   *Seattle Times*, 17 September 1968; Minutes of City Council, folder 8, box 2, BL-SMA; *Seattle Post-Intelligencer*, 18 September 1968; and *Seattle Times*, 14 February 1976.

9   *Argus*, 28 March 1969; *Seattle Post-Intelligencer*, 29 September 1968; *Seattle Times*, 24 August 1969; *Seattle Post-Intelligencer*, 20 September 1968; deposition of Dorm Braman, folder 2, box 3, *Washington et al. v. American League*, WANW; and deposition of Ted Best, folder 3, box 1, *Washington et al. v. American League*, WaNW.

10 Alan Ferguson, press release, 2 August 1965, and Dorm Braman to Seattle City Council, 12 August 1965, both folder 5, box 2, BL-SMA.

11 Folder 9, box 114, M-SMA; and Braman to Hy Zimmerman, 4 January 1966, and Marvin Milkes to Dorm Braman, 16 September 1966, both folder 8, box 114, M-SMA.

12 Alan Ferguson to Joe Gandy, 14 January 1966, folder 7, box 18, Gandy Collection, UWSC; and Narramore Plan for remodeling Sicks' Stadium, 27 May 1968, folder 7, box 1, BL-SMA.

13 Don Johnston to Dewey Soriano, 17 October 1968, folder 14, box 1, BL-SMA.

14 *Seattle Times*, 19 September 1968.

15 Minutes of 19 December 1968 meeting, folder 1, box 3, BL-SMA; and *Sporting News*, 11 January 1969.

16 Best, quoted in *Sporting News*, 11 January 1969; Halpin, "Our Musty, Crusty City Council," 48; and deposition of Dorm Braman, folder 2, box 3, *Washington et al. v. American League*, WaNW.

17 *Sporting News*, 24 August 1968; and deposition of Ted Best, folder 3, box 1, *Washington et al. v. American League*, WaNW.

18 Deposition of Dorm Braman, folder 2, box 3, *Washington et al. v. American League*, WaNW; Don Johnston to Charles Chisom, 9 January 1969, folder 1, box 1, BL-SMA; and Don Johnston to Dewey Soriano, 10 January 1969, folder 8, box 2, BL-SMA.

19 Don Johnston to Henry Berg, 19 November 1968, folder 37, box 1, BL-SMA; Henry Berg to Don Johnston, 3 June 1969, folder 34, box 1, BL-SMA; *Seattle Post-Intelligencer*, 21 March 1969; and *Seattle Times*, 9 April 1969.

20 Ed Johnson to Don Johnston, 17 March 1969, folder 9, box 2, BL-SMA; *Seattle Times*, 19 March 1969; and Lew Matlin to Don Johnston, 24 March 1969, and Don Johnston to Ken Hazelton, 14 March 1969, both folder 9, box 2, BL-SMA.

21 *Seattle Times*, 9 April 1969; Schaefer, "Play Ball!" 19; deposition of Dorm Braman, folder 2, box 3, *Washington et al. v. American League*, WaNW; *Seattle Times*, 4 February 1976; ibid., 10 April 1969; *Seattle Post-Intelligencer*, 6 April 1969; Job site visit by Gilbert Braida for Narramore et al., folder 1, box 2, BL-SMA; and *Seattle Post-Intelligencer*, 10 April 1969.

22 Brewster, "Is Floyd Miller Really Mayor?" 23; deposition of Dorm Braman, folder 2, box 3, *Washington et al. v. American League*, WaNW; Henry Berg to Robert Lavoie, 27 February 1970, folder 21, box 1, BL-SMA; and *Seattle Post-Intelligencer*, 11 April 1969.

23 Paul, quoted in *Seattle Times*, 26 March 1969; Lane, quoted in *Seattle Times*, 27 March 1969; deposition of Robert Short, folder 10, box 3, *Washington et al. v. American League*, WaNW; *Seattle Post-Intelligencer*, 7 February 1976; Kuhn *Hardball*, 91; and deposition of Joe Cronin, folder 4, box 3, *Washington et al. v. American League*, WaNW.

24 Henry Berg to staff, 2 May 1969, and work to do list, both folder 1, box 1, BL-SMA; Matlin to Johnston, 8 May 1969, folder 11, box 1, BL-SMA; Darrell "Righty" Eden (Strong, Eden and Robinson) to Matlin, 8 May 1969, and Matlin to Johnston, 8 May 1969, both DEPC; and Don Johnston to Robert Lavoie, 13 May 1969, correspondence file, Pilots, Miller Papers, UWSC.

25 Bouton, *Ball Four*, 275; Davis, quoted in Rousso, "An Exhilarating Big League Bust," 121.

26 *Seattle Times*, 6 April 1969.

27 Ken Hazelton to Gil Braida, 11 July 1969, folder 1, box 1, BL-SMA; Henry Berg to Ed Johnson, 5 June 1969, folder 8, box 1, BL-SMA; Lew Matlin to Floyd Miller, 19 September 1969, and Henry Berg to Lew Matlin, 21 November 1969, both folder 34, box 1, BL-SMA; Henry Berg to Ed Johnson, 11 March 1970, folder 30, box 1, BL-SMA; and Lew Matlin, telephone interview by author, 17 February 2009.

28 Henry Berg to staff, 27 June 1969, folder 11, box 2, BL-SMA; Henry Berg, handwritten report, 3 August 1969, folder 1, box 16, BL-SMA; and Bouillon, Christofferson, and Schairer Report, 8 August 1969, folder 21, box 1, BL-SMA.

29 Floyd Miller to Lew Matlin, 26 September, folder 34, box 1, BL-SMA; deposition of Ed Johnson, from *Washington et al. v. American League*, folder 22, box 4, BL-SMA; Marvin Milkes, memo to Ed Carlson, folder 3, box 3, *Washington et al. v. American League*, WaNW; "Sicks' Stadium Improvement," 22 October 1969, folder 11, box 1, BL-SMA; and Matlin to Renato Burkhart, 8 July 1969, DEPC.

30 Dewey Soriano to Don Johnston, 5 June 1969, folder 11, box 2, BL-SMA; *Seattle Times*, 7 June 1969; *Seattle Post-Intelligencer*, 6 June 1969; and Dewey Soriano to Floyd Miller, 9 June 1969, folder 1, box 3, *Washington et al. v. American League*, WaNW.

31 "Notes from discussion in Seattle Mayor's Office, Wednesday, 20 August 1959," personal collection of Lew Matlin; and deposition of Ed Johnson from *Washington et al. v. American League*, folder 22, box 4, BL-SMA.

32 *Seattle Post-Intelligencer*, 18 September 1969; *New York Times*, 13 October 1969; Max

Soriano interview; *Seattle Times*, 23 November 1969; and *Seattle Post-Intelligencer*, 12 November 1969.

33 *Seattle Times*, 28 October 1969; and Wes Uhlman on Pilots' complaints, folder 25, box 4, BL-SMA.

34 Uhlman on surety bond, folder 25, box 4, BL-SMA.

35 *Seattle Post-Intelligencer*, 16 September 1969; and *Seattle Times*, 16 September 1969.

36 *Tri-City Herald*, 3 April 1970; Mulvoy, "Baseball Booms Again," 17; *Wall Street Journal*, 9 September 1969; and Roger G. Noll, "Attendance and Price Setting," in *Government and the Sports Business*, 131. Miller complained that sportswriters were exaggerating when they wrote that Miller was threatening eviction, but the threat of changing the contract to, essentially, a daily rental agreement was not far from threatening eviction.

37 *Seattle Post-Intelligencer*, 17 July 1969; deposition of Charles Finley, folder 5, box 3, *Washington et al. v. American League*, WaNW; and *Seattle Post-Intelligencer*, 20 September 1968.

38 *Seattle Post-Intelligencer*, 8 April 1969; and Voigt, *From Postwar Expansion*, 289.

39 Bill Sears, interview by author, Edmonds, Washington, 31 May 2007; and "Gallery," SeattlePilots.com, http://seattlepilots.com/wheeldon.html.

40 *Seattle Post-Intelligencer*, 12 July 1970; *Seattle Post-Intelligencer*, 1 April 1970; and "Seattle Pilots 1969 Attendance," DEPC.

41 *Seattle Post-Intelligencer*, 28 May 1969; and Hogan, *The 1969 Seattle Pilots*, 79.

42 *Pilots Scorebook*, April 1969, DEPC; Rousso, "Exhilarating Big League Bust," 117; and *Seattle Post-Intelligencer*, 17 May 1970.

43 Mulvoy, "KC Is Back with a Vengeance," 79; *Seattle Post-Intelligencer*, 19 August 1969; Max Soriano interview; folder I, box 1, *Washington et al. v. American League*, WaNW; Bridge Restaurant Proposal, DEPC; Van Lindt, *The Seattle Pilots Story*, 152–53; Bouton, *Ball Four*, 288

44 *Seattle Post-Intelligencer*, 12 September 1969; Pilots Road Attendance (unidentified exhibit), folder III, box 1, *Washington et al. v. American League*, WaNW; and payouts to visiting teams, DEPC.

45 Scully, *Business of Major League Baseball*, 115–16; Jerry McNaul, interview by Mike Fuller, Seattlepilots.com, http://www.seattlepilots.com/mcnaul_int.html; Max Soriano, Statement to the Court, Pacific Northwest Sports, Inc., Debtor, Case File 6682; Soriano, quoted in Angeloff, "Are We Ready?" 15; and Sistek, "New 'Summer Sanity Index' Shows This Summer Wasn't So Bad," http://www.komonews.com/weather/blog/27743024.html?blog=y.

46 Euchner, *Playing the Field*, 136; Danielson, *Home Team*, 222; *Seattle Times*, 31 August 1969; and John Owen, telephone interview by author, Seattle, 2 January 2008.

47 Eddie O'Brien, interview by author, Seattle, 8 September 2008; *Seattle Times*, 3 February 1970; Bridge Restaurant Proposal, DEPC; and Robert Gladstone and Associates, "Basic Economic Indicators," 43, 57.

48 *Seattle Post-Intelligencer*, 28 August 1969; and Max Soriano interview.

Play by Play: June and July

1 *Seattle Post-Intelligencer*, 3 June 1969.
2 Bouton, *Ball Four*, 223; *Seattle Times*, 17, 9, 11, 14, and 16 June 1969; and *Seattle Post-Intelligencer*, 8 and 16 June 1969.
3 Bouton, *Ball Four*, 209; and *Seattle Times*, 14 June 1969.
4 *Seattle Times*, 15 June 1969.
5 Ibid., 16 June 1969; and *Seattle Post-Intelligencer*, 17 June 1969.
6 Bouton, *Ball Four*, 447; and *Seattle Post-Intelligencer*, 8 January 1970.
7 *Seattle Times*, 9 June 1969; and Bouton, *Ball Four*, 277, 211.
8 *Seattle Post-Intelligencer*, 17 June 1969.
9 Bouton, *Ball Four*, 248; and *Seattle Post-Intelligencer*, 9 July 1969.
10 Schultz, quoted in *Seattle Post-Intelligencer*, 18 July 1969.
11 *Seattle Times*, 21 July 1969; and Milkes, quoted in *Seattle Times*, 22 July 1969.
12 *Seattle Times*, 29 July 1969; and Schultz, quoted in *Seattle Post-Intelligencer*, 28 July 1969.

8. "Storm Clouds Gather over Pilots' Port"

1 "Ad Hoc Committee for the Seattle Center Stadium Site," folder 2, box 20, Gandy Collection, UWSC; and *Seattle Times*, 21 April 1968.
2 *Seattle Times*, 21 April 1968; and *Seattle Post-Intelligencer*, 9 March 1968.
3 *Seattle Times*, 12 May 1968.
4 Ibid., 29 April 1968.
5 Deposition of Dorm Braman and Braman to John O'Brien, 23 April 1968, folder 2, box 3, *Washington et al. v. American League*, WaNW; *Seattle Times*, 16 June 1968; *Tacoma News Tribune*, 21 June 1968; and various correspondence with Braman, folder 2, box 4, BL-SMA.
6 *Seattle Times*, 29 April 1968; and "To all consultants from Frank Hope," 7 March 1968, in deposition and evidence from John Spellman, folder 11, box 3, *Washington et al. v. American League*, WaNW.
7 James Ellis, telephone interview by author, 19 May 2008.
8 Western Management Consultants, "Report to the State of Washington," 2, 9–10, 30, 36, 47. Western Management Consultants used the following criteria and weighting: Market Area 10; Accessibility 10; Utility [likelihood of use] 10; Cost 8; Environment [impact] 8; Configuration 7; Public Acceptance [will people come to the stadium?] 6; Competition [with other facilities] 3; Availability [ease of land acquisition] 3; Flexibility [capable of enlargement] 3; and Climate 1.
9 Ibid., 4.
10 Frank Ruano, interview by Mike Fuller, January 1994, Seattlepilots.com, http://www.seattlepilots.com/ruano_int.html; *Seattle Times*, 12 June 1968; Braman, quoted in *Seattle Post-Intelligencer*, 13; *Seattle Post-Intelligencer*, 20 June 1968; and *Seattle Times*, 16 June 1968.

11   *Seattle Times*, 20 and 26 June and 26 July 1968.

12   Ibid., 7 August 1968; and Michener, "King of the Mountain," 48.

13   *Seattle Times*, 5 August 1968; "Ad Hoc Committee for the Seattle Center Stadium Site," folder 2, box 20, Gandy Collection, UWSC; "Let's Set the Record Straight," 13 February 1969, folder 11 box 20, Gandy Collection, UWSC; and cover letter of Ad Hoc Committee Report from Norman G. Jacobson Associates, 24 June 1968, folder 1, box 20, Gandy Collection, UWSC.

14   *Seattle Times*, 7 August 1968; "Ad hoc Committee for Seattle Center Stadium Site," 1–26; consultants report, folder 7, box 20, Gandy Collection, UWSC; *Seattle Post-Intelligencer*, 17 November 1968; *Seattle Times*, 8 and 24 August 1968; and Study City Team, Northwestern University, *Seattle*, 62.

15   *Seattle Post-Intelligencer*, 8 November 1968; and Narramore, Skilling, Praeger, "Schematic Design," unpaginated.

16   *Argus*, 21 June 1968; *Fortune*, March 1973, 106–7, folder 20, box 3, BL-SMA; and Ronna Smith to Dorm Braman, 18 November 1968, Joe Empens to Braman, 13 June 1968, Jack Waidman to Braman, 17 June 1968, and Braman to Waidman, 18 June 1968, all folder 2, box 4, BL-SMA.

17   *Sporting News*, 14 December 1968.

18   James Ellis to Edgar Christian, 24 February 1969, folder "Stadium 3," box 3, Ellis Collection, UWSC; and *Seattle Times*, 15 October 1969.

19   *Seattle Post-Intelligencer*, 23 September 1969.

20   *Seattle Times*, 19 February 1970; Frank Ruano to Ed Lackner, 4 May 1970, folder "Stadium Finance," box 3, Ellis Collection, UWSC; and *Seattle Post-Intelligencer*, 1 April 1970.

21   *Seattle Post-Intelligencer*, 8 May 1970; "Dome-Legal," Miller Papers, UWSC; *Seattle Post-Intelligencer*, 23 February and 19 May 1970; and *Seattle Times*, 16 and 14 May 1970.

22   Initiative Election of 19 May 1970 Certified, folder 13, box 4, Series 336, Record Group 011, KCA; *Seattle Post-Intelligencer*, 29 May 1970; and folder 8, box 16, Series 43 county department files, Record Group 137 County Executive, KCA.

23   Joe Gandy to Professor Bernard Brooms, 11 December 1970, folder 21, box 18, Gandy Collection, UWSC; *Seattle Times*, 21 May 1970; deposition and evidence from John Spellman, folder 11, box 3, *Washington et al. v. American League*, WaNW; and *Seattle Times*, 20 May 1970.

24   John O'Brien, interview by author, Seattle, 22 August 2008; and John Spellman, interview by author, Seattle, 30 July 2008.

25   Lloyd F. Hara, County Auditor, "Progress Report Fiscal and Performance Audit," folder 7, box 13, Series 872, Record Group 123, KCA; Ward and Associates, "Economic Feasibility: Multi Purpose Stadium" 1–2; Wilson, quoted in *Seattle Post-Intelligencer*, 22 September 1970; and *Seattle Post-Intelligencer*, 21 July 1970.

26   Narramore, Bain, Braley and Johanson, [Report on Sicks' Stadium], 2 April 1971, folder 21, box 27, Series 42 Bond and Commission Files, Record Group 137 County Executive, WaPS; Frank L. Hope and Associates, "Site Selection," 3-2–3-4, 7-1–7-8; and *Seattle Post-Intelligencer*, 21 January 1971.

27   Unidentified clipping, December 1971, Clippings scrapbook, KCA.

28 Poulson, quoted in Neil J. Sullivan, *The Dodgers Move West,* 143; and Ruano, quoted in unidentified newspaper clipping, December 1971, Clippings scrapbook, KCA.

29 *Seattle Times,* 23 December 1971; handwritten notes, 10 May 1971 [Joseph McGavick?], folder 9, box 18, Series 42 Bond and Commission Files, Record Group 137 County Executive, WaPS; Spellman interview; and *King County Multipurpose Stadium,* August 1972, box D-31, Series 491 Director's File, Record Group 502 Stadium Administration, KCA.

30 John W. Spangler to John Spellman, folder 3, box 46, Series 44 Subject Files, Record Group 137 County Executive, WaPS; and *Seattle Times,* 26 February 1976.

Play by Play: August and September

1 *Seattle Post-Intelligencer,* 7 and 8 August 1969.

2 *Seattle Times,* 19 August 1969; and *Seattle Post-Intelligencer,* 24 August 1969.

3 *Seattle Times,* 16 August 1969.

4 Milkes, quoted in *Seattle Post-Intelligencer,* 24 August 1969.

5 *Seattle Times,* 26 and 28 August 1969; and *Seattle Post-Intelligencer,* 31 August 1969 and 2 September 1969.

6 *Seattle Times,* 27 August 1969.

7 Ibid.

8 Ibid.

9 *Seattle Post-Intelligencer,* 27 August 1969.

10 Ibid., 3 September 1969.

11 Schultz, quoted in ibid., 11 September 1969.

12 Quirk and Fort, *Pay Dirt,* 111; Fort, *Sports Economics,* 137; *Seattle Post-Intelligencer,* 4 October 1969; *Seattle Times,* 27 November 1969; and Rousso, "An Exhilarating Big League Bust," 117.

13 *Seattle Post-Intelligencer,* 2 October 1969.

9. The Civic Leaders Strike Out

1 For more on this, see White, *Creating the National Pastime*; Danielson, *Home Team*; Quirk and Fort, *Pay Dirt*; and Voigt, *From Postwar Expansion.*

2 Folder 9, box 5, BL-SMA.

3 Soriano, quoted in *Seattle Post-Intelligencer,* 31 August 1969; Jerald Hoffberger to Joe Cronin, 18 August 1969, and American League Bulletin, 11 September 1969, both in deposition of Jerald C. Hoffberger, folder 7, box 3, *Washington et al. v. American League,* WaNW.

4 Daley, quoted in *Seattle Post-Intelligencer,* 31 August 1969.

5 *Seattle Times,* 27 May, 9 September 1969.

6 Ibid., 26 September 1969; and deposition of Joe Cronin, folder 4, box 3, *Washington et al. v. American League,* WaNW.

7 *Seattle Times,* 2 October, 29 September 1969.

8 *Seattle Post-Intelligencer,* 16 October 1969; Kuhn, *Hardball,* 91; *Seattle Post-Intelli-*

gencer, 28 September and 1 October 1969; and *Tacoma News Tribune*, 5 October 1969.

9   *Seattle Post-Intelligencer*, 22 June 1969; deposition of Allan Selig, folder 9, box 3, *Washington et al. v. American League*, WaNW; and W. G. Campbell to Roy Hamey, 18 February 1970, folder I, box 1, *Washington et al. v. American League*, WaNW.

10 Deposition of Joe Cronin, folder 4, box 3, *Washington et al. v. American League*, WaNW.

11 KIRO editorial, "Stadium Finance" folder, box 3, Ellis Collection, UWSC; and *Tacoma News Tribune*, 29 October 1969.

12 *Seattle Post-Intelligencer*, 16, 17, and 22 October 1969.

13 *Argus*, 24 October 1969.

14 Daley, quoted in *Milwaukee Journal*, 21 October 1969; Miller, quoted in *Seattle Times*, 15 October 1969; Henry Jackson and Warren Magnuson to Joe Cronin, 8 October 1969, folder 3, box 215, Jackson Papers, UWSC; Magnuson, quoted in *Seattle Post-Intelligencer*, 16 October 1969; Carroll, quoted in *Milwaukee Sentinel*, 21 October 1969; and Daley, quoted in *Milwaukee Journal*, 22 October 1969.

15 Deposition and evidence of John Spellman, folder 11, box 3, *Washington et al. v. American League*, WaNW; deposition of Joe Cronin, folder 4, box 3, *Washington et al. v. American League*, WaNW; deposition of Robert Short, folder 10, box 3, *Washington et al. v. American League*, WaNW; and *Milwaukee Journal*, 22 October 1969.

16 Affidavit of Fred Ruge, Pacific Northwest Sports, Inc., Debtor, Case File 6682; *Seattle Times*, 6 November 1969; and *Seattle Post-Intelligencer*, 20 November 1969.

17 *Seattle Post-Intelligencer*, 23 November 1969; and Fred Danz, interview by Mike Fuller, December 1993, Seattlepilots.com, http://www.seattlepilots.com/danz_int.html.

18 Edward Carlson to . . . [form letter], 23 October 1969, folder 3, box 3, *Washington et al. v. American League*, WaNW.

19 Meeting agenda, deposition of Edward Carlson, folder 3, box 3, *Washington et al. v. American League*, WaNW; and James Ellis, telephone interview by author, 19 May 2008.

20 Edward Carlson to William Daley, 28 October 1969, and deposition of Edward Carlson, both in folder 3, box 3, *Washington et al. v. American League*; Carlson to Daley, 28 October 1969, folder 19, box 4, BL-SMA; and *Seattle Post-Intelligencer*, 26 October 1969.

21 Leslie Curtis to Edward Carlson, 6 November 1969, Carlson to supporters, 10 November 1969, and Notes of contributions, 29 November 1969, all in deposition of Edward Carlson, folder 3, box 3, *Washington et al. v. American League*, WaNW; "Pilot Purchase Activities," folder 14, box 6, BL-SMA; Danz interview; Pacific Northwest Sports, Inc., Debtor, case 6682, folder 1; and *Seattle Post-Intelligencer*, 18 November 1969.

22 Danz, quoted in *Seattle Times*, 17 December 1969; "Pilot Purchase Activities," folder 5, box 7, BL-SMA; "Pacific Northwest Sports, Inc. Loan," folder 14, box 6, BL-SMA; and Frederic Danz to W. G. Campbell, 31 December 1969, folder 5, box 7, BL-SMA.

23 "Pilot Purchase Activities," folder 5, box 7, BL-SMA; and "Pacific Northwest Sports, Inc. Loan," folder 14, box 6, BL-SMA.

24 "Pacific Northwest Sports, Inc. Loan," folder 14, box 6, BL-SMA.

25 Press release, folder 5, box 197, Magnuson Papers, UWSC; *Seattle Post-Intelligencer*, 4 January 1970; folder 13, box 2, BL-SMA; and *Seattle Times*, 4 January 1970.

26 Uhlman's comment, folder 25, box 4, BL-SMA; *Argus*, 9 January 1970; Kauffman, quoted in *Seattle Times*, 13 January 1970; and Kuhn, quoted in *Milwaukee Sentinel*, 19 January 1970. For more on Uhlman and CHECC, see chapter 1.

27 Deposition of Edward Carlson, folder 3, box 3, *Washington et al. v. American League*, WaNW.

28 Reynolds and Kauffman, quoted in *Seattle Times*, 23 January 1970; *Milwaukee Sentinel*, 24 January 1970; deposition of Allan Selig, folder 9, box 3, *Washington et al. v. American League*, WaNW; and *Seattle Times*, 22 January 1970.

29 *Seattle Post-Intelligencer*, 22 January 1970; deposition of Wes Uhlman, folder 15, box 4, BL-SMA; and William Dwyer to Slade Gorton, 26 January 1970, folder 14, box 4, BL-SMA.

30 Pacific Northwest Sports, Inc., Debtor, case 6682, folder 6; and Jerry McNaul, interview by Mike Fuller, January 1994, Seattlepilots.com, http://www.seattlepilots.com/mcnaul_int.html.

31 Uhlman's comment, folder 25, box 4, BL-SMA.

32 *Seattle Times*, 27 January 1970; and telegram from Warren Magnuson and Henry Jackson to American League, 26 January 1970, folder 5, box 7, BL-SMA.

33 *Seattle Times*, 28 January 1970; and meeting transcripts, *Washington et al. v. American League*, folder 9, box 5, BL-SMA.

34 "Memorandum of Proposal for Purchase of Pacific Northwest Sports, Inc.," 10 February 1970; Van Lindt, *The Seattle Pilots Story*, 196; Watson, *Digressions of a Native Son*, 180; Carlson statement, T. E. Comer to Bowie Kuhn (no date), and deposition of Edward Carlson, all folder 3, box 3, *Washington et al. v. American League*, WaNW; Campbell, quoted in *Seattle Post-Intelligencer*, 10 February 1970; and deposition of Jack Zander, folder 12, box 3, *Washington et al. v. American League*, WaNW.

35 *Seattle Times*, 8 February 1970; and Soriano, quoted in *Seattle Times*, 10 February 1970.

36 *Seattle Post-Intelligencer*, 10 February 1970; *Milwaukee Journal*, 3 February 1970; Marvin Milkes to Edward Carlson, 31 January 1970, and Milkes to personnel, 3 February 1970, both deposition of Edward Carlson, folder 3, box 3, *Washington et al. v. American League*, WaNW; deposition of Charles Finley, folder 5, box 3, *Washington et al. v. American League*, WaNW; deposition of Robert Short, folder 10 box 3, *Washington et al. v. American League*, WaNW; deposition of Allan Selig, folder 9, box 3, *Washington et al. v. American League*, WaNW; and *Milwaukee Journal*, 8 February 1970.

37 James Ellis interview.

38 Kauffman, quoted in deposition of Charles Finley, folder 5, box 3 *Washington et al. v. American League*, WaNW.

39 *Seattle Times*, 27 January 1970.

40 Deposition of Edward Carlson, folder 3, box 3, *Washington et al. v. American League*, WaNW; *Tacoma News Tribune*, 23 February 1970; and *Seattle Times*, 8 March and 11 February 1970.

41 Folder 26, box D-31, Series 491 Director's File, Record Group 502 Stadium Admin-istration, KCA; deposition of Charles Finley, folder 5, box 3, *Washington et al. v. American League*, WaNW; Finley quotation in folder III, box 1, *Washington et al. v. American League*, WaNW; Robert Short quotation in folder VI, box 1, *Washington et al. v. American League*, WaNW; deposition of Joe Cronin, Pacific Northwest Sports, Inc., Debtor, case 6682; Allyn, quoted in *Seattle Times*, 12 February 1970; and *Seattle Post-Intelligencer*, 11 February 1970.

42 Cronin, quoted in *Seattle Post-Intelligencer*, 11 February 1970; and brief in support of renewed motion of baseball defendants, folder 10, box 5, BL-SMA.

43 Deposition of Joe Cronin, Pacific Northwest Sports, Inc., Debtor, case 6682; and deposition of Robert Short, folder 10, box 3, *Washington et al. v. American League*, WaNW.

44 Transcript of American League meeting, folder III and folder IV, box 1, *Washington et al. v. American League*, WaNW; and McNaul interview.

45 *Seattle Post-Intelligencer*, 10 March, 15 February, and 20 March 1970.

Chapter 10. Dropping the Pilots

1 Rockne, quoted in Rousso, "An Exhilarating Big League Bust," 121.

2 *Seattle Times*, 11 September 1969; Milkes, quoted in ibid., 21 August 1969; *Seattle Post-Intelligencer*, 2 October 1969; and *Seattle Times*, 14 October 1969.

3 Hogan, *The 1969 Seattle Pilots*, 175.

4 *Seattle Post-Intelligencer*, 12 February 1970; and *Seattle Times*, 19 February 1970.

5 Marvin Milkes to Joe Cronin, 23 February 1970, folder 14, box 2, BL-SMA; *Seattle Times*, 26 February 1970; deposition of Robert Short, folder 10, box 3, *Washington et al. v. American League*, WaNW; *Seattle Times*, 10 March 1970; T. E. Comer to Roy Hamey, 12 March 1970, folder 9, box 5, BL-SMA; and "Projected Cash Flow, February to October 1970," folder 14, box 2, BL-SMA.

6 Max Soriano, interview by Mike Fuller, January 1994, Seattlepilots.com, http://www.seattlepilots.com/msoriano_int.html; "Analysis of Meetings," [memo on radio], folder 1, box 6, BL-SMA; Jack Bankson to Pacific Northwest Sports, 19 February 1970, folder 6, box 4, BL-SMA; Marvin Milkes journal [?], in deposition of John Spellman, folder 11, box 3, *Washington et al. v. American League*, WaNW; and *Seattle Times*, 18 March and 12 March 1970.

7 *Seattle Times*, 18 March 1970.

8 *Seattle Post-Intelligencer*, 1 March 1970; and Eddie O'Brien, interview by author, Seattle, 8 September 2008.

9 Milkes, quoted in *Seattle Post-Intelligencer*, 18 March 1970; and *Seattle Post-Intelli-gencer*, 5 April 1970.

10 Cronin, quoted in *Seattle Post-Intelligencer*, 5 March 1970; *Seattle Post-Intelligencer*, 9 March 1970; Cronin, quoted in *Milwaukee Sentinel* 12 March 1970; *Milwaukee Jour-nal*, 8 March 1970; Daley, quoted in *Seattle Times*, 10 March 1970; *Milwaukee Journal*, 11 March 1970; and *Seattle Post-Intelligencer*, 11 March 1970.

11 Morgan, *Skid Road*, 281; *New York Post*, 11 March 1970; clipping and constituents'

letters, folder 39, box 243, Magnuson Papers, UWSC; copy of proposed bill, folder 3, box 215, Jackson Papers, UWSC; and Magnuson's review of baseball's antitrust status, folder 36, box 243, Magnuson Papers, UWSC.

12 Edward Carlson to Bowie Kuhn, folder 21, box 3, *Washington et al. v. American League*, WaNW; Carlson, quoted in *Seattle Post-Intelligencer*, 14 March 1970; and Kuhn, *Hardball*, 92.

13 *Seattle Times*, 24 March 1970; deposition of Jerald C. Hoffberger, folder 7, box 3, *Washington et al. v. American League*, WaNW; Slade Gorton to Cronin, William Daley, Dewey Soriano, Max Soriano, and Alexander Hadden, 10 March 1970, folder 15, box 2, BL-SMA; *Seattle Times*, 16 March 1970; and Alfred Schweppe to James Wilson, 27 March 1972, folder "Stadium 3," box 3, Ellis Collection, UWSC.

14 Transcript of American League meeting from *Washington et al. v. American League*, folder 9, box 5, BL-SMA; deposition of Joe Cronin, Pacific Northwest Sports, Inc., Debtor, Case File 6682; and *Milwaukee Journal*, 17 March 1970.

15 *Seattle Times*, 21 March 1970; deposition of Joe Cronin, Pacific Northwest Sports, Inc., Debtor, case 6682; and *Seattle Times*, 24 March 1970.

16 Petition for Bankruptcy, Pacific Northwest Sports, Inc., Debtor, case 6682; William Hutchinson notebook, in DEPC; Beeston, quoted in Euchner, *Playing the Field*, 48; Bill Sears, interview by Mike Fuller, January 1994, Seattlepilots.com, http://www. seattlepilots.com/sears_int.html; Peat Marwick analysis in deposition of Edward Carlson, folder 3, box 3, *Washington et al. v. American League*, WaNW; and Pacific Northwest Sports, Inc., Debtor, folder 1, case 6682.

17 John R. Tomlinson to Frederic Danz, 16 January 1970, folder I, box 1, *Washington et al. v. American League*, WaNW; Pacific Northwest Sports, Inc., Debtor, folder 1, case 6682; Jean Fisher to Robert Schoenbachler, 8 June 1970, DEPC; Campbell, quoted in *Seattle Post-Intelligencer*, 31 March 1970; Orlo Kellogg, quoted in SeattlePilots.com, http://www.seattlepilots.com/history3.html; Response of City of Seattle to Show Cause Order, Pacific Northwest Sports, Inc., Debtor, folder 1, case 6682; Van Lindt, *The Seattle Pilots Story*, 205; and *Seattle Times*, 24 March 1970.

18 Affidavit of Fred Ruge, folder 6, box 4, BL-SMA; and *Milwaukee Journal*, 31 March 1970.

19 Findings of fact and conclusions of law, 4 April 1970, folder 8, box 4, BL-SMA; Bankruptcy Court Ruling, 31 March 1970, Pacific Northwest Sports, Inc., Debtor, case 6682; Sidney Volinn, interview by Mike Fuller, January 1994, Seattlepilots.com, http://www.seattlepilots.com/volinn_int.html; and *Seattle Post-Intelligencer*, 3 April 1970.

20 *Milwaukee Journal*, 1 April 1970.

21 Ibid.

22 *Seattle Times*, 9 April 1970; *Seattle Post-Intelligencer*, 29 March 1970; *Seattle Times*, 2 April 1970; and *Tacoma News Tribune*, 7 January and 7 April 1970.

23 Schweppe, quoted in *Seattle Post-Intelligencer*, 18 March 1970; *New York Times*, 18 March 1970; Uhlman, quoted in *Milwaukee Journal*, 22 January 1970; *Seattle Times*, 19 March 1970; *Seattle Post-Intelligencer*, 27 January 1970; *Seattle Times*, 12 and 16 March 1970; and KIRO editorial, folder 3, box 215, Jackson Papers, UWSC.

24 *Seattle Times*, 29 March 1970; Red Smith, referenced in *Milwaukee Journal*, 22 March

1970; correspondence, folder 39, box 243, Magnuson Papers, UWSC; Soriano, quoted in *Tacoma News Tribune*, 8 February 1973; *New York Times*, 21 October 1969; and Anderson, referenced in Schaefer, "Play Ball!" 20.

25 Brabender, quoted in *Milwaukee Sentinel*, 18 March 1970; Sears interview by author, Edmonds, Washington, 31 May 2007; and Eddie O'Brien interview.

26 *Seattle Post-Intelligencer*, 26 March 1970; and Mary Soriano to Bob Schoenbachler, 24 June 1970, DEPC.

27 Dick Young, quoted in *Seattle Post-Intelligencer*, 18 March 1970; *Tacoma News Tribune*, 25 January 1970; Bill White, quoted in Whitford, *Playing Hardball*, 123–24; Quirk and Fort, *Pay Dirt*, 28; Whitford, *Playing Hardball*, 35; and Bouton, *Ball Four*, 441.

28 Dewey Soriano, interview by Mike Fuller, August 1994, Seattlepilots.com, http://www.seattlepilots.com/dsoriano_int.html; and Bill Dwyer, interview by Mike Fuller, Seattlepilots.com, http://www.seattlepilots.com/dwyer_int.html.

29 Sears interview by author; and Max Soriano interview.

30 Milkes, quoted in *Seattle Times*, 30 March 1970; [Final claims and payments], Pacific Northwest Sports, Inc., Debtor, folder 8, case 6682; and *Seattle Times*, 10 June 1970.

31 *Seattle Post-Intelligencer*, 9 February 1971.

32 Ibid,; and Max Soriano interview.

33 *Seattle Post-Intelligencer*, 28 January 1976; Fred Danz, interview by Mike Fuller, December 1993, Seattlepilots.com, http://www.seattlepilots.com/danz_int.html; *Seattle Post-Intelligencer*, 18 January 1970; King County Design Commission/Office of Architecture and City of Seattle, "Final Environmental Impact Statement," section 1–20.

34 John Owen, telephone interview by author, 2 January 2008; and Sears interview by author.

35 Bouton, "Reflections," 153; and Kahn, [no title], 14.

36 Bouton, *Ball Four*, 465; Armour, "The Revolution Started Here," 110; Bouton, *Ball Four*; McGimpsey, *Imagining Baseball*, 46; and Bouton, *Ball Four*, ix.

37 Armour, "The Revolution Started Here," 129.

38 Bouton, *Ball Four*, xii, xiv.

39 Ibid., 417, 447–48.

40 Ibid., xiv; Jim Bouton, "I'm Glad," 37–38; Bouton, "Reflections on Managing a Baseball Team," 153; and Bouton, *I'm Glad*, 80–89.

41 Press release quoted in Bouton, "I'm Glad," 37; Kuhn, *Hardball*, 73; and Bouton, *I'm Glad*, 67–79.

42 Parrott, *The Lords of Baseball*, 61; Schultz, quoted in *Seattle Times*, 21 November 1970; Owen interview; Schultz, quoted in Bouton, "I'm Glad," 46; Oyler, quoted in *Seattle Post-Intelligencer*, 25 October 1970; O'Brien, quoted in Bouton, *Ball Four*, 442; Bouton, *I'm Glad*, 136; and Bouton, *Ball Four*, 404.

43 Bouton, *Ball Four*, x–xi; comments of Halberstam in Armour, "The Revolution Started Here," 112, 139; Lipsyte referenced in Bouton, *I'm Glad*, 139; Kahn and Young referenced in Armour, "The Revolution Started Here," 111, 113. Armour's "The Revolution Started Here," a sensitive and thorough overview of critics' reactions to *Ball Four*, is well worth reading.

44 *Seattle Times*, 2 June 1970; *Seattle Post-Intelligencer*, 19 and 20 May 1970; and *Seattle Times*, 4 June 1970.

Play by Play: Spring Training 1970

1 Jim Kittilsby, telephone interview by author, 2 and 4 February 2009.
2 *Seattle Post-Intelligencer*, 17 and 20 March 1970; and Kittilsby interview.
3 *Seattle Post-Intelligencer*, 27 March 1970.
4 Kittilsby interview.
5 *Seattle Post-Intelligencer*, 8 April 1970.

Chapter 11. A Stadium at Last

1 *Bellevue American*, 11 December 1975.
2 *Seattle Post-Intelligencer*, 15 June 1975; *Seattle Times*, 26 August 1972; *Seattle Post-Intelligencer*, 24 February 1974; and John Spellman, interview by author, Seattle, 30 June 2008.
3 Folder 1, box 15, Series 277 Stadium Files, Record Group 137 County, WaPS.
4 *Bellevue American*, 19 July 1978.
5 Unidentified clipping, 1972 (?), clipping file, 1972–1975, KCA; and *Seattle Times*, 13 May 1972.
6 *Seattle Times*, 5 November 1972; and Chin, *Seattle's International District*, 80–81.
7 For a context for stadium building and city interest groups, see Curry, Schwirian, and Woldoff, *High Stakes*.
8 The District Design Group, "The International District–Seattle," unpaginated; Hara, County Auditor, "Progress Report Fiscal and Performance Audit," 4 January 1975, folder 7, box 13, Series 872, Record Group 123, KCA; and King County Design Commission, "Stadium Convention Center Impact Study," May 1972, box 97, Series 872, Record Group 465, KCA.
9 Thrush, *Native Seattle*, 175.
10 Chin, *Seattle's International District*, 81.
11 Wes Uhlman to Randy Revelle, 31 August 1972, folder 19, box 3, BL-SMA; Victor Steinbrueck to John Spellman, 29 August 1972, folder 5, box 4, BL-SMA; and *Seattle Times*, 13 December 1972.
12 Design Commission, "Impact Study," box 97, Series 872, Record Group 465, KCA; and *Seattle Times*, 15 July 1972.
13 *Seattle Times*, 14 July 1972; and *Seattle Post-Intelligencer*, 17 August 1972.
14 *Seattle Post-Intelligencer*, 4 February 1975; and Spellman interview.
15 Report on Impact, 5 September 1974, folder 2, box 15, WaPS; Examples of Stadium Impact, folder 7, box 6, Series 277 Stadium Files, Record Group 137 County Executive, WaPS; Brambilla and Longo, *Learning from Seattle*, 91; and John Spellman to Abrahma Aiditi, 4 September 1975, folder 10, box 7, Series 277 Stadium Files, Record Group 137 County Executive, WaPS.
16 *Seattle Times*, 19 May 1972; and Final Parking and Access Plan, 23 March 1976,

folder 10, box 8, Series 277 Stadium Files, Record Group 137 County Executive, WaPS.

17 "Prime Site, Prime Destination," Kingdome Kit, UWSC; and "King County Multi-purpose Stadium," August 1972, KCA.

18 "King County Multipurpose Stadium," February 1974, KCA.

19 *Seattle Times*, 19 July 1974.

20 Virginia Davis to Wes Uhlman and John Spellman, 29 March 1974, folder 5, box 4, Series 277 Stadium Files, Record Group 137 County Executive, WaPS.

21 *Seattle Weekly*, 12 July 1978; unidentified newspaper clippings from 12 and 20 December 197(7?), Series 45, Record Group 137 County Executive, KCA; and *Seattle Times*, 29 November 197(7?), Series 45, Record Group 137 County Executive, KCA.

22 *Seattle Times*, 5 October 1974.

23 Ibid., 6 December 1974.

24 Ibid., 13 December 197(7?), Series 45, Record Group 137 County Executive, KCA.

25 Ibid., 5 December 1974; and John Spellman to Paul Barden, 10 December 1974, folder 5, box 1, Series 277 Stadium Files, Record Group 137 County Executive, WaPS.

26 *Seattle Post-Intelligencer*, 4 December 1974 and 23 February 1978.

27 *Seattle Times*, 10 December 1974; and *Seattle Post-Intelligencer*, 12 December 1974.

28 *Seattle Times*, 3 December 1974; James Ellis to John Spellman, 24 December 1974, folder 13, box 3, Series 277 Stadium Files, Record Group 137 County Executive, WaPS; and *Seattle Times*, 11 December 1974.

29 John O'Brien, interview by author, Seattle, 22 August 2008; *Everett Herald*, 22 April 1978; and *Seattle Times*, 18 December 1974.

30 Johnson, "Kingdome Impact Study," 2-1.

31 *Seattle Post-Intelligencer*, 14 December 1974; and *Bellevue American*, 13 April 1978.

32 *Seattle Post-Intelligencer*, 19 February 1975.

33 Unsigned motion, folder 9, box 32, Series 304 Issue Files, Record Group 158 County Administrative Officer, WaPS.

34 *Seattle Times*, 25 January 1978; *Auburn Globe News*, 9 July 1978; and *Seattle Times*, 16 and 24 June 1980.

35 *Seattle Times*, 8 April 1975.

36 Unidentified clipping, folder 23, box 1, Department of Stadium Administration, Public Information Office, KCA; *Seattle Times*, 28 March 1976; John Spellman to Billy Graham, 11 October 1974, Series 277 Stadium Files, Record Group 137 County Executive, WaPS; and John O'Brien interview.

37 Johnson, "Kingdome Impact Study, 7-7-7-15.

38 *Argus*, 28 November 1975; "Movers . . . ," *Time*, 12 December 1978, 36; and *Louisville Times*, 24 May 1978.

39 *Seattle Times*, 11 January 1973.

12. *Out of Court Settlement: The Mariners*

1 Unidentified clipping, "Clippings 1972, 1973, 1974, 1975 [scrapbook]," KCA.

2 John O'Brien, interview by author, Seattle, 22 August 2008.

3 "Notes on Meeting with Ewing Kauffman," July 24, 1974, folder 15, box 4, BL-SMA; and John Spellman, interview by author, Seattle, 30 July 2008.

4 *Seattle Times*, 25 April 1974; unidentified clipping, [ca. June 1974], "Clippings 1972, 1973, 1974, 1975 [scrapbook]," KCA; and *Seattle Times*, 19 December 1975.

5 Watson, *Digressions of a Native Son*, 179; and unidentified clipping, 15 August 1975, and *Seattle Post-Intelligencer*, October(?) 1975, both "Clippings 1975–1976 [scrapbook]," KCA.

6 John Spellman to James Tamble, 16 May 1974, folder 12, box 5, BL-SMA; John Spellman to Lee McPhail, 5 September 1975, box D-31, Series 491 Director's Files, Record Group 502 Stadium Administration, KCA; Kuhn, *Hardball*, 91; and notes on baseball lease, box D-31, Series 491 Director's Files, Record Group 502 Stadium Administration, KCA.

7 Plaintiff's brief on a motion to remand, folder 19, box 2, *Washington et al. v. American League*, WaNW.

8 Complaint, folder 19, box 2, *Washington et al. v. American League*, WaNW; and Gorton, quoted in Thiel, *Out of Left Field*, 3.

9 Breakdown of losses, folder VI, box 1, *Washington et al. v. American League*, WaNW; city claim, folder 5, box 5, BL-SMA; and affidavit of Lowell R. Bassett, folder VIII, box 1, *Washington et al. v. American League*, WaNW.

10 *Washington et al. v. American League*, folder 2, box 5, BL-SMA; and Pre-trial arguments, folder 14, box 2, *Washington et al. v. American League*, WaNW.

11 Slade Gorton, interview by author, Seattle, 17 January 2008; Eskenazi, "Dwyer KO's American League"; *Everett Herald*, 30 January 1976; and Finley and Hoffberger, quoted in *Seattle Post-Intelligencer*, 18 February 1976.

12 Juror, quoted in *Seattle Post-Intelligencer*, 18 February 1976; Fred Brack, telephone interview by Mike Fuller, 1994, Seattlepilots.com, http://www.seattlepilots.com/brack_int.html; and *Seattle Times*, 8 February 1976.

13 Jerry McNaul, interview by Mike Fuller, January 1994, Seattlepilots.com, http://www.seattlepilots.com/mcnaul_int.html; deposition of Joe Cronin, folder 4, box 3, *Washington et al. v. American League*, WaNW; and deposition of Charles Finley, folder 5, box 3, *Washington et al. v. American League*, WaNW.

14 Plaintiff's brief , folder 11, box 2, *Washington et al. v. American League*, WaNW; and *Seattle Times*, 16 January 1976.

15 [Ellis's testimony], folder I, box 1, *Washington et al. v. American League*, WaNW; James Ellis, telephone interview by author, 19 May 2008; and *Everett Herald*, 30 January 1976.

16 State of Washington and City of Seattle v. American League and Pacific Northwest Sports, Inc., folder 2, box 6, BL-SMA; and *Washington et al. v. American League*, folder 3, box 6, BL-SMA; and Petition for Writ of Certiorari, 18 March 1974, *Washington et al. v. American League*, unnumbered folder, box 6, BL-SMA.

17 Folder 11, box 2, *Washington et al. v. American League*, WaNW; and Soriano quotation, in *Washington et al. v. American League*, folder 9, box 5, BL-SMA.

18 *Seattle Times*, 14 January 1976.

19 Short quotation, in folder V, box 1, *Washington et al. v. American League*, WaNW.

20 *Washington et al. v. American League*, folder 2, box 6, BL-SMA; and defendants memorandum, folder VI, box 1, *Washington et al. v. American League*, WaNW.

21 Jerry McNaul interview; Bill Dwyer, interview by Mike Fuller, December 1993, Seattlepilots.com, http://www.seattlepilots.com/dwyer_int.html; and brief in support of motion to compel production of documents, folder I, box 1, *Washington et al. v. American League*, WaNW.

22 Brief of defendants in opposition to remand, folder 19, box 2, *Washington et al. v. American League*, WaNW; Petition for Writ of Certiorari, *Washington et al. v. American League*, folder 3, box 6, BL-SMA; affidavit of John Weinberg, folder 18, box 2, *Washington et al. v. American League*, WaNW; plaintiff's brief opposing stay, folder 12, box 2, *Washington et al. v. American League*, WaNW; and McPhail, *My 9 Innings*, 132.

23 William Dwyer to Wes Uhlman, 1 December 1975, box D-2, #102, Series 491 Director's Files, Record Group 502 Stadium Administration, KCA.

24 *Seattle Times*, 23 January 1976; and *Seattle Post-Intelligencer*, 18 February 1976.

25 *Seattle Post-Intelligencer*, 27 January 1976; Lee McPhail, quoted in Danielson, *Home Team*, 197; and William Dwyer to David Wagoner, 26 January 1976, folder "Suit," box 11, Hill Special Collection, UWSC.

26 William Dwyer to Wes Uhlman and John P. Harris, 13 February 1976, folder "Suit," box 11, Hill Special Collection, UWSC; and Lease Agreement, box D-2, #125, Series 491 Director's Files, Record Group 502 Stadium Administration, KCA.

27 Press release, folder 10, box 233, Magnuson Papers, UWSC.

28 Thiel, *Out of Left Field*, 11; and Scully, *The Business of Major League Baseball*, 106.

29 Thiel, *Out of Left Field*, 14–15; and Zimbalist, *Baseball and Billions*, 131–32.

BIBLIOGRAPHY

Government and Quasi-public Documents

[Ad Hoc Committee for the Seattle Center Stadium Site]. "Ad Hoc Committee for the Seattle Center Stadium Site." Seattle, 1968.

A. T. Kearney and Company, Inc., "Economic Action Task Force, and Seattle–King County Economic Development Council. A Program for Economic Recovery." Seattle, 1971.

Baker, Miner. "A Reappraisal of the Seattle Area Industrial Council." In "A Reappraisal of the Seattle Area's Industrial Future," edited by Seattle Area Industrial Council, 3–13. Seattle, 1968.

Capitol Hill Community Study. "Proceedings."Seattle, 1969.

Century 21 Exposition. "Final Report of Century 21 Exposition, Inc., as Submitted to the Washington State World's Fair Commission." Seattle, 1962.

Council of Planning Affiliates. "Skid Road Study." Seattle, 1993.

The District Design Group. "The International District—Seattle: An Action Program for Physical Development." Seattle, 1973.

Duckstad, Eric E., and Bruce Waybur. *Feasibility of a Major League Sports Stadium for King County, Washington.* Menlo Park, CA: Stanford Research Institute, 1960.

Forward Thrust. "Developing a Capital Improvement Plan for King County: Part I, Background." [Seattle], 1967.

———. "Developing a Capital Improvement Plan for King County: Part II, Analysis, Sept. 1967." [Seattle], 1967.

———. "Developing a Capital Improvement Plan for King County: Part III, Recommendations." [Seattle], 1967.

———. "Developing a Capital Improvement Plan for King County: Part IV, Analysis and Recommendations, 1970." [Seattle], 1970.

———. *Forward Thrust Progress Report, 1973.* Seattle, 1973.

———. *Forward Thrust Progress Report, 1976.* Seattle, 1976.

———. "Selected Speeches on Forward Thrust and Feb 13, 1968 Election Results." [Seattle], [1968?].

———. *Forward Thrust Work, 1968–1970: A Report to the Residents of King County, Washington on Progress of 370 Forward Thrust Projects.* [Seattle], [1970?].

———. *Forward Thrust Work, 1968–1972: A Report to the Residents of King County, Washington on Progress of Forward Thrust Projects.* [Seattle], [1972?].

Forward Thrust Committee. [*Forward Thrust Progress Report*]. Seattle, 1980.

Frank L. Hope and Associates. "Site Selection: Multi-purpose Stadium, King County, Washington." Seattle, 1970.

Johnson, Virginia. "Kingdome Impact Study." Seattle, 1979.

Joseph B. Ward and Associates. "Economic Feasibility: Multi-purpose Stadium." Seattle, 1971.

Joseph B. Ward and Associates (for Downtown Seattle Development Association). "Central Business District Economic Impact Survey." Seattle, 1973.

King County, Washington. "The Capital Improvement Program for King County/Election Resolutions and Ordinances." Seattle, 1967.

———. "1970 Overall Economic Development Plan." Seattle, 1970.

———. *Official Statement $11,000,000 Various Purpose General Obligation Bonds 1970 Unlimited Tax, 2–40 Years.* Seattle, 1970.

King County, Washington, Design Commission/Office of Architecture and City of Seattle. "Final Impact Statement: King County Multipurpose Stadium." Seattle, 1972.

King County, Washington, Office of the County Auditor. "King County Domed Stadium: Progress Report, Fiscal and Performance Audit." Seattle, 1975.

Lawyers for Housing. "Skid Road Housing Survey." Seattle, 1972.

Merry, Calvo, Lane and Baker, Inc. "The 1970 Forward Thrust Bond Issues Press Book." Seattle, 1970.

Narramore, Skilling, Praeger. "Program for King County Multi-purpose Stadium." Seattle, 1969.

———. "Schematic Design: Phase I for the King County Multi-purpose Stadium." Seattle, 1969.

Port of Seattle. "Airborne Traffic of Sea-Tac International Airport and Its Impact on the Economy of King County." Seattle: Privately printed, 1974.

———. "Annual Report of the Seattle-Tacoma International Airport." Seattle, [1971?].

———. "History of Seattle-Tacoma International Airport." Seattle, [1991?].

———. "Port of Seattle Annual Report, 1968." Seattle: Privately printed, [1969?].

———. "1969 Annual Report." Seattle, [1970?].

Port of Seattle, Seattle-Tacoma International Airport. "Seattle-Tacoma International Airport Operations Report—1968." Seattle, [1969?].

Praeger-Kavanagh-Waterbury. "Engineering Study: Seattle–King County Stadium." Seattle: printed by author, 1966.

Robert Gladstone and Associates. "Basic Economic Indicators and Development Problems and Potentials for Seattle Model Cities Program: Final Report." Vol. 2. Seattle, 1970.

Seattle Area Industry Council. "Economic Information Reports: Annual Business Benchmarks, Seattle-Tacoma-Everett Area." Seattle, [1968].

Seattle Chamber of Commerce, Marine Exchange. "1971 Waterborne Foreign Trade for the Port of Seattle." Seattle, [1972?].

Seattle Chamber of Commerce, Research Department. "Business Economic Indicators." Seattle, [1974].

Seattle, Comptroller. "Annual Financial Report." Seattle, 1969.

———. Annual Financial Report. Seattle, 1970.

Seattle, Department of Community Development. "Sick's Stadium Development Prospectus." Seattle, 1978.

———. "A Statement of Seattle's Economic Condition." Seattle, 1971.

Seattle–King County Economic Development Council. "Seattle, U.S.A. in Perspective." Seattle, 1972.

Seattle, Mayor's Office. "Statement of Mayor Wes Uhlman Regarding International Business District." Seattle, 1972.

———. "Mayor J. D. Braman, 1969 Annual Budget." Seattle, 1968.

Seattle, Model City Program. "Seattle Model Neighborhood 1968 Household Survey." Seattle, [1968].

Seattle Municipal Reference Library. "Notes on Economic Effect of Seattle World's Fair (Century 21)." Seattle, [1962?].

University of Washington, Social Change Evaluation Project. "Patterns of Issue Generation and Community Responses on Public Policy Concerning the Poor and Minorities." Seattle, [1968?].

———. "A Study of Organizational and Institutional Change: Final Report." Seattle, [1968?].

———. "A Study of Organizational and Institutional Change: Part II." Seattle, [1968?].

Washington State, Major League Baseball Stadium Public Facilities District. *Comprehensive Reports*. Seattle: privately printed, 1996.

Washington State, Superintendent of Public Instruction. "Demographic and Socioeconomic Profiles of the American Indian, Black, Chinese, Filipino, Japanese, Spanish Heritage, and White Populations of Washington State in 1970." Seattle, 1974.

Western Management Consultants. "Economic Feasibility of a Multi-purpose Stadium for King County and Seattle, Washington: A Study for the Board of County Commissioners of King County and the Mayor and City Council of Seattle, Washington." Seattle, 1966.

———. "Report to the State of Washington Stadium Commission on Stadium Site Selection: Seattle–King County Washington." Seattle, 1968.

Manuscript Archives and Collections

PERSONAL COLLECTIONS

David Eskenazi, Personal Collection

Lew Matlin, Personal Collection

KING COUNTY ARCHIVES

Clipping books, 1972–76

King County Auditor, Progress Report, Fiscal and Performance Audit, 1975

King County Design Commission/Department of Architecture, "Stadium Convention Center Impact Study"

King County Design Commission/Department of Architecture in conjunction with City of Seattle, "Final Environmental Impact"

King County Multipurpose Stadium, Director's Files

Scrapbooks

NATIONAL ARCHIVES AND RECORDS ADMINISTRATION (NARA)— PACIFIC ALASKA REGION (SEATTLE)

Pacific Northwest Sports, Inc., Debtor, Case File 6682; United States District Court for the Western District of Washington, Northern Division (Seattle); Records of the District Courts of the United States, Record Group 21

SEATTLE MUNICIPAL ARCHIVES
City of Seattle Law Department Baseball Litigation Files
City of Seattle Legislative Information Service: Comptroller File
Records of the Office of the Mayor, 1956–70

SEATTLE PUBLIC LIBRARY, SEATTLE ROOM
Seattle King County Economic Development Council. "Economic Profile of Seattle."
  Manuscript Collection.
"Unemployment, October 30, 1967–March 4, 1970." Clipping File.

UNIVERSITY OF WASHINGTON LIBRARIES SPECIAL COLLECTIONS
Floyd Miller Collection
Henry M. Jackson Papers
J. D. Braman Collection
Joseph E. Gandy Collection
Joseph E. Gandy Inventory Folder
Kingdome Kit
Tim Hill Collection
Warren Grant Magnuson Papers

WASHINGTON STATE ARCHIVES, NORTHWEST REGIONAL BRANCH, BELLINGHAM
State of Washington et al. v. American League of Professional Baseball Clubs, Superior Court
  Case #110638, Snohomish County Clerk's Office

WASHINGTON STATE ARCHIVES, PUGET SOUND REGIONAL BRANCH, BELLEVUE
King County Administrative Officer
King County Executive: Board and Commission Files, Clipping Files, Stadium Files,
  Subject Files
King County Commissioners

Secondary Sources

Abbott, Carl. "Five Strategies for Downtown: Policy Discourse and Planning since 1943."
  In *Planning the Twentieth Century American City*, 404–27. Edited by Mary Corbin Sies
  and Christopher Silver. Baltimore, Md.: Johns Hopkins University Press, 1996.
———. *The New Urban America: Growth and Politics in Sunbelt Cities*. Rev. ed. Chapel Hill:
  University of North Carolina Press, 1987.
———. "Regional City and Network City: Portland and Seattle in the Twentieth Cen-
  tury." *Western Historical Quarterly*, August 1992, 293–322.
Adomites, Paul D. "Seattle Pilots–Milwaukee Brewers." In *Encyclopedia of Major League
  Baseball Team Histories: American League*, 183–204. Edited by Peter C. Bjarkman.
  Westport, Conn.: Meckler Books, 1991.

Amory, Cleveland. [No title]. *Saturday Review*, 1 August 1970, 10–11.

Anderson, Ralph. "Comments on the City." *Puget Soundings*, November 1968, 8–9.

Angell, Roger. "Scribe." *New Yorker*, 25 July 1970, 79–80.

———. "Sundown." *Sports Illustrated*, 6 January 1975, 74–81.

Angeloff, Sam A. "Are We Ready for the Big Leagues?" *Seattle: The Pacific Northwest Magazine*, January 1965, 10–16.

Anonymous. "Is Baseball Really Like That?" *Saturday Review*, 11 July 1970, 43–44.

———. "Knuckleballer." *New Yorker*, 24 October 1970, 39–40.

———. "Those Movers Who Shake Seattle." *Time*, 12 December 1977, 36.

Armour, Mark. "The Revolution Started Here." In *Rain Check: Baseball in the Pacific Northwest*, 108–13. Cleveland, Ohio: Society for American Baseball Research, 2006.

Ashe, Arthur. *A Hard Road to Glory: A History of the African American Athlete since 1946.* Vol. 3. New York: Amistad, 1988.

Axthelm, Pete. "Pitcher in the Wry." *Newsweek*, 15 June 1970, 59.

Baim, Dean. *The Sports Stadium as a Municipal Investment*. Westport, Conn.: Greenwood Press, 1994.

Banfield, Edward C. *Big City Politics*. New York: Random House, 1965.

Basseti, Fred. "The Pike Place Market." *Puget Soundings*, January 1968, 17, 31–32.

Bauer, Eugene E. *Boeing in Peace and War*. Enumclaw, Wash.: TABA Publishing, 1990.

Bavasi, Buzzie. *Off the Record*. Chicago: Contemporary Books, 1987.

Berner, Richard C. *Seattle in the Twentieth Century*. Vol. 1, *Seattle, 1900–1920: From Boomtown, Urban Turbulence, to Restoration*. Seattle: Charles Press, 1991.

———. *Seattle in the Twentieth Century*. Vol. 3, *Seattle Transformed: World War II to Cold War*. Seattle: Charles Press, 1999.

Bouton, Jim. *Ball Four*. Twentieth anniversary edition. Edited by Leonard Schecter. 1970; New York: Macmillan Publishing Co., 1990.

———. *I'm Glad You Didn't Take It Personally*. Edited by Leonard Schecter. New York: William Morrow and Company, 1971.

———. "I'm Glad You Didn't Take It Personally." *Look*, 15 June 1971, 35–46.

———. "Reflections on Managing a Baseball Team." *Esquire*, May 1973, 153–55, 220.

Bowker, Gordon. "Who's on First?" *Seattle: The Pacific Northwest Magazine*, January 1970, 32–37.

Bowman, John, and Joel Zoss. *Diamonds in the Rough: The Untold History of Baseball*. New York: Macmillan Publishing Co., 1989.

Braman, James D., Jr. "A New Idea for Cities." *Puget Soundings*, April 1970, 12–13.

Brambilla, Roberto, and Gianni Longo. *Learning from Seattle: What Makes Cities Livable?* [New York]: Institute for Environmental Action, 1980.

Brewster, David. "Can 'Culture' Survive in Seattle?" *Seattle: The Pacific Northwest Magazine*, October 1969, 26–34.

———. "Can We Stop Spread City?" *The Weekly*, April 1977, 9–10.

———. "A City to Live In." *Seattle: The Pacific Northwest Magazine*, June 1969, 16–23, 50.

———. "The Good, Gray Times." *Seattle: The Pacific Northwest Magazine*, November 1969, 32–41.

———. "Is Floyd Miller Really Mayor of Seattle?" *Seattle: The Pacific Northwest Magazine*, May 1969, 21–26, 47–51.

———. "Joy Comes to Mudville." *Seattle: The Pacific Northwest Magazine*, April 1969, 12–18, 54–56.

———. "The Making Up of a Mayor." *Seattle: The Pacific Northwest Magazine*, September 1970, 34–45.

———. "Seattle's Other Government." *Seattle: The Pacific Northwest Magazine*, December 1970, 70–77.

———. "Solidarity Forever." *Seattle: The Pacific Northwest Magazine*, December 1969, 35–41, 52–53.

Bunzel, Peter. "Antidisestablishmentarianism." *Seattle: The Pacific Northwest Magazine*, April 1968, 19–25.

———. "Why *Seattle Magazine* Didn't Make It." *Seattle: The Pacific Northwest Magazine*, December 1970, 20–30.

Burk, Robert F. *Much More Than a Game*. Chapel Hill: University of North Carolina Press, 2001.

Burke, Padraic. *A History of the Port of Seattle*. Seattle: Port of Seattle, 1976.

Carlson, Edward E. *Recollections of a Lucky Fellow*. Seattle: published by author, 1989.

Casserly, Brian Gerard. "Securing the Sound: The Evolution of Civilian-Military Relations in the Puget Sound Area, 1891–1984." Ph.D. diss., University of Washington, 2007.

Central Association. *The Emerging Downtown*. Seattle, [1970?].

Chin, Doug. *Seattle's International District: The Making of a Pan Asian American Community*. Seattle: International Examiner Press, 2001.

Clark, Tom. *Champagne and Baloney: The Rise and Fall of Finley's A's*. New York: Harper and Row, 1976.

Cline, Scott. "To Foster Honorable Pastimes: Baseball as a Civic Endeavor in 1880s Seattle." *Pacific Northwest Quarterly*, Fall 1996, 171–77.

Conway, Richard S., and William Beyers. "Seattle Mariners Baseball Club Economic Impact." Seattle, 1991.

Crowley, Walt. *Rites of Passage: A Memoir of the Sixties in Seattle*. Seattle: University of Washington Press, 1995.

———. "So Long, Wes." *The Weekly*, April 1977, 11.

Curry, Timothy John, Kent Schwirian, and Rachael A. Woldoff. *High Stakes: Big Time Sports and Downtown Redevelopment*. Columbus: The Ohio State University, 2004.

Danielson, Michael. *Home Team: Professional Sports and the American Metropolis*. Princeton, N.J.: Princeton University Press, 1997.

DeFord, Frank. "A Home with No Dome." *Sports Illustrated*, 12 August 1968, 14–17.

Demmert, Henry G. *The Economics of Professional Team Sports*. Lexington, Mass.: D.C. Heath, 1973.

Department of Stadium Administration. *Kingdome Master Plan, 1990*. Seattle: privately printed, 1990.

Douglas, Patrick. "A Brief Word of Thanks to Ed Devine." *Seattle: The Pacific Northwest Magazine*, January 1970, 38–41.

———. "County Government: Freeholders to the Rescue." *Seattle: The Pacific Northwest Magazine*, November 1967, 41–43.

———."Forward Thrust." *Seattle: The Pacific Northwest Magazine*, January 1968, 29–32.

———. "In the Lair of the Panthers." *Seattle: The Pacific Northwest Magazine*, October 1968, 36–47, 57–61.

———. "Is Seattle Just a Company Town?" *Seattle: The Pacific Northwest Magazine*, May 1970, 42–46.

———. "New Stirrings in the Central Area." *Seattle: The Pacific Northwest Magazine*, October 1967, 16–22, 57–58.

———. "Q: To Dome or Doom the Stadium." *Seattle: The Pacific Northwest Magazine*, February 1968, 12–13.

———. "Seattle: Spectacular Views, Resurgent Neighborhoods." *Saturday Review*, 21 August 1976, 10–12.

Dumovich, Eve. *The Boeing Logbook: 1916–1991*. Seattle: Boeing Historical Archives, [1991].

Duncan, Don. *Meet Me at the Center: The Story of Seattle Center from the Beginnings to the 1962 World's Fair to the 21st Century*. Seattle: Seattle Center Foundation, 1992.

Eagan, Michael, and Walt Crowley. *Seattle: Renaissance of America's Most Livable City*. Seattle, 1978.

Ellis, James. "Thrust toward Quality." *National Civic Review*, February 1969, 56–60, 75.

Ellis, John W. "The Last Time We Played on Real Grass." In *Diamond in the Emerald City: The Story of Safeco Field*, 1–4. Edited by John W. Ellis, Natalie Fobes, and Frank Wetzel. Seattle: Seattle Mariners, 1999.

Eskenazi, David. "Dwyer KO's American League," 25 October 2011, *Sportspress Northwest*, http://sportspressnw.com/2011/10/wayback-machine-bill-dwyer-kos-american-league/.

Euchner, Charles. *Playing the Field: Why Sports Teams Move and Cities Fight to Keep Them*. Baltimore, Md.: The Johns Hopkins University Press, 1993.

Findlay, John. *Magic Lands: Western Cityscapes and American Culture after 1940*. Berkeley: University of California Press, 1992.

———. "The Off-Center Seattle Center: Downtown Seattle and the 1962 World's Fair." *Pacific Northwest Quarterly*, January 1989, 2–11.

Fischer, John. "Seattle's Modern Day Vigilantes." *Harper's Magazine*, May 1969, 14–26.

Fizel, John, Elizabeth Gustafson, and Lawrence Hadle, eds. *Baseball Economics: Current Research*. Westport, Conn.: Praeger, 1996.

Fort, Rodney. *Sports Economics*. Upper Saddle River, N.J.: Prentice-Hall, 2003.

Garcia, Gilberto. "Beisboleros: Latin American Baseball in the Northwest, 1914–1937." *Columbia*, Fall 2002, 8–13.

Gastil, Raymond D. "The Pacific Northwest as Cultural Region." *Pacific Northwest Quarterly*, October 1973, 147–62.

Griffith, Thomas. "The Pacific Northwest." *Atlantic Monthly*, April 1975, 47, 58, 66.

Guttmann, Allen. *Sports Spectators*. New York: Columbia University Press, 1986.

Halpin, James. "The Auto's Terrible Tyranny." *Seattle: The Pacific Northwest Magazine*, April 1967, 45–48.

———. "Our Musty, Crusty City Council." *Seattle: The Pacific Northwest Magazine*, May 1965, 12–16, 46–48.

Halpin, James, and Patrick Douglas. "Viet Nam: What's at Stake for Seattle?" *Seattle: The Pacific Northwest Magazine*, March 1967, 10–12, 48–51.

Herrera, Philip. "Megalopolis Comes to the Northwest." *Fortune Magazine*, December 1967, 118–23, 194.

Hodges, Frederick William. "The Impact of Forward Thrust on Park Development in Seattle." Master's thesis, University of Washington, 1972.

Hogan, Kenneth. *The 1969 Seattle Pilots: Major League Baseball's One-Year Team*. Jefferson, N.C.: McFarland and Company, 2007.

Humphrey, Clark. *Images of America: Vanishing Seattle*. Charleston, S.C.: Arcadia Publishing, 2006.

James, Bill. *The Bill James Historical Baseball Abstract*. New York: Villard Books, 1986.

Jay, Kathryn. *More Than Just a Game: Sports in American Life since 1945*. New York: Columbia University Press, 2004.

Johnson, Arthur T., and James H. Frey. *Government and Sport: The Public Policy Issues*. Totowa, N.J.: Rowman and Allanheld, 1985.

Johnson, D. Grant. *The Seattle Mariners Story*. Seattle: Sunrise Publishing, 1977.

Jones, Nard. *Seattle*. New York: Doubleday and Co., 1972.

Kaese, Harold, and R. G. Lynch. *The Milwaukee Braves*. New York: G. P. Putnam's Sons, 1954.

Kahn, Roger. [No title]. *Esquire*, December 1970, 14–15.

Kaplan, Jim. "Jim Bouton's Instant Replay." *Sports Illustrated*, 31 August 1970, 36.

Kirkendall, Richard. "The Boeing Company and the Military-Metropolitan Industrial Complex, 1945–1953." *Pacific Northwest Quarterly*, October 1994, 137–49.

———. "Two Senators and the Boeing Company: The Transformation of Washington's Political Culture." *Columbia*, Winter 1997, 38–43.

Klingle, Matthew. *Emerald City: An Environmental History of Seattle*. New Haven, Conn.: Yale University Press, 2007.

Kuhn, Bowie. *Hardball: The Education of a Baseball Commissioner*. New York: Random House, 1987.

Lane, Bob. *Better Than Promised: An Informal History of the Municipality of Metropolitan Seattle*. Seattle: King County Department of Metropolitan Services, 1995.

Lapchick, Richard E., ed. *Fractured Focus: Sport as a Reflection of Society*. Lexington, Mass.: D. C. Heath, 1986.

LeSourd, Peter. "How a Slate Took Over the Seattle City Council." Crosscut.com, http://crosscut.com/2007/04/21/history/2233/How-slate-took-over-Seatttle-City-Council/.

LaWarne, Charles, and Robert Ficken. *Washington: A Centennial History*. Seattle: University of Washington Press, 1988.

Lee, Sohyun Park. "From Redevelopment to Preservation: Downtown Planning in Post-War Seattle." Ph.D. diss., University of Washington, 2001.

Lewis, Arthur. "The Worst American City." *Harper's*, January 1975, 67–71.

Lineberry, William, ed. *The Business of Sports*. New York: H. W. Wilson Company, 1973.

Lowenfish, Lee, and Tony Lupien. *The Imperfect Diamond*. New York: Stein and Day, 1980.

MacDonald, Norbert. *Distant Neighbors: A Comparative History of Seattle and Vancouver*. Lincoln: University of Nebraska Press, 1987.

Mansfield, Harold. *The Space Needle Story*. Mercer Island, Wash.: The Writing Works, 1976.

Marburger, Daniel R., ed. *Stee-rike Four! What's Wrong with the Business of Baseball?* Westport, Conn.: Praeger, 1997.

McCune, Cal. *From Romance to Riot: A Seattle Memoir*. Seattle: Cal McCune, 1996.

McGimpsey, David. *Imagining Baseball: America's Pastime and Popular Culture*. Bloomington: University of Indiana Press, 2000.

McPhail, Lee. *My 9 Innings: An Autobiography of 50 Years in Baseball*. Westport, Conn.: Meckler Books, 1989.

Michener, Charles T. "The Growing Cultural Crisis." *Seattle: The Pacific Northwest Magazine*, August 1967, 17–20, 55–56.

———. "King of the Mountain." *Seattle: The Pacific Northwest Magazine*, March 1969, 25–29, 48–49.

Mishler, Todd. *Baseball in Beertown: America's Pastime in Milwaukee*. Black Earth, Wis.: Prairie Oak Press, 2005.

Morgan, Murray. *Century 21: The Story of the Seattle World's Fair, 1962*. Seattle: University of Washington Press, 1963.

———. *Skid Road: An Informal Portrait of Seattle*. Rev. ed. Seattle: University of Washington Press, 1992.

Mullins, William H. *The Depression and the Urban West Coast, 1929–1933: Los Angeles, San Francisco, Seattle, and Portland*. Bloomington: University of Indiana Press, 1991.

Mulvoy, Mark. "Baseball Booms Again." *Sports Illustrated*, 4 August 1969, 12–17.

———. "KC Is Back with a Vengeance." *Sports Illustrated*, 26 May 1969, 75–81.

Nelson, Gerald B. *Seattle: The Life and Times of an American City*. New York: Alfred A. Knopf, 1977.

Newhan, Ross. *Anaheim Angels: A Complete History*. New York: Hyperion, 2000.

Noe, Cyrus. *Innocence Revisited: 20 Years after the Fair—a Flack Remembers*. Seattle: Pacific Search Press, 1982.

Noll, Roger G., ed. *Government and the Sports Business: Papers Prepared for a Conference of Experts, with an Introduction and Summary*. Washington, D.C.: The Brookings Institution, 1974.

Noll, Roger G., and Andrew Zimbalist, eds. *Sports, Jobs and Taxes: The Economic Impact of Sports Teams and Stadiums*. Washington, D.C.: Brookings Institution Press, 1997.

Okrent, Daniel. *Nine Innings*. Boston: Houghton and Mifflin, 1985.

O'Neil, Paul. "You're a Good Man, Charlie O." *Life*, 6 September 1968, 68–74.

Page, Richard. "Forward Thrust: Answer to Urban Crisis." *Puget Soundings*, January 1968, 12–13, 30–32.

Park, Sohyun. "Prescriptive Plans for a Healthy Central Business District: Seattle Downtown Design, 1956–1966." *Pacific Northwest Quarterly*, Summer 2007, 107–14.

Parrott, Harold. *The Lords of Baseball*. New York: Praeger Publishers, 1976.

Pascal, Anthony, and Leonard A. Rapping. "The Economics of Racial Discrimination in Organized Baseball." In *Racial Discrimination in Economic Life*, 119–56. Edited by Anthony Pascal. Lexington, Mass.: D. C. Heath, 1972.

Pearce, Neal R. *The Pacific States of America: People, Politics, and Power in the Five Pacific Basin States*. New York: W. W. Norton, 1972.

Peck, Janice. "Arts Activists and Seattle's Cultural Expansion, 1954–1965: Increasing in Beauty as It Increases in Size." *Pacific Northwest Quarterly*, July 1965, 82–94.

Peterson, John E. *The Kansas City Athletics: A Baseball History, 1954–1967*. Jefferson, N.C.: McFarland and Company, 2003.

Pieroth, Doris H. "With All Deliberate Caution: School Integration in Seattle, 1954–1968." *Pacific Northwest Quarterly*, April 1982, 50–61.

Quirk, James, and Rodney Fort. *Hard Ball: The Abuse of Power in Pro Team Sports*. Princeton, N.J.: Princeton University Press, 1999.

———. *Pay Dirt: The Business of Professional Team Sports*. Princeton, N.J.: Princeton University Press, 1992.

Rader, Benjamin G. *American Sports: From the Age of Folk Games to the Age of Spectators*. Englewood Cliffs, N.J.: Prentice-Hall, 1983.

———. *In Its Own Image: How Television Has Transformed Sports*. New York: Free Press, 1984.

Regalado, Samuel O. "'Play Ball': Baseball and Seattle's Japanese American Courier League." *Pacific Northwest Quarterly*, Winter 1995–96, 29–37.

Riess, Steven A. *City Games: The Evolution of American Urban Society and the Rise of Sports*. Urbana: University of Illinois Press, 1989.

Riley, Dan. "A Man Named Sick Made Seattle Well." In *Rain Check: Baseball in the Pacific Northwest*, 56–62. Edited by Mark Armour. Cleveland, Ohio: Society for American Baseball Research, 2006.

Roberts, Randy, and James S. Olson. *Winning Is the Only Thing: Sports in America since 1945*. Baltimore, Md.: Johns Hopkins University Press, 1989.

Robinson, Herb. "Community or Chaos?" *Puget Soundings*, October 1966, 8–9, 27.

Rodgers, Eugene. *Flying High: The Story of Boeing and the Rise of the Jetliner Industry*. New York: Atlantic Monthly Press, 1966.

Roe, Jo Ann. *Seattle Uncovered*. Plano, Tex.: Seaside Press, 1996.

Rosentraub, Mark S. *Major League Losers: The Real Cost of Sports and Who's Paying for It*. Revised ed. New York: Basic Books, 1999.

Rousso, Nick. "An Exhilarating Big League Bust: The Seattle Pilots." In *Rain Check: Baseball in the Pacific Northwest*, 116–22. Edited by Mark Armour. Cleveland, Ohio: Society for American Baseball Research, 2006.

Sale, Roger. *Seattle: Past to Present*. Seattle: University of Washington Press, 1976.

Santos, Bob. *Humbows Not Hot Dogs: Memoirs of a Savvy Asian American Activist*. Seattle: International Examiner Press, 2002.

Schaefer, Kurt. "Play Ball!" *Columbia*, Summer 2000, 14–22.

Scully, Gerald W. *The Business of Major League Baseball*. Chicago: University of Chicago Press, 1989.

Sell, T. M. *Wings of Power: Boeing and the Politics of Growth in the Northwest.* Seattle: University of Washington Press, 2001.

Serling, Robert J. *Legend and Legacy: The Story of Boeing and Its People.* New York: St. Martin's Press, 1992.

Silva, Joseph. "The Bank of California: Part of Seattle since 1905." [Seattle?]: Bank of California, 1973.

Sistek, Scott. "New 'Summer Sanity Index' Shows This Summer Wasn't So Bad." http://www.komonews.com/weather/blog/27743024.html?blog=y

Skinner, D. E. *Annals of Century 21 Center, Inc., Something to Build On.* [Seattle], [1971?].

"So Long, Wes." Panel discussion. *The Weekly,* January 1978, 11–12.

Speidel, Bill. *Through the Eye of the Needle.* Edited by Linda Lewis. Seattle: Nestle Creek Publishing, 1989.

Staff. "The First Hurrah: A Guide to the City Primaries." *Seattle: The Pacific Northwest Magazine,* September 1969, 42–53.

———. "They're Off and Running for the City Council." *Seattle: The Pacific Northwest Magazine,* September 1967, 37–41.

———. "Will the Real County Prosecutor Please Step Down?" *Seattle: The Pacific Northwest Magazine,* September 1968, 22–31.

Stenson, Barbara. "Restoring Pioneer Square: A Race with the Wrecking Ball." *Puget Soundings,* April 1970, 10–11, 34.

Study City Team, Northwestern University. *Seattle: City with a Chance.* Seattle, 1968.

Sullivan, Dean A., ed. *Late Innings: A Documentary History of Baseball, 1945–1972.* Lincoln: University of Nebraska Press, 2002.

Sullivan, Neil J. *The Dodgers Move West.* New York: Oxford University Press, 1987.

Taylor, Quintard. *The Forging of a Black Seattle Community: Seattle's Central District from 1870 through the Civil Rights Era.* Seattle: University of Washington Press, 1994.

Testa, Judith. *Sal Maglie: Baseball's Demon Barber.* DeKalb: Northern Illinois University Press, 2007.

Thiel, Art. *Out of Left Field: How the Mariners Made Baseball Fly in Seattle.* Seattle: Sasquatch Books, 2003.

Thornley, Stew. *Baseball in Minnesota: The Definitive History.* Saint Paul: Minnesota Historical Society Press, 2006.

Thrush, Cole. *Native Seattle: Histories from the Crossing-Over Place.* Seattle: University of Washington, 2007.

Torry, Jack. *Endless Summers: The Fall and Rise of the Cleveland Indians.* South Bend, Indiana: Diamond Communications, 1995.

Van Lindt, Carson. *The Seattle Pilots Story.* New York: Marabou Publishing, 1993.

Vandenbosch, Susanne Elaine. "The 1968 Seattle Forward Thrust Election: An Analysis of Voting on an Ad Hoc Effort to Solve Metropolitan Problems without Metropolitan Government." Ph.D. diss., University of Washington, 1974.

Voigt, David Quentin. *From Postwar Expansion to the Electronic Age.* Vol. 3 of *American Baseball.* University Park: Pennsylvania State University Press, 1983.

———. "Out with the Crowds: Counting, Courting and Controlling Ball Park Fans." In *Baseball History: An Annual of Baseball Research,* 92–129. Edited by Peter Levine.

Westport, Conn.: Meckler Books, 1989.

Waddingham, Gary. *The Seattle Rainiers, 1938–1942*. Seattle: Writers Publishing Service Co., 1987.

Warren, James R. *A Century of Seattle's Business*. Bellevue, Wash.: Vernon Publications, 1989.

———. *King County and Its Emerald City: Seattle*. [Tarzana, Calif.]: American Historical Press, 1997.

———. *Seattle: 150 Years of Progress*. Carlsbad, Calif.: Heritage Media, 2001.

Watson, Emmett. *Digressions of a Native Son*. Seattle: The Pacific Institute, 1982.

———. *My Life in Print*. Seattle: Lesser Seattle Publishing, 1993.

———. *Once upon a Time in Seattle*. Seattle: Lesser Seattle Publishing, 1992.

Weiner, Jay. *Stadium Games: Fifty Years of Big League Greed and Bush League Boondoggles*. Minneapolis: University of Minnesota Press, 2000.

White, G. Edward. *Creating the National Pastime: Baseball Transforms Itself, 1903–1953*. Princeton, N.J.: Princeton University Press, 1996.

Whitford, David. *Playing Hardball: The High Stakes Battle for Baseball's New Franchises*. New York: Doubleday, 1993.

Wilkinson, Robert David. "Forward Thrust." Master's thesis, University of Washington, 1972.

William S. Harper and Son and Co. and Blyth and Company. *Forward Thrust Program*. [Seattle], [1969?].

Williams, DeCharlene. *History of Seattle's Central Area*. Seattle: Central Area Chamber of Commerce, 1990.

Wilson, James, et al. *Whatever Happened to the World's Fair Dream? A Paper to Promote Discussion on the Future of Seattle Center*. Seattle: Seattle Center, [1974].

Wilson, John. *Playing by the Rules: Sport, Society, and the State*. Detroit, Mich.: Wayne State University, 1994.

Wilson, Lyle Kenai. *Sunday Afternoons at Garfield Park: Seattle's Black Baseball Teams, 1911–1951*. Everett, Wash.: The Print Shop, 1997.

Wolf, Ruth. "Freeways under Fire." *Seattle: The Pacific Northwest Magazine*, February 1969, 30–36.

———. "The Spectre of Violence in Seattle." *Seattle: The Pacific Northwest Magazine*, August 1969, 25–27.

———. "The Urban League on a Tightrope." *Seattle: The Pacific Northwest Magazine*, July 1969, 27–30, 46–47.

———. Whizzing Along toward the 21st Century." *Seattle: The Pacific Northwest Magazine*, June 1969, 32–42, 65.

Zimbalist, Andrew. *Baseball and Billions: A Probing Look inside the Big Business of Our National Pastime*. Updated ed. New York: Basic Books, 1992.

Zingg, Paul J., and Mark Medeiras. *Runs, Hits, and an Era: The Pacific Coast League, 1903–1958*. Urbana: University of Illinois Press, 1994.

INDEX

Abbott, Carl, 22

accounting principles, baseball, 231

Adcock, Joe, 100

Ad Hoc Committee Seattle Center Stadium Site, 171–72

admissions taxes, 134–35

Aero Mechanics, 45

Aker, Jack: April games, 88; exhibition games, 66, 67, 70, 71; player representative position, 71; spring training, 116; trading of, 93, 152

Alaska-Yukon-Pacific Exposition (1909), 28

Allen, William, 10–11, 30

Allied Arts, 18

Allison, Bob, 118

All Star Game, 163–64

Allyn, John, 89, 210, 211

Alvis, Max, 227, 249

Amdur, Neil, 21–22

American League: attendance declines, 149; expansion draft process, 112; and Forward Thrust campaign, 80–81; franchise management power, 190–91; post-Kingdome team discussions, 270; revenue sharing structure, 111, 152–53

American League, Seattle's franchise: in bankruptcy proceedings, 232–33, 273; community responses to, 55, 58; competition process, 54; Danz-led purchase initiative, 200, 203; during domed stadium planning, 191–92; Finley and Symington roles, 53–54, 56; in franchise failure analysis, 234, 236, 237–38; granting of, 54–55, 57–59; incentives for, 52–53, 56–57; litigation against, 204, 205, 229–31, 268, 271–80; nonprofit corporation ownership idea, 206, 208–9, 228–29; oversight process, 225; ownership change requirement, 197; ownership group development, 59–65; PNSI ownership revocation/reversal, 197, 211–12; responses to sale agree-

ment, 194–95, 196–97; Sicks' Stadium remodel, 138, 139, 142–43, 145–46

amphetamine use, 159, 242

Anderson, Lenny (writing on): Boston game, 183; Bristol's coaching style, 227; D. Soriano, 236; franchise arrival context, 55; franchise possibility, 13; home run pattern, 91; Milkes, 100; Milwaukee ownership group, 194; Pilots' departure, 234, 247; relocation/sale speculation, 193; stadium campaigns, 84

Angels, Seattle, 20, 64, 136

Anson, Paul, 137

antitrust laws: in American League litigation, 204, 270–71, 274–75, 277, 278; baseball's exemption, 190; franchise expansion impact, 53, 190–91; as senators' leverage, 53–54, 194, 196; Supreme Court ruling, 190

April games, 88–91, 124–25*f*

Argus (article/editorial topics): Danz-led purchase initiative, 202–3; franchise sale, 195; Kingdome impact, 266; Seattle Center site, 173–74; Sicks' Stadium remodel, 135; siting process, 30; stadium campaign, 84; style of, 19; Uhlman's election, 16–17

Argyros, George, 281

Arizona State University, 67–68

Arnold, Lawrence, 29

Ashford, Emmett, 81

Astrodome, 83

Atlantic Monthly, 9, 14

attendance patterns: Husky football, 20; influences on, 153; minor league baseball, 20, 149; in stadium feasibility studies, 43; SuperSonics games, 51; World's Fair, 32

attendance patterns, major league baseball: declines, 149; Milwaukee Brewers, 194, 234, 249; Montreal Expos, 195; Oakland A's, 195; and revenue sharing,

Diablos, 133
DiMaggio, Joe, 150
dirt problem, Sicks' Stadium, 140, 143
division standings, Milwaukee Brewers,
234
division standings, Seattle Pilots: and
attendance patterns, 153; exhibition
season, 67; expectations, 68, 117–18;
final rankings, 287; Milkes' obsession, 100, 134, 184–85; during regular
season, 91, 95, 156, 158, 161, 182, 186,
188; Schultz' prediction, 99, 117–18,
184, 187
Donaldson, John, 157, 159, 161, 164
Donohoe, Ed, 45
Douglas, James: civic leader role, 29; in
Danz-led purchase initiative, 198, 200;
in nonprofit corporation ownership
initiative, 219f, 228–29; Space Needle
project, 24; in stadium siting process,
172; ticket drive, 107
draft selections, 112–15
Drake Construction, 253, 256–61
drug culture, 159, 242
Duckstad, Eric, 26
Dudley, Jimmy, 108–9, 110, 141, 225
Duncan, Don, 266
Dupar, Frank, 29
Durslag, Melvin, 39
Durso, Joe, 228
Duwamish Waterway location, 167,
169–70
Dwyer, William, 204, 220f, 237–38, 262,
271–80

Eaton, Cyrus, 61
Eckert, William, 56–57, 60, 82, 97–98
Edgerton, Bill, 68, 90
Edwards, Myrtle, 29
Ehrlichman, Ben, 29
electrical problems, Sicks' Stadium, 145
Ellis, James: in American League litigation, 273, 274; characterized, 14, 75–76,
216f; in Danz-led purchase initiative,
198, 199; Forward Thrust campaigns,
76–79, 175–76; at injunction hearing,

230; in multipurpose stadium siting,
84, 169, 174–75, 219f; in nonprofit
corporation ownership initiative, 207,
228–29; on Spellman's leadership,
260–61; urban sprawl focus, 251
Empens, Joe, 174
employment patterns, Seattle, 9, 11, 154
Environmental Protection Agency, Washington State, 255
Ermer, Cal, 224
Evans, Dan: on Boeing, 11; Finley negotiations, 49; during NFL franchise competition, 46; opening game festivities, 89;
Stadium Commission appointments,
84–85, 217f; World's Fair project, 40
Evergreen Point Floating Bridge, 17
eviction threat, Miller's, 146–47, 191, 194

Facts, 84, 153–54
Fair Feasibility Committee, 28–30
Falls, Joe, 242–43
falsework, Kingdome, 222f, 259–60
Family Night sponsorships, 151
fan base, 19–20, 34, 37, 43, 87, 236
farm system, overview, 103
fences, Sicks' Stadium, 90, 143–44
Ferguson, Alan, 35, 136, 137, 192
Ferguson, John, 272
Ferguson, Tommy, 233
Ferrari, Ray, 144
Ferraro, Mike, 4, 67, 69, 71, 90
Ferrucci, Tony F., 174
Fetzer, John, 196
Field, Wayne, 269
field manager. See Schultz, Joe
finances: bond election amounts, 44; in
Danz-led purchase initiative, 199–203,
205, 231; domed stadium planning,
175, 192; Finley negotiations, 49, 50;
Forward Thrust campaigns, 78, 79, 81,
231; Kingdome operations, 264–65;
Kingdome siting/construction, 179,
252–53, 258, 259–60, 261–63; Mariners
ownership, 281; for Mariners' stadium,
281–82; for multipurpose functions,
169; NFL franchise negotiations, 269;

Golden West Broadcasting: in bankruptcy proceedings, 233; contract negotiations, 104, 108–9, 208, 226; in Forward Thrust campaign, 83–84; in litigation process, 276. *See also* KVI radio

Golub, Stan, 280–81

Gomez, Lefty, 89

Goossen, Greg, 164, 189

Gorton, Slade, 10, 204, 229, 271–72, 276, 279

Gosger, Jim, 67, 71, 88, 90, 114, 157

Governor's Sports Advisory Council, 25

Graham, Billy, 83, 264–65

Graham, Jack, 24

Green, Joshua, 29, 172

Griffith, Cal, 196

Gura, Larry, 67

Guzzo, Lou, 170, 198

Hadden, Sandy, 203, 211, 229, 268

Halberstam, David, 244

Hall, John, 132

Hamey, Roy, 225, 226, 227, 246, 273, 276

Haney, Fred, 118

Haney, Larry, 66, 96, 157

Hanley, Bridget, 89, 124*f*

Hardwick, Bob, 68

Harper, Tommy: at bat, 130*f*; contract negotiations, 226; drafting of, 113; exhibition games, 66, 67, 68, 71, 247; music favorites, 158; promotional activities, 128*f*, 150, 225; stolen base totals, 189

Harper, Tommy (regular season games): April, 88, 89; August, 182, 183, 184; July, 161, 163, 164; June, 156, 159, 161; May, 91, 94, 95, 96

Harper-O-Graph, 92

Harper's magazine, 8, 75–76

Harris, John, 278

Harrison, Roric, 186

Hatton, Grady, 100

Hauberg, John, 18–19

Hazelton, Kenneth, 140

Hegan, Jim, 67

Hegan, Mike: All Star Game, 164; batting average, 189; exhibition games, 67, 71, 247; game day routine, 93; house purchase, 227; signing of, 111; spring training arrival, 226; winter tours, 225

Hegan, Mike (regular season games): April, 88; August, 182, 183; July, 161, 162, 163, 164, 182; June, 156, 158, 161; May, 91, 94, 96; September, 187

Helix, 84

Hendricks, Ellie, 184

Henke, Henry, III, 219*f*

Henry, Bill, 66–67, 70

Herr, Gordon, 174

Hershberger, Mike, 224, 248

Hill, Tim, 16, 135, 136, 256, 280

Hirsch, Elroy, 40

Ho, Chinn, 62

Hoffberger, Jerry: in franchise failure analysis, 236; in litigation activity, 230, 272, 273; on PNSI capabilities, 63; responses to franchise retention initiatives, 196–97, 209, 211; on stadium campaigns, 80–81, 190–91

Home Games: Two Wives Speak Out (B. Bouton and N. Marshall), 243

Home Run for the Money, 151

Hoosier Dome, Indianapolis, 80

Hope, Frank, 169

Horlen, Joel, 118

Houk, Ralph, 92

Houston, in NFL franchise competition, 40

Houston Astros, 240

Houston Chronicle, 191

Houston Colt .45s, 52, 149, 186

Houston Oilers, 82

Houston Post, 83

Hovley, Steve: Bouton relationship, 240; drafting of, 114; exhibition games, 248; on franchise failure blame, 231; July games, 161, 162, 163, 164; spring training arrival, 116, 226; Vancouver demotion, 69

Howard, Elston, 243

Howard, Frank, 278

Howell, Lem, 255

Hunt, Lamar, 36, 191, 204

Seattle Pilots: initial player selection, 111–15; regular season games, 88–96, 124–25f, 154–65, 182–87, 189; spring training, 3–5, 66–71, 116, 132–34, 226, 246–49; team statistics, 287–89. *See also specific topics, e.g.,* Pacific Northwest Sports, Inc.; trading/purchasing activity, Milkes'; *specific players*

Seattle Pilots, sale of: and bankruptcy proceedings, 230–33; blame framework for, 234–39; Danz-led initiative, 196, 198–204; initial responses to, 194–97; litigation against, 204, 205, 229–31, 268, 271–80; Milwaukee agreement, 194, 229–30; nonprofit corporation ownership initiative, 205–11, 228–29; retention barriers summarized, 212–13; Ruge's offers, 197, 232; speculation about, 190–94, 227–28

Seattle Post-intelligencer, booster role, 19

Seattle Post-Intelligencer (article/editorial topics): American League expansion, 55; bankruptcy proceedings, 233; booster role, 19; Danz-led purchase initiative, 200; division standings, 67; draft process, 112; exhibition games, 248; Forward Thrust campaign, 82–83, 84; Harper's play, 92, 225; Marshall interview, 91; NFL franchise competition, 40, 45, 46; 1960 stadium campaign, 27; nonprofit corporation ownership idea, 207, 212; Pierce County proposal, 85; potential ownership changes, 197; sale of Pilots, 191; Schultz poll, 185; season expectations, 117, 118; Spellman's leadership, 261; stadium importance, 38–39; stadium siting process, 168, 170–71, 173, 176, 177. *See also* Anderson, Lenny; Owen, John; Watson, Emmett

Seattle Rainiers, 6, 20, 35, 239

Seattle Seahawks, 63, 269

Seattle Sounders, 264, 269

Seattle Spirit: Danz-led purchase initiative, 197, 198–204, 208; during 1960 stadium campaign, 25–27; Space Needle's role, 24–25; World's Fair impact, 27–33. *See also* Forward Thrust campaign (1968); nonprofit corporation approach, ownership structure

Seattle Times: booster role, 19; Bouton's *Ball Four,* 244; in civic leadership role, 14; during NFL franchise competition, 44, 46; World's Fair support, 28

Seattle Times (article/editorial topics): Danz-led purchase initiative, 199, 204; exhibition games, 248; Forward Thrust campaign, 84; franchise loss, 195; franchise public opinion, 58; Kingdome opening, 264; litigation activity, 278–79; 1960 stadium campaign, 27; Pierce County proposal, 85; potential ownership changes, 197; Sicks' Stadium remodel, 140; Spellman's leadership, 250, 260; SRI study, 13; stadium incentives, 56; stadium siting process, 168, 170, 171, 176; ticket prices, 109. *See also* Zimmerman, Hy (writing on)

Seattle World's Fair, 13, 18, 27–33, 40, 215f

Security Pacific Bank, 281

Segui, David, 128f

Segui, Diego: drafting of, 113; innings totals, 189; at kids' game, 128f; on Maglie, 102; spring training period, 66, 67, 68, 71, 129f; trade of, 92, 157, 224

Segui, Diego (regular season games): April, 88, 89; August, 184, 186; July, 163, 164; June, 156, 157; May, 91, 94; September, 187, 188

Selig, Bud, 142, 194, 201, 204, 229, 233

September games, 187–89

sex, in Bouton's *Ball Four,* 242–43

Sharp, Morell, 263

Sherman Antitrust Act. *See* antitrust laws

Short, Bob, 142, 196, 206, 210, 276, 278

Sick, Emil, 29, 136

Sicks' Stadium: aerial view, 124f; in American League litigation, 271, 273, 274, 279–80; in bankruptcy proceedings, 238; Carroll's upgrade proposal, 39; Cleveland Indians negotiations, 35, 37; during domed stadium siting process, 178, 179;